Oracle7 SQL Commands

SQL Command	Description
CREATE DATABASE	Creates a database.
CREATE DATABASE LINK[†]	Defines a named path to a remote database. Available without the Distributed Database option, but for read operations only.
CREATE FUNCTION	Creates a stored function.
CREATE INDEX	Creates an index for a table.
CREATE PACKAGE	Creates a stored package specification.
CREATE PACKAGE BODY	Creates a stored package body.
CREATE PROCEDURE	Creates a stored procedure.
CREATE PROFILE	Creates a named profile of resource limits.
CREATE ROLE	Creates a role to group related privileges.
CREATE ROLLBACK SEGMENT	Creates a rollback segment.
CREATE SCHEMA	Creates a number of tables and views, all in one statement, in a current database account.
CREATE SEQUENCE	Creates a named sequence of numbers.
CREATE SNAPSHOT[†]	Creates a snapshot of a remote table.
CREATE SNAPSHOT LOG[†]	Creates a refresh log for a snapshot.
CREATE SYNONYM	Creates a synonym for a database object.
CREATE TABLE	Creates a new database table.
CREATE TABLESPACE	Creates a new tablespace.
CREATE TRIGGER	Creates a database trigger for a table.
CREATE USER	Creates a new database username and password.
CREATE VIEW	Creates a view of a table or other views.
DELETE	Deletes one or more rows from a database table.
DROP CLUSTER	Drops an indexed or a hash cluster.
DROP DATABASE LINK[†]	Drops a named path to a remote database. Available without the Distributed Database option, but for read operations only.
DROP FUNCTION	Drops a stored function.
DROP INDEX	Drops an index on a table.
DROP PACKAGE	Drops a stored package specification and body.
DROP PACKAGE BODY	Drops a stored package body.
DROP PROCEDURE	Drops a stored procedure.
DROP PROFILE	Drops a named profile of resource limits.

[†]Available only with the Oracle7 Distributed Database option

MASTERING™

ORACLE7® & CLIENT/SERVER

COMPUTING

SECOND EDITION

Steven M,

Steve Bobrowski

SYBEX®

San Francisco • Paris • Düsseldorf • Soest

Associate Publisher: Amy Romanoff
Acquisitions Editor: Kristine Plachy
Developmental Editor: Melanie Spiller
Editor: Marilyn Smith
Project Editor: Lee Ann Pickrell
Technical Editor: Aaron Kushner
Book Series Designer: Suzanne Albertson
Electronic Publishing Specialist: Deborah A. Bevilacqua
Graphic Illustrator: Kelly Jonick
Production Coordinator: Kim Wimpsett
Indexer: Matthew Spence
Cover Designer: DesignSite
Cover Photographer: David Bishop

Library of Congress Card Number: 96-67844

ISBN: 0-7821-1840-2

Manufactured in the United States of America

10 9 8 7 6 5 4 3 2 1

Warranty

Sybex warrants the enclosed disk to be free of physical defects for a period of ninety (90) days after purchase. If you discover a defect in the disk during this warranty period, you can obtain a replacement disk at no charge by sending the defective disk, postage prepaid, with proof of purchase to:

Sybex Inc.
Customer Service Department
2021 Challenger Drive
Alameda, CA 94501
(800) 227-2346
Fax: (510) 523-2373

After the 90-day period, you can obtain a replacement disk by sending us the defective disk, proof of purchase, and a check or money order for $10, payable to Sybex.

Disclaimer

Sybex makes no warranty or representation, either express or implied, with respect to this medium or its contents, its quality, performance, merchantability, or fitness for a particular purpose. In no event will Sybex, its distributors, or dealers be liable for direct, indirect, special, incidental, or consequential damages arising out of the use of or inability to use the medium or its contents even if advised of the possibility of such damage.

The exclusion of implied warranties is not permitted by some states. Therefore, the above exclusion may not apply to you. This warranty provides you with specific legal rights; there may be other rights that you may have that vary from state to state.

Copy Protection

None of the files on the disk is copy-protected. However, in all cases, reselling or making copies of these files without authorization is expressly forbidden.

To my Kathleen, who unselfishly supports me in the wonderful adventure of life.

ACKNOWLEDGMENTS

I'd like to thank the many people who helped me produce this book.

First of all, writing this book would not have been possible if not for endless contributions of time, effort, and software from my many friends at Oracle Corporation. I'd especially like to thank Ken Jacobs, Vice President of Product Strategy, Server Technologies, for his foreword to the book. I'd also like to thank my friends at Oracle for their significant contributions to this book: Robert Dell'Immagine, Steve Erlich, Gary Hallmark, Mark Herring, Gordon Larimer, Dennis Moore, Merrill Holt, Mike Hartstein, Scott Hollows, John Frazzini, Tim Smith, Bhushan Fotedar, Gordon Smith, Stuart Read, and Wynn White.

While Oracle software is the primary focus of this book, you can't take advantage of Oracle software without a great operating system to support it. For this I'd like to extend my gratitude to the folks at The Santa Cruz Operation for their SCO UNIX software and support, especially Sal Bruno, Yasmin Kureshi, Barbara LoFranco, and Bob Walsh.

Many of my esteemed colleagues and friends in the industry helped me with specific areas of this book. Thanks to Beth Marcum, who helped me get SQL*Net just right, and David Kalman, editor-in-chief of *DBMS* magazine, for his opinions concerning the database industry.

Editing a book this large, and one that covers such diverse topics, is no small task. I can't begin to express my gratitude to the primary editors for this book: Dusty Bernard (for the first edition) and Marilyn Smith (for this edition), for their patience and extreme attention to detail while combing the manuscript for my goofs, and Walter Lindsay and Aaron Kushner, for their outstanding technical reviews and invaluable input, which contributed significantly to the technical value of this book.

Last but not least, I'd like to thank the many folks at SYBEX for extending me the opportunity to write this book, especially Melanie Spiller, for getting the book started in the right direction, and Lee Ann Pickrell, for her calmness and patience while coordinating the editing of the book. I'd also like to thank Kelly Jonick for her fine work in translating my pencil-scribbled drawings into meaningful graphics that help illustrate the tough concepts of Oracle7 and client/server computing. Thanks also to Deborah A. Bevilacqua, electronic publishing specialist; Kim Wimpsett, production coordinator; and Suzanne Albertson, book series designer.

CONTENTS AT A GLANCE

TABLE OF CONTENTS

5 Client and Server Communication: SQL and PL/SQL   111

PART II   Database Administration in an Oracle7 System   **153**

6 Understanding Oracle7 Database Administration and Administrative Utilities   **155**

12 Monitoring and Tuning Database Server Performance   381

FOREWORD

Occasionally, computer technology makes a dramatic break with the past. The relational model of database management, with its simple, tabular data structures and powerful data manipulation operations, is one such revolution. The year 1994 marked the twenty-fifth anniversary of the introduction of the relational model by Dr. E.F. Codd, then of IBM Research. The relational model has helped focus computer science research on the problems of data management, and relational database management system products have resulted in tremendous improvements in accessing data and developing applications. Although object databases have recently received much attention, the industry consensus is that leading relational database management systems will successfully incorporate object database ideas as an extension of the basic relational model; the extended relational model of database management will survive and thrive for years to come.

Another revolution in computing technology, client/server computing, took place in the last decade with the spread of minicomputers and microcomputers. These highly cost-effective and flexible open systems have made client/server computing possible. In the early 1980s, the introduction of minicomputers made it economically feasible to dedicate computing resources to departmental applications. Before, computer resources were dedicated to centralized mainframes running corporate applications. Then, microcomputers lowered the cost of computing so much that desktop computers became attractive for personal productivity applications. Along with these advances in computing platforms came improvements in networking technology, permitting widely dispersed computers to communicate reliably and efficiently with each other.

These hardware changes were accompanied by significant changes in software technology. Modern graphical user interfaces (GUIs) increasingly are replacing traditional character-mode screens, providing dramatic gains in ease of use and flexibility. New application development tools reduce and may one day eliminate altogether the need for traditional programming. Today, most companies are designing and using applications that employ a client/server architecture, in which the application runs on the user's PC or workstation and accesses a centrally maintained and managed file or database server. This approach exploits the client machine's ability to provide highly responsive and intuitive presentation services while using a powerful server to manage shared data securely and efficiently.

In 1979, a tiny Silicon Valley company introduced Oracle, the first commercial relational database incorporating the SQL data-access language. Today, Oracle Corporation is the world's largest supplier of database management systems and associated products. Oracle version 5, released in 1985, was the very first client/server database system. Oracle7 is the latest version of the Oracle database server. This product, introduced in 1992, represents the industry's most advanced product, implementing both the extended relational model and the client/server architecture.

Oracle7 includes a full-featured and government-certified implementation of the ANSI/ISO standard SQL language. The Oracle7 server can be an active part of applications, enforcing data integrity and business rules through "declarative means" (that is, without programming) as well as through the industry's most complete and robust set of programming features, such as stored procedures and triggers. Oracle7 also includes industrial-strength distributed database facilities, enabling enterprise-wide access to data, no matter where it is stored or on what kinds of platforms. Last but not least, Oracle7 maximizes the performance and reliability of on-line transaction processing (OLTP) applications through a range of architectural features, such as row-level locking, online backup and recovery, and support for a wide variety of platforms.

Oracle Corporation is also a leader in another revolution taking place in computer technology: the emerging use of parallel computing platforms, which can deliver unprecedented levels of performance with significant cost effectiveness. These platforms are constructed of low-cost components, with tens, hundreds, or even thousands of highly interconnected independent CPUs, each with its own memory. Historically, such massively parallel platforms were considered applicable only to scientific computing problems, such as weather simulation or other highly computer-intensive operations. As Oracle Corporation has shown, data management is also an application well suited for these machines.

For transaction-processing applications, the Oracle parallel server allows multiple CPUs to access a single database. The parallel server and appropriate hardware can provide extraordinary levels of transaction processing throughput.

The newest updates of Oracle7, releases 7.1, 7.2, and 7.3, exploit the power of parallel platforms for processing sets of records, a common requirement in relational databases. On either shared-memory symmetric multiprocessors or massively parallel platforms, Oracle7 greatly speeds creating and querying large databases by decomposing bulk data operations and executing them in parallel on multiple CPUs. With open systems and parallel technology, Oracle Corporation is lowering the cost of decision-support applications, just as it has done for transaction-processing applications.

Oracle Corporation's experience in building portable data-management software for massively parallel computers has enabled it to take a leadership role in the most recent and exciting computing technology revolution: the construction of the so-called information highway. The information highway will bring to our daily lives vast quantities of multimedia data—for home shopping, video conferencing, video-on-demand, personalized electronic newspapers, and other applications. These changes may well affect society as significantly as did the telephone and the automobile. The Oracle relational database management system, as well as specialized, massively parallel software produced by Oracle Corporation, will be critical components of the information highway.

Steve Bobrowski has written *Mastering Oracle7 & Client/Server Computing* to give you an in-depth understanding of the Oracle7 relational database server and its use in a client/server environment, without burdening you with esoteric information you might never need. You will quickly learn just what you need to know to design, build, and employ applications using the Oracle7 server and Oracle's Cooperative Development Environment (CDE) tools.

If you are designing a new application to run on Oracle7, you will appreciate the thorough treatment of Oracle7's SQL language and extensive facilities for enforcing data integrity through declarative referential integrity and procedurally through PL/SQL stored procedures and triggers. This book also provides an excellent overview of database administration, including the vital issues of database security, backup and recovery, and performance tuning.

Steve Bobrowski is especially qualified to explain how to use the Oracle7 server and application development tools in a client/server environment. Steve worked closely with the developers, product managers, and technical writers associated with the development of Oracle7 and was the principal author of the extensive Oracle7 server documentation published by Oracle Corporation. Few people understand Oracle7 better than he does, and no one can do a better job of making the technology understandable to others. It's been a particular pleasure for me to have known and worked with Steve for over five years.

Part of the excitement in working with database management as a technology, and Oracle in particular, comes from participating in a revolution, contributing to the development of products that empower people, and from imparting to others our enthusiasm for these products. Steve shares with many people at Oracle this special passion for the technology. It is his fond hope, as it is mine, that you will also share that feeling as you come to know and use the technology we call Oracle7.

Ken Jacobs
VP Product Strategy, Server Technologies
Oracle Corporation

April 1996

INTRODUCTION

All businesses, small and large, must manage the company data in a fashion that allows the business to run smoothly. Some businesses might use file cabinets to manage their data, but most companies choose to use computerized database management systems that efficiently store, retrieve, and manage large amounts of data. Oracle7 is a multi-user database management system—a software product that specializes in managing a single, shared set of information among many concurrent users. This book explains how to configure and use Oracle7 in an information management system, with a special focus on using Oracle7 in a client/server system—one that operates among a number of computers that work together and communicate using a network.

Is This Book for You?

Mastering Oracle7 and Client/Server Computing is of interest to a broad audience. If you fall into one or more of the following categories, this book is for you:

- You would like to learn about the world of client/server computing, its advantages and disadvantages, and whether or not it's right for you and your company.

- You want to learn the basics of relational and multi-user database management systems, with a special focus on the features of the Oracle7 relational database management system.

- You want to master the many jobs necessary to administer an Oracle7 client/server system, from basic tasks—such as using Server Manager (Oracle7's administrative utility), controlling database availability, and database backup—to more advanced operations—such as configuring, monitoring, and tuning Oracle7, SQL*Net V2 (Oracle's networking product), and the Oracle7 Parallel Query option.

- You would like to learn what end-user database applications are and how you can develop custom applications for an Oracle7 system.

- You want a quick introduction to the most important application development tools in Oracle's Developer/2000, Designer/2000, and Discoverer/2000 development suites.

- You are an application developer who wants a clear understanding of the key Oracle7 features to take advantage of when developing applications specifically for a client/server system—such as integrity constraints, procedures, triggers, database alerters, and SQL functions.

- You are an end user who wants more insight into how database management systems, especially client/server systems, and Oracle7 work to serve your processing needs.

The Technology

The pace at which new technology is being introduced in the computing industry is nothing less than astonishing. As companies compete for market share and profits, they quickly deliver new innovations in hardware, software, and computing paradigms that drive forward the overall state of information management technology. But the real winner in this race is you, the consumer. That's because if you can grasp new technology as it becomes available and then use it to your benefit, your business gains a significant advantage over those competitors of yours who do not do the same.

The evolution of database management system (DBMS) software is a perfect example of how pervasive the new technology is. Whether or not you realize it, every segment of society benefits from electronic database management systems that allow for the quick storage and retrieval of various types of information. For example, airline companies use databases to track flight reservations; banks use databases to accurately manage bank transactions; and video stores and their customers benefit from database systems that allow for quick and easy check-in and check-out of video tape rentals. In all these examples, database management systems benefit both the companies and their consumers.

Client/Server Computing

What is client/server database computing, and how can it benefit those who choose to take advantage of it? Client/server computing, a relatively new computing model, is nothing more than the distribution of a multi-user database application's processing requirements across a number of networked computers, such as PCs and workstations. What does client/server offer that the traditional mainframe (single-computer) computing environment does not? If you correctly implement a client/server system, the result is an information management system that delivers a much better price/performance ratio and one that can grow and adapt easily to ever-changing business needs. And these are just a couple of the reasons you can benefit from understanding client/server and implementing it in an information management system.

How Does Oracle7 Fit In?

Oracle7 is one of the many servers that you can plug into a client/server database system. And because a client/server system depends heavily on the features of its server, it's important for you to understand how it works and what it can do.

This book provides an in-depth discussion of client/server systems, with a special focus on the features available when you use Oracle7 as the server in the system.

What You Need to Use This Book

This book's primary focus is the central component of an Oracle client/server system: the Oracle7 database server. However, the book also examines the other Oracle products useful for assembling a complete Oracle7 client/server database system. If you want to follow along with all the examples in the book, you'll need the following:

- Oracle7 database server (includes Server Manager and SQL*Loader)
- Oracle7 Parallel Query option
- SQL*Net (version 2)

- Developer/2000
- Designer/2000

Organization of This Book

This book is organized in three parts:

- Part I, Introduction to Client/Server Computing and Oracle7, covers the basic components of client/server communication, including the server, the client, networking issues, and the SQL language.
- Part II, Database Administration in an Oracle7 System, covers all aspects of Oracle7 database administration, including using the administrative utilities, configuring the server, securing databases, and performing other database administrator tasks.
- Part III, Application Development in an Oracle7 System, describes how to design an application's schema, tune applications, centralize application logic in the server, and secure applications. The final chapter contains a tutorial for using Oracle7 Designer/2000 tools for rapid application development.

It also has three appendices. Appendix A provides quick reference lists for Oracle7, including SQL commands, PL/SQL commands, SQL functions, data dictionary views, datatypes, and system and object privileges. Appendix B covers configuring and using the Oracle7 Parallel Query option for parallel processing, and Appendix C provides an overview of the companion disk's contents.

About the Examples in This Book

Learning by example is perhaps one of the fastest ways to understand new things. This book includes literally hundreds of code examples and screen shots to illustrate the workings of Oracle7 and companion products. If you want to experiment yourself, the listings in the book and supporting scripts are on the disk that accompanies the book. Read the README.TXT file on the disk to learn more about the contents of the disk.

Many of the examples in this book appear in the form of code examples—specifically, SQL and PL/SQL statements. (If you aren't familiar with SQL or PL/SQL, don't worry; you'll learn about them in the book.) SQL and PL/SQL are not case-sensitive; that is, you can enter command words in uppercase, lowercase, or a mix of both. However, the sample statements in this book, such as the following SQL statement, contain a mix of uppercase and lowercase words:

```
SELECT id FROM customer;
```

To help you distinguish between keywords of the SQL and PL/SQL languages and user-inserted words, all language *keywords* (words key to the language) appear in uppercase letters (for example, SELECT and FROM). User-inserted words usually appear in lowercase letters (for example, id and customer). The only exception occurs when a user-inserted word is case-sensitive (for example, if it is an operating system filename).

The preceding example also includes a *statement terminator*—a character or set of characters that indicates the end of a statement. The terminator for Oracle SQL statements is the semicolon. Depending on the environment in which you issue statements, SQL statements may or may not require terminators. As a matter of convention, this book uses terminators only where absolutely necessary for technical accuracy in all situations.

PART I

Introduction to Client/Server Computing and Oracle7

Chapters 1 through 5 constitute the introductory part of this book. In reading these chapters you'll get a clear understanding of the "big picture" of an Oracle7 client/server system. This part of the book introduces client/server computing, describes how the Oracle7 server fits into a client/server computing system, and provides an overview of Oracle7's features. You'll also learn about the role of clients in an Oracle7 client/server system and about networking issues, and you'll get an introduction to the Oracle SQL and PL/SQL languages.

What Are Client/Server and Oracle7 Anyway?

- ■ The evolution of corporate computing models from centralized to distributing computing

- ■ The client/server computing model

- ■ Advantages and disadvantages of client/server computing

- ■ How Oracle7 fits into a client/server system

If you or your company works with computers, you have no doubt heard terms such as "database," "database server," and "client/server." Do you really know what they mean and why they are so important in management information systems circles? If you don't know, don't worry; this chapter introduces each of these terms and explains how Oracle7 fits into the picture.

Evolution of Corporate Computing Models

Why is client/server computing so important in the information systems industry? One way to answer this question is to study the evolution of corporate computing models. The next few sections introduce the evolution from the host-based computing model to the client/server computing model.

The Mainframe/Minicomputer Computing Model

First, let's go back to the days of corporate computing when a centralized *host computer* (that is, a corporate mainframe or minicomputer) was boss. In this setting, any company employee could use an application on the corporate mainframe by pulling up a chair to a *dumb terminal* that was physically connected to the mainframe. It's called a "dumb" terminal because that's what it is—a terminal that has no processing capability. It can only send information to the central mainframe and display information given to it by that mainframe. Figure 1.1 illustrates two host-based computing models.

As you can see in Figure 1.1, the mainframe application is a single component responsible for both the interaction with the user and the management of data in a multi-user environment. It quickly became apparent that this application development strategy was inefficient because developers needed to reinvent the same data management component with each new application. Therefore, mainframe and minicomputer applications evolved so that the application's processing was split into two parts: a *front end*, responsible for interaction with the user, and a *back end*, responsible for management of data. The back end, a *database management system*

FIGURE 1.1:

Centralized host-based computing models allow many users to share a single computer's applications, databases, and peripherals.

(*DBMS*), is a central component that can be used with each new front-end application. The separation of the front and back ends of an application also allows more system flexibility because multiple front ends can access the database managed by a single back-end DBMS.

Like anything else, the host-based computing models have both advantages and disadvantages. On the positive side, a mainframe computer is centralized. Therefore, dedicated system administrators can reliably manage the single computer to make sure that data is available when users need it and that valuable corporate data is being backed up for protection. Centralized systems also allow users to share expensive hardware peripherals, such as disk drives, printers, and modems.

However, there are also many negatives to the mainframe model. For example, the greater the number of company workers who need to access the mainframe, the more horsepower the mainframe needs to adequately serve the company's ongoing business. Traditionally, a few companies control the mainframe and minicomputer industries, meaning that they can charge large amounts of money for the proprietary operating systems, processors, applications, memory, and disk storage necessary to make the mainframe or minicomputer work for a company. The more you need, the more you pay.

The Disconnected, Personal Computing Model

Something happened in the 1980s that forever changed the corporate computing model: the introduction of personal computers and workstations. With IBM's introduction of the PC and its operating system (DOS), Apple's introduction of the Macintosh, and, later, the introduction of UNIX workstations from companies like Hewlett-Packard and Sun Microsystems, independent computing workstations quickly became prevalent throughout corporations, ending the centralized control that mainframes once had on all corporate data.

Independent personal workstations are popular because they have several advantages over a mainframe system:

- Personal workstations are inexpensive and easy-to-use computers that deliver the processing power and performance once available only with expensive mainframes.

- A user can make a computer workstation "personal" by picking the type of workstation, operating system, and application that best fits the user's needs.

- PC applications (such as word processors, spreadsheets, graphics, and database management systems) are abundant and typically inexpensive. A user who cannot find a prebuilt application that meets a requirement can create a custom application with an easy-to-use development tool.

- A workstation's data is an autonomous set of information that is personal. Each workstation user is responsible for managing it and backing up the data to protect it. Individual users, not a high-priced data center engineer, administer their own PCs.

Unfortunately, the move toward independent personal computing and away from centralized mainframe computing also introduces problems as well as advantages. Most notably, corporate information, once centralized and available to all employees on a mainframe, is now distributed among the mainframe and personal workstations throughout a company. The data on PCs is not readily available to all users who may need it. Therefore, the gains in the price/performance ratio and ease of use from personal computing can easily be nullified by the loss in productivity of workgroups that need access to information dispersed throughout a corporation. Figure 1.2 shows the problems of a disconnected personal computing model.

Besides not being able to share data, disconnected personal workstation users cannot share other expensive resources that mainframe system users can share: disk drives, printers, modems, and other peripheral computing devices.

The Network/File Server Computing Model

The data- and peripheral-sharing problems of independent, personal PCs and workstations quickly led to the birth of the *network/file server computing model*. In fact, if you use a personal computer or workstation at work today, chances are that your computer is connected to a *local-area network* (*LAN*). A LAN lets a workgroup continue to reap the benefits of easy-to-use PCs but also permits the workgroup to share data and peripherals as in a mainframe system. Figure 1.3 shows the network/file server computing model.

FIGURE 1.2:

Disconnected, independent personal computing models allow processing loads to be removed from a central computer but isolate data sources throughout a company.

FIGURE 1.3:

Network/file server computing models link PCs together so they can share data and peripherals.

To share data in a LAN, users store files on a *file server*. A file server is a central *node* (computer in the network) that stores data files where all users can access them. Typically, the file server in a LAN is also the central hub for sharing peripherals such as printers, print queues, and modems. Because the file server is an independent computer in the network, it's best to specialize it for its job by giving it lots of disk storage space.

In a LAN, an application running on a workstation reads and writes files on the LAN's file server. In many cases, entire files are pumped across the network on behalf of the operations taking place on LAN PCs. A file server plays no part in the processing of an application. The file server does nothing more than store files for applications that run on LAN PCs. For example, you might have a personal database manager on your LAN PC. First, you start your personal database manager and request information in a file on the file server. The LAN's file server sends all or part of the data file across the network to your workstation. As you work with your personal database manager and the database on your workstation, the file server doesn't participate at all. When you save the file, you copy the data file back to the file server across the network.

Unfortunately, the inherent design of the LAN/file server computing model prevents it from adequately servicing demanding multi-user, shared-data applications that mainframes can easily support. Two flaws limit a file server system for multi-user applications:

- The file server model does not deliver the *data concurrency* (simultaneous access to a single data set by multiple users) that is required by multi-user applications. That's because the file server operates in files, which are very large data sets, and prevents a user from sharing a file when another user has it locked out. In short, users that operate on the same data usually bump into each other and are forced to wait in line to access a file.

- File processing and file storage do not typically take place on the same computer; file processing occurs on workstations that store and retrieve files from a central file server. If many workstations request and send many files in a LAN, the network can quickly become saturated with traffic, creating a bottleneck that degrades overall system performance.

The Client/Server Computing Model

The problems of the LAN have led to the genesis of the *client/server computing model*. Client/server computing (also called *distributed application processing* and *cooperative application processing*) delivers the benefits of the network computing model along with the shared data access and high-performance characteristics of the host-based computing model.

A client/server system has three distinct components, each focusing on a specific job: a database server, a client application, and a network. Figure 1.4 shows how the client/server computing model works.

FIGURE 1.4:

Client/server database systems share data in small sets (rows), which allows for a high degree of data concurrency and system performance.

Many users can update the same table at the same time.

A *database server,* (or back end) focuses on efficiently managing a resource, such as a database of information. The server's primary job is to manage its resource optimally among multiple clients that concurrently request the same resource from the server. Database servers concentrate on tasks such as the following:

- Managing a single database of information among many concurrent users
- Controlling database access and other security requirements
- Protecting database information with backup and recovery features
- Centrally enforcing global data integrity rules across all client applications

A *client application* (the front end) is the part of the system that users employ to interact with data. The client applications in a client/server database system focus on jobs such as the following:

- Presenting an interface a user can interact with to accomplish work
- Managing presentation logic such as pop-up lists on a data-entry form or bar graphs in a graphical data presentation tool
- Performing application logic, such as calculating fields in a data-entry form
- Validating data entry
- Requesting and receiving information from a database server

Last but not least, the *network* and *communication software* are the vehicles that transmit data between the clients and the server in a system. Both the clients and the server run communication software that allows them to talk across a network.

A client/server system can deliver better performance than a file server system because a client application and a database server work together to split the processing load of an application (thus the term *distributed application processing*). The server manages the database among a number of clients, while the clients send, request, and analyze the data they receive from the server. In a client/server application, the client application works with small specific data sets, such as rows in a table—not files, as in the file server system. A database server is intelligent, locking and returning only the rows a client requests, which ensures concurrency, minimizes network traffic, and improves system performance.

Benefits and Pitfalls of Client/Server Computing

Now that you understand what the client/server computing model is and how it came about, let's take a look at the benefits and problems of the client/server computing model. This will help you understand the model well and use it appropriately in an information system design.

Distributing an Application's Processing for Flexibility and Scalability

Several benefits of the client/server model stem from the fact that the client and server portions of a system usually run on separate computers. One advantage is that each computer in the system can be selected to best meet the requirements of each component. For example, it's best to use a computer with powerful processors and lots of disk space and memory to run the database server. This way, the server can store large amounts of data and adequately handle many simultaneous client requests. In contrast, it's best to use a less expensive computer with minimal disk storage and memory, a mouse, and excellent graphics capabilities to run the client application. This way, a company can inexpensively equip scores of users with a productive, easy-to-use tool to enter and analyze data.

Another benefit is that the system is very responsive and flexible to all the inevitable types of hardware and software changes. For example, suppose that you want to replace the server with a new type of computer that delivers twice the computing performance of your system's current server at half the price. In a client/server system, it's easy to take out the old server and plug in the new one without disturbing the functionality of client applications or the productivity of users.

Also, it's easy to scale the system to accommodate changes in a workgroup. For example, when a department hires several new workers, they can immediately plug into the network system with new client workstations.

Focusing on Areas of System Development

Each functional component in the client/server system can specialize to do something the best way it can. For example, to develop a client application, a programmer concentrates on the presentation and analysis of data. Meanwhile, the database server concentrates on the management of data. In short, developers do not need to design and code a database management system every time they create a new application.

Delivering Cost Savings

A widely believed benefit of client/server computing is cost savings versus the cost of mainframe or minicomputer systems. In the past, the only choice for running a demanding multi-user database application was to use an expensive, powerful mainframe or minicomputer. This meant using nonintuitive character-based end user terminals, hiring a team of well-paid programmers to get an application up and running, and then maintaining the complicated system around the clock with a team of specialized and pricey administrators. Initial and ongoing expenses for such a system can be astronomical.

In many cases, a client/server system can support a mainframe application with greatly reduced cost. That's because a client/server system distributes the processing load of a large application across many inexpensive computers connected by a network. The application itself is easier to develop and use because of user-friendly workstation graphical user interfaces (GUIs) and object-oriented application development tools (see Chapter 3 for information about user interfaces and object-oriented programming).

Some Disadvantages

Now, a dose of reality. Client/server computing does have its disadvantages. First, anticipated cost savings of a client/server may not actually appear in real-world situations. When projecting the cost of a computer system, system designers must include many factors, not just hardware expenditures. For example, the productivity of users—end users, developers, and administrators—is an important consideration in measuring cost.

Developers may notice improved productivity by using the GUIs and *computer-aided software engineering* (*CASE*) development tools available for client/server database computing. However, application users and administrators may actually notice a drop in productivity. Why? The reliability of a client/server system, a mix of independently developed, manufactured, and managed hardware and software components, is inherently less than that of a homogenous, centrally managed mainframe or minicomputer. And who do you call for technical support when something goes wrong? Downtime due to an unreliable system takes away from end user and administrator productivity. And as the old saying goes, time is money. Figure 1.5 illustrates the heterogeneity of client/server systems.

FIGURE 1.5:

The inherent heterogeneity of client/server systems makes system integration, administration, and maintenance a formidable challenge.

The key factor in realizing a cost saving is choosing the correct type of application to run on a client/server system. For example, it might be unrealistic to run and manage a massive, mission-critical airline reservation system completely on a client/server database system, considering the hundreds of thousands of reservation terminals and dial-in hookups that stretch across the world. However, it is perfectly reasonable to run a company's or department's localized accounting and manufacturing applications on a client/server database system.

Client/server computing is a very important part of an overall corporate information strategy, but it isn't the right choice for every application. As you learn more about client/server database systems in this book, use your understanding to correctly apply client/server where you think it will work and when it will save your company money.

Oracle7 and Client/Server Computing

What about Oracle7—how does it figure into the client/server model? Oracle7 is one of many database servers that you can plug into a client/server equation. Oracle7 works to efficiently manage its resource, a database of information, among the multiple clients requesting and sending data in the network. As this book explains, Oracle7 has many important features that make it not only an exceptional database management system but also an excellent database server choice for client/server database computing. Here are some of those features:

- Oracle7 supports all major operating systems for both clients and servers, including MS-DOS, NetWare, Windows NT, MacOS/2, and most flavors of UNIX. Oracle networking software, SQL*Net, also supports all major network communication protocols, including TCP/IP, SPX/IPX, Named Pipes, and DECNet. Therefore, Oracle7 can be the link that joins the many data stores and networks throughout the heterogeneous computing systems prevalent in most corporations.

- Oracle7 has client/server features developers can use to minimize network traffic between clients and servers. Therefore, applications based on Oracle7 can deliver the performance that users require to be productive in their jobs.

- Oracle7 has features that make it easy to administer a complicated client/server system. Therefore, Oracle7 can deliver the advantages of client/server computing and keep the administration cost in a large, complicated system within reason.

There aren't many specifics about Oracle7 in the preceding list, but don't worry—
you'll learn all you need to know about Oracle7 and client/server database computing as you continue to read this book.

This chapter has given you a quick overview of client/server computing and has
shown how Oracle7 fits into the client/server model. The remaining chapters in
Part I are a broad overview of each of the three different components in an Oracle7
client/server database system: the database server, the client, and the communication between the server and its clients.

### TWO

The Server in Client/Server

- The structure of an Oracle7 database

- Data integrity

- Oracle7 security features

- Data availability

- Oracle7 database protection

Now that you understand the term *client/server*, let's learn some specifics about each of the components that make up a client/server system. This chapter focuses on the database server part of the client/server equation. After reading this chapter, you'll have a broad understanding of the most important issues that are addressed by the database server:

- Databases, relational databases, and Oracle7 databases

- The structure of an Oracle7 database, including tables, views, tablespaces, and data files

- Data integrity and how to enforce it in an Oracle7 database using integrity constraints, stored procedures, and triggers

- Oracle7's concurrency mechanisms, which allow multi-user access to a single database

- Oracle7's security features, such as database usernames and passwords, privileges, and roles

- Control of data availability with database startup and shutdown and online and offline tablespaces

- Protection of an Oracle7 database with a transaction log and backups, and using these features to recover from damaging circumstances

- Database administration in an Oracle7 client/server database system

Databases and Relational Database Management Systems

We've all been exposed to a countless number of databases. For example, every time you pick up the phone book to find a number, you're using a database. And every time you get a piece of junk mail, it is the result of someone using a mailing list, which is a database of names.

In simple terms, a *database* is a set of related information. Using our previous examples, a phone book is a database of names and phone numbers, and a mailing list is a database of prospective customer names and addresses.

One of the most common ways to manage a database is the file cabinet. Neatly organized with hanging file folders and name tags, a file cabinet is an example of a paper database. Although the file cabinet does a fine job of organizing data, it has many limitations. For example, what if you need to use a file someone else is already using? In this case, you have two options: you can wait until the other person finishes with the file or you can make your own copy of the file. If you are the patient type and decide to wait for the file, you can hope that the other person is a fast worker and will promptly return the file so you don't need to wait too long. If you can't wait and decide to make a copy of the file, you must gamble that your work won't depend on the other person's work.

The paper database in a file cabinet has other disadvantages. Think about all the office space a series of full-size file cabinets can consume. And what if a fire destroys your building? Do you have a set of file cabinets at home to keep up-to-date copies of important files, such as employee lists, customer names, product orders, and billing information? Your answer is probably no, especially if your business is larger than a lemonade stand.

Database Servers

You probably already know that computers can do a much better job than a file cabinet. Using a network of computers or a multi-user computer, many users can concurrently share the same set of data. Computers can store billions of characters of information on a single magnetic or optical disk, which makes it easy to protect valuable data from catastrophes. And the affordability and power of the personal computer allows even the household bill payer to manage a database by computer.

What you might not realize is that you need the correct piece of computer software to actually manage data. This software is the database management system (DBMS), or database server. And just as file cabinets come in many different colors and sizes, each type of database server has its own characteristics. If you understand the characteristics of your database server, you'll no doubt make better use if it, no matter what type of user you are.

The Relational Database Model

The Oracle7 database server is based on the relational database model. The *relational database model* is a well-defined theoretical model of working with and managing a set of data (a database) that attends to three specific things: data structure, data integrity, and data manipulation. Let's learn about Oracle7's presentation of the relational database model by studying the components of Oracle7 that address the four fundamental areas of the relational model: tables, integrity constraints, data access, and transactions.

Data Structure: Tables

The fundamental rule of the relational model is that data is seen as *tables,* and nothing but tables. Because the concept of a table is simple and intuitive, the relational model is easy to understand.

There are several specific rules for tables in the relational model. For example, a table, formally called a *relation,* has a fixed number of *columns* (also called *fields* or *attributes*) and can have a variable number of *rows* (also called *records* or *tuples*). Figure 2.1 shows examples of typical tables in a relational database.

Data Integrity: Integrity Constraints

The relational model also concerns itself with data integrity. If a relational database has *data integrity,* it means that all of the data in the database is valid according to a set of rules. For example, all customers in the CUSTOMERS table must have a unique customer ID; otherwise, you would not be able to distinguish between two customers with the same name and same address. This standard data integrity rule of the relational model is called *entity integrity,* which implies that you can uniquely identify each row in a table.

You can define standard data integrity rules of the relational model within an Oracle7 relationship using *integrity constraints.* When you create a table in an Oracle7 relational database, you *declare* (specify) integrity rules with simple command options. Once declared, integrity constraints are a statement about the integrity of the data in an Oracle7 relational database because they automatically prohibit invalid data from existing in the database.

FIGURE 2.1:

The ORDERS, ITEMS, CUSTOMERS, and PARTS tables are examples of tables in a relational database.

Customers Table

ID	COMPANY NAME	LASTNAME	FIRSTNAME	ADDRESS	CITY	STATE	ZIPCODE	...
1	NBC	Brokaw	Thomas	Park Ave.	New York	NY	01002	...
2	CBS	Rather	Daniel	Park Ave.	New York	NY	01002	...
3	CNN	Shaw	Bernard	Pixie Dr.	Atlanta	GA	21002	...
4	ABC	Jennings	Peter	Rodeo Dr.	Los Angeles	CA	94200	...
...	...	...	...	...	...	...	...	

Columns
(fields or attributes)

Parts Table

ID	UNITPRICE	ONHAND	REORDER	...
1	8.97	178200		...
2	21.40	223150		...
3	87.12	4850		...
4	6.03	638450		...

Orders Table

ID	CUSTOMERID	ORDERDATE	SHIPDATE	...
1	4	06/23/95	06/23/95	...
2	2	06/23/95	06/23/95	...
3	3	06/23/95	06/24/95	...
4	1	06/24/95	06/24/95	...
...	...	...	...	...

Items Table

ID	ORDERID	PARTID	QUANTITY	TOTAL
1	1	4	1	...
2	1	2	4	...
3	1	3	2	...
1	2	1	2	...
2	2	2	3	...
...	...	...	...	...

Rows (records or tuples)

Data Manipulation: Structured Query Language (SQL)

The relational model also describes how users can manipulate data within tables using relational algebra. *Relational algebra* is a finite set of operators that are used on tables to manipulate database data. For example, the *restrict relational operator* collects specific rows from a table, the *project relational operator* collects specific columns from a table, and the *join relational operator* creates a new table by joining related data from two or more tables. Relational algebra is a set of mathematical principles that precisely controls how to manipulate data in a relational database.

To interact with a relational database, you must use an access language that embodies the principles of relational algebra. Although not part of the relational model, the industry-standard data access language for relational databases is called *SQL* (pronounced either as "es-que-el" or "sequel"), for Structured Query Language. SQL is an easy-to-use, English-like language that has all the commands necessary to work with a relational database server like Oracle7. Following are some quick examples of SQL commands that retrieve table data using restrict, project, and join relational operators.

> **NOTE** Comments in a SQL statement begin with two hyphen characters (--) and proceed to the end of the line.

```
-- example of restrict relational operator in SQL
SELECT *
  FROM customers
  WHERE ID = 3

-- example of project relational operator in SQL
SELECT id, lastname, firstname
  FROM customers

-- example of join relational operator in SQL
SELECT items.orderid, items.id, parts.description
  FROM items, parts
  WHERE items.partid = parts.id
```

SQL also has other types of commands that permit users to create and drop data structures, manipulate table data, and control access to specific database data. Here are a few quick examples:

```
CREATE TABLE orders ...
DROP TABLE items ...
INSERT INTO orders VALUES (...)
UPDATE items SET quantity = 2 WHERE orderid = 2345 AND id = 2
DELETE FROM orders WHERE id = 597
GRANT SELECT ON customers TO rnixon
REVOKE SELECT ON orders FROM gbush
```

Query is a common term used when discussing relational databases and SQL. Some use *query* to mean any type of SQL statement that manipulates data (for example, to insert, update, delete, or retrieve data). Others use the term specifically to mean a SELECT statement that retrieves data from a database. In this book, we'll use the term to mean a SELECT statement.

Data Manipulation: Transactions

Before the age of the automated teller machine (ATM) and phone banking systems, you went to the bank and talked to a human being when you needed to transfer money between your savings and checking accounts. A transfer of money between accounts is a banking transaction that consists of several different but related operations. For example, first you go up to the teller and say, "Hi, I'd like to transfer some savings into my checking account." Then you hand the teller your bankbook and the transaction slip. After the teller increments your checking account and decrements your savings account, the teller records the transfer in a log or journal. Finally, you get a receipt of the transfer for your records.

Each operation of the transfer banking transaction is important in the grand scheme of things. Think what would happen if some steps were completed but others left undone. In your favor but at the expense of the bank, you might get extra funds in your checking account if the teller forgets to record the savings funds withdrawal. Even worse, you may come out behind if the teller withdraws the savings funds but forgets to credit your checking account. Therefore, the banking transfer transaction is not complete unless the teller carries out all the steps.

Banking and other operations are no different with SQL; the language incorporates the important concept of a transaction. A database *transaction* is a unit made up of the work done by one or more SQL statements. For example, to complete the several related steps of the banking transfer action using a relational database and SQL, you perform the following steps:

1. Update the ACCOUNT table to reflect the new savings account balance after the transfer.

2. Update the ACCOUNT table to reflect the new checking account balance after the transfer.

3. Insert a new entry into the JOURNAL table, recording your ID, the account numbers, the transaction type, the transfer data, and the transfer amount.

4. Commit the transaction as complete (make the changes permanent).

Before step 4 takes place, the changes of steps 1, 2, and 3 are considered temporary, because the transaction has not yet been committed. Step 4 is the critical step. You *commit* a transaction using the SQL command COMMIT, which marks the end of the current transaction. At this point, the database server makes all the changes of the current transaction permanent.

SQL also gives you another choice for transaction control. If in step 4 you decide that you don't want to commit the transaction, you can *roll back* the transaction using the SQL command ROLLBACK. This command undoes any effects caused by the SQL statements in the current transaction as if they had never happened.

So far, we've covered the basics you need to understand the foundations of the Oracle7 relational database server: tables, integrity constraints, SQL, and transactions. The following sections describe the specifics of an Oracle7 relational database management system.

Oracle7 Relational Database Structure

Just as a company organizes a warehouse of goods, Oracle7 structures a database both logically and physically. An Oracle7 database's *logical structure* is the set of tables in the database. A database's *physical structure* is the set of operating system files that store the bits and bytes of database information on disk.

One of the characteristics of a relational database system is *data independence*. An Oracle7 relational database's physical structure is independent of and hidden from an end user's logical view of the data. The benefit is that users can easily access data in logical structures (tables) by using simple SQL commands, without needing to know anything about the physical organization of the data. Oracle7 takes care of mapping columns and rows of table data to files and physical bytes on disk.

NOTE   In contrast, database systems that are not relational require users to program applications to access data by using complicated physical addressing mechanisms. The major drawback of such *data-dependent* database systems is that database applications have compiled access paths to data. Therefore, when someone changes the physical location or organization of the data, it's likely that all applications will need major modifications to account for such changes. Because relational database systems have data independence, they don't fall prey to similar problems.

To take complete advantage of Oracle7's data-independence qualities, it's important to understand the logical and physical components in an Oracle7 database. The next few sections describe these components, including tables, views, tablespaces, and data files.

Tables: Oracle7's Logical Storage Building Blocks

The Oracle7 relational database system stores and presents all data in tables like those shown in Figure 2.1. A table is a focused collection of related information—a set of data records that all have the same attributes. The attributes of a table are the table's columns, and the data records are the table's rows. For example, all the records in the CUSTOMERS table in Figure 2.1 have the same attributes: ID number, company name, last name, first name, address, city, state, zip code, phone number, and fax number. The CUSTOMERS table can have any number of customer records, but each customer must have the same set of fixed attributes.

Column Datatypes

Each table column, or attribute, contains a specific type of data. For example, the ID column in the CUSTOMERS table stores numbers, and the remainder of the columns store text strings. (The zip code field is a text string to allow for leading zeros, and the phone and fax number columns are text strings to allow for hyphens and other delimiting characters.) When a user creates a table, the user specifies the table's columns and the *datatype* for each column.

Oracle7 supports many different datatypes. Table 2.1 describes some of them.

TABLE 2.1: Some Oracle7 Datatypes

Datatype	Description
CHAR (*size*)	Stores fixed-length character strings
VARCHAR2 (*size*)	Stores variable-length character strings
NUMBER (*precision, scale*)	Stores numbers of all types, including integer and, floating-point, and so on
DATE	Stores time-related information, including dates and times
LONG	Stores large, variable-length character strings, up to 2 gigabytes
RAW (size)	Stores small binary strings, less than 2000 bytes
LONG RAW	Stores long binary strings, up to 2 gigabytes

Administrators need to pay particular attention when specifying the datatypes for columns. The datatype for a column can significantly affect the amount of space Oracle7 uses to store the column's data. Chapter 10 explains how to choose the correct datatypes for the columns of a table.

Tablespaces and Data Files: Oracle7's Physical Storage Building Blocks

When a user creates a new table, the user tells Oracle7 where to physically store the table's data. The user does this by specifying a tablespace for the new table. A *tablespace* is a partition or logical area of storage in a database that directly corresponds to one or more physical *data files*. After an administrator creates a tablespace in a database, users can create one or more tables in the tablespace. Figure 2.2 illustrates the relationship among tables, tablespaces, and data files.

The table-tablespace-data file chain is what gives Oracle7 the inherent relational database characteristic of data independence. After a user creates a table, other users

FIGURE 2.2:

A tablespace is a logical database division that maps to one or more physical data files. Table data in each tablespace therefore maps to the tablespace's data files.

can insert, update, and delete rows in the table just by naming the table in a SQL statement. Oracle7 takes care of mapping a SQL request to the correct physical data on disk.

The SYSTEM Tablespace: The Tablespace of All Tablespaces

Every Oracle7 database has at least one tablespace: the SYSTEM tablespace. When creating a database, the administrator specifies the names and sizes of the initial data files for the database. These files are the physical storage for the SYSTEM tablespace.

Oracle7 uses the SYSTEM tablespace to store the data dictionary. The *data dictionary* is a set of internal system tables that holds all sorts of information about the database itself. For example, there are data dictionary tables that provide information about the tables, tablespaces, and data files in the database.

Why Use Multiple Tablespaces?

After creating an Oracle7 database, the administrator will want to create other tablespaces to physically partition the data planned for the database. For example, there will likely be many client applications that access a database in your client/server system. When adding each new client application to the system, it's best to create one or more new tablespaces to hold each application's data separate from the data dictionary and the data of other applications.

Why should an administrator bother to use tablespaces to organize data storage? There are many good reasons. Here are a few:

- Oracle7 allows administrators to control the availability of a database's data on a tablespace-by-tablespace basis. Therefore, they can effectively take an application offline by taking the application's tablespace offline, making its tables inaccessible.

- Oracle7 allows administrators to back up a database at the tablespace level. When administrators want to back up just a specific application's data, not the entire database, it's easy; they can back up just the application's tablespace.

- Administrators can improve the performance of client applications if they use tablespaces wisely. For example, by placing the data files of each application's tablespace on different disks of a database server, the administrator can ensure that applications won't contend with each other for disk access and space.

If you will administer your Oracle7 client/server system, you will want to learn more about designing and managing your database's tablespaces and data files. Chapter 7 explains how to configure these components of a database.

Now let's take a look at some of the other components in an Oracle7 database system.

Views: Looking at Table Data in Different Ways

When you look into the night sky, you see stars. When you look into a telescope at night, you also see stars. As you know, the stars aren't actually in the telescope; you're just looking at the stars in the sky with a different perspective—a much closer view.

A *view* and tables in a relational database are analogous to the telescope and the stars. When users open a view, they see the same data that's in database tables, but with perhaps a different perspective. And just as the telescope doesn't contain any stars, a view doesn't contain any data. Instead, a view is a *virtual table*, deriving its data from *base tables*. Figure 2.3 illustrates the concept of a view.

You can think of a view as a *stored query*. That's because you define a view with a query. Here is the SQL definition of the REORDER view shown in Figure 2.3:

```
CREATE VIEW reorder AS
  SELECT id, onhand, reorder FROM parts
  WHERE onhand < reorder
```

The CREATE VIEW statement defines the REORDER view. Its query corresponds only to those rows in the PARTS table where the part's current inventory quantity is lower than its reorder point.

As stated earlier, one of the primary rules of a relational model is that all data must be seen as tables. Therefore, a view maintains the characteristics of a table. For example, the defining query names the columns of the view. And users can employ data-manipulation SQL statements against a view just as they can with a table (with some restrictions). Because a view derives its data from a base table, Oracle7 manipulates the data of the base table when a user queries, inserts into, updates, or deletes from a view. Unless you specifically know you're using a view, it's hard to distinguish a view from a table.

FIGURE 2.3:

A view is a virtual table. You see information derived from one or more tables, but the view itself doesn't store any information.

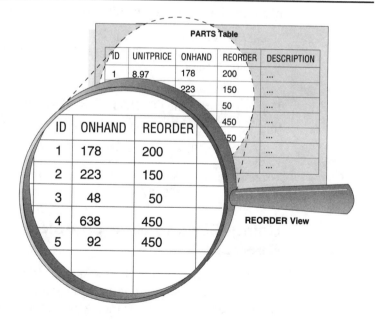

Views are a powerful tool in a relational database such as Oracle7. The next few sections discuss some of the ways administrators and developers can use views in a database.

Using Views to Increase Security

If an administrator allows an ordering clerk to query the PARTS table, the clerk can see all the information about all the parts in inventory. However, if the security administrator allows the clerk to query only the REORDER view, the clerk can see only the part numbers, quantity, and reorder point for the parts that need reordering. Therefore, restricting the user's access to only the REORDER view increases the security of the PARTS table. Developers can limit access to specific table columns using a view and create value-based security by defining a view for specific rows. The REORDER view is an example of both options.

Using Views to Present Additional Information

A developer can use a view to derive other columns not present in any table. For example, you can create calculated fields using a view. Here is the SQL definition of a view that calculates the total for all the line items in each order:

```
CREATE VIEW ordertotal AS
  SELECT orderid, SUM(total) "ORDER TOTAL"
  FROM items
  GROUP BY orderid
```

If a user queries the ORDERTOTAL view, Oracle7 calculates the totals for the requested orders. Here is a typical output when querying the ORDERTOTAL view:

```
SELECT * FROM ordertotal WHERE orderid = 1

ORDERID    ORDER TOTAL
1          265.87
```

Using Views to Hide Complex Queries

Developers can hide complicated queries from users by using a view. The benefit is that users issue simple queries against the view and the view takes care of all the complicated work. For instance, a developer might create a view to hide a join query—a query that pulls together related information. A developer might create a view to join order and corresponding line item information from the ORDERS and ITEMS tables. Here is a view with a join and a typical output when a user queries the view:

```
CREATE VIEW orderreport AS
  SELECT orders.id "ORDER ID", orders.orderdate, items.id "LINE
ID", partid
  FROM orders, items
  WHERE items.orderid = orders.id

SELECT * FROM orderreport WHERE "ORDER ID" = 2

ORDERID ORDERDATE LINEID PARTID
2       06/23/95  1      1
2       06/23/95  2      2
```

The previous sections explained just three examples of how to use views in an Oracle7 database.

Limitations When Using Views

There are certain limitations when using views. For example, users can't insert, update, or delete records using the ORDERTOTAL view described earlier. Oracle7 doesn't allow you to manipulate data using views that have a defining query with a group operator (for example, the GROUP BY operator in the ORDERTOTAL view). In this case, it's not clear to the database server how to map a data-manipulation operation back to the underlying base table(s) of a view.

Other limitations apply to views. If you are an administrator or application developer, you'll want to learn more about the powers and limitations of views. Chapter 15 explains how to use views effectively in an Oracle7 database.

Ensuring Data Integrity

It's important to make sure that the data in a database has integrity, or that the data is valid according to a set of rules. The relational model describes several intrinsic rules that must be enforced to guarantee data integrity in a relational database: domain integrity, entity integrity, and referential integrity. Figure 2.4 shows the integrity rules in our sample database, and the following sections explain these rules in more detail.

FIGURE 2.4:

Several related tables and their associated data integrity rules

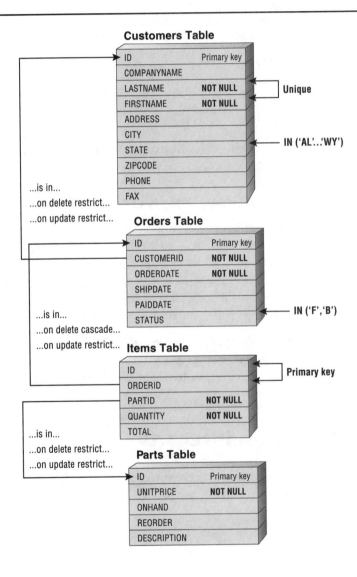

Domain Integrity: Making Sure Every Field Value Is a Member of a Domain

Domain integrity makes sure that a database doesn't contain any nonsense values. It ensures that a value in a column is a member of the column's *domain,* or legal set of values.

A row cannot be in a table unless each of the row's column values is a member in the domain of the corresponding column. For example, there can't be a row in the ORDERS table with the character *A* for an ID field, because the ID column holds numbers and *A* is not a member of the domain of numbers.

Entity Integrity: Making Sure Each Row Is Unique

Another intrinsic data integrity rule is entity integrity. *Entity integrity* means that every row in a table must be unique. If a table has entity integrity, you can uniquely identify every row in the table because there are no duplicate rows.

To ensure entity integrity, a developer designates a column or a set of columns in a table as its *primary key.* Each row in a table must contain a unique primary key value. Implicitly, this means that every row in a table must indeed have a primary key value (a complete set of values in the case of a composite primary key, a key made of two or more columns) because the absence of value, a *NULL,* is not distinguishable from another NULL. For example, the ID column is the primary key of the ORDERS table in Figure 2.4. Therefore, every order has a unique order ID.

A table can have only one primary key. In many cases, developers need to eliminate duplicate values from other columns as well. For this, a developer can designate a non-primary key column (or set of columns) as an *alternate key* or a *unique key.* A table can't have duplicate values in a unique key, just as it can't have duplicates in a primary key. For example, every record in the CUSTOMERS table has a unique last name and first name combination.

Referential Integrity: Making Sure Related Tables Stay in Sync

Referential integrity, or relation integrity, is another elemental data integrity rule of the relational model. *Referential integrity* defines the relationships among different columns and tables in a relational database. It's called referential integrity because the values in one column or set of columns refer to or must match the values in a related column or set of columns.

For example, the CUSTOMERS and ORDERS tables in Figure 2.4 track different, but related, information. The CUSTOMERS table keeps track of customer names, addresses, and phone numbers. Each customer record has a unique customer ID. The ORDERS table keeps track of orders that customers place. ORDERS has a column to indicate the customer, by customer ID, who places each order. As you can see, the customer ID column in ORDERS refers to the customer ID column in CUSTOMERS. Referential integrity simply makes sure that at all times, each order has a customer ID that matches a customer ID in the CUSTOMERS table.

Several terms are used when discussing referential integrity. The dependent column or set of columns is a *foreign key*. The referenced column or set of columns is a *parent key*, which must be a primary key or unique key. The foreign key is in the *child*, or *detail*, table; the parent key is in the *parent*, or *master*, table. If the parent and foreign keys are in the same table, it is called *self-referential* integrity. For example, Figure 2.5 shows how the MANAGER column of the EMPLOYEE table refers to the primary key of the same table.

The ability to relate values in different tables and maintain referential integrity is an important characteristic of relational databases. Relational database servers are

FIGURE 2.5:

Self-referential integrity occurs when one column of a table refers to the values in another column of the same table.

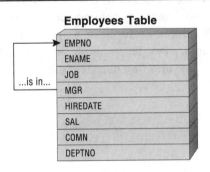

Employees Table

very efficient at storing data because of this ability to link different tables. For example, consider the amount of redundant customer data our sample database would need to keep track of if it couldn't relate the ORDERS and CUSTOMERS tables. Without a relational database, every order would require a full set of customer information, including customer name, address, and phone number. Additionally, if a customer's phone number changed, someone would need to go back and update every one of the customer's orders to indicate the new number. Fortunately, no one will need to do this with an Oracle7 relational database (if the developer has set it up correctly), because it is very flexible and efficient at storing data.

Business Rules: Custom Data Integrity Rules

So far, we've learned about the standard data integrity rules that are built into the relational database model. However, every company's database has its own unique set of *business rules* that are just as important as the standard set of data integrity rules. For example, a security administrator might want to disallow changes to a table during abnormal business hours or derive a value for a column when a user inserts or updates a record.

To ensure complete database integrity, there must be a way for the system to enforce custom business rules as well. The following sections explain the features of Oracle7 that developers and administrators can use to enforce standard and complex data integrity rules.

Enforcing Data Integrity with Oracle7

One way to enforce data integrity rules is to code every integrity rule inside each application that accesses your database. Although this approach works, two significant problems arise:

- Developers must code, test, and debug the same integrity rules into each database application. If a rule changes, developers need to modify all applications. As you can imagine, this is a time-consuming and unproductive development process.

- An application must request a great deal of data from the database to enforce data integrity rules inside the application. If a client application and database server operate on different machines joined by a network, the server must ship lots of data across the network so that each application can enforce integrity rules; consequently, this generates excessive traffic that can saturate the network and diminish system performance.

For these two reasons alone, it's important to enforce data integrity rules inside the server instead of in the application when you use a client/server database system. Oracle7 has a number of features that developers and administrators can use to enforce standard and complex data integrity rules at the database server: datatypes, integrity constraints, and triggers.

Using Column Datatypes to Enforce Domain Integrity

Oracle7 automatically enforces domain integrity using the datatypes for the columns in a table. A record can't be in a table unless the data for each column is the correct type. For example, a record can't be in the ORDERS table with an alphabetic character in the ID column because the ID column holds numbers, and an alphabetic character isn't in the domain of valid numbers.

Oracle7 allows developers to declare the datatype or domain for a column. Some datatypes allow further limitation of the domain of a column (see Table 2.1, shown earlier in the chapter). For example, the NUMBER datatype can define the *precision* (total number of significant digits) and *scale* (total number of significant digits to the right or left of the decimal place) of acceptable numbers in the column. Oracle7 doesn't allow a row in a table if the row has a number in a column that exceeds the column's precision. Oracle7 automatically rounds all acceptable numbers to match the scale you specify for the column.

The character datatypes also allow additional domain integrity control by specifying the maximum length of acceptable text strings for the column. Oracle7 doesn't allow a row in a table if the row has a text string in a column that is longer than the length specified for that column.

Using Integrity Constraints to Enforce Standard Data Integrity Rules

Integrity constraints allow relational database systems to enforce the standard data integrity rules that are part of the relational model. Integrity constraints are simple to use because developers declare standard data integrity rules as part of a table's definition. Here are some Oracle7 CREATE TABLE statements that include the declaration of several integrity constraints:

```
CREATE TABLE customers
( id NUMBER(5,0) PRIMARY KEY,
  companyname VARCHAR2(50),
  lastname VARCHAR2(50) NOT NULL,
  firstname VARCHAR2(50) NOT NULL,
  address VARCHAR2(100),
  city VARCHAR2(50),
  state CHAR(2),
  zipcode VARCHAR2(10),
  phone VARCHAR2(20),
  fax VARCHAR2(20),
  UNIQUE (lastname, firstname),
  CHECK (state IN

    ('AL','AK','AZ','AR','CA','CO','CT','DE','DC','FL','GA','HI','ID',
     'IL','IN','IA','KS','KY','LA','ME','MD','MA','MI','MN','MS','MO',
     'MT','NE','NV','NH','NJ','NM','NY','NC','ND','OH','OK','OR','PA',
     'PR','RI','SC','SD','TN','TX','UT','VT','VA','WA','WV','WI','WY') ) )

CREATE TABLE orders
( id NUMBER(5,0) PRIMARY KEY,
  customerid NUMBER(5,0) NOT NULL,
  orderdate DATE NOT NULL,
  shipdate DATE,
  paiddate DATE,
  status CHAR(1),
  CHECK (status IN ('F','B')), -- F is filled, B is backlogged
  FOREIGN KEY (customerid) REFERENCES customers )
```

```
CREATE TABLE parts
( id NUMBER(5,0) PRIMARY KEY,
  unitprice NUMBER(10,2) NOT NULL,
  onhand NUMBER(5,0),
  reorder NUMBER(5,0),
  description VARCHAR2(2000))

CREATE TABLE items
( id NUMBER(5,0),
  orderid NUMBER(5,0),
  partid NUMBER(5,0) NOT NULL,
  quantity NUMBER(5,0) NOT NULL,
  total NUMBER(10,2),
  PRIMARY KEY (id, orderid),
  FOREIGN KEY (orderid) REFERENCES orders ON DELETE CASCADE,
  FOREIGN KEY (partid) REFERENCES parts )
```

Eliminating NULLS

In many cases, it's necessary to narrow the acceptable domain of a column's values further than datatyping permits. A common requirement is to eliminate absent values, or NULLs, from the domain of a column. This way, every row in a table has a value for the column. The developer can eliminate NULLs from the domain of a column by declaring a NOT NULL integrity constraint with the column's definition. For example, the preceding CUSTOMERS table definition declares NOT NULL integrity constraints for both the LASTNAME and FIRSTNAME columns to make sure every customer record has a complete customer name. If someone tries to insert or update a row with a NULL in a column designated as NOT NULL, Oracle7 will not accept the row.

Defining Complex Domains

After datatyping and handling NULLs, a developer might find it necessary to narrow a column's domain even more, defining the specific values that are acceptable in a column. For example, only valid state code abbreviations—'AL', 'AK', 'AZ', ... 'WY'—should be in the STATE column of the CUSTOMERS table. This example of domain integrity is an expression that specifically defines the domain of a column.

A developer can express a custom domain integrity rule using a CHECK integrity constraint. For example, the preceding CUSTOMERS table declares a CHECK constraint to enforce the custom domain integrity expression for valid state codes in the STATE column.

Declaring PRIMARY KEY and UNIQUE Constraints

A developer can declare a PRIMARY KEY integrity constraint to define a table's primary key and enforce entity integrity. Every table definition above declares a PRIMARY KEY integrity constraint to enforce entity integrity. The CUSTOMERS table also declares a UNIQUE integrity constraint to enforce uniqueness of customer names.

Declaring Referential Integrity Constraints

A developer can establish referential integrity by declaring a referential or FOREIGN KEY integrity constraint to define a foreign key in a table. The column(s) of a foreign key must match the datatypes of the column(s) in the parent key.

Remember that referential integrity makes sure that each foreign key value always matches a parent key value. Therefore, a referential integrity constraint not only determines acceptable data in the foreign key of the child table, it defines the *referential action* when operating on the parent key. For example, there are two referential integrity constraints in the ITEMS table in the previous example. The first referential integrity constraint references the ORDERS table. The *delete cascade referential action* of this constraint is to cascade the deletion of a parent row to all dependent child rows. Therefore, when a user deletes an order from the ORDERS table, Oracle7 automatically deletes the line items for the order.

It's not apparent, but by not including the ON DELETE CASCADE option, the second referential integrity constraint restricts all operations on a parent key that has dependent child rows. Therefore, Oracle7 prohibits a user from updating a part number or deleting a part from the PARTS table if the part has dependent order line items. This rule is called the *restrict referential action*.

Using Stored Procedures and Triggers to Enforce Custom Business Rules

Integrity constraints can enforce a large percentage of the data integrity rules in a database. However, there will always be business rules that developers cannot enforce with integrity constraints. Developers need to enforce these custom integrity rules as well to ensure complete database integrity. And as we've already learned, it's best to be able to centralize the enforcement of all integrity rules inside the database server of a client/server system.

Stored Procedures

To enforce a complex business rule, Oracle7 offers stored procedures. A *stored procedure* is a compiled collection of SQL statements, flow control statements, variable declarations, assignment operators, and so on, that a developer creates and stores in a database. Developers can use procedures to enforce complex data integrity because when a user performs an operation using a procedure, Oracle7 forces the user to handle data in a prescribed or predefined manner.

For example, let's assume we need to enforce the following business rule: When a user deletes a customer record from the CUSTOMERS table, the user should log the customer ID and name in a history table. Here is the definition of a stored procedure that enforces this business rule:

```
CREATE PROCEDURE deletecustomer (custid IN INTEGER) AS
  last VARCHAR2(50);
  first VARCHAR2(50);
BEGIN
  SELECT lastname, firstname INTO last, first
    FROM customers WHERE id = custid;
  INSERT INTO customerhistory VALUES (custid, last, first);
  DELETE FROM customers WHERE id = custid;
EXCEPTION
  WHEN NO_DATA_FOUND THEN
    raise_application_error (-20123, 'Invalid Customer ID');
END deletecustomer;
```

The preceding example introduces statement terminators for SQL statements. A *statement terminator* is a character or set of characters that indicates the end of a statement. For example, the terminator used to indicate the end of Oracle SQL statements is the semicolon. Depending on the environment in which you issue statements, SQL statements may or may not require terminators. As a matter of convention, this book uses terminators only where absolutely necessary for technical accuracy in all situations.

To enforce our business rule, we should not allow users and applications to issue DELETE statements against the CUSTOMERS table. Instead, give users only the privilege to execute the DELETECUSTOMER procedure; this way, when someone executes this procedure, it automatically logs the removal of a customer record before deleting the specified customer.

Database Triggers

If you want to allow users to delete rows from the CUSTOMERS table but still automatically enforce your business rule, you can use a trigger instead. A *trigger* is a stored procedure that Oracle7 automatically *fires* (executes) under the appropriate conditions. The following example is a trigger that automatically enforces the same business rule as the DELETECUSTOMER procedure:

```
CREATE TRIGGER deletecustomer
BEFORE DELETE ON customers
FOR EACH ROW
BEGIN
  INSERT INTO customerhistory
    VALUES (:old.id, :old.lastname, :old.firstname);
END deletecustomer;
```

The *trigger condition* for the DELETECUSTOMER trigger is a DELETE statement that targets the CUSTOMERS table. A *trigger body* is the procedure in a trigger that includes the logic for a business rule. Oracle7 fires the trigger body of the DELETECUSTOMER trigger when someone issues a statement to delete a row from the CUSTOMERS table. For each row that Oracle7 deletes, it executes the trigger body immediately before removing the row. Note that if a user deletes multiple rows with one SQL statement, the DELETECUSTOMER trigger fires once before the deletion of each customer record.

By enforcing custom data integrity rules using stored procedures and triggers, developers centralize the enforcement of complex business rules at the database server instead of inside individual applications. Therefore, applications keep the amount of network traffic to a minimum so that network performance isn't a bottleneck in a client/server system. Figure 2.6 illustrates this benefit of stored procedures and triggers.

FIGURE 2.6:

By centralizing complex data integrity rules inside the database using triggers and stored procedures, you can minimize network traffic generated from SQL statements.

Procedures and triggers can also increase development productivity. That's because a single developer codes, tests, and debugs each integrity rule once in the server instead of once per application that accesses the server.

You now have a solid introduction to data integrity and how to enforce it in your Oracle7 client/server database system. To learn more about integrity constraints, stored procedures, and triggers, read Chapters 14 and 17. Now let's learn about one of the most important functions of the database server in a client/server database system: data concurrency.

Managing Data Concurrency in a Multi-User Database System

So far, our discussions of data integrity, SQL statements, and transactions consider database operation in *isolation* only, as though a user executes the statements of a transaction operating in a single-user database system. The only requirement mentioned so far is that all statements in a transaction must leave the database in an acceptable state of data integrity. If a statement violates an integrity constraint or an integrity rule in a trigger, Oracle7 automatically rolls back the statement to preserve database integrity. Simple, right?

Unfortunately, single-user databases don't cut it for workgroups, even when you use a file cabinet. Consider the problem of interference with file cabinets noted at the beginning of the chapter. You want to use the same file someone else is already using. If you want to see all the work done by the other person, you need to wait. If you want to gamble that the work the other user is doing won't affect your work, you can make a copy of the file. In either case, there is a penalty—waiting for the other user to finish work or incurring the risk of inaccurate work because you can't see what the other person does. The file cabinet illustrates the concurrency problems involved when many users attempt to use the same database.

A computerized multi-user database system, like a file cabinet, must solve the problem of *contention,* or concurrent attempts by many users to use the same data. In fact, the job of data concurrency (managing concurrent access to the same set of data) is one of the most important and perhaps the most apparent jobs of a database server. A database server must manage data so that contending users wait the least amount of time for each other to complete work without sacrificing data integrity. If a database server fails at either objective, users surely notice the repercussions, especially during times of heavy system use; as many transactions contend for the same data, users observe poor application performance or get inaccurate results from their work.

Now that I've scared you with all of these data concurrency problems, here's some good news. Oracle7 has an automatic concurrency control system, so developers don't need to worry about the problems just described. Let's take a quick look at how Oracle7 solves the problems of data concurrency in a multi-user client/server database system.

Using Data Locks to Prevent Destructive Interference

Consider what can happen if you and your spouse want to withdraw the remaining balance of your checking account at the same time from different ATMs. If the database server permits you both to update your checking balance in an ACCOUNT table at exactly the same time, one of two very bad things can happen: one of the updates is lost or the account has a final checking balance that is negative. The former result translates to the bank giving you and your spouse a bonus every time you pull this trick. The latter result violates a cardinal business rule of the bank database: Don't carry credit for checking accounts.

This scenario illustrates *destructive interference*, when two operations contending for the same data interfere with each other to produce inaccurate results or sacrifice data integrity. Most database systems use locks to prevent destructive interference when different users concurrently access the same data. Just as the lock on an airport locker prevents two people from using the same locker at the same time, *data locks* prevent destructive interference in a multi-user database system. The following sections explain the different types of locks Oracle7 uses to control data concurrency.

Exclusive and Share Locks

When you get the key to an airport locker, you have the exclusive right to use it. No one else can store stuff in your locker until you return the key. Alternatively, it's likely that there is more than one key to the lock on the front door of your house or apartment because you share the use of your house with a spouse, relative, or roommate. This notion of exclusive and shared locks is similar to how Oracle7 locks data.

When a user attempts to operate on some data, Oracle7 automatically acquires a lock on the data to prevent the possibility of destructive interference. Oracle7 always acquires a *share lock* on the data if doing so leaves no possibility of destructive interference. A share lock allows other transactions to acquire share locks as well on the same data, thereby maximizing the level of concurrency in the database.

However, if acquiring a share lock would leave open the possibility of destructive interference, Oracle7 must acquire an exclusive lock on the data that your transaction requests. An *exclusive lock* prevents other locks of any type on the same data to preserve data integrity at the expense of eliminating concurrent access to the same data. The following examples demonstrate when Oracle7 uses share locks and exclusive locks.

Let's assume you want to update the balance for account 65 in the ACCOUNTS table. When you update the row for account 65, Oracle7 gives your transaction a share lock on the ACCOUNTS table. If another user wants to update account 71 at the same time you're updating account 65, the other transaction also gets a share lock on the ACCOUNTS table. Therefore, Oracle7 allows you both concurrent shared access to the same table because you are not interfering with each other. So far, so good.

Now let's assume another user wants to update account 65 at the same time you're updating it. If you try to update the account first, Oracle7 gives your transaction an exclusive lock on the row for account 65. Until you decide to commit or roll back your transaction, you hold the exclusive lock on the row for account 65. When the other user's transaction tries to update account 65, Oracle7 won't allow it. That's because your transaction holds the exclusive lock on the row that the other user's transaction requests.

This example illustrates how Oracle7 creates *serializability* in a multi-transaction environment. Oracle7 processes concurrent transactions that contend for the same resource on a first-come-first-serve basis in a serial fashion. In the example, you requested to update account 65 first, so Oracle7 prevents the other user from updating the row until you're finished with it.

Hidden in the example is one of Oracle7's nicest concurrency features, *row-level locking*. To maximize concurrency by minimizing data conflicts, Oracle7 always locks data row by row, which is great for data concurrency. Unless two users attempt to update the same row in the same table at the same time, they'll be able to go about their business without interfering with each other's work.

> **NOTE**   Many database servers don't offer the row-level locking that Oracle7 provides. Instead, other systems use *page-level locking.* If a server uses page-level locking and a user updates a row, the server exclusively locks the entire page (or data block) that stores the row that the user's transaction updates. Unfortunately, this means all of the rows in the page are exclusively locked from other transactions, resulting in less data concurrency because of the increased potential that two transactions will interfere with each other's work.

Queries, Read Consistency, and Multi-Versioning: Reporting Accurate Data with Excellent Data Concurrency

The previous examples show how Oracle7 handles two different updates that contend for the same set of data. But what about queries, which are read-only statements? How does Oracle7 address contending queries and queries that contend with updates and still return accurate results?

Oracle7 uses an interesting approach to address these situations. First, a transaction doesn't acquire row locks of any type for queries. This means that two transactions can issue exactly the same query at the same time without any contention for the same set of rows. No row locks also means that a query can never block an update, and vice versa. But how can Oracle7 return accurate results if it doesn't take locks on behalf of queries? You would think that without row locks for queries, an update that contends with a query could create an inaccurate set of results for the query, as in the example in Figure 2.7.

Oracle7 can do without row locks for queries and still return accurate results because Oracle7 has a timepoint-based *multi-versioning mechanism.* For a query, Oracle7 returns a result set that is consistent with the way that the data looks at the time you issue the query.

FIGURE 2.7:

Inconsistent query data can result from a contending update in a multi-transaction system that does not use multi-versioning. Oracle7 rollback segments are the key component that delivers multi-versioning.

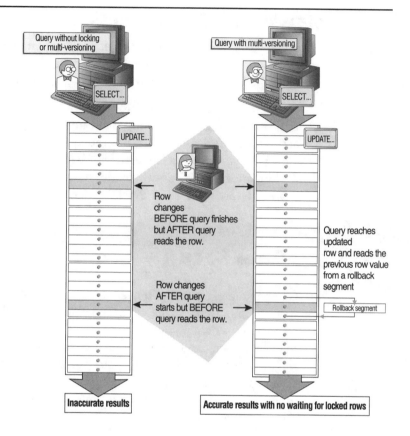

Rollback Segments

Oracle7 can create *read-consistent snapshots* (result sets) of data for queries using the data it stores in rollback segments. A *rollback segment* is a storage area Oracle7 uses to temporarily store old data values of rows that a transaction updates or deletes. If a user rolls back a transaction, Oracle7 reads the rollback segment assigned to the transaction and changes the affected rows to their previous state. Oracle7 also uses rollback segments for its multi-versioning mechanism. If a query requests data that changes during the execution of the query, Oracle7 generates a timepoint-based, read-consistent snapshot using data in the rollback segments. Figure 2.7, shown earlier, illustrates how Oracle7 uses the data in rollback segments to generate a read-consistent snapshot for a query.

Relax, It's All Automatic!

If you've used another relational database system that requires you to consider complicated locking strategies, I'm sure you'll agree that one of the nicest things about Oracle7's locking and multi-versioning mechanisms is that they are all automatic.

Developers don't ever need to worry about complex locking mechanisms and multi-versioning to make sure that multiple applications and users concurrently access the same database with both adequate system performance and complete accuracy. However, if developers want to squeeze out every last drop of application performance, Oracle7 does provide controls to override the default locking mechanisms. To learn more about Oracle7's manual concurrency controls, read Chapter 16.

Ensuring Data Security

Can anyone get into an Oracle7 database and start using the data, reading table data and modifying it at a whim? Of course not! If this were the case, users would be able to see data not intended for their eyes (such as the manager's salary), and malicious users could erase or change data to their liking (such as giving themselves salary raises). Part of the job of a database server is making sure that all the data in a database is secure. Whether you want to protect your data from the eyes of unauthorized users or from malicious intent, security is an important function of a database server.

Oracle7 maintains database security using a system of *discretionary access controls*. This simply means that at an administrator's discretion, the administrator creates registered database users and then grants them the privileges to perform specific database operations and use specific data. The next few sections introduce the different security controls of Oracle7.

Granting Access to Database Users

Have you ever used your bank's 24-hour phone banking system? To access your account, you first call the system's phone number. However, you can't do anything until you actually get inside the system by indicating your account number and a password using the keypad on your touch-tone phone. Once you pass these system access controls, you can do things such as check the balance of your accounts and transfer money among your accounts.

Accessing an Oracle7 database is similar to accessing your phone banking system. First, a user needs to get general access to the database. To give someone access to an Oracle7 database, an administrator registers the person by creating a new *username* in the database. To maintain database access security, the new username has a corresponding password. A user must give both a username and password to connect to the database. This SQL statement creates a new user:

```
CREATE USER gwashington IDENTIFIED BY P1ew2w
```

Administrators should choose meaningful usernames. In this example, the username is the concatenated string of the user's first initial and last name. Users should choose complicated, meaningless passwords so malicious users cannot easily determine their passwords. For example, George Washington should not have the password "cherrytree" or "president."

After a user gains access to an Oracle7 database, other security controls limit what the user can do inside the database. The next section discusses these controls.

Extending and Restricting Privileges

Once you are in the 24-hour phone system for your bank, you can do only a limited number of things. For example, you can request the balance of your checking and savings accounts, but you can't get the balance of other users' accounts. You are privileged to look at the information regarding your accounts only.

Again, Oracle7's security system is much like the phone banking system. The administrator can control all database operations and data access, including which users can create tables and views, which users can create and modify tablespaces, and which users can read and modify the various tables and views in the database. Administrators do this by granting and revoking different *privileges*, or rights of access. Here are examples of the SQL GRANT and REVOKE commands:

```
GRANT CREATE SESSION, CREATE TABLE TO gwashington

REVOKE CREATE TABLE FROM alincoln
```

The GRANT statement gives the user GWASHINGTON the privilege to connect to the database (that is, start a database session) and create tables. The REVOKE statement takes away ALINCOLN's ability to create tables.

Oracle7 has two broad classifications of privileges: system privileges and object privileges. These are described in the next two sections.

System Privileges: Controlling Powerful System Operations

A *system privilege* is a broad, powerful privilege that gives a user the right to perform an operation on a database-wide basis. Here are some examples:

- A user with the ALTER DATABASE system privilege can alter the physical structure of the database by adding new files to it.

- A user with the DROP TABLESPACE system privilege can drop any tablespace (with the exception of the SYSTEM tablespace) in the database.

- A user with the SELECT ANY TABLE system privilege can query any table in the database.

These are just a few of the many Oracle7 system privileges. Chapter 9 covers system privileges in more detail, and Appendix A includes a complete list of these privileges.

> **WARNING** Because system privileges are very powerful, administrators should consider granting system privileges to other administrators and application developers only.

Database Object Privileges: Controlling Access to Data

A *database object privilege* controls a database operation on a specific database object. An *object* is something inside a database, such as a table, view, role, procedure, or user. For example, an administrator can control who can query the CUSTOMERS table by granting only specific users the SELECT privilege for the CUSTOMERS table. Similarly, there are INSERT, UPDATE, and DELETE object privileges for each table, just to mention a few.

See Chapter 18 for a complete list of the object privileges available for each type of database object. The important thing to remember is that database object privileges give the administrator the ability to control data access at a very granular level.

Using Roles to Manage Security

Managing the job of database security in a large client/server database is a challenge, to say the least. The many users and applications in the system require specific sets of privileges to do their jobs. Without some type of administrative tool, security management can become a nightmare.

Fortunately, Oracle7 has just the answer for privilege management in a large, complicated client/server system. A *role* is a collection of related privileges that an administrator can grant collectively to database users and other roles.

For example, let's say that your company uses an accounting application, and the 100 users of the accounting application will need the privileges to query and modify the data in the ACCOUNTSRECEIVABLE and ACCOUNTSPAYABLE tables. Without roles, the administrator would need to grant four object privileges (SELECT, INSERT, UPDATE, and DELETE) on two tables to 100 users. That is equivalent to 800 individual grants:

$$4 \times 2 \times 100 = 800$$

You could make it two GRANT statements, because you can grant multiple object privileges for a single object to multiple users in the same GRANT statement. However, these would be huge GRANT statements!

With roles, an administrator can dramatically simplify privilege management. For example, these statements show how to manage the security for the accounting application using a role:

```
CREATE ROLE accounting

GRANT SELECT, INSERT, UPDATE, DELETE
  ON accountspayable
  TO accounting
```

```
GRANT SELECT, INSERT, UPDATE, DELETE
  ON accountsreceivable
  TO accounting

GRANT accounting TO user1, user2, user3 ...
```

When your company hires a new accounting clerk, just grant the new person the accounting role. If the privileges for the accounting application change, simply modify the privilege set of the role. All users who have the role automatically see the changes in the role's privilege set. These are just a few examples of how roles can simplify privilege management in a large client/server database system.

Simplified privilege management is not the only benefit of using roles. Perhaps even more significant, developers can use roles to dynamically change the *privilege domain* (the current privilege set) of users as they use different applications. An application can ensure that all of its users have the correct privilege domain when using the application simply by enabling the appropriate role at application startup. For example, the accounting application would include this SET ROLE statement:

```
SET ROLE accounting
```

When a user starts the accounting application, it enables the ACCOUNTING role and disables all other roles granted to the user. This way, the user has all the privileges needed to work with the ACCOUNTSRECEIVABLE and ACCOUNTSPAYABLE tables but can't use privileges that aren't intended for use with the accounting application.

To learn more about system and application security issues, see Chapters 9 and 18.

Understanding Schemas in Oracle7

When working with Oracle7, you'll often come across the term *schema*. This word has a very distinct meaning. Just as administrators can physically organize the tables in an Oracle7 database using tablespaces, they can logically organize tables and views in a relational database using schemas. A *schema* is a logical collection of related tables and views (as well as other database objects, as we'll see later in the book). For example, when adding a new application to a client/server database system, the administrator should create a new schema to organize the tables and views that the application will use. Figure 2.8 shows the schema for a sales application.

FIGURE 2.8:

Related collections of objects can be logically organized into schemas within an Oracle7 database.

Oracle7 doesn't really have a true implementation of database schemas. With Oracle7, an administrator creates a new database user, which effectively creates a default database schema for the user. When a database user creates a new table or view, the object becomes part of the user's schema by default. In fact, with Oracle7 schemas, you can say that a user *owns* all the objects in his or her default schema.

> **NOTE** Relational database systems with a more advanced schema implementation allow users to switch their default schema among the different schemas in a database and perform various operations that correspond to their current schema. Perhaps future versions of Oracle will allow such features.

Data Availability: Making Sure Data Is Available When Users Need It

With any computer program, a user cannot access a file unless the user starts an instance of the application and then opens the file. For example, to open a report created with a word processor, the computer's operating system must start the word processor and then open the word processing file that contains the report. Working with an Oracle7 database system is somewhat similar, as the following sections explain.

Controlling General Database Availability with Startup and Shutdown

As in a multi-user operating system startup, in an Oracle7 database no one can use the data until the administrator starts up the server to make the database available. This requires several steps:

1. The administrator starts up an instance of the database. An *instance* is a collection of *memory buffers* (temporary data caches in the random-access memory of a computer) and *operating system processes* (tasks or jobs scheduled by the operating system) that work together to provide multiple users access to an Oracle7 database.

2. The administrator *mounts* (associates) the database to the instance.

3. The administrator opens the database.

During the phases of database startup, Oracle7 opens the different files it needs to make the database available.

To make a database unavailable to normal database users, an administrator closes the database, dismounts the database from the instance, and then shuts down the instance. During database shutdown, Oracle7 closes the operating system files that make up the database. Figure 2.9 illustrates the cycle of database availability.

FIGURE 2.9:

An Oracle7 database server undergoes database startup to make the system available for use and database shutdown to take the system offline.

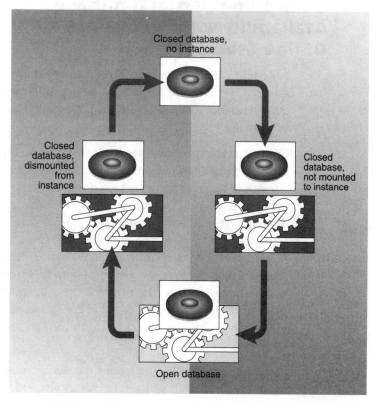

Closed database, no instance

Closed database, dismounted from instance

Closed database, not mounted to instance

Open database

Database shutdown   Database startup

After an administrator starts a database instance and opens the database, privileged users can connect to the database instance and create a new *session*. You can think of a database session as the time that elapses between a user's connecting to and disconnecting from a database instance. A session in a database is just like a session at a doctor's office—when you enter the office, the session begins; when you leave the office, the session ends.

Parameter Files and Instance Startup

Each time an administrator starts a new instance, Oracle7 reads an initialization parameter file to configure the new instance. For example, an administrator can set different parameters to control the size of an instance's various memory buffers.

Controlling Partial Database Availability with Online and Offline Tablespaces

An administrator can also control the availability of the data in an open database on a tablespace-by-tablespace basis. If a tablespace is *online*, privileged users can query and modify the tables in the tablespace. However, if a tablespace is *offline*, no one can use the data in the tablespace.

Oracle7's tablespace availability feature can be quite useful for many administrative operations. For example, if all of an application's tables are in a tablespace, an administrator can effectively take down the application by taking the application's tablespace offline. As another example, suppose a tablespace contains historical data that is useful only in very rare circumstances, and the administrator needs extra disk space to store data for other tablespaces. To free some disk space, the administrator can take the historical tablespace offline, back up the tablespace's data files, and then remove the historical data files from disk. (The administrator must make sure to store the data file backups of the offline historical tablespace in a safe place in case it's necessary to bring the tablespace back online.) Meanwhile, there is now free disk space an administrator can use to store information for other tablespaces.

The administrators of an Oracle7 database system should be the only users who control the availability of a database and its tablespaces. For details on controlling database availability, see Chapter 7.

Data Backup and Recovery

Probably almost every reader of this book has lost some data and work at one time or another by losing an important computer file. If your boss accidentally formats a hard disk and you have neglected to make a backup copy of an important report on that disk, you've lost that report, along with the hard work it took to produce it. And in this case, the fault is as much yours as your boss'.

Accidents and problems are inevitable, so an administrator needs to prepare to be able to recover from them. The next few sections introduce the different protective mechanisms built into the Oracle7 database server.

Protecting Transaction Work:
The Transaction Log

The flight log of a commercial airliner records what goes on in the cockpit during a flight. An almost indestructible box houses the flight log recorder to protect the log if the airplane crashes. After a crash, investigators can use the flight log to reconstruct the incidents leading up to the crash and discover what went wrong.

Oracle7 keeps a log, similar to a flight log, of the changes that occur in a database. Each time a user issues a SQL statement that makes a change to the database, Oracle7 records the change in its *transaction log* (also called the *redo log*). When a user commits a transaction, Oracle7 immediately writes a record to the log stating that the transaction and its changes are now permanent.

Oracle7 uses the transaction log to recover from different failures that might occur. For example, if a power failure suddenly crashes the current database instance, there might be some committed data that Oracle7 hasn't yet written to the data files. Not to worry. During the next instance startup, Oracle7 automatically performs crash recovery to recover the database as it was just after the very last transaction committed before the power failure. Oracle7 applies the committed changes in the transaction log to the data files to reconstruct the lost transactions.

The section "Database Backups" a little later in this chapter describes how Oracle7 uses the transaction log, along with data file backups and rollback segments, to recover from more serious problems such as disk crashes. However, first let's learn a little about the transaction log.

Structure of the Transaction Log

A database's transaction log contains two or more *groups* of fixed-size *log files*, or *members*, that Oracle7 uses to physically record changes to the database. Figure 2.10 illustrates the physical structure of a database's transaction log.

A transaction log has one or more groups. After transactions fill up the log space in one group, Oracle7 switches to the next available group to continue logging ongoing changes to the database. Meanwhile, Oracle7 automatically *archives* (backs up) the filled group in parallel (at the same time), without interfering with ongoing transaction logging. As Oracle7 switches groups to continue logging, it increments the database's *log sequence number* to keep track of current and archived log groups. After Oracle7 backs up a filled log group, the group will be available the next time

FIGURE 2.10:

A database's transaction log contains two or more log groups, and each group contains one or more members (files) that are exactly the same but are stored on different disks.

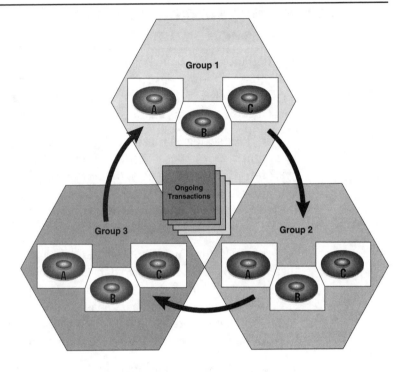

Oracle7 needs a group to log ongoing transactions. The cyclical reuse of the log groups allows Oracle7 to continually log transactions using a very small, fixed amount of disk space. And the archiving of filled log groups builds a permanent, offline, sequential transaction log for the database.

Because it is a vital component in the Oracle7 database-recovery mechanism, the transaction log itself has protective features. To protect against a single point of failure (such as a disk crash), an administrator can *mirror* a database's log groups. An administrator mirrors a log group by creating the group with multiple members, physically placing the members on different disks. As Oracle7 logs transactions to a mirrored group, it writes the changes in parallel to all members of the group. If a disk crashes, the group member on the damaged disk becomes unavailable. However, this won't stop Oracle7; it can continue logging changes to the other, intact members of the current log group.

Database Backups

For serious problems like a disk crash or an accidental file drop or disk format, an administrator needs more than just the transaction log to recover an Oracle7 database. An administrator needs physical backups of all the files that make up the database.

Data File Backups

The data files of an Oracle7 database hold all the table data for that database. As users modify the data in tables or add new objects to the database, Oracle7 updates the data files to record the changes. An administrator should back up data files on a regular basis to make sure that there are always relatively fresh data file backups.

Oracle7 gives an administrator several options to back up a database's data files. The simplest option is to back up all the data files after closing a database. However, many systems need continuous availability and can't afford to shut down the database to perform regular backups. For such high-availability systems, Oracle7's online tablespace backup feature permits the backup of data files while the system is online and in use.

Transaction Log Backups

As the previous section mentions, an administrator can configure Oracle7 to automatically archive or back up transaction log groups as they fill.

Other File Backups

Besides data files and log files, there should always be a copy of the parameter files for a database. Another file the administrator will want to back up is the database's *control file*. This is a very small file that Oracle7 uses to keep track of the physical structure of the database, storing the names of all data and log files of the database and the current log sequence of the transaction log. Oracle7 uses the control file during database startup to identify the database's data and log files and during recovery operations to guide the application of the transaction log groups.

Oracle7 allows an administrator to configure a database to mirror the control file to protect against single points of failure. However, an administrator will also want to make a backup of a database's control file every time there is a change to the database's physical structure (such as adding a new data or log file) just in case a catastrophe damages all copies of the control file.

Recovering from Disk Failures

With luck, no one will format a hard disk by accident or damage the disk, causing an Oracle7 database to be damaged. But if trouble does strike, an administrator can recover an Oracle7 database without losing any work at all. Here's how it's done:

1. The administrator fixes the hardware problem, if necessary. This might mean replacing a damaged disk with a new one.

2. The administrator restores any damaged data files with the most current backup copies and restores archived transaction log groups to any available disk, if necessary.

3. The administrator starts the recovery process, which includes roll-forward and rollback recovery. *Roll-forward recovery* is the application of the necessary transaction log groups to the backup copies of the damaged data files. *Rollback recovery* is the rolling back of any uncommitted transactions that are left after roll-forward recovery.

Figure 2.11 illustrates these steps.

Once the administrator finishes the recovery process, Oracle7 leaves the database in a transaction-consistent state, as it once appeared just after the last committed transaction, right before the disk was damaged.

If you want to learn more about Oracle7's backup and recovery features, see Chapter 11.

The Oracle7 Product Options

The Oracle7 relational database management system ships as a base product that comes with several options to enhance the functionality of the base database server. The following sections briefly explain the features in the base Oracle7 database server and each of the available options.

FIGURE 2.11:

Oracle7 database recovery is the
process of restoring a damaged data
file and then applying information in
the transaction log to redo lost work.

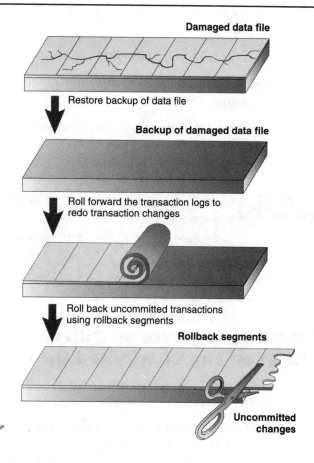

Damaged data file

Restore backup of data file

Backup of damaged data file

Roll forward the transaction logs to
redo transaction changes

Roll back uncommitted transactions
using rollback segments

Rollback segments

**Uncommitted
changes**

The Base Product: The Oracle7 Database Server

The base Oracle7 database server supports most of the features you'll read about
in this book, including the following:

- Basic relational database features, including SQL, tables, integrity constraints, and views

- Server-side application development features, such as stored procedures,
functions, packages, and triggers

- Supplemental performance features, such as sequences, indexes, and hash data clusters

- Data concurrency features, such as row-level locking and multi-versioning

- Security controls, such as system privileges, object privileges, roles, and resource limit profiles

- Protective features, such as online database backups and database recovery features

NOTE Only in releases 7.1, 7.2, and 7.3 of Oracle7 does the base version of Oracle7 allow you to store blocks of application logic inside the database server using PL/SQL extensions to Oracle SQL. With the original 7.0 release of Oracle7, such functionality is available only with the now extinct Procedural option.

Distributing Data on Different Servers: The Distributed Option

The Oracle7 Distributed option supports distributed database functionality. A *distributed database* is a collection of related but physically independent databases.

Let's take another look at our paper database example, the file cabinet. First, assume that a small, one-office company uses a single set of file cabinets to store its information. If an employee needs some information, there's no problem because the information is right there at the company's office. Now consider a larger company with branch offices. Each branch office has its own set of file cabinets to keep track of information specific to the branch office. Therefore, as a whole, the large company's database is distributed among the file cabinets in the branch offices. When you need information stored in a file at another branch office, you must somehow get a copy of that file.

Large companies that use computer databases experience the same problem. For example, each department in a company might have its own Oracle7 database to manage information that is relevant to its work. But an employee in one department might occasionally need some information in another department's database.

Oracle7 supports such distributed databases with the Oracle7 Distributed option. If the different databases are on different computers, you must connect the database servers using a network. With the Distributed option, you can access and change the information in any Oracle7 database, including the data your local database server manages and the data remote database servers manage. Figure 2.12 shows an Oracle7 distributed database.

FIGURE 2.12:

A distributed database is two or more physically separate databases that logically make up one database. Users of any server can access information throughout the distributed database.

The features of the Oracle7 Distributed option address the needs of a somewhat select audience—those who need to link separate Oracle7 databases. Distributed database technology an d the features available using the Oracle7 Distributed option are not discussed in detail in this book.

Replicating Data among Servers: The Advanced Replication Option

Distributed database technology allows an institution to decentralize its data while still allowing applications access to all data as if it were in a single database. However, the availability and performance of an application that uses a distributed database system is directly dependent on the availability and performance of the networks that link servers in the system. Often, applications with high availability and fast performance requirements cannot depend on a distributed database system. In such environments, data replication is a good alternative.

Data replication is the process of copying and maintaining redundant information in the databases that compose a distributed database system. By distributing copies of the same data at several servers in a distributed database, applications can locally access distributed database information and avoid slower network access to data at remote servers, even when a network between two servers fails.

Oracle7 supports many types of data replication with the Oracle7 Advanced Replication option. As with the Oracle7 Distributed option, the features of the Oracle7 Advanced Replication option address the needs of a more select audience, and it is not covered in this book.

Providing Parallel Access to an Oracle7 Database: The Oracle7 Parallel Server Option

In a typical Oracle7 database server configuration, a single Oracle7 database server or instance accesses a single database. Users connect to the database server to perform any work with the Oracle7 database. With the Oracle7 Parallel Server option, more than one instance can access a single database in parallel (at the same time). This makes multiple access points available to a single Oracle7 database.

What are the benefits of using the Oracle7 Parallel Server option? One advantage is availability. If one instance of the database crashes because of a software or memory failure, other instances are available to provide access to the Oracle7 database. If an administrator correctly configures an Oracle7 Parallel Server system and applications, another possible benefit is increased performance.

You can't take advantage of the Oracle7 Parallel Server option unless the system you use (or plan to use) to run Oracle7 is a loosely coupled *multiprocessor computer*—one that has multiple processors to perform work. A *loosely coupled computer system* is a type of multiprocessor computer that gives each processor its own private area of memory but allows all processors to share files on all disks. In terms of the Oracle7 Parallel Server option, the memory used by each Oracle7 instance is private to a specific processor or cluster of processors, while all instances can share a single database—that is, the files that make up the database on disk.

The Parallel Server option pertains to a select audience seeking its specific features for loosely coupled hardware systems, and it is not covered in this book.

The Ultimate Data Security Fortress: Trusted Oracle7

Many users require more security features than those present in the base version of Oracle7. Some organizations require access controls based on the sensitivity or classification of data. For example, government agencies often classify information in levels such as "top secret." To satisfy particular security requirements of a select group of users, Oracle offers a special release of Oracle7 called Trusted Oracle7. This is another specialized feature that is not discussed in this book.

Parallelizing Database Operations for Speedup: The Oracle7 Parallel Query Option

The Parallel Query option allows Oracle7 to take full advantage of all types of multiprocessor computer systems to dramatically increase the performance of many types of database operations.

Without the Parallel Query option, Oracle7 uses a single processor to perform all steps necessary to complete a database operation, such as a query or a database-recovery operation. If a database operation is complicated or involves large amounts of data, completion time can be long; Oracle7 is limited by the speed with which a single processor can accomplish work. With the Parallel Query operation, Oracle7 automatically breaks down complicated database operations into smaller subtasks that it then hands off to multiple processors, which complete each task in parallel. Because Oracle7 uses multiple processors to reduce the overall time needed to process individual database requests, application performance is dramatically improved, especially for complicated operations or those operations that touch large amounts of data.

The Oracle Parallel Query option is available for all types of multiprocessor computer systems, so many users can gain significant benefits from using this option. Appendix B focuses on configuring and using the Oracle7 Parallel Query option.

Miscellaneous Options for Specialized Applications

Oracle7 release 7.3 offers several miscellaneous options that are useful for specialized application systems:

- The Text option includes features that allow Oracle7 to better manage textual data. With the Oracle7 Text option, applications can store, index, and search large text fields and different types of document formats, and automatically create abstracts of documents.

- The Spatial Data option allows Oracle7 to serve applications that must store and manage access to multidimensional data, such as geographical, demographic, spatial, and temporal data.

- The Video Server option supports Oracle7 applications that work with binary multimedia data, such as video and sound.

- The Web Server option includes special features that permit Oracle7 to serve Internet applications that function as part of the World Wide Web.

These features are not discussed in detail in this book.

Database Administrators and Oracle7

At this point, you can see that Oracle7 is a very powerful and complex database management system. That's why there needs to be a *database administrator,* who is responsible for managing an Oracle7 client/server database system. The administrator of a client/server database system can be responsible for some or all of the following jobs:

- Planning the database and making sure the database server has enough memory and disk storage to accommodate the proposed system

- Configuring or aiding in the configuration of the computer network

- Installing Oracle7 and other software on the database server

- Creating Oracle7 databases

- Managing the space requirements for a database

- Working with application developers to create database objects such as tables and views

- Creating new users and managing user privileges

- Backing up all databases on a regular basis and performing recovery operations when necessary

- Controlling access to the database using operating system, network operating system, and Oracle7 security features

- Monitoring and tuning Oracle7 databases

There may be other jobs the administrator can handle as well.

In large systems, administration is typically split among a team of administrators. For example, one administrator might be responsible only for the operating system, another for the network, another for database backups, and still another for system security.

Administrators of Oracle7 need to concentrate on managing the database server. Part II of this book describes all facets of the tasks necessary to manage an Oracle7 client/server database system.

Part of the job of database administration is daily interaction with application developers and end users. Therefore, in addition to knowing Oracle7 thoroughly, an administrator needs a good understanding of users' requirements. Part III of this book describes many different topics regarding client application development.

This chapter has provided an introduction to many of the important concepts of a relational database management system and the components of the Oracle7 relational database server. We've covered these topics:

- How users interact with an Oracle7 database using SQL and transactions

- What tables are and what the Oracle7 column datatypes are

- How Oracle7 table data is physically organized using tablespaces and data files

- How to use views to present table data with a different look and to increase security

- How to ensure complete data integrity inside an Oracle7 database using integrity constraints, stored procedures, and database triggers

- How the Oracle7 server automatically delivers a high level of data concurrency within a multi-user database system using row-level locking and multi-versioning mechanisms

- How to manage database security using usernames, passwords, privileges, and roles

- How to control the availability of an Oracle7 database using startup and shutdown procedures as well as online and offline tablespaces

- How to protect all the work and data in an Oracle7 database with the transaction log, database backups, and database recovery

- What an Oracle7 distributed database is

- Who an Oracle7 database administrator is and what that person does

Now that we know a little about the *server* in client/server, let's learn more about the *client*.

CHAPTER

THREE

The Client in Client/Server

- Different categories of client applications

- Client applications in the Oracle tool set

- Application development tools

- Database administrative utilities

- Client application user interfaces

- Object-oriented programming

A database server is just one part of the picture in a client/server system. Another significant component is the clients—the applications that interface with the database server to input, modify, and retrieve database data. This chapter provides an introduction to the basics of the client portion of a client/server system.

Your Window to Database Access: Client Applications

A *client application* is the front-end component of a database system that users work with to input, retrieve, and analyze data. Client applications come in all shapes and sizes. For example, the primary client application in a sales department might be an order-entry application that salespeople use to record customer orders. In the product warehouse, the primary work tool might be an inventory management and tracking application. In short, whatever data a workgroup must track, there is usually a client application to suit the job at hand.

Chapter 2 showed how a back-end database server focuses on managing a database and the data requests of many front-end client applications. A client application uses SQL statements to send information to and request information from the database server (usually across a network). It is the job of the client to present or analyze information. A client application does not include data management components; the database server is responsible for these management operations.

The division of responsibilities between client and server is what makes a client/server system so effective. For example, a company's order-entry application and inventory application both need to work with the same set of product inventory data. Instead of requiring each application to have its own database manager and database of inventory information, the client/server system allows them both to work with a single database server, such as Oracle7, to manage a single inventory database. Custom application development is straightforward and productive because the most complicated part of the system—a multi-user database management system—is a predeveloped software package that someone can install right out of a box.

Because client applications are the front end of a database system, all types of users must use client database applications. Administrators use utilities to manage a database server, end users run applications to get work done, and developers make custom client database applications.

There are many categories of client applications for a database system. For example, end users run form applications for data entry and reporting applications for generating database reports. The next sections describe forms, reporting, and other types of client applications. You'll also find an overview of Oracle's set of integrated tools you can use in an Oracle7 client/server system.

Data Entry and Online Transaction Processing Using Form Applications

Forms are all around us—forms to order a product, forms to apply for a loan, forms to pay taxes, even forms to get more forms. When you fill out the fields of a paper form, you are entering data that eventually ends up in some sort of database.

In a computer database system, users can use a *form application* to enter, view, and print reports of database data. Figure 3.1 shows examples of two forms in a form application: one for recording customer information and one for entering customer orders.

A form application in a computer system is relatively simple to learn and use because, for the most part, the form appears on a computer screen the same way it would on a piece of paper. However, form applications have several important advantages over standard paper forms. Aside from the advantages of using a computer database, form applications are vastly more versatile and powerful than paper forms. Here are some of the advantages of form applications:

- A form can read a database server's data dictionary to learn about data integrity rules. As a user enters data in the fields of a form, the application automatically validates data according to the integrity rules.

- An entry field in a form can present a list of valid values from which users can pick to fill out the field easily.

FIGURE 3.1:

Form applications, such as this order-entry application, permit users to input and display information using a database system.

- An area on a form can display a picture that is associated with the current record(s) displayed on the form.

- A button on the form can play a sound file that is associated with the current record(s) displayed on the form.

- A form can display context-sensitive instructions (such as help notes), reducing training time.

- A form can adjust its input fields based on data the user enters.

Form applications are often *online transaction processing* (*OLTP*) applications. OLTP applications are characterized by short, simple transactions to input or update data in a database. A bank's ATM is a perfect example of an OLTP form application. Thousands of ATM users can simultaneously withdraw money from bank accounts. Each user simply enters an identification number and a withdrawal amount. The ATM application then sends data-manipulation requests to a database server to update the account balance and record the user's transaction.

Oracle Forms

Oracle Forms, part of Oracle's Developer/2000 application development suite, is an Oracle tool that both end users and application developers use. A developer uses the Oracle Forms development system to create visually appealing, client data-entry applications that can integrate text and graphics and deliver high-transaction throughput in a demanding OLTP environment. Using Oracle Forms on a client workstation, an end user can run a form application for data entry and on-screen reporting with an Oracle7 database. The screen shown earlier in Figure 3.1 is from an Oracle Forms application. Chapter 19 introduces you to developing and using Oracle Forms applications.

Analysis and Decision Making Using Query and Reporting Applications

Analyzing and presenting data are just as important as entering and storing it. Computer systems use reporting and query applications to retrieve database data and present it in a way that provides useful information, drives decision making, and supports business projects. For example, monthly account statements help bank customers balance their checkbooks; quarterly sales and financial reports of publicly owned businesses drive the stock markets of the world; and mailing labels make it easy for a company to conduct a direct-mail advertising campaign.

Reporting applications can present data in different ways. Custom text reports with a multiple-column listing of some records in a database table are probably the most common type. For example, printed bank statements typically have columns that list the date, description, amount, and resulting account balance corresponding to monthly bank transactions. To generate a bank statement for a customer, a reporting application pulls a customer's transaction records from a database and then calculates a running account balance for each new transaction. Other types of text reports list only a single table record per printed page. For example, a mailing label is a record of a person's name, company, address, city, state, and zip code.

In many cases, standard reports do not show the exact piece of information that someone needs to help make an important decision; no compiled reporting application can anticipate every possible question you might want to ask a database server. In these cases, query reporting tools come in handy. For example, a giant corporation may need to make a sudden decision on whether or not to renew the contract of its advertising firm. The CEO says, "I need sales trend information regarding the new series of advertisements that our company has been printing in the trade rags. And I need the report in five minutes!" There's no time to make a fancy report. But by using a query tool to issue an ad hoc query, the person under the gun can get the information quickly and help the CEO make the correct decision.

Graphical representations of data are another type of report. In many cases, graphs and charts present database data more effectively than text. For example, a company's financial report might include a pie chart to illustrate the percentage of total revenues in different countries. A bar or line graph can show trends in sales revenues, profits, and expenses from quarter to quarter.

The next sections give an overview of the query and reporting tools available from Oracle: Oracle Reports, Oracle Graphics, SQL*Plus, and Oracle Browser.

Oracle Reports

Oracle Reports, part of Developer/2000, is a tool that both application developers and end users can use for reporting applications. A developer uses the complete Oracle Reports development system to design custom reports of data in Oracle7 databases. An end user runs a runtime version of Oracle Reports and a prebuilt report application to generate and print reports. Figure 3.2 shows an example of an invoice report in an Oracle Reports application.

Oracle Graphics

Oracle Graphics, also part of Developer/2000, is a tool developers and end users use for visual reporting applications. Developers can use Oracle Graphics to design graphical reports that present Oracle7 database information using text, charts, drawings, and images. End users can then use Oracle Graphics applications to view these reports using database data and make intelligent decisions. Figure 3.3 shows examples of graphical reports in an Oracle Graphics application.

FIGURE 3.2:

An example of an invoice report in an Oracle Reports application

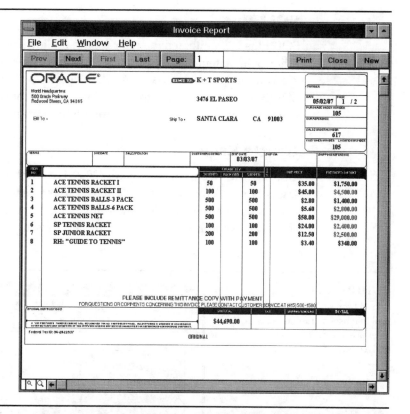

FIGURE 3.3:

Examples of reports in an Oracle Graphics application

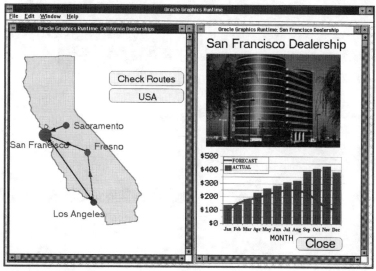

SQL*Plus

SQL*Plus is an interactive query tool that allows you to issue ad hoc queries and other SQL statements to a database as you think of them. SQL*Plus has a simple command-line interface. At the command prompt, you can type a SQL or SQL*Plus command and then execute it. You must know the syntax of SQL to use SQL*Plus effectively. (See Chapter 5 for a primer on SQL.)

Oracle Browser

Oracle Browser, part of Discoverer/2000, is a graphical, interactive data-access tool. Users can use Browser's graphical user interface to build and send ad hoc queries to Oracle7 while insulating themselves from the complexity of SQL. Figure 3.4 shows an example of a screen in Oracle Browser.

FIGURE 3.4:

Oracle Browser is an ad hoc query tool that uses a graphical user interface to hide the complexity of SQL commands.

Developing Custom Applications with Application Development Tools

An *application development tool* is an application that developers use to create custom client applications that end users can use to access a database system. Application development tools come in two varieties: 3GL (third-generation language) and 4GL (fourth-generation language).

A developer can create a client application with procedural programming techniques by using a 3GL development tool along with a third-generation programming language such as C, Ada, or COBOL. To develop a 3GL client database application, the developer programs the source code of the application using the procedural commands of a 3GL compiler along with embedded SQL statements that make calls to a database server. Alternatively, a developer can use a 4GL application development tool to develop a client application with nonprocedural programming techniques, such as visual form layout and screen painting.

So what are the primary differences between a 3GL and 4GL client application development environment? One major difference is in the ease of use and productivity of application developers. 3GL development environments require the developers to know how to program in a 3GL and to know the functional extensions provided by the 3GL development tool. For example, to display a box on a form, a developer must be able to call library functions inside the form application to make the box appear. On the other hand, 4GL tools use nonprocedural techniques to make most areas of application design much easier and more productive. For example, to draw a box on a form, the developer simply needs to know how to use a line-drawing tool in the 4GL application development tool.

Even though 3GL tools may be more difficult to use, they do have certain advantages. Because 3GLs such as C are flexible and developers can program anything imaginable, they are inherently more powerful than their 4GL counterparts. For example, C might be more appropriate than a 4GL for developing a scientific application that performs many intensive calculations. That's because developers can use C's low-level bit operations to perform calculations more efficiently (and thus more quickly) than a 4GL. Additionally, if a client application uses the standard commands of a 3GL and SQL, the application source code is automatically portable across (the application will work with) any operating system that supports the programming language. Oracle provides both 3GL and 4GL application development tools.

Oracle Precompilers

The Oracle precompilers work with a standard 3GL compiler to develop custom applications that have embedded SQL statements. A developer uses a precompiler to do a first pass on a source program to identify and translate all embedded SQL statements and generate a modified source program that the 3GL compiler can understand. Then the developer uses a standard language compiler to compile and link the program to its finished and executable form. To aid in the development of portable client database applications, each Oracle precompiler includes a flagger to detect and mark source code statements that do not conform to ANSI-standard SQL syntax.

Oracle Call Interfaces

Like the Oracle precompilers, the Oracle Call Interfaces (OCIs) let you use a 3GL and embedded SQL statements to create custom applications that access data in an Oracle7 database. However, the OCIs also provide low-level, proprietary procedure and function calls that can give you more power and flexibility than the precompilers when developing Oracle7 applications. For example, an OCI program can control the actual steps of SQL statement processing (parse, bind, execute, rebind, reexecute, and so on) to achieve absolute optimal application performance and minimal network traffic between the client application and the database server.

Oracle 4GL Application Development Tools

Oracle Forms, Oracle Reports, and Oracle Graphics are examples of 4GL application development tools in Oracle's tool set. As explained earlier in this chapter, developers use these 4GL tools to develop custom forms and reporting applications that allow end users to enter and access data in an Oracle7 client/server database system.

Computer-Aided Systems Engineering (CASE) Tools

As you might have already gathered from this book, a computer database and application system for a business is a very complex thing to plan, develop, validate, and manage. Computer-aided systems engineering (CASE) tools can dramatically simplify all stages of the business system life cycle, including system analysis, design, implementation, and maintenance.

CASE tools are based on many different modeling techniques that make it easy to develop a business computer system. Using different diagrammers that work in a graphical user interface, CASE tools usually allow you to model the different processes and data that make up the system. For example, Figure 3.5 shows a screen from the Entity Relationship Diagrammer of Oracle's Designer/2000.

FIGURE 3.5:

Entity Relationship Diagrammer of Oracle's Designer/2000

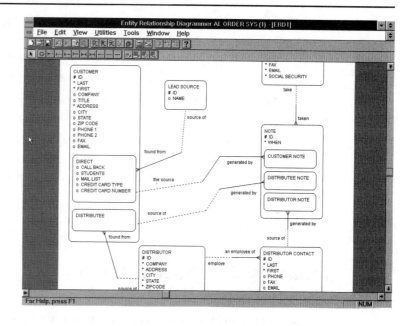

To keep track of the data they generate, CASE tools have a special component called a repository. A *repository* is a dictionary of *metadata*—information about the processes, data, and relationships in a business system. A repository is the fundamental component of a CASE tool set because it provides the information necessary to automatically create the system's underlying database and generate front-end client applications.

Designer/2000

Designer/2000 is Oracle's suite of CASE products that addresses several different areas of systems development, including process modeling, systems modeling, systems design, application generation, and repository management. Designer/2000's areas and products are as follows:

Design Area	Product
Process modeling	Process Modeler
Systems modeling	Entity Relationship Diagrammer, Function Hierarchy Diagrammer, and Dataflow Diagrammer
Systems design	Data Diagrammer, Module Structure Diagrammer, Module Data Diagrammer, Module Logic Navigator, Preferences Navigator, and Design Wizards
Application generation	Forms Generator, Reports Generator, and Server Generator
Repository management	Repository Object Navigator, Matrix Diagrammer, Repository Administration Utility, and Repository Reports

See Chapter 19 to learn more about rapid application development using the tools in Designer/2000.

Managing Databases Using Administrative Utilities

An *administrative utility* is an application a database administrator uses to manage a database system. Oracle Corporation ships a number of utilities with the Oracle7 database server, including Server Manager, Enterprise Manager, SQL*Loader, Import, and Export. These utilities are described briefly in the following sections. For more detailed information about the administrative utilities, see Part II of this book, which discusses many of the different operations performed by a database administrator using the Oracle7 utilities, particularly Server Manager and SQL*Loader.

Server Manager

Server Manager is an Oracle7 utility administrators can use for most administrative operations. Within Server Manager, Administration Manager allows administrators to perform all basic administrative operations, such as database startup and shutdown, tablespace management, transaction log configuration, and system security. Administration Manager presents a graphical user interface of drawers and folders that permits you to easily access its many features, as shown in Figure 3.6.

FIGURE 3.6:

Server Manager's Admistration Manager component provides a graphical user interface for basic administrative operations.

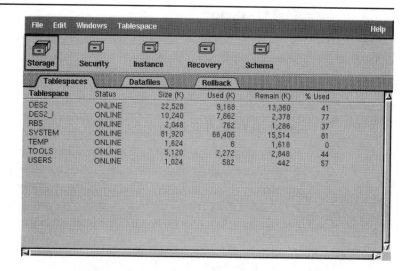

The Server Manager utility also allows you to use a *SQL worksheet*, which is a simple, ad-hoc query tool. Another Server Manager tool is its *monitors*, which let the administrator look at database performance and system usage statistics. Figure 3.7 shows an example of a Server Manager monitor screen. See Chapter 6 for more information about Server Manager.

FIGURE 3.7:

The Server Manager monitors let Oracle administrators take a look at real-time database server status.

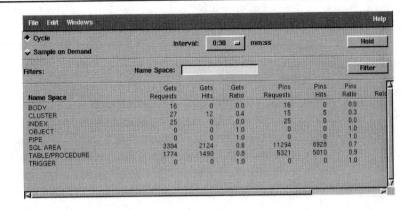

Name Space	Gets Requests	Gets Hits	Gets Ratio	Pins Requests	Pins Hits	Pins Ratio	Rel
BODY	16	0	0.0	16	0	0.0	
CLUSTER	27	12	0.4	15	5	0.3	
INDEX	25	0	0.0	25	0	0.0	
OBJECT	0	0	1.0	0	0	1.0	
PIPE	0	0	1.0	0	0	1.0	
SQL AREA	3304	2124	0.6	11294	8928	0.7	
TABLE/PROCEDURE	1774	1490	0.8	5321	5010	0.9	
TRIGGER	0	0	1.0	0	0	1.0	

SQL*Loader

SQL*Loader is a utility that administrators use to load data from external files into tables in an Oracle7 database. For example, SQL*Loader can load data from an ASCII fixed-format or delimited file into an Oracle7 table. See Chapter 6 for more information about using SQL*Loader.

Import and Export

Administrators use Oracle's Import and Export utilities to move data in and out of Oracle7 databases not connected by a network. Export writes data from an Oracle7 database to operating system files. Import reads the data from Export files back into an Oracle7 database. The Export utility is also useful for creating supplemental database backups for added recovery flexibility.

Vertical Client Applications

Vertical client applications are prebuilt applications that work right out of the box. Oracle Corporation offers many vertical client applications for different tasks. For example, Oracle offers these tools in the area of financial and human resources applications:

- Oracle General Ledger
- Oracle Order Entry

- Oracle Inventory

- Oracle Personnel

- Oracle Payables

- Oracle Receivables

- Oracle Purchasing

- Oracle Assets

- Oracle Alert

Oracle also offers the following vertical applications in the area of manufacturing:

- Oracle Work in Process

- Oracle Bills of Material

- Oracle Engineering

- Oracle Master Scheduling/MRP

- Oracle Capacity

NOTE Oracle7 has an "open" architecture, which means that other companies can create development tools, utilities, and applications for Oracle7. Third-party companies offer all types of client applications that work in an Oracle7 client/server system.

Client Application User Interfaces

The presentation and interaction methods of a client application are perhaps its most important features. The *interface* defines the way a user works with the application. The two types of user interfaces are character-based and graphical, which are explained in the following sections.

Character-Based User Interfaces

Character-based user interfaces (*CUIs*) use lines of simple alphanumeric characters to present an application to a user. For example, in mainframe and minicomputer environments, typical dumb terminal screen applications use CUIs.

CUIs are usually not easy to use because the interface is made up of screens with nonintuitive text and numbers. Therefore, a user has a significant learning curve with each new application.

CUIs also usually lack flexibility, forcing an application to be process-driven and to rigidly control the flow of the program. For example, an application that uses a CUI might ask a question, wait for a response, ask another question, wait for a response, and so on. It is the program that determines what questions to ask and in which order to ask them.

In many cases, an application uses a CUI that is nothing more than a command-line interface with a prompt that waits for a user to enter a command. For example, operating systems such as MS-DOS, UNIX, and VAX VMS use command-line interfaces. Figure 3.8 shows a screen from Oracle's SQL*Plus, which is an example of a client database application that uses a command-line interface.

FIGURE 3.8:

The command-line interface of SQL*Plus requires that users know the syntax of SQL statements.

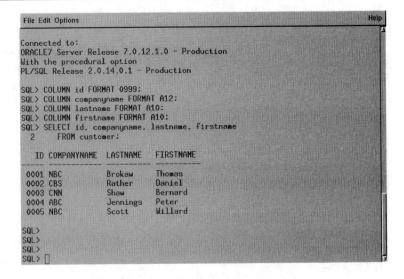

The obvious drawback of an application that uses a simple command-line interface is that the user needs to know the available commands and corresponding syntax (language) rules for that application. For example, to use SQL*Plus, a user needs to know how to use SQL commands.

Graphical User Interfaces (GUIs)

Just as computing models have evolved, so have user interfaces. Apple Computer is widely recognized as the first company to offer a commercial operating system with a *graphical user interface* (*GUI*). GUIs make users more productive for several reasons:

- Instead of requiring a user to know application commands, a GUI uses an intuitive, easy-to-use shell with a pointing device (such as a mouse), as well as application windows, menus, dialog boxes, buttons, and so on, which hide the complexity of commands from the user.

- GUIs can typically display multiple applications in different windows at the same time. This way, users can see what is happening in one application while working with another or transfer information between different applications with cut-and-paste operations.

- Well-defined GUIs have specifications with which all applications must conform to make the look and feel of every application consistent. This way, users can easily learn new applications because they recognize certain functions from application to application.

The power and ease of use of a GUI is available with almost every computer operating system you can buy. Popular GUIs include MacOS on Apple computers, Microsoft Windows on IBM PCs and compatibles, and Motif on UNIX machines. Figure 3.9 shows an example of the Motif GUI used in SCO UNIX's Open Desktop (ODT).

Each ODT application has its own window, and every application window has corner and side border handles to size the window, as well as a menu bar across the top. The first items in every application's menu bar are File and Edit, and the last item is Help. These are all examples of conformance specifications that help make GUIs easy to use. SCO's ODT is a particularly powerful GUI because it can display

FIGURE 3.9:

SCO UNIX's Open Desktop is an example of a powerful GUI that is intuitive to learn and use.

another GUI within Motif; Microsoft Windows applications can run in a Motif window at the same time other Motif applications are running.

Many mainframe and minicomputer terminal applications now use pseudo-GUIs for applications, but these GUIs are constrained by the hardware limitations of the terminal. Specifically, the older variety of dumb terminals can display hardware-encoded characters only.

More expensive bitmapped display terminals—monitors that can display bitmapped graphics—are much better suited for GUIs because they can display text in several different fonts, line art, and images in a WYSIWYG (what you see is what you get) format. WYSIWYG is obviously a big advantage for applications such as desktop publishing and graphic design, because you can see the layout of printed material as you work with it on a display screen.

Object-Oriented Programming for Application Development

In most business environments, several related applications are required to help run the business. Consequently, programmers spend time coding each application to the specifications of different parts of the system. However, while each application may have its own unique, high-level purpose, it is more than likely that individual parts of each application will perform the exact same or similar functions. These are functions that can be reused, allowing the programmers to avoid duplicate coding and testing throughout the business's application development process.

To address the opportunities for improving programmer productivity, today's programming environments now embrace what is called *object-oriented programming* (*OOP*). To supplement your existing knowledge about the application development process, let's learn a little about the principles of object-oriented programming so you can understand how it can help you when you create applications for a database system.

Data Abstraction, Classes, and Objects

From what you already know about database systems (tables, rows, columns, datatypes, and so on), you'll probably agree that the associated terms and concepts can get rather abstract when compared with everyday business terms. One principle of object-oriented programming is to raise the level of data abstraction so it more closely matches human terminology (for example, business terminology). Data abstraction in an object-oriented system centers around the definition of classes and objects.

A *class* is an abstract datatype that closely matches something in the real world. For example, you might have a class PERSON, which encapsulates common attributes, such as LASTNAME, FIRSTNAME, ADDRESS, and so on. An *object* is a specific instance of a class. For example, just as you would declare a variable of a specific datatype in a traditional programming language, you can declare an object of a specific class in an object-oriented language. BILL and SAMANTHA might be examples of objects of class PERSON.

Methods and Messages

Once you define a class in an object-oriented system, you also need to define the methods (functions) that will act upon objects of that class. For example, in a traditional programming language, you can add, subtract, multiply, and divide variables declared of a simple NUMBER datatype.

Likewise, for an object-oriented programming system, you might define a method CHANGE_ADDRESS that can act upon objects of class PERSON. When you want to change a person's address, the program sends a message (calls a specific method) to the object for the specific person to get the job done.

Inheritance and Class Hierarchy

When you declare classes in an object-oriented system, you can create a class hierarchy by declaring classes as subclasses of others. Consequently, a subclass inherits the properties of its parent class. For example, the classes EMPLOYEE and CUSTOMER are both subclasses of PERSON. In this case, the EMPLOYEE and CUSTOMER classes are both PERSONs (people) and can inherit the structure of the base PERSON class (LASTNAME, FIRSTNAME, ADDRESS, and so on), as well as the methods of the PERSON class (CHANGE_ADDRESS and others).

A powerful characteristic of inheritance in the class hierarchy is that the inheritance descends down the class tree, not up it. This is important because a subclass typically extends the structure and/or functionality of its base class with additional attributes and methods, which would not necessarily have meaning if the class hierarchy allowed inheritance to extend upward.

For example, in addition to using the attributes of the base class PERSON, the EMPLOYEE subclass might also have some unique attributes such as SALARY, DEPARTMENT, and so on. Another subclass of PERSON might not necessarily have a use for these attributes that are specific to EMPLOYEE. Additionally, the EMPLOYEE subclass can have some unique methods (CHANGE_SALARY, CHANGE_DEPARTMENT, and so on) of its own that would not make sense for all subclasses of PERSON.

A new subclass method can even override the functionality of an inherited base class method of the same name if necessary. In this case, the subclass version of the method affects the behavior of only the subclass, not the base class or any of its other descendants. For example, there may be some special requirement to consider that justifies a special version of the CHANGE_ADDRESS method for objects of class CUSTOMER, but all other subclasses of PERSON can use the standard CHANGE_ADDRESS method.

Other than the obvious benefit of reducing the complexity of class definition and minimizing the number of methods in the system, inheritance can also make the system easier to maintain. For example, if you decide that you want an attribute to record the middle name of all the people in the system, you don't need to modify the PERSON class as well as all of its subclasses. Simply add the MIDDLENAME attribute to the PERSON class, and all subclasses, including EMPLOYEE and CUSTOMER, can automatically inherit the new attribute from the parent.

Polymorphism

As explained in the previous section, behavioral inheritance allows subclasses in the hierarchy to inherit the methods of their parents. Therefore, an object-oriented system's methods must be *polymorphic,* or generic enough so that they act appropriately upon objects that traverse down the target class hierarchy.

For example, the CHANGE_ADDRESS method is said to be polymorphic because it performs the correct behavior (changes a person's address) when a program sends a change address message to objects of class PERSON or any of its subclasses, including EMPLOYEE and CUSTOMER.

How Does Object-Oriented Programming Help Application Development Productivity?

The benefits of object-oriented programming quickly become apparent when a business requires many related application systems. Related applications should all have the same look and feel and, in many cases, might overlap in function.

Therefore, there are potentially many situations where an object-oriented programming environment can save time for programmers. The generation of windows, dialog boxes, menus, and business functions are just a few examples of code segments that can be reused throughout the business's different applications. As a result, all applications have a standard appearance and behavior, and the overall amount of code needed to generate the system's applications can be kept to a minimum.

Due to its inheritance qualities, object-oriented programming also reduces the costs associated with application maintenance. For example, if you need to change a standard menu that all applications use, a single code update modifies all applications at once.

Most application development tool vendors have or will have object-oriented programming features in their products to help you be more productive in developing your system. Be sure to look for these features and make good use of them so your application systems are the best they can be, as fast as they can be.

Client Application End Users and Developers

The two types of users most involved with client applications are developers and end users. If you are a developer, there's a good chance you will not find a prebuilt Oracle7 application that does what your business needs to accomplish. In this case, you can use one of the development tools described in this chapter to create a custom client application. Your responsibilities will include designing the data structures (such as tables and views) for the application; programming the application using a development tool; coordinating storage, security, and design issues with the database administrator; and tuning the application after implementation.

NOTE　To develop good client applications, you need to take advantage of the features in Oracle7 that are designed specifically for client/server systems. Part II of this book provides a sound overview of Oracle7, and Part III presents the information you need to develop client applications for Oracle7.

If you are an end user, you don't really need to know anything about how Oracle7 manages data, how the network relays data between a client and a server, or how to develop efficient client applications. You just need to know how to use an application to get a job done. You can refer to the user documentation for the application or to other books that explain your application.

This chapter has given you the basics of the client portion of a client/server system:

- You use client applications to input, modify, retrieve, or report information that the database server manages.

- Client applications come in all varieties, including form applications for data input, retrieval, and display, and reporting applications for textual and graphical reports of database information.

- To develop custom client applications, you can use the different Oracle tools, including Oracle Forms, Oracle Reports, and Oracle Graphics in the Developer/2000 suite, and the CASE tools in Oracle's Designer/2000.

Between Client and Server: Networking Issues

- Star, bus, and ring network topologies

- Network configurations: LANs and WANs

- Network hardware and software

- Middleware: the software layer for system communication

- Client and server processes

As you learned in the previous chapters, a client/server system is a distributed application processing system in which the processing load of a single application is split between a client component and a server component. Implicit in the design of a distributed application processing system is the ability of the client and the server components to communicate with one another so they can work together to perform the overall function of the business application.

Although communication between clients and servers may be an implicit requirement of a distributed application processing system, it is not something that you can forget about when you design your client/server system. This chapter examines the critical communication issues for an Oracle7 client/server system:

- Network hardware, topologies, and communication software

- Middleware, which is software that resides on both the clients and servers and translates the messages sent between them

- Client and server processes in the Oracle7 client/server software architecture

First, let's learn more about the network that connects the clients and servers and the hardware and software you need for an Oracle7 client/server system.

The Network in a Client/ Server System

The client and server components of an Oracle7 client/server database system can operate on physically different computers. When this is the case, there must be a *network* to connect the clients and servers so they can communicate and work together.

If you use a personal computer in a workgroup, chances are your workstation is connected to other computers in a local-area network (LAN). A *LAN* is one in which all the computers are close together and physically connected by wiring of some sort. For example, if all of a department's employees work together in the same building, they might use a LAN to connect their personal computers so they can share files and a printer, communicate using an electronic-mail system, and have access to a central Oracle7 database server.

LANs can have many different *topologies*, or configurations:

- In the *star topology*, there is a central node that serves as a common connection point for all other nodes. All nodes in a star network can communicate *synchronously* (at the same time) through the central network node (that is, as long as the central node is available).

- The *bus topology* does not depend on a central node for network availability and permits only asynchronous (one-at-a-time) network communication among the nodes in the network.

- A *ring topology* offers the advantages of both the star and bus network topologies: synchronous communication without reliance on a central network node.

Figure 4.1 illustrates the star, bus, and ring network topologies.

When a network includes remote computers that go beyond a small geographic area, the network becomes a *wide-area network* (*WAN*). For example, if a company's departments are physically dispersed across the country, the company might use leased phone lines to connect department LANs so the entire company can communicate using an electronic-mail system and have access to each other's local Oracle7 database servers.

A LAN or WAN consists of several different parts, including network hardware, network software, and communication software.

Network Hardware

The first thing necessary to form a network is some special *network hardware* so different computers can communicate. In a LAN, each computer has a network adapter card. A *network adapter card* has one or more outlets to plug in some sort of network cable that joins a computer to the network.

There are several types of network cable you can use in a network: coaxial (coax) cable, twisted-pair cable (for example, a standard phone line), and fiber-optic cable. Although it is the most expensive, the best of the bunch is fiber-optic cable, because it supports the fastest communication rates with the least amount of noise interference.

Bus, star, and ring network topologies

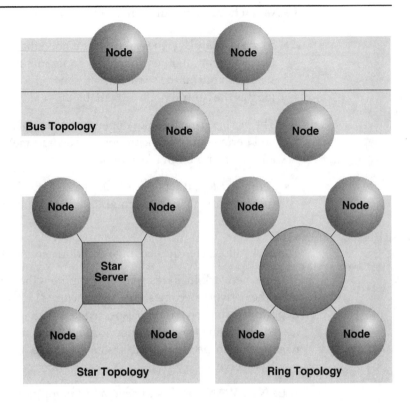

Coax cable is a bit more expensive than twisted-pair cable, but coax can support faster communication rates with less noise interference. Another possibility is the use of *wireless network adapter cards,* which allow different computers to communicate with each other using wireless communication mechanisms, such as high-frequency radio signals instead of physical cables.

In a WAN, computers are too far apart to use network cables. Therefore, WANs typically use leased phone lines, routers, and high-speed modems. To support long-distance communication, a computer might use an internal modem card or an external modem that you attach to a computer through a communications (COM) port. A modem has phone connections where you can plug in standard twisted-pair phone lines to gain access to the outside world.

Network Software

Every network has special *network software* that controls the operations specific to the network. For example, most networked environments include software to control things like user security, print queues, space allocation for user files, and mail exchange.

If a network server uses an operating system that is not designed for networking (such as DOS), it typically uses a special network operating system, such as Novell's NetWare. If a network server uses an operating system designed for networking (such as UNIX), it can use the built-in networking capabilities without a special network operating system.

Communications Software

In addition to network software, computers in a network need communications software. *Communications software* allows different computers connected in a network to send and receive packets of information on the network. The language the computers speak across a network is called the network *communication protocol*. For example, *TCP/IP* (Transmission Control Protocol/Internet Protocol) is the most common communication protocol in UNIX networks, while *IPX/SPX* (Internet Package Exchange/Sequenced Packet Exchange) is the protocol for Novell NetWare LANs.

If a client and a server must be able to talk directly to each other, both computers need to use the same communication protocol. If the clients and the servers cannot use the same protocol, special equipment, such as a *communications bridge* or a *router*, may allow the clients and servers to communicate.

Middleware for Client/Server Database Systems

Imagine the complexity of writing an application for a database system if a developer needed to consider all the different network layers—the hardware, topology, operating system, and communication system. Luckily, developers are not required to think about network considerations because client/server systems use *application middleware,* a software layer that makes it easy for different components of a distributed processing system to communicate. Middleware sits on both the clients and servers in a client/server system and translates the messages sent between them.

> **NOTE**
>
> In distributed database systems, middleware allows different servers to communicate with one another. For example, a *database gateway* is middleware that heterogeneous distributed database systems use so one vendor's database server can talk to another vendor's database server (for example, Oracle7 and IBM's DB2). This book focuses on the role of middleware in client/server systems.

A client/server system can use two different types of middleware to pass messages between clients and servers:

- With *conversational middleware,* a client and server connect and then pass a series of messages to complete a communication. Both components remain active during a conversation, which is usually asynchronous (messages go only one way at a time). Conversational middleware is typically not very efficient because of its back-and-forth message-passing scheme and its asynchronous communication method.

- With *remote procedure call (RPC) middleware,* one component communicates with a remote component using simple procedure calls. For example, a client requests information from a server by connecting to the server, making the request by calling a low-level procedure native to the database server, and then disconnecting. To respond to a request, the server connects to the application and calls a low-level procedure in the application. RPC middleware is typically transparent to a user, making it easy to use.

Figure 4.2 illustrates these two types of middleware.

FIGURE 4.2:

Conversational and RPC
middleware communication methods

SQL*Net: Oracle's Own Middleware Product

If a client/server system includes only Oracle products (for example, the Oracle7 database server and Oracle tools), the system uses Oracle's own middleware product, SQL*Net. The most common middleware product in an Oracle7 client/server database system, SQL*Net runs on both the clients and the server in a system to hide the complexity of the network.

Like Oracle7, SQL*Net works with almost every operating system and communication protocol and does not care which network topology is in use. In fact, SQL*Net's *multiprotocol interchange* even allows client/server connections to span multiple communication protocols without the need for expensive bridges and routers. Systems engineers can design a client/server system without ever considering which computers, operating systems, and protocols to use; SQL*Net will work in any configuration design. Given the heterogeneous nature of client/server systems, this is an especially important feature of SQL*Net. Figure 4.3 illustrates SQL*Net's function in a client/server system.

FIGURE 4.3:
SQL*Net in a client/server system

Other Examples of Middleware

If you use non-Oracle software in a client/server system, you might use another company's middleware product rather than Oracle's SQL*Net. For example, if you choose Centura Corporation's SQLWindows instead of Oracle Forms to develop and run client form applications, client PCs must use Centura's own middleware product, SQLRouter/Oracle, so SQLWindows can connect to Oracle7 across the network.

In addition, there are other types of middleware that attempt to standardize the application programming interface (API) between client application development tools and many different types of database servers (Oracle7, Sybase SQL Server, Informix, and so on). In the client/server context, an API is simply a specification of a set of functions that allows client and server processes to communicate. An example of a standard API is *ODBC*, Microsoft's Open Database Connectivity standard. Using tools and database servers that support standard API middleware when developing applications for a client/server system has both advantages and disadvantages.

The primary advantage of developing a client application using a standard API is that the resulting application can use any back-end database server rather than just a specific server. Therefore, you have more choices when considering your database server. If you decide to buy or switch to or from Oracle7, DB/2, Microsoft SQL Server, Sybase SQL Server, Informix, or another server, your application continues to function without modification, because all of these database servers support the standard API.

The primary disadvantage of standard APIs is that they generally include only the "common denominators" of all tools and database servers that support the standard. Therefore, when you develop a client application, you might not be able to take advantage of all the unique and special features that any one database server offers. This can result in applications that perform poorly or are unusable.

In conclusion, consider the use of standard API middleware only if your client/server system has or will include two or more different database servers. Even if your client/server environment falls into this category, do not commit to the use of a standard API for all of your applications until you perform serious testing to validate that the standard API will deliver the performance your applications require to make them useful.

Network hardware, communication software, and middleware enable clients and servers to distribute application processing. The next few sections explain more about the actual processing components that communicate using the network.

Client/Server Processing

Processing in a computer system is done by one or more operating system processes. A *process* is a task that a computer's operating system schedules and executes. A *multitasking operating system* can process different tasks simultaneously. Multitasking operating system technology makes it possible for Oracle7 to serve multiple users concurrently. As you might guess, the database server in a client/server system uses a multitasking operating system, such as UNIX, Windows NT, OS/2, or VMS.

A client/server system splits processing between two different components—client processes and server processes—and the network funnels the data between the two. Figure 4.4 illustrates the different types of processes and related components in an Oracle7 client/server system. Let's learn more about each of these different types of processes.

Client Processes

A *client process* is responsible for executing a client application on a workstation. For example, when you start Oracle Browser, your workstation's operating system creates a process in which to run the application. This client process executes the compiled application program that sends and receives data to and from the server across the network, redraws the application display when necessary, and so on.

You cannot do any work with a client database application like Oracle Browser unless you first connect to the database server across the network. Therefore, one of the first things a client process does is to send an initial *connect request* across the network to the address of the database server. The initial connect request includes your Oracle username and password, which the application typically requests when you start the application. If the database server is available and you provide a valid username/password combination, Oracle7 connects you to the database. Now you can use your application and the corresponding client process to run the application.

Processes in a client/server system

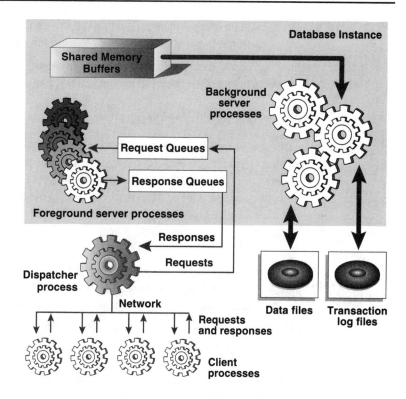

Server Processes

Server processes work to handle the requests sent by client processes and operate the many functions of an Oracle7 database server. As you can see in Figure 4.4, Oracle7 makes a distinction between foreground server processes and background server processes. *Foreground server processes* directly handle requests from client processes. *Background server processes* handle other specific jobs of the database server, such as writing data to data files and transaction log files.

Processing in an Oracle7 client/server system works like this:

1. When a client process sends a request to the database server, the dispatcher background process receives the request and puts it into a request queue. The dispatcher places requests in the queue on a first-in/first-out basis.

2. The next available foreground server process picks up the oldest request in the queue and processes it. After the foreground server process finishes processing the request, it places the results in the response queue.

3. The dispatcher monitors the response queue and sends back any request results to the client process that made the request.

Oracle7 Foreground Processes

During transaction processing, Oracle7 automatically adjusts the number of foreground server processes to match the processing load on the system. When requests build up in the request queue, Oracle7 starts more foreground processes so no user needs to wait to accomplish work. When foreground processes sit idle because of a lack of requests in the queue, Oracle7 terminates some foreground processes to eliminate unnecessary and unused system process overhead.

NOTE This chapter provides a quick overview of the Oracle7 process architecture. For more information about configuring and tuning the different Oracle7 server processes, see Chapter 8.

A single process can have multiple threads of execution. This simply means that a single multithreaded process can do the work of multiple single-threaded processes. The advantage of a multithreaded process is that it can do the work of many single-threaded processes but requires far less system overhead.

If a database server uses multithreaded server processes, it can support large numbers of clients with minimal system overhead. In your Oracle7 documentation, you will notice that the process architecture just described is classified as a multithreaded server. Technically, this is correct because, overall, a small number of foreground server processes can process the requests that come from many client processes. But don't take this to mean that the foreground server processes in Oracle7 are multithreaded themselves, because they are not; they execute only one thread per process.

Oracle7 Background Processes

As dispatchers and foreground server processes handle client requests, other background server processes work on other important database server operations. Here's an overview of the operations of the important Oracle7 background processes.

Database Writer (DBWR)   When a user transaction modifies some database data, a foreground server reads the data into the database server's shared memory buffer and makes the modification. The *database writer* (*DBWR*) writes data blocks that transactions modify in memory back to the appropriate data files.

DBWR does not immediately write modified blocks from memory to disk as transactions commit. To eliminate unnecessary I/O and boost server performance, DBWR writes a block in memory back to disk only when DBWR sits idle for a few seconds, a foreground server wants to read a new block into memory but there is no free space available, or Oracle7 performs a database or tablespace checkpoint (discussed shortly).

Log Writer (LGWR)   The *log writer* (*LGWR*) logs all Oracle7 database transaction activity to the database's transaction log. As transactions generate log information in the database's *transaction log buffer*, or *redo log buffer* (a shared memory area that temporarily stores log information), LGWR reads the log buffer and physically writes the log entries to the current transaction log group.

Like DBWR, LGWR writes information from the log buffer to disk only at certain times to keep disk I/O to a minimum. LGWR protects the commit of a transaction by immediately writing a commit record to the transaction log.

Archiver (ARCH)   The *archiver* (*ARCH*) is an optional process that automatically backs up transaction log groups when they become full. An administrator who uses ARCH doesn't need to worry about backing up a filled log group so it will be available the next time LGWR needs the log group for transaction logging. After Oracle7 switches from a filled log group to the next log group, ARCH notices that there is a group for archiving and makes a copy of the group in a configurable destination.

System Monitor (SMON)   The *system monitor* (*SMON*) carries out many internal operations as Oracle7 processes transactions. For example, SMON performs different space management operations as transactions free space or request more space for database data. SMON accomplishes its job with minimal impact on system performance because it requests processing time only when it is needed; otherwise, it sleeps.

Process Monitor (PMON) The *process monitor* (*PMON*) is a wake-and-sleep process responsible for cleaning up after a front-end server process terminates abnormally. For example, if a user's connection to the database is broken, PMON wakes up to roll back the user's dead transaction and release the transaction's locks so they won't prevent other transactions from accessing the same data.

Checkpoint (CKPT) As you just learned, DBWR does not necessarily write modified data blocks to disk when transactions are committed. However, DBWR periodically performs a *checkpoint* (*CKPT*), or *consistency point*, to make sure all modified information in memory is physically stored on disk.

The main purpose of a checkpoint is to serve as a post that indicates how much of the transaction log Oracle7 needs to apply should the system require crash recovery. Because Oracle7 knows that all data blocks before the last recorded checkpoint are present on disk, it needs to apply only the transaction changes since the last checkpoint.

During a checkpoint, LGWR stamps the headers in all the data files in the database with the most recent checkpoint's internal information. Normally, LGWR updates data file headers during a checkpoint. However, if your database has a large number of data files, you can improve the performance of transaction logging during checkpoints by configuring the instance with the optional CKPT background server process to update data file headers during checkpoints.

Dispatcher The *dispatcher* routes client process requests to the request queue and then returns the results from the response queue back to the appropriate clients. If the system load is heavy, you can start additional dispatchers dynamically without bringing down the current instance.

This chapter has presented a broad introduction to the important communication issues in a client/server system, including the following:

- The different types of networks, specifically local-area networks (LANs) and wide-area networks (WANs)

- The different types of network topologies, including star, bus, and ring topologies

- The types of hardware and software necessary for networks to function

- The role of middleware in a client/server system, and an introduction to Oracle's middleware product, SQL*Net, as well as the standard API middleware specification ODBC (Microsoft's Open Database Connectivity standard)

- The processes that cooperate to form a distributed application processing system, including client processes, foreground server processes, and background server processes

At this point, you have a basic understanding of all the primary components in an Oracle7 client/server database system, including the database server, the client, and the communication that occurs between clients and the server. The final chapter in Part I of this book provides a quick introduction to the language that you need to use to interact with Oracle7, SQL, and Oracle's procedural language extensions, PL/SQL.

CHAPTER

FIVE

5

Client and Server Communication: SQL and PL/SQL

- Common SQL commands

- Built-in SQL functions

- The block structure approach of PL/SQL

- PL/SQL variables, constants, and datatypes

- PL/SQL flow control statements

- Error handling with PL/SQL

- Different types of PL/SQL programs

Oracle7 is like a person who speaks only one language because users can interact with it using only one language: the Structured Query Language (SQL). Other than using SQL, there is no way for a user or application to enter or retrieve data from an Oracle7 database. That's why most database users—and especially developers and administrators—need to know SQL commands to get work done with Oracle7.

This chapter provides a broad overview of SQL, including the following:

- Data manipulation language (DML) commands, such as SELECT, INSERT, UPDATE, and DELETE

- Transaction control commands, such as COMMIT, ROLLBACK, and SAVEPOINT

- Data definition language (DDL) commands, such as CREATE, ALTER, and DROP

- Data control language (DCL) commands, such as GRANT, REVOKE, and SET ROLE

This chapter also provides a solid foundation for understanding and using PL/SQL, Oracle's extensions to the SQL standard. You'll learn about the following:

- The block structure approach of PL/SQL

- PL/SQL variables, constants, and datatypes

- Flow-control statements

- Different types of PL/SQL programs, including anonymous PL/SQL blocks, database procedures, functions, packages, and triggers

NOTE This chapter is by no means intended to be a complete SQL reference. For a complete syntax description of all SQL commands, see Martin Gruber's two books, *Understanding SQL* (1990) and the *SQL Instant Reference* (1993), both from Sybex.

A Quick Note about ANSI/ISO Standard SQL

Many, but not all, commercially available relational database servers support some version and level of the ANSI/ISO SQL standard. (ANSI is for American National Standards Institute, and ISO is for International Organization of Standards.) Support of industry-standard SQL allows users and SQL database applications to work identically with many different relational database servers.

To enhance the capabilities of the standard SQL language, each commercial relational database server has extensions to the ANSI/ISO SQL standard. Oracle7 is no different. Extensions to SQL can be in the form of nonstandard commands or nonstandard options to standard SQL commands. You are free to use the extensions of any commercial relational database server's SQL implementation, but understand that SQL extensions may not be the same or even present when you use another database server.

NOTE Oracle7 is 100 percent compliant with the entry-level ANSI/ISO SQL-92 standard, including the integrity enhancement feature, which outlines specifications for integrity constraint syntax and behavior.

Data Manipulation Using SQL

Data manipulation or *data modification* SQL commands are the SQL commands almost everyone uses when working with an Oracle7 database. Data manipulation language (DML) commands let users move data into and out of a database. DML commands include SELECT, INSERT, UPDATE, and DELETE.

The SELECT Command

To query data from tables in a database, use the SQL command SELECT. The SELECT command has many different options you can use to generate a report of data. You can use the SELECT command in its simplest form to retrieve all data from a table. For example, this query requests the data in all columns of all rows in the CUSTOMERS table:

```
SELECT * FROM customers
```

The wildcard character * indicates that you want to retrieve all columns in the table. If you want to narrow a query's *result set* (set of data that the server returns for a query) to specific columns of a table, you can include a column list:

```
SELECT id, lastname, firstname FROM customers
```

You can further narrow a query's result set to specific rows using a WHERE clause and a condition that limits the rows in the result set:

```
SELECT id, lastname, firstname FROM customers WHERE id = 32
```

A condition in a WHERE clause can take many forms. In the preceding example, the condition is a simple comparison expression that specifies only the row where the ID field contains the value 32. The following are all examples of a query with different types of expressions in the WHERE clause:

```
SELECT lastname, firstname, address, state, zipcode
  FROM customers
  WHERE state IN ('CA', 'FL', 'AZ')

SELECT id FROM orders
  WHERE orderdate BETWEEN '01-JUN-96' AND '30-JUN-96'

SELECT id, lastname FROM customers
  WHERE (firstname IS NULL) OR (address IS NULL)

SELECT id, lastname, firstname FROM customers
  WHERE id NOT IN (SELECT customerid FROM orders)
```

NOTE The sample statements above show that when you specify literals in SQL statements, it is necessary to delimit the literal with single quotation marks.

The last two examples are of particular interest. The next-to-last example includes a compound expression that is joined with the OR conjunction. As you might guess,

Oracle7 includes a row in the query's result set if the row satisfies either of the conditions separated by the OR conjunction in the WHERE clause. If you use the AND condition (not shown in the examples), Oracle7 includes a row in a query's result set only if the row satisfies both conditions in the WHERE clause.

The last example of WHERE conditions includes a *subquery*, which is a query nested within another statement. The example is a query to return the ID and name of all customers who have never placed an order.

You've probably guessed that the FROM clause indicates the target table, which is the CUSTOMERS or ORDERS table in the examples. If the database has two different tables with the same name that are owned by different users, you can prefix the table name in the FROM clause with the name of the user who owns the table, as shown here:

```
SELECT id, lastname, firstname FROM gwashington.customers

SELECT id, lastname, firstname FROM wclinton.customers
```

The SELECT command also has options for formatting the output of the result set. For example, the ORDER BY clause allows you to order the rows in a query's result set:

```
SELECT id, lastname, firstname FROM customers
  ORDER BY lastname, firstname
```

You can even concatenate the output of two columns and give the concatenated column an alias column name:

```
SELECT CONCAT(CONCAT(firstname,' '),lastname) "NAME"
  FROM customers
```

The SQL function CONCAT concatenates the first name and last name, separating them with a space (because the space character is specified within single quotation marks).

The INSERT Command

To insert new rows into a database, use the SQL command INSERT:

```
INSERT INTO orders
  VALUES (239, 2, '06-JUN-96', '06-JUN-96','23-JUN-96','F')

INSERT INTO orders (id, customerid, orderdate, status)
  VALUES (240, 7, '06-JUN-96', 'B')
```

The INTO clause specifies the target table and an optional list of column values, and the VALUES clause specifies the different column values for the new row. If you don't explicitly specify a list of the column values you will supply when inserting a new row, you must supply a value for every column in the table (as in the first example above).

You can also use a subquery instead of the VALUES clause to copy multiple rows from one table to another:

```
INSERT INTO orderhistory
  (SELECT * FROM orders WHERE orderdate < '31-MAY-96')
```

The UPDATE Command

To update rows in a table, use the SQL command UPDATE:

```
UPDATE customers SET fax = NULL
```

This example updates every customer's fax number to NULL. The SET clause includes an expression to update the target table. If you want to target specific rows, you can include a WHERE clause:

```
UPDATE customers SET address = '134 Rodeo Drive' WHERE id = 87
```

You can also use a subquery in the expression of the SET clause of an UPDATE statement:

```
UPDATE orders
  SET customerid = (SELECT id FROM customers
    WHERE lastname = 'King' AND firstname = 'Martin')
  WHERE id = 562
```

This statement updates the customer ID of order 562 to the customer ID of Martin King.

The DELETE Command

To delete rows from a table, use the SQL command DELETE:

```
DELETE FROM orderhistory
```

Be careful—the sample statement deletes all the rows in the ORDERHISTORY table. If you want to delete specific rows from a table, you must include a WHERE clause:

```
DELETE FROM items WHERE orderid = 739
```

That's your quick introduction to the DML commands in SQL. You should now be able to understand most of the examples in this book.

Transaction Control Using SQL

Transaction control commands let you determine the outcome of your transaction. Transaction control commands include COMMIT, ROLLBACK, and SAVEPOINT.

The COMMIT Command

To *commit* the changes made by your current transaction (to make the changes permanent and irreversible) and release any locks the transaction is holding, use this SQL command:

```
COMMIT
```

After you commit a transaction, you implicitly end the transaction and begin a new transaction.

The ROLLBACK Command

To *roll back* the changes made by your current transaction (to undo the changes as if they had never happened) and release any locks the transaction is holding, use this SQL command:

```
ROLLBACK
```

After you roll back a transaction, you implicitly begin a new transaction. In the next section, you'll see another option of the ROLLBACK command.

The SAVEPOINT Command

Within a long transaction, you can declare intermediate *savepoints* to divide the work in the transaction, as in this example:

```
INSERT ...
UPDATE ...
  .
  .
  .
DELETE ...
SAVEPOINT one
INSERT ...
UPDATE ...
DELETE ...
SAVEPOINT two
INSERT ...
UPDATE ...
DELETE ...
  .
  .
  .
```

Using the savepoints you declare, you can roll back parts of a transaction and leave other parts intact:

```
ROLLBACK TO SAVEPOINT two
```

This statement rolls back the effects of all statements after savepoint TWO. Your transaction also releases any locks that rolled back statements acquired so other transactions can modify the data. After a rollback to a savepoint, the transaction is still active.

NOTE It's important to understand how to design good transactions in an Oracle7 database application. See Chapter 16 for more information about designing transactions.

Data Definition Using SQL

Data definition language (DDL) commands are the SQL commands you use to create, alter, and drop (delete) different database objects in an Oracle7 database. Most types of database objects (tables, views, procedures, triggers, tablespaces, users, and so on) have CREATE, ALTER, and DROP commands; in other words, there are many DDL commands. In earlier chapters, you saw examples of the CREATE TABLE, CREATE VIEW, CREATE PROCEDURE, CREATE TRIGGER, CREATE USER, and CREATE ROLE commands.

Data Control Using SQL

Use the SQL data control language (DCL) commands to control which users can access an Oracle7 database and specific data (tables, views, and so on) within it. Data control statements include the GRANT and REVOKE commands, which you use to grant and revoke privileges, as well as the SET ROLE command, which enables or disables roles in your current session.

The GRANT Command

To grant a privilege or a role to a user or a role, use the SQL command GRANT:

```
GRANT CREATE TABLE, CREATE VIEW TO gwashington, alincoln

GRANT placeorders, updateorders, deleteorders TO orderentry

GRANT SELECT ON customers TO tjefferson
```

As these examples show, you use the GRANT clause to specify what you want to grant: a privilege, a role, or a comma-separated list of privileges or roles. Use the TO clause to specify a target or a list of the targets. Valid targets include roles and users.

The first example grants the system privileges CREATE TABLE and CREATE VIEW to the users GWASHINGTON and ALINCOLN. The second statement grants the roles PLACEORDERS, UPDATEORDERS, and DELETEORDERS to another role, ORDERENTRY. The third statement grants the SELECT privilege for the CUSTOMERS table to the user TJEFFERSON.

If you want to grant all object privileges for a particular object, use the keyword ALL:

```
GRANT ALL ON customers TO tjefferson
```

If you are granting system privileges or roles, you can grant them with the ADMIN option to allow the grantee the ability to pass the privilege or role to other users and roles:

```
GRANT CREATE TABLE TO rreagan WITH ADMIN OPTION
```

Now RREAGAN can grant the CREATE TABLE privilege to other users and roles. For example, RREAGAN might use this statement:

```
GRANT CREATE TABLE TO gbush
```

Similarly, if you are granting object privileges, you can grant them with the GRANT option to allow the grantee the ability to pass the privilege to other users and roles:

```
GRANT SELECT, INSERT, UPDATE, DELETE ON customers
   TO jkennedy WITH GRANT OPTION
```

The REVOKE Command

To revoke a privilege or role from a user or role, use the SQL command REVOKE:

```
REVOKE CREATE TABLE FROM alincoln
```

```
REVOKE placeorders FROM orderentry
```

```
REVOKE SELECT ON customers FROM tjefferson
```

With the REVOKE command, you can specify the privilege or role you want to revoke in the REVOKE clause. Use the FROM clause to indicate which user or role should no longer have the privilege or role. If you want to revoke all object privileges from a user or a role, use the ALL keyword:

```
REVOKE ALL ON customers FROM rnixon
```

The SET ROLE Command

To enable or disable roles in your current session, use the SQL command SET ROLE:

```
SET ROLE orderentry
```

If a role is protected by a password, you must indicate the password in an IDENTI-FIED BY clause to enable the role:

```
SET ROLE orderentry IDENTIFIED BY Y10wer
```

You can enable more than one role using the ALL option:

```
SET ROLE ALL
```

If you use the EXCEPT clause with the ALL option, Oracle7 enables all roles except those listed:

```
SET ROLE ALL EXCEPT orderentry
```

For the ALL option to work successfully, with or without the EXCEPT clause, the roles must not have passwords.

When you enable a specific role or number of roles, you implicitly disable all other roles granted to you. You can disable all roles using the NONE option of the SET ROLE command:

```
SET ROLE NONE
```

NOTE Application developers typically use the SET ROLE command as one of the first SQL statements in a client application. If you use the SET ROLE command, an application can set the correct privilege domain for application users when they start the application and connect to Oracle7.

For more information about security and DCL commands, see Chapters 9 and 18.

Using SQL Functions

Oracle7 SQL includes an extensive set of built-in SQL functions you can use to operate on data. The following are some examples of how you can use some of the many SQL functions.

To return the square root of 120:

```
SELECT SQRT(120) FROM dual;
```

Every Oracle7 database has a publicly accessible data dictionary table named DUAL. The DUAL table has a single column, DUMMY, and a single row, with a value of X. You can think of the DUAL table as a scratchpad you can use to return the result of a SQL function. This example shows a query that uses DUAL to return the value of the square root.

To return the total order amount of line items for order 32:

```
SELECT SUM(quantity * unitprice)
  FROM items, parts
  WHERE orderid = 32 AND items.partid = parts.id
```

To return the total number of customers in the CUSTOMERS table:

```
SELECT COUNT(*) FROM customers
```

To insert your username into a table:

```
INSERT INTO ... VALUES (USER, ...)
```

To return 'NONE AVAILABLE' if the customer address is NULL:

```
SELECT lastname, NVL(address,'NONE AVAILABLE') "ADDRESS"
  FROM customers
```

To insert today's date with a new order:

```
INSERT INTO orders (id, customerid, orderdate)
  VALUES (34, 534, SYSDATE)
```

TIP SQL functions are especially beneficial in a client/server database system because they allow you to perform more of the data processing at the server instead of in a client application. Consequently, you can improve overall system performance because less data is sent between the client and the server.

These are just a few examples of the SQL functions. Look for more SQL functions in the examples in this book. For a complete list of Oracle7 SQL functions, see Appendix A.

SQL and PL/SQL: What's the Difference?

SQL is a *nonprocedural language*, which means that you simply tell the database server to do something, not how to do it. The database server translates SQL commands into internal procedures to process the request. SQL is easy to use because it hides all the details of data processing.

C, Ada, and Pascal are examples of procedural languages. *Procedural languages* require you to know how to access data and create programs using a very structured design. Although a procedural language is more complex to use than a nonprocedural language, it can offer more flexibility and power.

To merge the advantages of both procedural and nonprocedural languages, Oracle7 offers *procedural language extensions* to SQL. The Oracle7 procedural language extensions are collectively called PL/SQL.

PL/SQL is an integrated component in many Oracle products. So you can create and use stored procedures and database triggers in the database server, Oracle7 includes PL/SQL and Oracle Forms includes PL/SQL so you can create form triggers as part of a client application. (These topics are covered later in the chapter.) PL/SQL programs in the different parts of an Oracle7 client/server system can work together. For example, a trigger in a form application can call a database procedure to accomplish some work.

If you are developing applications for a client/server database system, learning how to take advantage of PL/SQL is mandatory. With PL/SQL, you can improve application and system performance because you use fast-executing compiled programs rather than uncompiled SQL statements. Also, you significantly reduce network traffic between clients and servers.

The Basics of PL/SQL

The following sections provide a guide to the basics of PL/SQL. If you already know how to use a procedural language such as C or Ada, the information here should be familiar. It will be very familiar if you use Ada, because Oracle has modeled PL/SQL using the Ada programming language.

Blocking Code for Clarity

PL/SQL is a block-structured language. In a single PL/SQL program, you can group related sets of statements in *blocks* for easier programming and readability. Here is an example:

```
DECLARE
   ... set of statements ...
BEGIN
   ... set of statements ...
   BEGIN
     ... set of statements ...
   END
... set of statements ...
EXCEPTION
   ... set of statements ...
END
```

This PL/SQL program has four blocks. The DECLARE block is the section where you declare the variables, constants, and user-defined datatypes you want to use in the program body. The first BEGIN statement marks the beginning of the main program body. Nested within the main program body is another block that starts with another BEGIN statement and finishes with the END statement. Finally, the EXCEPTION block is where you write any exception handlers to handle error conditions in the program (explained in the section titled "Error Handling" later in this chapter). A final END statement indicates the end of the main program body.

Using Variables, Constants, and Datatypes

As part of a PL/SQL program, you can declare *variables* and *constants*. Any variable or constant you declare must have a datatype.

```
DECLARE
  currentcustomer VARCHAR2(15);   --variable for name of current user
  discount CONSTANT INTEGER := 0.1;   --constant for sales discount
```

> **NOTE** You can include comments in a PL/SQL program. Comments start with the characters – – and proceed to the end of the current line.

You can use any of the standard Oracle7 datatypes. The first of the preceding examples declares a variable using the VARCHAR2 datatype with a maximum length of 15 bytes. In addition to standard Oracle7 datatypes, PL/SQL supports other datatypes and subtypes. Table 5.1 lists all the PL/SQL datatypes, including the standard Oracle7 datatypes.

TABLE 5.1: Datatypes Available in PL/SQL

Datatype	Subtypes	Description
NUMBER (*precision, scale*)	DEC, DECIMAL, DOUBLE PRECISION, FLOAT, INT, INTEGER, NUMERIC, REAL, SMALLINT	Use this datatype to create variables and constants that store fixed or floating-point numbers. Precision is 38 by default; valid values are 0–38. Scale is 0 by default; valid values are –84–12.7. If you specify a negative scale, Oracle7 rounds values to the left of the decimal point.
BINARY_INTEGER	NATURAL, POSITIVE	Use this datatype to create variables and constants that store signed integers. Binary integers range from $-2^{31}-1$ to $2^{31}-1$. You can improve application performance if you use binary integer variables because Oracle7 avoids converting binary integers in calculations.
CHAR (*size*)	CHARACTER	Use this datatype to create variables and constants that store fixed-length text strings. Maximum length is 32,767 bytes; however, the maximum length of a CHAR column in a database table is only 255 bytes.

TABLE 5.1: Datatypes Available in PL/SQL (continued)

Datatype	Subtypes	Description
VARCHAR2 (*size*)	STRING, VARCHAR	Use this datatype to create variables and constants that store variable-length text strings. Maximum length is 32,767 bytes; however, the maximum length of a VARCHAR2 column in a database table is only 2000 bytes.
DATE		Use this datatype to create variables and constants that store time-related information, such as dates, hours, minutes, and seconds.
BOOLEAN		Use this datatype to create variables and constants that store the logical values TRUE and FALSE.
LONG		Use this datatype to create variables and constants that store large variable-length text strings. Maximum length is 32,767 bytes; however, the maximum length of a LONG column in a database table is 2 gigabytes.
RAW		Use this datatype to create variables and constants that store small binary strings. Maximum length is 32,767 bytes; however, the maximum length of a RAW column in a database table is only 255 bytes.
LONG RAW		Use this datatype to create variables and constants that store large binary strings. Maximum length is 32,767 bytes; however, the maximum length of a LONG RAW column in a database table is 2 gigabytes.
RECORD		Use this datatype to create your own record datatypes.
TABLE		Use this datatype to create PL/SQL table datatypes.

Of particular interest are the RECORD and TABLE PL/SQL datatypes because they allow you to create your own user-defined datatypes. The following sections explain these datatypes in more detail.

Creating User-Defined RECORD Datatypes

Using the RECORD datatype, you can create a user-defined datatype as a record that matches the attributes of a table, as shown here:

```
DECLARE
  TYPE orderrecordtype IS RECORD
  ( id NUMBER(5,0) NOT NULL := 0,     -- field for order's ID
    customerid NUMBER(5,0) NOT NULL := 0,   -- field for order's customer
    orderdate DATE NOT NULL := SYSDATE);    -- field for order's date
```

NOTE This example declares a user-defined record datatype that matches the columns of the ORDERS table. Notice that you can include the NOT NULL constraint for a field declaration in a record to prevent the assignment of NULLs to the field. If you use the NOT NULL constraint for a field declaration, you must initialize the field.

Once you create a user-defined datatype, you can use it to declare *record variables,* or arguments for procedures and functions:

```
DECLARE
  currentorder ORDERRECORDTYPE;

PROCEDURE placeorder (currentorder ORDERRECORDTYPE) ...
```

The second example shows how easy it is to pass a number of related values in a row as a single-record argument in procedures and functions.

In a PL/SQL program, you reference the fields in a record by indicating both the record and field names. This example assigns the current date and time to the ORDER-DATE field of the CURRENTORDER record variable:

```
currentorder.orderdate := SYSDATE;
```

Creating User-Defined TABLE Datatypes

You can use the TABLE datatype to create a user-defined datatype as a single-column table. The following examples create a user-defined datatype for order numbers and a variable that stores a table of order numbers:

```
DECLARE
  TYPE ordernumbertype IS TABLE OF NUMBER(5,0)
    INDEX BY BINARY_INTEGER;

  ordernumbers ORDERNUMBERTYPE;
```

A variable that you declare with a table datatype is called a *PL/SQL table*. Like database tables, PL/SQL tables can grow to an unlimited number of rows. You can reference a specific row in a PL/SQL table using its primary key number:

```
currentorderid := ordernumbers(1)
```

Like records, tables are especially useful for passing data sets as a single argument in procedures and functions.

PL/SQL offers two special attributes you can use to declare variables and user-defined datatypes that match table attributes: %TYPE and %ROWTYPE. Here are examples of their use:

```
DECLARE
  TYPE orderrecordtype IS RECORD
  ( id orders.id%TYPE NOT NULL := 0,
    customerid orders.customerid%TYPE NOT NULL := 0,
    orderdate orders.orderdate%TYPE NOT NULL := SYSDATE);

DECLARE
  currentorder orders%ROWTYPE;
```

These declarations are alternatives to the explicit declarations of the same record datatype shown at the beginning of the previous section. The first example explicitly declares each field of ORDERRECORDTYPE, depending on the datatypes of the matching columns in the ORDERS table. The second example declares a record variable CURRENTORDER to match the row structure of the ORDERS table, without declaring a record type.

Assigning Database Values to Variables

To allow a PL/SQL program to work with database data, you can assign database values in the result set of a query to PL/SQL variables. There are two different methods, depending on the number of rows the query returns: by using the SELECT command with the INTO clause or by declaring cursors.

SELECT... INTO...

To assign a single table value to a variable in a PL/SQL program, you can use a special clause of the SELECT command: the INTO clause. This example retrieves an order into a record variable:

```
DECLARE
   currentorder orders%ROWTYPE;
BEGIN
   SELECT id, customerid, orderdate
     INTO currentorder.id,
     currentorder.customerid,
     currentorder.orderdate
     FROM orders
     WHERE id = 453;
   .
   .
   .
other statements
   .
   .
   .
END
```

You can use the INTO clause to assign a table value to a variable only when the SELECT statement returns a single row. The next section explains how to assign values from queries that return more than one row.

Cursors

If a PL/SQL program includes a query that returns multiple rows from the database, you must declare a cursor for the statement. A *cursor* is essentially a name for a multi-row query. You use a cursor to process individual rows of the query's result set, one by one, as Oracle7 returns them from the database, as shown here:

```
DECLARE
  TYPE orderrecordtype IS RECORD
    ( id orders.id%TYPE NOT NULL := 0,
      customerid orders.customerid%TYPE NOT NULL := 0,
      orderdate orders.orderdate%TYPE NOT NULL := SYSDATE);
  currentorder ORDERRECORDTYPE;
  CURSOR ordercursor IS
    SELECT id, customerid, orderdate FROM orders;
```

This example declares a cursor for the rows in the ORDERS table. Once you declare a cursor, you use several different PL/SQL statements to process the rows in the cursor. The first step is to open the cursor:

```
OPEN ordercursor;
```

After you open a cursor, you can *fetch* rows one by one into a variable that can receive the data from the cursor:

```
FETCH ordercursor INTO currentorder;
```

To narrow the result set of a cursor to a specific set of rows, you can declare *cursor parameters,* which you can then use in the WHERE clause of the cursor query:

```
DECLARE
  CURSOR ordercursor (ordernumber NUMBER) IS
    SELECT id, customerid, orderdate
      FROM orders
      WHERE id >= ordernumber;
```

You set the value for a cursor parameter when you open the cursor:

```
OPEN ordercursor(3);
```

In the preceding examples, the result set of ORDERCURSOR includes all of the rows in the ORDERS table with an order ID greater than 3.

PL/SQL also provides methods for testing *cursor attributes,* including %ISOPEN, %ROWCOUNT, %NOTFOUND, and %FOUND.

- %ISOPEN simply tests a cursor to see if it is open. If the cursor is open, %ISOPEN evaluates to TRUE; if the cursor is closed, %ISOPEN evaluates to FALSE.

```
IF ordercursor%ISOPEN
  THEN CLOSE ordercursor;
END IF;
```

- %ROWCOUNT keeps a count of how many rows you fetch after you open a cursor. When you open a cursor, the cursor's %ROWCOUNT attribute is 0.

- %NOTFOUND and %FOUND are opposing attributes that reveal the state of the current cursor position. For example, %NOTFOUND always evaluates to FALSE (and %FOUND to TRUE) if the last fetch returned a row. %NOTFOUND evaluates to TRUE (and %FOUND to FALSE) only when the last fetch fails to return a row. %NOTFOUND eventually evaluates to TRUE, once you fetch the last row in the result set.

The following function is an example of the PL/SQL statements for creating and using a cursor. The ITEMTOTAL function returns the total price of all items for a specific order number.

```
CREATE FUNCTION itemtotal (ordernumber IN NUMBER)
RETURN NUMBER IS
  CURSOR ordercursor (ordernumber NUMBER) IS
    SELECT items.total
      FROM items
      WHERE items.orderid = ordernumber;
  ordertotal NUMBER (5,2) := 0;
  linetotal NUMBER (5,2) := 0;
BEGIN
  -- Add each linetotal to ordertotal.
  -- Exit loop after last line item.
  OPEN ordercursor (ordernumber);
  LOOP
    FETCH ordercursor INTO linetotal;
    EXIT WHEN ordercursor%NOTFOUND;
    ordertotal := ordertotal + linetotal;
  END LOOP;
  CLOSE ordercursor;
  RETURN ordertotal;
END itemtotal;
```

Using Flow Control Statements

Procedural language programs are said to have flow; that is, they execute statements, one by one, in the order that the program issues them. Procedural languages usually have *flow control statements* that allow you to control the flow of statement execution within a program. For example, flow control statements typically allow a program to execute one or more statements based on a specific condition, repeatedly execute a number of statements in a loop, or skip a number of statements by moving to another part of the program.

Oracle's PL/SQL has several flow control statements that allow you to control the flow of execution in a PL/SQL program, including IF...THEN, LOOP, WHILE, FOR, and GOTO. The next few sections explain the PL/SQL flow control statements.

The IF...THEN... Statement

The IF...THEN... statement lets you test for a condition and, depending on whether the condition is TRUE or FALSE, perform different blocks of statements. For example, this statement tests if the QUANTITY value is more than 5:

```
IF quantity > 5 THEN ... END IF
```

You can extend conditional testing using the ELSE and ELSIF structures of the IF statement, as shown here:

```
IF quantity > 15
   THEN ... ;    -- discount 15%
ELSIF quantity > 10
   THEN ... ;    -- discount 10%
ELSIF quantity > 5
   THEN ... ;    -- discount 5%
ELSE ... ;    -- no discount
END IF;
```

The LOOP Statement

Use the LOOP statement to execute a sequence of statements a number of times. Loops are useful for processing multiple rows in a cursor, as shown by this excerpt from the ITEMTOTAL function in the earlier section about using cursors:

```
LOOP
  FETCH ordercursor INTO linetotal;
  EXIT WHEN ordercursor%NOTFOUND;
  ordertotal := ordertotal + linetotal;
END LOOP;
```

There are several ways to exit a loop. The preceding example shows the EXIT WHEN construct. Alternatively, you can test for a condition with an IF statement and use the EXIT statement. The next example is a rewrite of the previous loop, using IF and EXIT to exit the loop after you fetch the last row of ORDERCURSOR:

```
LOOP
  FETCH ordercursor INTO linetotal;
  IF ordercursor%NOTFOUND
    THEN EXIT;
  END IF;
  ordertotal := ordertotal + linetotal;
END LOOP;
```

WHILE Loops

WHILE loops are yet another option for iterative flow control. They allow you to execute statements while a condition is TRUE. Here is another rewrite of the preceding loop:

```
WHILE ordercursor%FOUND LOOP
  FETCH ordercursor INTO linetotal;
  ordertotal := ordertotal + linetotal;
END LOOP;
```

For Loops

You can use any of the preceding loop structures when you don't know how many times you need to iterate the loop. You use a FOR loop when you know exactly how many times you need to execute a loop:

```
FOR counter IN 1 .. 5 LOOP
  ... set of statements ...
END LOOP;
```

Loops are so useful for processing cursors that PL/SQL includes a special type of FOR loop called a *cursor FOR loop*. A cursor FOR loop significantly simplifies coding when processing the rows of a cursor. It implicitly declares a variable or record to receive the rows in the cursor, opens the cursor, fetches rows from the cursor with each iteration of the loop, and closes the cursor after the last row has been fetched. Here is a rewrite of the ITEMTOTAL function using a cursor FOR loop:

```
CREATE FUNCTION itemtotal (ordernumber IN NUMBER)
RETURN NUMBER IS
  CURSOR ordercursor (ordernumber NUMBER) IS
    SELECT items.total
      FROM items
      WHERE orderid = ordernumber;
  ordertotal NUMBER (5,2) := 0;
BEGIN
  FOR line IN ordercursor(ordernumber) LOOP
    ordertotal := ordertotal + line.total;
   END LOOP;
  RETURN ordertotal;
END itemtotal;
```

Notice that cursor FOR loops also support cursor parameters.

The GOTO Statement

The GOTO statement allows you to continue program processing at a specific label in your program. You can label any part of a PL/SQL program using a unique identifier enclosed in double angle brackets. The following example shows how to label a loop and then go to the loop from another part of the program after checking for a condition:

```
<<orderitemloop>>
LOOP
  FETCH ordercursor INTO linetotal;
  IF ordercursor%NOTFOUND
    THEN EXIT;
  END IF;
  ordertotal := ordertotal + linetotal;
```

```
END LOOP orderitemloop;
.
.
.
other statements
.
.
.
IF ...
   THEN GOTO orderitemloop;
END IF;
```

Error Handling

Because we are all human, error conditions are inevitable in every type of data processing environment. For example, the user might mistakenly enter an incorrect spelling of a name when asking a database for a customer's address. To account for such errors when you develop programs such as PL/SQL blocks, you must pay specific attention to possible error conditions and plan programs so they react appropriately.

Good programming languages have specific mechanisms you can use to identify and handle error conditions separately from normal program processing. PL/SQL has an extensive error-handling mechanism called *exceptions*, which you can use to trap and process error conditions in a program. When a PL/SQL program encounters a defined error condition, PL/SQL *raises* the corresponding exception. You can specifically handle processing for an individual exception by defining an exception handler in the EXCEPTION block of a PL/SQL program. There are two types of exceptions: built-in and user-defined.

Built-In Exceptions

PL/SQL has built-in exceptions for common error conditions. For example, PL/SQL has a built-in exception that identifies when a program issues a SQL statement without first connecting to an Oracle7 database. Table 5.2 lists the built-in PL/SQL exceptions.

TABLE 5.2: Predefined PL/SQL Exceptions

Exception	Description
CURSOR_ALREADY_OPEN	You tried to open a cursor that is already open.
DUP_VAL_ON_INDEX	You tried to insert a duplicate value into a unique column.
INVALID_CURSOR	You referenced an invalid cursor or attempted an illegal cursor operation.
INVALID_NUMBER	You tried to use something other than a number where a number is required.
LOGIN_DENIED	Your connect request has been denied.
NO_DATA_FOUND	No data matches the request of your SELECT INTO statement.
NOT_LOGGED_ON	You are not connected to Oracle7.
PROGRAM_ERROR	You encountered a PL/SQL internal error.
ROWTYPE_MISMATCH	Your host cursor variable and PL/SQL cursor variable have incompatible return types.
STORAGE_ERROR	You encountered a PL/SQL memory error.
TIMEOUT_ON_RESOURCE	You reached a timeout while waiting for an Oracle7 resource.
TOO_MANY_ROWS	Your SELECT INTO statement returned more than one row.
VALUE_ERROR	You encountered an arithmetic, a conversion, a truncation, or a constraint error.
ZERO_DIVIDE	You tried to divide a number by 0.

The following example shows how you might use the NO_DATA_FOUND and TOO_MANY_ROWS built-in PL/SQL exceptions:

```
CREATE FUNCTION customerid (last IN VARCHAR2, first IN VARCHAR2) RETURN
INTEGER AS
-- This is a function to return the ID of a customer
-- given the customer's last and first names.
  customerid     INTEGER;
  errnum         INTEGER := -20000;
  errmess        VARCHAR2(2000) := 'Standard error';
BEGIN
  SELECT id INTO customerid FROM customers
    WHERE lastname = last AND firstname = first;
```

```
RETURN customerid;
EXCEPTION
  WHEN NO_DATA_FOUND THEN    -- if no matching customer, return user error
    SELECT errornumber, errormessage INTO errnum, errmess
      FROM usererrors
      WHERE errormessage LIKE ('Invalid cust%');
    raise_application_error(errnum, errmess);
  WHEN TOO_MANY_ROWS THEN    -- if there are multiple customers, then ...
    SELECT errornumber, errormessage INTO errnum, errmess
      FROM usererrors
      WHERE errormessage LIKE ('Multiple cust%');
    raise_application_error(errnum, errmess);
  WHEN OTHERS THEN    -- for undefined errors, return standard error message
    raise_application_error(errnum, errmess);
END customerid;
```

When a PL/SQL program encounters a built-in exception, PL/SQL automatically raises the exception. This means that processing of the main program body stops and transfers to the corresponding exception handler in the EXCEPTION block, if present. The code in an exception handler determines what happens from that point forward.

For example, in the previous example of the CUSTOMERID function, if the SELECT statement in the main program body fails to find a customer record with the given last and first names, the program automatically raises the NO_DATA _FOUND exception—processing of the main program body terminates and transfers to the NO_DATA_FOUND exception handler in the EXCEPTION block of the program. The exception handler chooses to retrieve a user-defined error number and message from a table and then return them to the calling environment after rolling back the effects of the CUSTOMERID function.

Notice in the EXCEPTION block of the CUSTOMERID function that PL/SQL includes a special OTHERS exception handler. You use the OTHERS exception handler to generically handle any exceptions you don't otherwise explicitly handle in the EXCEPTION block. This is a very convenient way to trap unexpected errors and prevent unhandled exceptions.

User-Defined Exceptions

You can also name your own user-defined exceptions in the DECLARE block of a PL/SQL program. For example, you might declare a user-defined exception to handle a specific business rule in a PL/SQL program.

You declare user-defined exceptions in the DECLARE block of PL/SQL. For example, the following statement declares an exception AFTERHOURS:

```
afterhours EXCEPTION
```

When you declare a user-defined exception, you must also define a corresponding exception handler in the EXCEPTION block of a program. The exception handler for the AFTERHOURS exception might be similar to the following:

```
WHEN afterhours THEN
   SELECT errornumber, errormessage INTO errnum, errmess
     FROM usererrors
     WHERE errormessage
     LIKE ('Operation not allowed before 8 A.M. or after 6 P.M.');
   raise_application_error(errnum, errmess);
```

In the main program body, you typically check for user-defined errors at the appropriate time using conditional statements (IF…THEN). When a user-defined error is detected, you raise a user-defined exception with the PL/SQL RAISE statement to transfer program processing to the corresponding exception handler.

```
IF (TO_CHAR(SYSDATE, 'HH24')) < 8 OR (TO_CHAR(SYSDATE, 'HH24')) > 28 THEN
RAISE afterhours;
END IF;
```

Unhandled Exceptions

If you don't explicitly handle an exception in a PL/SQL block and don't use the OTHERS exception handler to trap it, PL/SQL rolls back the operations performed by the block and returns the *unhandled exception* to the calling environment. For example, procedure A calls procedure B, which calls procedure C. If procedure C encounters an unhandled exception, PL/SQL rolls back the effects of procedure C and returns the unhandled exception to procedure B. If procedure B doesn't handle the exception either, PL/SQL rolls back the effects of procedure B and returns the exception to procedure A, and so on.

An unhandled exception can eventually step all the way back to a client application. However, a well-designed PL/SQL program handles all exceptions the program might raise unless there is a specific reason for not doing so. Well-designed PL/SQL programs that correctly handle exceptions are especially important for an application in a client/server database system that calls database-stored procedures. To eliminate network traffic for unhandled exceptions that return to a client, PL/SQL programs in the database should handle their own exceptions.

NOTE If an application doesn't explicitly handle an unhandled exception returned from another program, the application typically rolls back the effects of the PL/SQL program call only, not the entire application.

Creating Your Own Application Error Messages

Oracle7 includes a set of programming utilities you can use when designing client applications. You can use one utility—the RAISE_APPLICATION_ERROR procedure—to create your own application error numbers and messages. You can have up to 1000 valid user-defined error numbers that range between –20000 to –20999.

If you decide to use the RAISE_APPLICATION_ERROR procedure extensively throughout your programs, it's a good idea to centralize user-defined error numbers and corresponding error messages in a database table. This way, programmers won't make up unnecessary error messages and all user-defined error messages will be consistent across all applications. Here is an example:

```
CREATE TABLE usererrors
( errornumber     NUMBER(5,0) PRIMARY KEY,
  errormessage    VARCHAR2(2000));

INSERT INTO usererrors VALUES (-20000, 'Standard error');

INSERT INTO usererrors VALUES (-20001, 'Invalid customer ID');

CREATE PROCEDURE deletecustomer (customerid IN NUMBER) AS
  errnum     NUMBER := -20000;
  errmess    VARCHAR2(2000) := 'Standard error';
BEGIN
  DELETE FROM customers WHERE id = customerid;
  IF SQL%NOTFOUND THEN    -- if no customer is found, return error message
    SELECT errornumber, errormessage INTO errnum, errmess
      FROM usererrors
      WHERE errormessage LIKE ('Invalid cust%');
      raise_application_error(errnum, errmess);
  END IF;
```

```
EXCEPTION
  WHEN NO_DATA_FOUND THEN    -- if no matching error message, use standard error
    raise_application_error(errnum, errmess);
END deletecustomer;
```

When you call the RAISE_APPLICATION_ERROR procedure in a program, you raise an exception (roll back the effects of the surrounding program) and return the error number and message to the calling environment (for example, the client application).

Creating PL/SQL Programs

Now that you have a broad overview of the PL/SQL language components, let's see how they all fit together. The next few sections discuss different types of PL/SQL programs you can create.

Anonymous PL/SQL Blocks

An *anonymous PL/SQL block* is an unnamed PL/SQL program in an application. For example, you can send the DELETECUSTOMER procedure as an anonymous block of statements to the server when you use SQL*Plus, as shown here:

```
SQL>   DECLARE
SQL>     errnum    ' NUMBER := -20000;
SQL>     errmess     VARCHAR2(2000) := 'Standard error';
SQL>   BEGIN
SQL>     DELETE FROM customers WHERE id = 12;
SQL>       IF SQL%NOTFOUND THEN    -- if no customer is found, return
              error message
SQL>         SELECT errornumber, errormessage INTO errnum, errmess
SQL>           FROM usererrors
SQL>           WHERE errormessage LIKE ('Invalid cust%');
SQL>         raise_application_error(errnum, errmess);
SQL>       END IF;
SQL>   EXCEPTION
SQL>     WHEN NO_DATA_FOUND THEN    -- use standard error if no
              matching error
SQL>       raise_application_error(errnum, errmess);
```

```
SQL>  END deletecustomer;
SQL>    /
```

As shown in this example, when you are using SQL*Plus (or Server Manager) to send an anonymous block, you need to include a special program terminator (/) on a line by itself, immediately following the END statement that concludes the program. The program terminator signals SQL*Plus that you have finished typing the statements in the program, so SQL*Plus can process the program and send it to the database server as a single unit.

A client application sends an anonymous block to the database server as a single network I/O, greatly reducing network traffic that would otherwise be present if you send individual SQL statements one by one. However, each time the server receives a new anonymous block, it must compile the block before it can execute it. To overcome this performance problem, you can store the PL/SQL program inside a database (see the next section).

In summary, anonymous blocks are useful for procedures that you want to issue just once and won't use again. If you will repeatedly use a PL/SQL program from a client application, it's better to store the PL/SQL program as a compiled procedure or function in the database server.

Using Procedures and Functions

Oracle7 allows you to create and store compiled PL/SQL programs inside a database, including procedures, functions, and packages (packages are explained in the next section). *Functions* differ from *procedures* only in that a function returns a single variable to the calling environment, while a procedure does not return anything to the calling environment.

Your client/server application environment benefits tremendously from using procedures and functions:

- Developer productivity is better because you code, test, and debug common application logic once and store it centrally, where all client applications can use it.

- Application performance is better because an application calls and executes a compiled block of code stored in the database rather than sending an uncompiled block of statements across the network to be compiled by the server.

- Network overhead is reduced because client applications send a procedure call and a set of parameters rather than individual SQL statements or an entire anonymous PL/SQL block.

You create procedures and functions with the CREATE PROCEDURE or CREATE FUNCTION command, respectively. (See the examples of the CREATE PROCEDURE and CREATE FUNCTION commands earlier in this chapter.)

Defining Procedure and Function Parameters

When you create a procedure or function, you can give it values with which to work using *parameters*. Most of the CREATE PROCEDURE and CREATE FUNCTION statements in this book specify parameters. When you specify a parameter, you must indicate its datatype. You can use any valid PL/SQL datatype to declare a parameter.

When you specify a procedure or function parameter, you should indicate whether it is an IN, OUT, or IN OUT parameter. An *IN parameter* is one you want to assign a value to when you call the procedure but don't want to allow the procedure to change its value in the outside calling environment. As you might guess, an *OUT parameter* is the opposite of an IN parameter. You don't assign an OUT parameter a value when you call a procedure, but the procedure can assign the OUT parameter's value in the outside calling environment. An *IN OUT parameter* is one you can both assign a value to when you call the procedure and change inside the body of the procedure. Review the procedures in this book for examples of IN, OUT, and IN OUT parameters.

Executing Procedures and Functions

The way in which a client-side application calls a database procedure or function is specific to the development tool with which you create the application. You'll need to read the documentation for your client application development tool to learn the specifics. Here is a client-side PL/SQL block that calls the previously shown CUSTOMERID function and the DELETECUSTOMER procedure to find and delete a customer from the CUSTOMERS table:

```
DECLARE
  custid NUMBER(5,0);
BEGIN
```

```
-- Assign return value of CUSTOMERID function call
-- to CUSTID, and then use the returned value to
-- delete the customer.
  custid := customerid('Hamilton','Alexander');
  deletecustomer(custid);
END;
```

Using Packages

You can create and store related procedures, functions, and other PL/SQL constructs together in a *package*. Among other things, packages allow you to organize related PL/SQL programs for easier application development and for improved security and performance. Packages also allow you to create *global variables* that have persistent state. Here is a package for processing parts in a company's inventory:

```
CREATE PACKAGE partmanager AS
PROCEDURE newpart( price IN REAL, initnum IN INTEGER,
reorderpt IN INTEGER, descr IN VARCHAR2);
PROCEDURE updatepart( fieldcode IN CHAR, partid IN INTEGER,
numberupdate IN NUMBER, descupdate IN VARCHAR2);
FUNCTION checkpart(partid IN INTEGER) RETURN NUMBER;
PROCEDURE restockpart( partid IN INTEGER);
PROCEDURE deletepart(partid IN INTEGER);
END partmanager;

CREATE PACKAGE BODY partmanager AS
--------------------------DECLARE  BLOCK-----------------------------
-- Private global variables to hold user-defined error numbers and messages
-- for all package procedures and functions.

  errnum     INTEGER;
  errmess    VARCHAR2(2000);
--------------------------RETURNERROR FUNCTION-----------------------
-- This private procedure sets the error number and message for the error
-- asked for by a package procedure or function.

PROCEDURE returnerror (errorstring IN VARCHAR2) IS
BEGIN
  SELECT errornumber, errormessage INTO errnum, errmess
    FROM usererrors
    WHERE errormessage LIKE errorstring||'%';
  raise_application_error(errnum, errmess);
```

```
EXCEPTION
  WHEN NO_DATA_FOUND THEN -- if no matching error message, use standard
    error
  raise_application_error(-20000, 'Standard error');
END returnerror;
-------------------------NEWPART PROCEDURE-------------------------
-- This public procedure creates a new part in the PARTS table, given
the new
-- part's price, initial quantity, reorder point, and description.

PROCEDURE newpart  (price IN REAL, initnum IN INTEGER,
reorderpt IN INTEGER, descr IN VARCHAR2) IS
BEGIN
  INSERT INTO parts
    VALUES (partsequence.NEXTVAL, price, initnum, reorderpt, descr);
END newpart;
-------------------------UPDATEPART PROCEDURE-------------------------
-- This public procedure updates a part record given the part number and
-- either a number or a string for the update (one or the other is NULL),
-- and the code of the field to update (P = unitprice, O = onhand,
-- R = reorder, D = description).

PROCEDURE updatepart ( fieldcode IN CHAR, partid IN INTEGER,
numberupdate IN NUMBER, descupdate IN VARCHAR2) IS
codetype CHAR := fieldcode;
BEGIN
  IF codetype IN ('P','p') THEN
    UPDATE parts SET unitprice = numberupdate WHERE id = partid;
  ELSIF codetype IN ('O','o') THEN
    UPDATE parts SET onhand = onhand + numberupdate WHERE id = partid;
  ELSIF codetype IN ('R','r') THEN
    UPDATE parts SET reorder = numberupdate WHERE id = partid;
  ELSIF codetype IN ('D', 'd') THEN
    UPDATE parts SET description = descupdate WHERE id = partid;
  ELSE
    returnerror('Invalid operation code');
  END IF;
  IF SQL%NOTFOUND THEN
    returnerror('Invalid part');
  END IF;
END updatepart;
```

```
--------------------------CHECKPART FUNCTION------------------------
-- This public function gets the difference between a given
       part's current
-- quantity and reorder point.

FUNCTION checkpart(partid IN INTEGER) RETURN NUMBER IS
  quantity INTEGER;
BEGIN
  SELECT (onhand - reorder) INTO quantity FROM parts WHERE id = partid;
  RETURN quantity;
EXCEPTION
  WHEN NO_DATA_FOUND THEN
    returnerror('Invalid part');
    quantity := NULL;
    RETURN quantity;
END checkpart;
--------------------------RESTOCKPART PROCEDURE---------------------
-- This public procedure puts the given part's ID in the REORDER table
along
-- with the current quantity and reorder point.

PROCEDURE restockpart (partid IN INTEGER) IS
  reorderstatus    INTEGER := 0;
  quantity     INTEGER := 0;
  reorderpt    INTEGER := 0;
BEGIN
-- First, check to see if part hasn't already been reordered.
  SELECT count(*) INTO reorderstatus FROM reorder WHERE id = partid;
-- If the part hasn't already been reordered, then reorder it now.
  IF reorderstatus = 0 THEN
    SELECT onhand, reorder INTO quantity, reorderpt
      FROM parts WHERE id = partid;
    INSERT INTO reorder VALUES (partid, quantity, reorderpt);
  END IF;
EXCEPTION
  WHEN NO_DATA_FOUND THEN
    returnerror('Invalid part');
END restockpart;
--------------------------DELETEPART PROCEDURE---------------------
-- This public procedure deletes a part from the PARTS table. A foreign
key
-- in the ITEMS table prevents the deletion of a part if it is refer-
enced in
-- a line item for an order.
```

```
PROCEDURE deletepart(partid IN INTEGER) IS
BEGIN
  DELETE FROM parts WHERE id = partid;
IF SQL%NOTFOUND THEN
    returnerror('Invalid part');
  END IF;
END deletepart;

END partmanager;
```

You create a package in two parts: a package specification and a package body.

- In the *package specification,* you declare those procedures, functions, and global variables you want to make available to the outside world. Constructs that you declare in a package's specification are *public.*

- In the *package body,* you define all procedures, functions, and global variables, including those that you don't declare in the package specification. Constructs that you define in a package's body but do not declare in the package's specification are *private.*

Applications cannot use private package constructs; only procedures and functions within the package can use them.

In the PARTMANAGER package, all the procedures and functions are public except the RETURNERROR procedure. The package body also declares two private global variables, ERRNUM and ERRMESS, that work with the RETURNERROR procedure.

Oracle7 has a useful feature called the *sequence generator* that an application can use to quickly generate unique numbers. You can use this facility to create primary keys whenever you insert a new row into a table. First, you must define and name a specific sequence of numbers:

```
CREATE SEQUENCE partsequence
  START WITH 1
  INCREMENT BY 1
```

This statement creates a sequence of numbers an application can use to generate new part numbers for rows in the PARTS table.

The INSERT statement in the definition of the PARTMANAGER.NEWPART procedure given earlier uses PARTSEQUENCE to create a new part number when someone calls the procedure. To generate the next available sequence number, the procedure references the sequence using the NEXTVAL suffix.

NOTE   To learn more about the sequence generator and using sequences, see Chapter 15.

Executing Package Procedures and Functions

To call a public procedure or function in a package, simply preface the call with the package name. The following examples call public procedures in the PARTMANAGER package.

```
partmanager.newpart(24.00, 100, 15, 'blue widget');

partmanager.updatepart('P', 304, 72.00, NULL);

partmanager.updatepart('D', 21, NULL, 'yellow-green widget');

partmanager.deletepart(31);
```

Using Database Triggers

A *database trigger* is a PL/SQL procedure that you associate with a table. When you issue a SQL statement for a table that meets a trigger condition, Oracle7 automatically fires (executes) the trigger's body (PL/SQL program body). As Chapter 2 mentions, you can use triggers to program the Oracle7 server to react to specific situations. For example, you can use triggers to enforce complex data integrity rules or to derive specific column values.

You can create a trigger using the CREATE TRIGGER command. The next example is a trigger that derives the total for each line item in the ITEMS table.

```
CREATE TRIGGER linetotal
BEFORE INSERT OR UPDATE OF quantity ON items
FOR EACH ROW
```

```
DECLARE
  itemprice REAL;
BEGIN
  SELECT unitprice INTO itemprice
    FROM parts WHERE id = :new.partid;
  :new.total := :new.quantity  * itemprice;
END linetotal;
```

Defining Trigger Conditions

A *trigger condition* has a triggering statement and an optional trigger restriction. A *triggering statement* is an INSERT, UPDATE, or DELETE statement that references a specific table. The LINETOTAL trigger's statements are an INSERT statement or an UPDATE statement that references the QUANTITY column of the ITEMS table. When you issue either of these statements, Oracle7 fires the LINETOTAL's trigger body to calculate the line item total for every row the statement touches.

You can further limit the firing of a trigger by using a trigger restriction. A *trigger restriction* is a simple Boolean condition that you specify in an optional WHEN clause of the CREATE TRIGGER command. A triggering statement also must satisfy the restriction for Oracle7 to fire the trigger's body. Here is an example:

```
CREATE TRIGGER reorder
AFTER UPDATE OF onhand, reorder ON parts
FOR EACH ROW
WHEN (new.onhand <= new.reorder)
BEGIN
  INSERT INTO reorder
    VALUES (:new.id, :new.onhand, :new.reorder);
END;
```

Firing Options

When you create a trigger, you can specify several options that determine how Oracle7 fires the trigger's body when the trigger's condition is met. You specify how many times you want the trigger body to execute and whether the trigger's body should fire before or after the execution of the triggering statement.

Statement and Row Triggers   To indicate the number of times you want the trigger body to be executed for each triggering statement, Oracle7 lets you create two different types of triggers: *statement triggers* and *row triggers*. Oracle7 fires a statement trigger's body once, no matter how many rows the triggering statement touches. Oracle7 fires a row trigger's body once for every row the triggering statement touches. When you create a trigger, you need to think about the behavior you want and decide which type of trigger is correct for your application.

The following PARTCHANGES trigger creates a single, simple record of every statement issued against the PARTS table:

```
CREATE TRIGGER partchanges
AFTER INSERT OR UPDATE OR DELETE ON parts
DECLARE
  dmltype VARCHAR2(6);
BEGIN
-- Set dmltype to the type of statement issued against the PARTS table.
  IF INSERTING THEN
    dmltype := 'INSERT';
  ELSIF UPDATING THEN
    dmltype := 'UPDATE';
  ELSE
    dmltype := 'DELETE';
  END IF;
-- Insert the statement user's name and the dmltype into the log table.
  INSERT INTO partchangelog VALUES (USER, dmltype);
END partchanges;
```

But what if you want more extensive logging of the changes to the PARTS table? Let's say you want to log every change to every part. In this case, you need to write the PARTCHANGES trigger as a row trigger:

```
CREATE TRIGGER partchanges
AFTER INSERT OR UPDATE OR DELETE ON parts
FOR EACH ROW
DECLARE
  dmltype VARCHAR2(6);
BEGIN
-- Set dmltype to the type of statement issued against the PARTS table.
  IF INSERTING THEN
    dmltype := 'INSERT';
  ELSIF UPDATING THEN
    dmltype := 'UPDATE';
  ELSE
    dmltype := 'DELETE';
  END IF;
```

```
-- For every row that's changed in the PARTS table, insert the old and new
-- column values for the row.
  INSERT INTO partchangelog VALUES (dmltype,
:old.id,:old.unitprice,:old.onhand,:old.reorder,:old.description,
:new.id,:new.unitprice,:new.onhand,:new.reorder,:new.description);
END partchanges;
```

BEFORE and AFTER Triggers   You can also specify whether you want the trigger's body to fire before or after the execution of the triggering statement. Again, you need to consider the behavior you want and then create the appropriate type of trigger for your application.

For example, the LINETOTAL trigger shown earlier is a BEFORE row trigger; Oracle7 fires the trigger's body once before inserting or updating each row in the ITEMS table. A BEFORE row trigger is the correct trigger type for this application because you want to derive the line item total *before* inserting or updating a row in the trigger's table.

The PARTCHANGES trigger (either version) is an AFTER trigger. This is appropriate since Oracle7 doesn't need to roll back the changes to the PARTCHANGELOG table if the triggering statement fails against the PARTS table.

Special PL/SQL Extensions for Trigger Bodies

To enhance the capabilities of triggers, there are several special PL/SQL extensions you can use in a trigger body: *conditional predicates* and *correlation values*.

The predicates INSERTING, UPDATING, and DELETING allow you to conditionally execute different blocks of statements depending on the type of triggering statement that fires a trigger. You need to use conditional predicates only when a trigger's condition includes two or all three types of triggering statements. The previous examples of the PARTCHANGES trigger (both versions) demonstrate the use of the conditional predicates.

Correlation values allow a row trigger to use the old and new column values of the row the trigger is currently positioned on when it is firing. For example, the second version of the PARTCHANGES trigger logs the old and new column values when you issue a DML statement against the PARTS table. When the triggering statement is an INSERT statement, the old correlation values are NULLs (there is no old row from which to obtain values); when the triggering statement is a DELETE statement, the new correlation values are NULLs (there is no new version of the row from which to obtain values); and when the triggering statement is an UPDATE statement, both old and new correlation values are available.

NOTE You can reference correlation values in a row trigger's restriction. Correlation values are not available for statement triggers.

The last few sections have given you an overall sense of PL/SQL's capabilities to help you understand the remainder of this book, no matter what job you perform. See Chapter 17 for more information and examples of using PL/SQL in an Oracle7 client/server database system.

This chapter has given you a quick introduction to SQL and PL/SQL. It covered how to work with some of the most commonly used Oracle7 SQL commands, such as SELECT, INSERT, UPDATE, DELETE, COMMIT, ROLLBACK, SAVEPOINT, GRANT, REVOKE, and SET ROLE. The chapter also described how to extend the functionality of Oracle7 SQL using the procedural language extensions provided through PL/SQL, such as program variables and constants, flow control statements (IF...THEN, LOOP, and so on), and the different types of PL/SQL programs you can create (procedures, packages, triggers, and so on). The discussions in this chapter should help you understand the SQL and PL/SQL examples seen throughout this book.

This chapter concludes the introductory portion of this book. You should now have a solid understanding of the big picture in an Oracle7 client/server database system—what the server, client, and network portions of the system do, and how clients can get work done using SQL and PL/SQL programs to communicate with the server. Parts II and III of this book focus on different jobs you might have in an Oracle7 client/server database system. To learn more about database administration, turn to Part II; to learn more about application development, turn to Part III.

PART II

Database Administration in an Oracle7 Client/Server System

Now that you have a foundation of knowledge about the scope of an Oracle7 client/server system, it's time to focus on the tasks of one of the key users of an Oracle7 system, the database administrator. Chapters 6 through 12 reveal detailed information about the job of managing an Oracle7 database, with a special emphasis on client/server database administration.

CHAPTER

SIX

Understanding Oracle7 Database Administration and Administrative Utilities

- **Responsibilities encompassed by the title of database administrator**

- **Security concerns for Oracle7 database administrators**

- **An overview of Server Manager, Oracle7's primary administrative utility**

- **Data transfer with Oracle's SQL*Loader utility**

An Oracle7 database server is the central part of an Oracle7 client/server database system. If the database server has not been installed properly or configured correctly, or if it goes down because of a power failure or disk crash, or if it is not performing well, the productivity of many company workers will be hampered. Because the database server plays such an important role as the central manager of data in a client/server system, organizations typically designate one or more people as responsible for the administration of this special system component.

To get you started and to begin this part of the book, which is devoted to Oracle7 database administration, this chapter explains the following:

- The role of a database administrator

- Database administrator security

- Server Manager, Oracle's primary database administration tool

- SQL*Loader, the utility for loading data into an Oracle7 database

What Does a Database Administrator Do?

A database administrator may be responsible for a wide assortment of tasks:

- Planning the database

- Configuring your system

- Creating the database

- Managing database space

- Planning and installing applications

- Administering security

- Managing database backup and recovery

- Monitoring and tuning database performance

- Dividing administrator responsibilities

The following sections describe these responsibilities.

Planning a Database

One key to a successful client/server system design is planning. The more planning you do up front, the more you will know about your system requirements and the better prepared you will be when you need to make important decisions.

Always start the planning of a computer system by clearly identifying the goals and requirements of your application(s). Remember to include both current and future goals in your requirements list so you pick a system design that can grow with your business in the near future.

In the planning phase, you need to pick the correct hardware and software components for your system. These include client workstations (or dumb terminals), the database server, operating systems, network hardware, and the network operating system. Answering the questions presented in the following sections will help you decide how to equip your database system properly. If you are going to use a computer system that you already have for a new application, the answers to these questions will help you make sure your current system will work for a new application. If you are building a new system, it might be best to plan and purchase a small development system first so you can test your planning before buying the full-blown production system for all system users.

Choosing Client Workstations

To decide which type of client workstations to buy, you'll need to examine the applications you are planning. For example, if your applications will use a bitmapped GUI, make sure the workstations you buy have the correct type of display and a pointing device, such as a mouse. In this case, you'll need to outfit the workstations with an operating system that uses a GUI.

You'll also need to consider your applications to plan the memory and disk-space requirements for your client workstations. For example, make sure the client workstations have at least enough memory to run both the operating system and the proposed application(s). If you will install the application locally on each workstation, you'll need to determine how much disk space is necessary. If you don't want users to store any applications or work locally on the workstation, you may decide to buy inexpensive diskless workstations.

Planning the Database Server

The type of computer and operating system you use for your database server is critical. You need to know, on the average, how many transactions a second an application will need to process. Additionally, you must consider any background batch processing that might be necessary. Knowing these facts can help you decide how much processing power your database server will require. For example, if an application's transaction rate is relatively small, you may decide a single processor machine will suffice. If an application's transaction-processing rate is high and you need good performance, you may need to use more powerful computer configurations, such as a multiprocessor computer that can increase system throughput.

When choosing components, answer these questions to help you plan the amount of memory your database server needs:

- How many users will use the system?

- On the average, how many users will be using the system at the same time?

- How much database data would you like to be able to cache in the memory of the database server to help reduce disk I/O and boost system performance?

Answering these questions will help you plan the amount of disk space your database server needs:

- On the average, how much data do you expect the application(s) to generate?

- What are the characteristics of the application's data needs? Will your database continue to grow and require more disk space, or can you incrementally take older, historical data offline to free disk space?

To help you decide whether you should purchase additional disks and/or tape storage devices for your database server, answer this question:

- How will you protect your system from possible failures?

Choosing a Network and Network Operating System

Answer these questions to help you decide on the correct network and network operating system for your new applications:

- What type of operations do you want to be able to control on your computer network?

- Does your company's building already have network wiring and a computer network you can use for your new system?

- Is speed or ease of use more important to you?

Configuring Your System

After you decide on and buy the components of your system, the next thing to do is to put them together. Installing the computer system, wiring the network, and integrating the components is a big job. If you work in a medium or large company that has specialists to do this work, or if you hire an independent consultant to help you, system integration may not be your responsibility. If you must configure the system yourself, refer to other documentation that can assist you.

Installing Oracle7

With the computer hardware, operating systems, network, network operating system, and communications software in place, you are ready to install the central software component of your system, Oracle7. Again, this job may not be your responsibility if there is a system administrator or consultant to do it for you.

If Oracle7 installation is your responsibility, follow the directions in the Oracle7 installation guide that comes with the software. As part of the Oracle7 installation procedure, you have the option of installing other Oracle software tools and utilities that you may have purchased. If you want to install this software at the same time, follow the directions. Alternatively, you can install additional software at a later time. For a client/server system, you'll definitely want to install your SQL*Net drivers for the communication protocol you'll be using.

Creating a Database

As the database administrator, you are responsible for planning and creating the databases for your Oracle7 system. The next few sections discuss some of the issues involved with database creation. Chapter 7 provides step-by-step procedures for database creation.

The Initial Oracle7 Database

The Oracle7 installer offers you the choice of automatically creating an initial database on your database server. During installation, you can mold the initial database to meet the requirements for your application(s). If you choose the default database during installation and find later that it doesn't meet your needs, you can delete the initial database and start from scratch.

> **WARNING**   If you decide to delete the initial database and start from scratch, be aware that there is no "delete database" command to make this a simple operation. You need to identify the files that make up the initial database and delete them using the operating system commands.

Single or Multiple Databases?

When you plan your system and applications, you must decide whether all applications will use a single physical database or whether it is better to use multiple physical databases. If several applications need to use the same or related sets of data, it is much simpler to organize your information in a single database. Even if applications use independent sets of tables, you can logically and physically separate the data for different applications in different tablespaces (that is, partition) within a single Oracle7 database. In most cases, it's best to use a single database for all applications because you will need to configure only one Oracle7 instance and transaction log for all applications.

Use multiple databases when you want to insulate *production database* applications from *test database* application environments. It's a good idea to create a test database for application developers so they can have an unrestricted application development environment that won't affect the ongoing productivity of other workers who are using production applications. For example, if you create a test database for application developers, you can grant them the powerful system privileges to start up and shut down the test database but prevent them from controlling the availability of the production database.

Database Migration

If want to upgrade to Oracle7 with a database you created with a previous version of Oracle, you might need to follow special *database migration* steps listed in the installation guide that comes with your Oracle7 software. If you want to use Oracle7 with data originating from a non-Oracle database, you'll need to load the data into an Oracle7 database using the SQL*Loader utility. For example, SQL*Loader allows you to load data from flat files (text files) into an Oracle7 database. For more information about data loading and SQL*Loader, see the section "Using SQL*Loader" later in this chapter.

Managing Database Space Requirements

An ongoing database administrator job is managing the space that is available to the database system. Space management encompasses many different but related tasks:

- Tablespace creation and growth: When you install a new application in your system, you typically create one or more new tablespaces in the Oracle7 database so you can physically separate the application's data from other application data. If the data in a tablespace approaches the boundary of them tablespace's preallocated space, you can create additional data files for the tablespace to increase its storage capacity, or you can configure the data files of the tablespace to grow dynamically.

- Tuning space usage: Application developers are typically responsible for designing the data structures of a database (tables, views, and so on). However, the database administrator is responsible for implementing the production database design, including consideration of the space implications of the tables in the production database. Specifically, the administrator needs to understand and correctly set the storage parameters for tables and other database objects when creating them so the database will make the best use of space and deliver optimal performance regarding disk I/O.

- Monitoring of space usage: After you create a database, the job of space management is not finished. You need to consistently monitor storage structures for growth characteristics, anomalies, and so on. For example, if a table needs more space, Oracle7 will automatically extend it according to the table's space parameters; however, you might decide that you want to manually extend the table with specific storage parameters.

Planning and Installing an Application

As mentioned in the preceding section, a developer is typically responsible for designing an application's underlying tables, views, procedures, roles, and so on. After validating an application in a test environment, the developer can contact the production database's administrator and arrange to move the new application to the production environment.

As the database administrator, you are responsible for reviewing the *scripts* (batch command files) a developer provides to create the database objects for the new application. When reviewing an application script, consider things like the space parameters for the application objects (as the previous section mentions), object naming, schema design, and so on. After you edit the script, you can run it using Server Manager or SQL*Plus to create the application objects. After running the script, you must also consider the security operations necessary to get the application running and a backup strategy for the application's data, as described in the next two sections.

Deployment of an application on client workstations may or may not be your job, depending on your organization. If the client/server system is large, the database administrator typically focuses on managing the database server and lets special system administrators deploy applications. However, if a system is small (for example, a departmental application), the administrator may be the only person capable of installing the new application.

Administering Security

Administrators are responsible for controlling access to a database using operating system, network operating system, and Oracle7 security features. Once you let someone inside an Oracle7 database, you need to control how that person can use the data within a database. If a system has many users and applications, the job of security administration may justify a full-time *security administrator*.

As the security administrator, you are responsible for creating new database user accounts and controlling the privilege domain of each user. When you add a new application to the client/server system, you need to empower users to use the application by creating the application's role(s) and by granting the application role(s) to users and/or other roles, as necessary. For more information about database security, see Chapters 9 and 18.

Backing Up and Recovering the Database

Perhaps the most common administrator function is backing up a database's data to protect it. To adequately protect a database from damaging situations, you first must configure a database's transaction log and control files. Next you must devise, test, implement, and automate a backup strategy for your database. If your site has extreme high-availability requirements, you should consider configuring a standby database in case a catastrophic disaster completely destroys the primary database location.

If a failure damages your database at some time, it's your job as the database administrator to recover the database as quickly as possible so user productivity does not suffer. For more information about database backup and recovery, see Chapter 11.

Monitoring and Tuning Database Performance

Another primary job of a database administrator is monitoring and tuning the performance of Oracle7 databases. This can include monitoring and adjusting instance settings, such as process and memory buffer configurations, as well as space management operations, such as setting space parameters for database objects, regenerating object statistics for the Oracle7 optimizer, and rebuilding indexes when necessary. See Chapter 12 for more information about database performance tuning.

Dividing Administrator Responsibilities

In large systems with many databases, users, or applications, administration may be too big a job for one person. In these cases, it may be necessary to split database administration tasks among a team of administrators. For example, one administrator might be responsible for only the operating system, another for the network, another for database backups, and still another for system security.

Database Administrator Security

Not everyone who uses your client/server database system should have the power of a database administrator. If everyone had administrator privileges, they would be able to perform such powerful operations as starting up and shutting down Oracle7 databases, creating new tablespaces, creating new users, dropping users, killing user sessions, and so on. You must maintain tight control over the power of a database administrator by using user accounts and database administrator privileges. The next few sections explain the default administrator accounts of every Oracle database and privileged administrator connections that permit important operations such as server startup and shutdown.

The SYSTEM Administrator Account

When you create a database, Oracle7 automatically creates the SYSTEM user for database administration connections. The Oracle7 installer prompts you to supply a password for this account in the initial database. When you create other databases, the initial password for this account is MANAGER.

If you don't create customized administration user accounts after installation and database creation, always connect to a database as SYSTEM to complete most database administration tasks. The next few sections describe specific exceptions to this rule.

The SYS Administrator Account

When you create a database, Oracle7 automatically creates the SYS user for special database administration connections. The Oracle7 installer prompts you to supply a password for this account in the initial database. When you create other databases, the initial password for this account is CHANGE_ON_INSTALL.

SYS is the "owner" of an Oracle7 database's data dictionary tables. This means that when you connect to an Oracle7 database as the SYS user, you have the potential of adversely affecting the database's data dictionary, thus preventing normal operation. Therefore, use the SYS account only in these situations:

- When you want to supplement or remove some data dictionary tables using scripts provided with the Oracle7 installation kit

- When you install a new Oracle application and must connect as SYS

The headers in all Oracle7 scripts typically indicate when you must run a script as SYS. The installation documentation for Oracle and non-Oracle applications also indicates when to use the SYS account.

WARNING   To protect system security, change the default passwords for both the SYSTEM and SYS users immediately after you create an Oracle7 database.

Enhancing Security with Individual Administration Accounts

Once a database is operational, it's best to create individual administration accounts for all the administrators of the system and avoid giving group access to the standard administrative accounts SYSTEM and SYS. This policy has two primary justifications:

- Individual accounts are typically more secure than a group account because only one user knows the password for an individual account; multiple users know the password for a group account.

- If access is given to multiple users for a single administrative account, it's difficult to audit which administrator does which operation.

Privileged Administrative Connections

For most administrative duties, database administrators can connect to Oracle7 using their own accounts to perform work. However, Oracle7 is designed so unauthorized users cannot affect database availability. For this reason, several important administration tasks, such as server startup, shutdown, and database recovery, require a database administrator to establish a *privileged administrative connection* to the database server.

Several steps are necessary to configure support for privileged administrative connections. Make sure to read the section "Configuring Privileged Connections" in Chapter 9 for complete information.

Using Server Manager

Let's take a good look at the primary utility you use to administer an Oracle7 database system: Server Manager. When you, as the database administrator, install Oracle7 on your database server, you automatically install Server Manager. Here, you will get an overview of the capabilities of Server Manager and how to use it in your Oracle7 system. The other chapters in this part of the book provide more specific examples of using Server Manager to manage an Oracle7 database system.

The Server Manager User Interface

The method for starting Server Manager depends on the operating system your database server or client workstation uses. When you start Server Manager, it first presents you with a connection dialog box so that you can immediately connect to the Oracle database server with which you want to work. Once you connect to an Oracle Server, you can accomplish your work using the three main components of Server Manager: the Administration Manager, SQL worksheets, and system monitors. The following sections take a look at each component.

The Administration Manager

The Administration Manager, shown in Figure 6.1, is the primary interface component of Server Manager. When you start a new session, Server Manager presents you with the Administration Manager by default.

FIGURE 6.1:

The drawers and folders of Server Manager's Administration Manager allow you to accomplish most database administration tasks with ease.

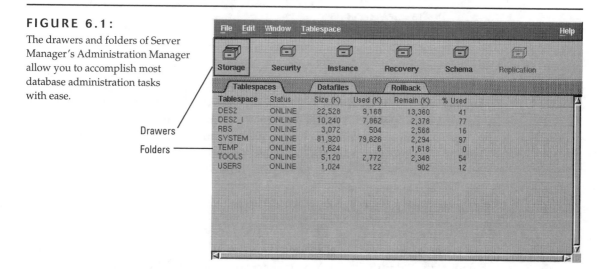

Tablespace	Status	Size (K)	Used (K)	Remain (K)	% Used
DES2	ONLINE	22,528	9,168	13,360	41
DES2_I	ONLINE	10,240	7,862	2,378	77
RBS	ONLINE	3,072	504	2,568	16
SYSTEM	ONLINE	81,920	79,626	2,294	97
TEMP	ONLINE	1,624	6	1,618	0
TOOLS	ONLINE	5,120	2,772	2,348	54
USERS	ONLINE	1,024	122	902	12

The Administration Manager drawers and folders allow you to access its many features with ease and without cluttering up the screen. Just below the main menu bar is a set of labeled drawer icons (Storage, Security, and so on). Each drawer relates to a different set of administrative operations, such as storage management, database security, and so on.

When you click on a drawer, Server Manager "opens" the drawer and presents a set of corresponding folders below. For example, when you select the Storage drawer, Server Manager presents folders labeled Tablespaces, Datafiles, and Rollback.

After you open a drawer to display its folders, the next step is to click on the tab of a folder. When you click on a tab, Server Manager displays a list of important data dictionary information relevant to the topic of the folder. For example, clicking on the Tablespace folder tab causes Server Manager to issue a query that returns a list of all tablespaces, along with corresponding availability and space information (as you can see in Figure 6.1). Click on any column of the folder display, and Server Manager promptly sorts the rows by ascending values of the selected column.

> **TIP**
>
> Server Manager's folder displays are a great way to quickly view important system information without knowing the structure of the Oracle7 data dictionary.

In most cases, the Administration Manager folder displays are more than just read-only lists of information from the Oracle data dictionary. To alter an object in a display, you can simply double-click on the object in the display list, or you can select the object and choose an item from the main menu. In either case, Server Manager displays an appropriate dialog box that allows you to manipulate the selected object. For example, you can take a tablespace offline by double-clicking on the tablespace in the Tablespace folder and using the dialog box that appears.

SQL Worksheets

The Administration Manager drawers have a fixed set of folder displays that address many of the concerns of an Oracle administrator. When you need to do something that the Administration Manager doesn't automatically support, you can use a Server Manager SQL worksheet. A SQL worksheet, as Figure 6.2 shows, is a simple ad hoc query tool. To start a new SQL worksheet, select New Worksheet from the File menu of any Server Manager component (for example, the Administration Manager).

FIGURE 6.2:

A SQL worksheet is an ad hoc query tool that lets you query specific information.

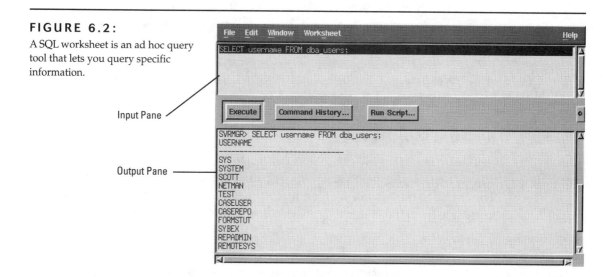

The Input pane of the worksheet window is where you can enter SQL and Server Manager commands. The Output pane is where the worksheet displays the output generated by the corresponding commands. In between the two panes is a split bar with several push buttons:

- The Execute button executes the command in the Input pane.

- The Command History button displays past commands that you can either execute again or paste into the Input pane for modification and subsequent execution.

- The Run Script button displays a file selection dialog box that you can use to select and run a command script located on your client machine.

> **NOTE**
>
> Server Manager automatically creates separate sessions as you work with the different components of the product. For example, Server Manager opens one server connection for your work in the Application Manager and distinct sessions for each SQL worksheet that you open. You can even start multiple, concurrent Administration Managers that each connect to different Oracle7 servers available in the network. Because each window has its own session (and thus transaction), work in one window won't affect operations taking place in other windows.

System Monitors

Another component of Server Manager is a group of system monitors. A monitor is a convenient display that reports information about ongoing database activity. For example, the System I/O monitor shows the database I/O load split among current users of the system. Figure 6.3 shows the System I/O monitor.

FIGURE 6.3:

The System I/O monitor shows the processing loads currently in demand by different system users.

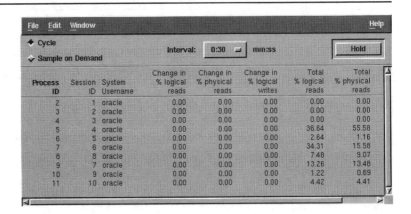

To start a new monitor, select Monitor from the File menu of any Server Manager component (for example, the Administration Manager or a SQL worksheet).

WARNING After you start a monitor, it repeatedly issues its query at specific timed intervals to refresh the information in the monitor display. If you have several monitors running at once and they all issue their queries frequently (say, every 5 seconds), the negative impact on the system performance can be significant. To avoid monitors hurting system performance, run only the monitors you need, and terminate or pause them when you no longer need to update them. You can also update each monitor's display on demand, and adjust each monitor's query cycle interval using widgets in the monitor itself.

Essential Server Manager Dialog Boxes and Menus

The following sections introduce some of Server Manager's most commonly used dialog boxes and menus:

- The Connect dialog box
- The Startup Database dialog box
- The Shutdown Database dialog box
- The Disconnect Session dialog box
- The Create Tablespace dialog box
- The Start Online Backup and End Online Backup menus
- The Create User dialog box

Connecting to a Database

When you start Server Manager, you must first connect to an Oracle7 database using the Connect dialog box, shown in Figure 6.4.

FIGURE 6.4:

The Connect dialog box allows you to connect to Oracle7 using your username and password.

Enter your username or a predefined administrator username and a password. If you are connecting to a database across a network, you must also indicate the service name of the Oracle database server. See Chapter 9 for a description of the Connect As option list, which allows you to establish privileged versus nonprivileged administrative connections. After you complete the dialog box entries, select the Connect button.

> **TIP**
>
> You can also change a connection to a server when working with any component of Server Manager. From any Server Manager component, select File ➤ Connect. Additionally, you can quickly display certain Server Manager dialog boxes using the hot-key sequence shown next to the option in a menu. For example, on UNIX ports, the hot-key sequence for the Connect dialog box is Ctrl-O.

Starting a New Instance

After you establish a privileged connection to an Oracle Server, you can use the Startup Database dialog box to start a new Oracle7 instance and optionally mount and open a database. To access this dialog box from the Administration Manager, select the Instance drawer, click on the Database folder tab, then select Database ➤ Startup from the menu bar. Figure 6.5 shows the Startup Database dialog box.

FIGURE 6.5:

Server Manager's Startup Database dialog box allows you to start up an Oracle7 database server so other users can connect to and use the database.

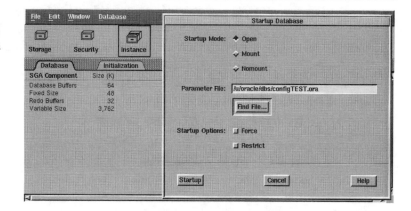

The Startup Mode radio button list in the Startup Database dialog box determines to what degree you start Oracle7. Normally you want to start a new instance and mount and open the database all in one operation so that the database is available to users. To perform a complete startup in one operation, select the Open radio button. Consider the other options, Mount and Nomount, only when you have specific administration operations in mind. For example, you should use Nomount when creating a new database.

The other options of the Startup Database dialog box allow you to customize your startup. In general, you won't use these other options unless you have special circumstances to address during startup. An exception, however, is the Parameter File entry field. This field allows you to specify the name of the parameter file to use when configuring the new instance. If you don't enter anything in the Parameter File entry field during startup, Server Manager uses the default parameter file for your system to start up the database. In most cases, you'll have a special parameter file for each database, and that is what you should enter in this field. When you do not recall the name of a specific parameter file, you can use the Find File button to browse the server's directories for the file.

> **NOTE**
>
> The default parameter file varies, depending on your operating system. For example, if you run Oracle7 on a UNIX platform, the default parameter file is *ORACLE_HOME*/dbs/init*ORACLE_SID*.ora, where *ORACLE_HOME* and *ORACLE_SID* correspond to specific UNIX environment variables. For more information about environment variables, ORACLE_HOME, ORACLE_SID, and default settings for your server's initialization parameter file, see Chapter 7.

Shutting Down the Database

After you establish a privileged connection to an Oracle server, you use the Shutdown Database dialog box to stop an Oracle7 database. To access this dialog box from the Administration Manager, select the Instance drawer, click on the Database folder tab, then select Database ➤ Shutdown from the menu bar. Figure 6.6 shows the Shutdown Database dialog box.

FIGURE 6.6:

The Shutdown Database dialog box permits you to stop an Oracle7 database server so it is not available for normal use.

The Normal option in the Shutdown Database dialog box is the most user-friendly way of shutting down; it waits for all database users to disconnect before shutting down the database. In situations in which you can't be patient when shutting down a database, you can use the Immediate option to disconnect all users, roll back their open transactions, and commence database shutdown. Use the Abort Instance option only when something has hung the system and the Immediate option doesn't work. See Chapter 7 for more information about shutting down a database.

TIP

> If your session hangs while you are trying to shut down a database (that is, because it is waiting for users to log off before commencing database shutdown), consider aborting your last command using your terminal's normal interrupt key combination, such as Ctrl-C, and then using the Immediate option.

Killing a User Session

One of the more useful dialog boxes in Server Manager is the Disconnect Session dialog box, shown in Figure 6.7. Many times in a client/server configuration, a client can abnormally disconnect from the Oracle7 server and Oracle7 can't detect this event because the network does not indicate a disconnection. As a result, the user's

FIGURE 6.7:

Using the Disconnect Session dialog box, you can terminate remnant client user sessions that waste system resources on the server.

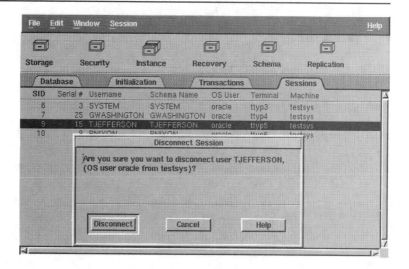

remnant session wastes overhead on the server. You can use the Disconnect Session dialog box to kill such sessions and release the unused overhead. You might also want to kill a user session if you suspect that the session is causing some sort of problem. For example, a application developer's user session may be in an endless loop and wasting server processing time.

To access the Disconnect Session dialog box from the Administration Manager, select the Instance drawer and click on the Sessions folder tab to display a list of the current database sessions. Select the session to kill from the folder list, and then select Session ➤ Disconnect from the menu bar.

NOTE   If a user has multiple sessions and you're not sure which one to kill, you can also use the different monitors of Server Manager to help determine the problem session.

Creating a New Tablespace

You can use the Create Tablespace dialog box to create a new tablespace for your database. To access this dialog box from the Administration Manager, select the Storage drawer, click on the Tablespaces folder tab, then select Tablespace ➤ Create from the menu bar. Figure 6.8 shows this dialog box.

TIP   As you work with Server Manager dialog boxes, notice the Show SQL button. You can use this feature to reveal and edit the underlying SQL commands that Server Manager uses to perform the administrative operations that you request.

The General folder of the Create Tablespace dialog box allows you to enter a name for the new tablespace, build a list of data file specifications to store the tablespace's data, and determine whether or not you want the tablespace to be online after creation. Optionally, you can use the Default Storage folder of the same dialog box to set the new tablespace's default storage options. See Chapter 7 for more information about creating tablespaces. For more information about building file specification lists and setting tablespace storage parameters, see Chapter 10.

The Create Tablespace dialog box allows you to create a new tablespace and determine its storage settings.

Backing Up the Database

Perhaps the database administrator's most frequently performed operation is database backup. Server Manager's Start Online Backup and End Online Backup menus help you begin and end the process of backing up specific tablespaces in your database.

The Backup folder of the Recovery drawer in the Administration Manager lists all the tablespaces of a database, along with their current backup mode status. Figure 6.9 shows this folder.

To begin the backup of an online tablespace, select the tablespace from the folder list, and then select Backup ➤ Start Online Backup. This simply tells Oracle7 to prepare the tablespace for backup; it doesn't actually back up the data files of the tablespace. To do the physical file backups, you must use an operating system command or a backup utility. Although this might seem like an inconvenience, it can actually be quite useful and make backup much faster. For example, you can back up different files in parallel to different disk drives or tape devices to speed up the tablespace backup operation. And if your operating system or utility lets you compress the files during the backup, you can save lots of space on your backup media.

FIGURE 6.9:

The Backup folder of the Recovery drawer lists all of a database's tablespaces and their backup mode status. Use the options on the Backup menu to mark any online tablespace for a backup operation.

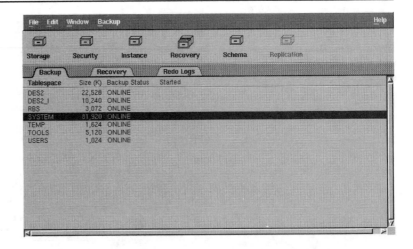

> **TIP**
>
> You can automate your backups by creating scripts that you can run from Server Manager. You can use the options of the File menu of a SQL worksheet to build and execute SQL scripts quickly. Chapter 11 shows specific examples of how to build database backup scripts and execute them automatically using operating system utilities.

After you finish backing up an online tablespace's data files, you must let Oracle7 know. To mark the end of an online tablespace backup, select the tablespace from the folder list and then select Backup ➤ End Online Backup. See Chapter 11 for complete information about backing up online and offline databases, as well as documenting, automating, planning, and testing your backups.

Creating a New User

You use the Create User dialog box to create a new user for your database. To access this dialog box from the Administration Manager, select the Security drawer, click on the Users folder tab, and then select User ➤ Create from the menu bar. Figure 6.10 shows the Create User dialog box.

FIGURE 6.10:

The Create User dialog box allows you to create new database users along with their security settings.

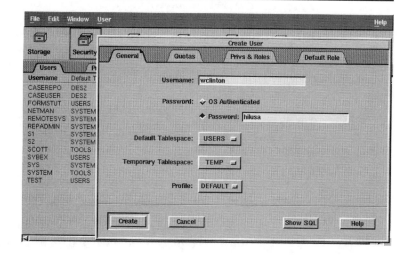

For every new user, you must specify some general information about the user in the General folder of the Create User dialog box. First, enter a new username and then indicate how you want to authenticate the user using the Password list. If you want the user to enter a password at connect time, select the Password radio button and then enter an initial password for the new user. Alternatively, select the OS Authentication radio button when you want an external service such as the server's operating system to authenticate the new user when the user attempts to connect to the database.

The remaining fields in the General folder of the Create User dialog box are optional and control security settings:

- The Default Tablespace field allows you to specify a new user's default tablespace, which Oracle7 uses, for example, if the user neglects to include a tablespace specification when creating a new table.

- The Temporary Tablespace field allows you to specify a new user's temporary tablespace, which Oracle7 uses for temporary work space—for example, when executing a complicated query.

- The Profile field allows you to assign a resource limit profile to a user. Resource limits control, for example, how many CPU cycles and how much disk I/O a user can use.

The other folders in the Create User dialog box provide access to other optional security settings:

- The Quotas folder allows you to indicate the tablespaces in which a new user can create objects and how much space in the corresponding tablespaces is available to the user.

- The Privs & Roles folder allows you to grant any number of privileges and roles to a user.

- The Default Role folder allows you to determine a user's initial security domain after connecting to the database by enabling a set of one or more default roles.

Before you create users for a database, you should learn more about how the options in the Create User dialog box affect database security. See Chapter 9 for complete information about securing an Oracle7 database, including creating and managing users.

Using SQL*Loader

Many times, you'll want to load data from a preexisting data source into a table in an Oracle7 database. For example, assume that each salesperson in a sales department uses a personal database manager on his or her PC to keep track of customers. When the department moves to an Oracle7 client/server database, it's best to centralize all of the customer information in a single table so every person in the company can share a single source of information. SQL*Loader is a simple administrative utility you can use to load data that you output from non-Oracle data sources into an Oracle7 database.

SQL*Loader Data Sources

To load data into an Oracle7 database using SQL*Loader, the data must be in a text file with the data records in a format that SQL*Loader can read: fixed-length or variable-length. These text file formats are described in the next sections.

Fixed-Length Format

A text file containing data records in a *fixed-length format* is one in which each field of each data record is a fixed length. Fields in a fixed-length format are delimited by their position. Field values shorter than a field's maximum value are padded with blank spaces to adjust the field length of every record to exactly match the others. For example, customer records in a fixed-length format might look like this:

```
1    NBC              Brokaw           Thomas
2    CNN              Shaw             Bernard
```

Variable-Length Format

A text file containing data records in a *variable-length format* is one in which each field of each data record is its real length. To indicate the beginning and end of each field in a variable-length format, the fields must be delimited by special characters, such as commas and quotation marks. For example, customer records in a variable-length format might look like this:

```
1,"NBC","Brokaw","Thomas"
2,"CNN","Shaw","Bernard"
```

NOTE Most programs that store data in a tabular format—specifically, database managers and spreadsheet programs—allow you to output data into standard text files. Furthermore, such programs allow you to specify whether you want to dump data to a text file in a fixed- or variable-length format. If you have the option, choose to dump a file using a variable-length format; it is slightly easier to configure SQL*Loader to accept such data.

SQL*Loader Control Files

Along with your text file containing your data, you need to create another text file, called a SQL*Loader control file. A *control file* is a very small text file containing a number of options and clauses that tell SQL*Loader how to load the data from a text file into an Oracle7 database. You can specify many, many clauses and options in a SQL*Loader control file to precisely control data loads. In this section, we'll cover just a few of the more important options so you can get a quick start on using SQL*Loader.

The LOAD/CONTINUE_LOAD Options

The LOAD option is usually the first statement in a control file. It signals the beginning of a new data load. The CONTINUE_LOAD option signals the continuation of an interrupted data load so you can pick up a data load from the point at which it ended earlier (for example, because of an error).

The INFILE Parameter

The INFILE parameter specifies the location of the data you want to load. After the INFILE parameter, specify a valid operating system filename. You can specify an asterisk (*) instead of a filename to indicate that the data to load is contained in the control file itself:

```
INFILE '/u/usr/oracle/rdbms/business.dat'

INFILE *
```

The BEGINDATA Option

The BEGINDATA option indicates the beginning of a block that contains data to load from within the control file itself. Specify the BEGINDATA option only if the INFILE parameter specifies an * to indicate that the data is within the control file and not in an external file. To include data in a control file, make sure the BEGINDATA option is the last control file keyword followed by the fixed- or variable-length data rows.

The INTO TABLE Clause

The INTO TABLE clause specifies the target table for the data load. Specify the target table using standard SQL table name specifications (for example, *owner.table*):

```
INTO TABLE customers
```

The INSERT, APPEND, and REPLACE Options

The INSERT option indicates that the target table is empty. Use this option if you just created a new table in preparation for a data load. If the table is not empty, SQL*Loader returns an error and cancels the load.

The APPEND option indicates that the target table may or may not already have rows and that you want to load the data into the table without affecting any current table data.

The REPLACE option indicates that you want to delete all rows in the table before inserting the data from the load. Use the REPLACE option if you periodically refresh a table in the database using data from an external source.

The FIELDS Clause

Use the FIELDS clause if you plan to load data from a variable-length format data source. In this clause, specify the character that delimits different fields using the TERMINATED BY parameter. Also, use the OPTIONALLY ENCLOSED BY parameter to indicate special characters that enclose different fields. Then specify an ordered list of the names of the columns in the target that correspond exactly to fields in the data to load. Enclose the column list within parentheses:

```
FIELDS TERMINATED BY ' , ' OPTIONALLY ENCLOSED BY ' " '
(id,companyname,lastname,firstname,address,city,state,zipcode,phone,fax)
```

SQL*Loader Command-Line Options

For most operating systems, you execute SQL*Loader by invoking the program from the command line of the operating system. When you invoke SQL*Loader, you can specify several command-line options. Here are a few of the most important options to consider:

Option	Description
USERID=	Specifies the name and password of the user to connect to Oracle7 when performing a data load. Be sure to specify a user who has the privilege to select and insert records into the target table. Additionally, if the control file specifies the REPLACE option, be sure the user you specify also has the privilege to delete records from the target table. If you don't specify a user account when you invoke SQL*Loader, the program prompts you for one.
CONTROL=	Specifies the name of the control file to use to perform the data load. The filename you give must be a valid operating system filename. If you don't specify a control file when you invoke SQL*Loader, the program prompts you for one.
DATA=	Specifies the name of the data file that contains the data to load into the target table. Specify the DATA option only if you don't include the INFILE parameter in the control file or if you want to override the INFILE setting in the control file.
LOG=	Specifies the name of the file in which to log information about the data load. If you don't specify a log filename, SQL*Loader automatically creates a log file that has the same name as the control file, with the file extension .LOG.
BAD=	Specifies the name of the file in which to store data records that are improperly formatted or records that SQL*Loader cannot insert because of errors during the data load. If you don't specify a "bad filename," SQL*Loader automatically creates a file that has the same name as the control file, with the file extension .BAD.

> **NOTE** The SQL*Loader command-line options CONTROL, DATA, LOG, and BAD are not case-sensitive themselves; however, their inputs (filenames) may be case-sensitive depending on your operating system. For example, DOS does not support case-sensitive filenames, but UNIX does.

This example shows how to use these command-line options of SQL*Loader:

```
sqlload USERID=gwashington/P1ew2w
CONTROL=/u/usr/oracle/cust.ctl
  LOG=/u/usr/oracle/cust.log BAD=/u/usr/oracle/cust.bad
```

Example of Loading Variable-Length Data

The following example shows a control file—the CUST.CTL control file that also contains the data to load—that loads data from a set of customer records in variable-length format into the CUSTOMERS table of an Oracle7 database:

```
LOAD DATA
INFILE *
INSERT
INTO TABLE gwashington.customers
FIELDS TERMINATED BY ',' OPTIONALLY ENCLOSED BY '"'
(id,companyname,lastname,firstname,address,city,state,zipcode,phone,fax)
BEGINDATA
1,"NBC","Brokaw","Thomas","Park Avenue","New York","NY","01002",
"1-800-NBC-NEWS","1-800-NBC-FAXS"
2,"CBS","Rather","Daniel","Park Avenue","New York","NY","01002",
"1-800-CBS-NEWS","1-800-CBS-FAXS"
3,"CNN","Shaw","Bernard","Dixie Drive","Atlanta","GA","21002",
"1-800-CNN-NEWS","1-800-CNN-FAXS"
4,"ABC","Jennings","Peter","Park Avenue","New York","NY","01002",
"1-800-ABC-NEWS","1-800-ABC-FAXS"
5,"NBC","Scott","Willard","Park Avenue","New York","NY","01002",
"1-800-NBC-NEWS","1-800-NBC-FAXS"
```

To load the data, execute SQL*Loader using this command:

```
sqlload USERID=gwashington/P1ew2w CONTROL=/u/usr/oracle/cust.ctl
```

This simple example shows just a few of the many options you can use to load data into an Oracle7 database using SQL*Loader. SQL*Loader has many control file options that let you customize data loads. For example, you can use control file options for the following:

- To specify a condition to selectively discard rows in the data source and store discarded rows in a separate file (for example, to load only the records with customer IDs > 25).

- To specify multiple target tables for a single data load

- To set a column to NULL or 0 if it meets a condition

- To apply SQL functions to fields in a data load

- To specify indexes on which to sort data and then have SQL*Loader build the indexes in presorted order as a load proceeds

Conventional and Direct Path Data Loads

SQL*Loader can load data into a database using two different paths: conventional path loads and direct path loads.

A *conventional path load* proceeds through the normal SQL processing layer of Oracle7. SQL*Loader creates arrays of records to insert and then ships the insert arrays to the database server using the SQL command INSERT.

A *direct path load* bypasses the SQL processing layer of Oracle7 to minimize the time necessary to complete a data load. When you use a direct load, SQL*Loader creates data blocks in the Oracle7 format and directly adds them to the data files in a database. Consequently, a direct path load is typically much faster than a comparable conventional data load.

The example in the previous section performs a conventional load. If you want to perform a direct path load, simply specify DIRECT=TRUE on the command line when invoking SQL*Loader:

```
sqlload USERID= ... CONTROL= ... DIRECT=TRUE
```

Choosing between the Different Types of Data Loads

When should you use a conventional load and when should you use a direct load? In most cases, a direct path load is the right choice because it is faster than a conventional path load. However, there are certain restrictions or conditions that justify choosing a conventional path load over a direct path load. Use a conventional path load instead of a direct path load under the following conditions:

- You are loading data across a network in a client/server system.

- The target table must be available to DML transactions during the load.

- The target table has an index and the table must be available to queries during the load.

- The target table is stored in a cluster.

- The target table is being appended and it has frequent delete activity. A conventional load can reuse available space in existing data blocks.

Integrity Constraints, Database Triggers, and Data Loads

When you use SQL*Loader, you must plan for integrity constraints and triggers, the mechanisms you use to maintain data integrity in an Oracle7 database. For example, if integrity constraints and INSERT triggers are enabled on the target table during a conventional path data load, the data load is slowed down; as SQL*Loader uses the INSERT statement to insert a new row, Oracle7 must check the row for integrity violations. Both conventional and direct path loads are subject to integrity constraints and triggers.

TIP

> To speed a data load, you can disable constraints and INSERT triggers during the load (UPDATE triggers don't affect data loads), and then reenable them after the load is complete.

If you are going to perform a conventional path load, be sure to disable all of the target table's integrity constraints and INSERT triggers. You can do this by using several forms of the ALTER TABLE command:

```
ALTER TABLE customers DISABLE CONSTRAINT sys_c00123
-- disables a constraint by its name
ALTER TABLE customers DISABLE PRIMARY KEY
-- disables a table's primary key
ALTER TABLE customers DISABLE UNIQUE (lastname, firstname)
-- disables a table's unique key
ALTER TABLE customers DISABLE ALL TRIGGERS
-- disables all of a table's triggers
```

If you try to disable a parent key before a data load and the dependent keys are enabled, you must either disable the dependent keys first or use the CASCADE option of the DISABLE clause to disable the parent key and all of its dependent keys:

```
ALTER TABLE customers DISABLE PRIMARY KEY CASCADE
```

SQL*Loader automatically disables check and referential integrity constraints and INSERT triggers before commencing a direct path data load. However, SQL*Loader does not automatically disable other types of constraints, including NOT NULL, PRIMARY KEY, and UNIQUE. You must use the ALTER TABLE statements above to disable any other integrity constraints before a data load.

After a data load is complete, you can reenable any disabled constraints and triggers using the ALTER TABLE command. Remember to enable any related dependent keys that are not in the target table:

```
ALTER TABLE customers ENABLE CONSTRAINT sys_c00123
-- enables a constraint by its name
ALTER TABLE customers ENABLE PRIMARY KEY
-- enables a table's primary key
```

```
ALTER TABLE customers ENABLE UNIQUE (lastname, firstname)
-- enables a table's unique key
ALTER TABLE customers ENABLE ALL TRIGGERS
-- enables all of a table's triggers
```

If all rows in the table pass the integrity rule that you enable, Oracle7 enables the constraint without error. However, if the table contains *exceptions* to (rows in violation of) the integrity rule after a data load, Oracle7 cannot enable the constraint. When enabling an integrity constraint, you can generate a report of exceptions using the EXCEPTIONS INTO parameter of the ENABLE clause:

```
ALTER TABLE customers
 ENABLE PRIMARY KEY EXCEPTIONS INTO exceptions
```

If no exceptions exist, Oracle7 enables the constraint. However, when exceptions exist for the constraint you specify, Oracle7 generates a report of exceptions as rows of information in a specially formatted table called EXCEPTIONS. You must run the UTLEXCPT.SQL script in your account to create the EXCEPTIONS table before trying to create an exceptions report. For example, assume that after a data load, there are two rows with the same primary key value. A query of the EXCEPTIONS table would provide information similar to the following to help you discover which rows violate the integrity constraint:

```
SELECT * FROM exceptions

ROW_ID              OWNER                TABLE_NAME           CONSTRAINT
-----------         --------------------  --------------------  ----------
00000005.0004.0005 GWASHINGTON          CUSTOMER             SYS_C00337
00000005.0005.0005 GWASHINGTON          CUSTOMER             SYS_C00337
```

You can automatically configure a SQL*Loader control file to reenable constraints after a data load by using the REENABLE control file keyword. You can even add an EXCEPTIONS parameter to specify an exceptions table to report constraint exceptions:

```
REENABLE EXCEPTIONS INTO exceptions
```

Checking data integrity after reenabling INSERT triggers is a different story. When you reenable a trigger, Oracle7 doesn't check the rule against all table rows before enabling the trigger. Therefore, it's up to you to check the integrity of your table with regard to triggers after a data load.

This chapter has presented an overview of the responsibilites of Oracle7 database administrators. It also introduced two utilities that are frequently used by database administrators: Server Manager, the primary administration utility, and SQL*Loader, a utility for loading data into a preexisting database. The next chapter discusses basic Oracle7 database administration procedures, including how to create an Oracle7 database and control its availability.

CHAPTER

SEVEN

Basic Database Administration

- **Operating system account settings**

- **Initialization file settings**

- **Database planning and creation**

- **Server availability controls**

- **Tablespace data availability controls**

- **Techniques for extending database storage capacity**

- **Methods for reducing the size of databases**

- **Database structural and space reports**

As you read through the chapters in Part II of this book, you'll quickly learn that database administration is a big job. To get you started, this chapter explains the most basic database administration tasks, including the following:

- Working with operating system settings

- Creating and customizing initialization parameter files for databases

- Planning and creating a new Oracle7 database

- Starting and stopping an Oracle7 database server

- Controlling the availability of individual tablespaces within an Oracle7 database

- Extending the storage capacity of an Oracle7 database

- Reducing the size of an Oracle7 database

Establishing Operating System Settings for Database Administration

Before you perform any type of administrative function, it is important to configure several operating system session variables for your operating system session to make database administration easier. *Operating system session variables* serve as a kind of shorthand and provide file and device independence for files and directories.

Most operating systems have operating system session variables, although each operating system refers to them by a different name: UNIX calls them *environment variables*, VAX VMS uses *logicals*, and Novell NetWare refers to them as *CONFIG* parameters. Whatever your operating system calls them, there are two important operating system session variables for you to set when working with Oracle7:

- ORACLE_HOME specifies the home directory where Oracle7 is installed. During the installation procedure for Oracle7, ORACLE_HOME is configured, so it is likely that you will never need to adjust the setting for this operating system session variable on the server. However, each operating system has a different way of configuring ORACLE_HOME on the client.

- ORACLE_SID (on UNIX) or ORACLE_SRVNAME (on Novell NetWare) identifies the database to work with in an operating system session. This operating system variable is especially important if one central server has more than one database. ORACLE_SID's value may change, depending on the database currently of interest. The ORACLE_SID for a particular database is typically the same as the database's name, although it can be different.

NOTE Each operating system has its own method for setting operating system session variables. Use your operating system documentation to determine how to set these variables.

Creating and Editing Database Initialization Parameter Files

Before creating and starting up an Oracle7 database, you must create an initialization parameter file for the database. A database's initialization parameter file has many settings specific to the database, several of which must be configured before you actually create the database.

One way to create a parameter file for a new database is to make a copy of the sample parameter file called INIT.ORA. You can find INIT.ORA in the DBS directory of ORACLE_HOME on UNIX systems and in the RDBMS73 directory of ORACLE _HOME on Novell NetWare systems. Copy INIT.ORA to a filename that corresponds somehow to the name of the new database.

You can customize a parameter file for a database by using a text editor to change the settings for the parameters in the file. When you use a text editor to open a copy of the INIT.ORA initialization parameter file, you will see many initialization parameters. Oracle has conveniently included commented lines (lines that start with #) that suggest several parameter settings for small, medium, and large databases.

Choose the parameter settings that best work for your database and uncomment them (remove the #s at the beginning of the lines).

When you customize your new database's initialization parameter file, it is crucial that you properly set the CONTROL_FILES and DB_NAME parameters.

- The CONTROL_FILES parameter determines the name and location of each copy of the database's control file. It is important to specify at least two control file names on different disks. This way, Oracle7 mirrors the database's control file to protect it against an isolated disk failure.

- The DB_NAME parameter sets the name of the database. A database's name is a literal of eight characters or less. It is made up of alphabetic characters (case is insignificant), numbers, underscores (_), sharps (#), and dollar signs ($).

TIP

In many cases, the setting for the COMPATIBLE parameter can be important. This parameter determines what level of server functionality is available to an Oracle instance on a release-by-release basis. For example, if you are using release 7.2.0.0 of Oracle7 and want to have access to all the features available in this release, set COMPATIBLE to 7.2.0.0. However, if COMPATIBLE remains set to 7.2.0.0 after you upgrade to release 7.3.0.0 of Oracle7, newer features found only in release 7.3 will not be available to the server until you adjust COMPATIBLE to 7.3.0.0.

Here is an excerpt from an initialization parameter file, INITACCTING.ORA, that corresponds to a database named ACCTING (short for ACCOUNTING) on an Oracle7 for SCO UNIX database server:

```
        .
        .
        .
DB_NAME = accting
CONTROL_FILES = /usr/oracle/dbs/controlaccting.ora,
/u2/usr/oracle/dbs/controlaccting.ora
        .
        .
        .
```

In this case, the two copies of the ACCOUNTING database's control file are on different disk drives. The first copy is in the root file system, and the second copy is in the /u2 file system on a different disk drive.

Creating an Oracle7 Database

Creating an Oracle7 database is a lot like building a new house. Both jobs have two major phases: the design phase and the creation phase. The database design phase includes planning file limits and file placements for the new database. The database creation phase is the execution of the plan using the SQL command CREATE DATABASE and some scripts. The following sections explain the design and creation phases for an Oracle7 database.

Planning an Oracle7 Database

Before constructing a new house, an architect must consider several things to create a quality design. Among other considerations, the lot and house foundation must account for water drainage; the house's infrastructure must meet local building electrical, plumbing, and earthquake codes; and the house's floor plan must suit the owner's taste. If the architect does not draft a good plan beforehand, it is difficult to go back and change the house after it is built.

Similarly, an Oracle7 administrator must plan several things about a database's foundation—its file structure—before creating the database, because it is hard or impossible to make changes later. As an administrator, you perform the following tasks:

- Determine appropriate values for the file-limit parameters of the CREATE DATABASE command.

- Plan the size and location of the initial data files of the new database's SYSTEM tablespace.

- Plan the size and location of the new database's transaction log groups and members.

- Determine the character set to store database data.

- Create an initialization parameter file for the new database and specify the filenames of the database's control file.

The following sections discuss each topic in planning a new Oracle7 database.

Determining Database File Limits

The SQL command CREATE DATABASE has several optional parameters that determine the maximum number of different types of files you will be able to create for a new database. These file-limit parameters include the following:

Parameter	Description
MAXDATAFILES	Determines the maximum number of data files that can ever be allocated for the database
MAXLOGFILES	Determines the maximum number of log groups for the database
MAXLOGMEMBERS	Determines the maximum number of members for each log group

When planning a database, it is crucial to set the file limits for the new database correctly; it is difficult to go back and change them after you create the database.

All file-limit parameters of the CREATE DATABASE command have default and maximum values. If you do not specify a particular file-limit parameter, Oracle7 uses the default value when creating the database. The default and maximum values for file limits vary, depending on the operating system you use to run the Oracle7 server. For example, the default and maximum values for MAXDATAFILES on Oracle7 SCO UNIX are 30 and 1022, respectively. For Oracle7 on Novell NetWare, the default and maximum values for MAXDATAFILES are 1 and 254.

NOTE   All file-limit parameters directly affect the size of the database's control file. Higher file limits allocate more space in the control file to make it slightly larger. However, considering the minimal effect on the control file's size and the difficulty of changing a database's file limits after database creation, it is much better to err on the high side when setting file-limit parameters.

Planning File Sizes and Placements

An architect must determine the best size and placement for doors and windows in a house to make the house functional and aesthetically appealing. Similarly, a database administrator must plan the size and placement of a database's initial data files and log files to ensure maximum database performance and fault tolerance. Although Oracle7 allows you to correct poor choices for file sizes and placement after database creation, it is easier to plan and get it right during database creation.

The CREATE DATABASE command allows you to indicate the names, sizes, and locations for two different types of files for a new database:

- The DATAFILE parameter specifies the initial data file(s) for the database's SYSTEM tablespace.

- The LOGFILE parameter specifies the database's initial transaction log groups and members.

File size is an important consideration when creating Oracle7 files because of the way Oracle7 allocates space to store database data. Oracle7 preallocates sized files to eliminate data fragmentation within a single file. *Preallocated files* are like empty buckets that a database server fills with data as users create tables and carry out transactions. This disk I/O optimization technique ensures that all of a file's data blocks are allocated at the same time and in a relatively contiguous location on disk. This reduces disk head movement during system operation, so the database server can deliver good disk I/O performance.

Early releases of Oracle7, including releases 7.0 and 7.1, do not allow data files to grow, so it's especially important to size database files correctly when using these releases. Data files must be big enough to store the proposed data but not so large that they waste valuable disk space. Newer releases of Oracle7, including releases 7.2 and 7.3, allow you to create data files that can automatically grow, when necessary. However, initial data file sizing is still important if you want to get the maximum performance from your I/O subsystem. Data files that dynamically grow can become *fragmented* across the sectors of a disk; that is, different data blocks of the file might be scattered in different sectors across a disk.

There are several important considerations when specifying the initial data file(s) of the SYSTEM tablespace. First of all, there is no advantage to specifying more than one initial data file for the SYSTEM tablespace. It is typically better to use fewer large data files than many small data files for a tablespace, to keep tablespace data fragmentation to a minimum.

Regarding size, the SYSTEM tablespace's initial data file must have enough space to hold all data dictionary tables. Additionally, you might also plan to install client tools and applications that create more data dictionary tables and require space in the SYSTEM tablespace. Also consider that Oracle7 automatically stores all database procedures and triggers in the SYSTEM tablespace. Therefore, you must make sure there is enough space for the procedures and triggers your system's applications will require. See Chapter 10 for some help with planning space for procedures and triggers.

The placement of Oracle7 database files is important for both performance and fault tolerance. For example, the different members of each mirrored transaction log group should be on different physical disks to protect the transaction log against isolated disk failures.

Determining the Database Character Set

When creating a new database, you can use the CHARACTER SET parameter of the CREATE DATABASE command to specify the character set Oracle7 will use to store database data. It is important to make the correct choice because you cannot change a database's character set after the database is created. A database's character set is usually the character set most users employ when interacting with Oracle7. For example, those of you who live and work in the U.S. most likely will use the US7ASCII character set for Oracle7, a set of characters that corresponds to the English language as used in the U.S.

Creating the Database Initialization Parameter File

Before you can create a new database, you must create and customize an initialization parameter file for the database. See the section "Creating and Editing Database Initialization Parameter Files" earlier in this chapter for details. As explained in that section, the CONTROL_FILES and DB_NAME parameters in the database initalization parameter file must be set properly.

Special Considerations

There are additional CREATE DATABASE command parameters and initialization parameters that apply to special circumstances. If your system supports the Oracle7 Parallel Server option, you will want to plan settings for the following CREATE DATABASE command parameters:

- The MAXLOGHISTORY parameter specifies the amount of space to reserve in the control file for names of archived transaction log groups. These names are used by the Parallel Server option if instance-recovery operations are necessary.

- The MAXINSTANCES parameter specifies the maximum number of instances to which the database can ever be simultaneously mounted.

If you plan to make your new database part of a distributed database, it is also important to set the DB_DOMAIN initialization parameter to an appropriate *Internet network address*. A typical Internet network address for an Oracle7 database server is the IP address of the host computer. The DB_DOMAIN parameter takes this form:

```
servername.companyname.com
```

An Example of Database Planning

Now that you have a good idea of what to plan before creating an Oracle7 database, let's look at a comprehensive, integrated example to demonstrate proper database planning.

Assume that a dentist's office is creating a database to track patient records and billing information. The database server will have two different client applications: one for tracking insurance billing and another for tracking medical information about patients. Both client applications use database procedures and triggers to centralize common application logic and business rules.

The database server has these characteristics:

- Oracle7 runs on a computer using UNIX.

- The server has two different disk drives, with the root file system on one disk drive and the /u2 file system on the other.

- The native user language is U.S. English.

- The expected database growth rate is 12MB/year, approximately 50K/day.

Given this information, here's a good plan for the initialization parameter file settings:

```
CONTROL_FILES /usr/oracle/dbs/patient.ctl,
/u2/usr/oracle/dbs/patient.ctl
DB_NAME patients
```

And here's an acceptable CREATE DATABASE command for the new database:

```
CREATE DATABASE patients
LOGFILE
  GROUP 1 ('/usr/oracle/dbs/patient1a.log',
  '/u2/usr/oracle/dbs/patient1b.log') SIZE 50K,
  GROUP 2 ('/usr/oracle/dbs/patient2a.log',
  '/u2/usr/oracle/dbs/patient2b.log') SIZE 50K
```

```
MAXLOGFILES 10
MAXLOGMEMBERS 4
DATAFILE '/usr/oracle/dbs/patientsystem1.ora' SIZE 40M
   AUTOEXTEND ON NEXT 500K MAXSIZE UNLIMITED
MAXDATAFILES 100
CHARACTER SET us7ascii
```

MAXDATAFILES can be set to 100 because the dentist's database grows very slowly and predictably. It is a reasonable assumption that with proper planning, you can allocate space for one year's worth of records on a yearly basis to slowly extend the tablespace that stores patient records and insurance billing information. A setting of 100 for MAXDATAFILES is more than reasonable for the growth characteristics of this database.

DATAFILE specifies a single data file for the SYSTEM tablespace:

```
'/usr/oracle/dbs/patientsystem1.dbf' SIZE 40M
```

The size 40MB is ample space for data dictionary tables, as well as for many stored procedures and triggers. The AUTOEXTEND clause configures the data file for automatic extension. After creation, Oracle will allow the data file to automatically extend in 500K chunks to an unlimited size, if necessary.

Given the daily generation of data, the dentist's database probably needs only two or three log groups, with a small file size for each. MAXLOGFILES is set to 10 just in case the future demand on the database grows and more log groups are necessary. Since the database server has only two disk drives, it makes sense that the maximum number of members per group will be two; however, MAXLOGMEM-BERS is set to 4 in case additional disks are available in the future.

CHARACTER SET is set to us7ascii because all users on the system will use U.S. English as their language.

A Planning Aid

Use Table 7.1 to help you plan a new Oracle7 database. This table includes the most important items of database planning, a short description of each item, and a blank space where you can make notes about the setting for a new database.

TABLE 7.1: Checklist for Database Creation Parameters

Parameter	Description	Your Setting
ORACLE_HOME—Operating system session variable	Points to the directory location where Oracle7 is installed.	_____ _____ _____
ORACLE_SID (or ORACLE _SRVNAME)—Operating system session variables	Identifies the Oracle7 database of interest.	_____ _____ _____
CONTROL_FILES— Initialization parameter	Determines the names of the database's control files. Specify at least two filenames, each on a different disk.	_____ _____ _____
DB_NAME—Initialization parameter	Determines the name of the database	_____ _____ _____
MAXDATAFILES—CREATE DATABASE command parameter	Determines the maximum number of data files you can ever create for the database. Consider that every time you create a new tablespace or need to extend the storage space in a current tablespace, you create one or more datafiles.	_____ _____
DATAFILES—CREATE DATABASE command parameter	Identifies the names and sizes of the initial datafiles in the SYSTEM tablespace. It is better to create fewer large files than many small files, to reduce data fragmentation.	_____ _____ _____
MAXLOGFILES—CREATE DATABASE command parameter	Determines the maximum number of log groups you can ever create for the database.	_____ _____ _____
MAXLOGMEMBERS— CREATE DATABASE command parameter	Determines the maximum number of log members you can create for each log group. Therefore, MAXLOG-MEMBERS determines how many levels of mirroring you can use to protect the transaction log.	_____ _____ _____
CHARACTER SET—CREATE DATABASE command parameter	Determines the character set Oracle7 uses to store data in the new database.	_____ _____ _____

Using CREATE DATABASE to Create an Oracle7 Database

After you have planned a new Oracle7 database, you can execute your plan using the SQL command CREATE DATABASE.

To use the CREATE DATABASE command, first you must start a Server Manager SQL worksheet and connect to the Oracle7 database server using a privileged administrative connection (see Chapter 9 for instructions on establishing a privileged administrative connection). Then, using the parameter file for the new database, start up a new instance only; do not mount or open the database, because it is not there! (If you are not familiar with database startup, see the section "Starting the Oracle7 Server" later in this chapter.)

After you complete the prerequisite steps, you can issue a CREATE DATABASE statement (see the previous section "An Example of Database Planning" for an example of the CREATE DATABASE command).

A CREATE DATABASE statement takes a while to complete because Oracle7 must allocate disk space for several database files and create the internal data dictionary tables in the SYSTEM tablespace. After the statement completes, Oracle7 leaves the database mounted and open.

What to Do After Creating the Database

After you create a database, you'll probably want to run some scripts to build additional data dictionary tables and public views for the data dictionary. On UNIX systems, the following scripts can be found in the RDBMS/ADMIN directory underneath ORACLE_HOME. On Novell NetWare systems, the scripts can be found in RDBMS70\ADMIN directory underneath ORACLE_HOME.

- The CATALOG.SQL script creates data dictionary tables and views. Run this script as SYS for all databases.

- The CATPROC.SQL script creates additional data dictionary tables and views for the stored procedures, database triggers, and so on. Run this script as SYS.

Both scripts build many data structures and will take some time to complete.

After you create a new database with the CREATE DATABASE command, the database has only one tablespace—the SYSTEM tablespace. To keep data dictionary information in the SYSTEM tablespace separate from application data, you'll want to create additional tablespaces for the new database, as explained in the section "Creating New Tablespaces" later in this chapter.

Another important step after database creation is to turn on media recovery. When Oracle7 creates a database, media recovery is disabled by default to avoid unnecessary logging of the database creation step and make database creation proceed more quickly. However, to fully protect a new database after creation, you need to enable media recovery. For more information about this operation, see Chapter 11.

Controlling Database Availability

Now that you have a database, the next step is to open it so people can use it. One of the most basic administrative operations for an Oracle7 administrator is controlling the availability of a database. Until an administrator opens a database, users cannot employ applications to interact with an Oracle7 database server. The following sections explain how to control the general availability of an Oracle7 database, as well as how to control the availability of individual tablespaces within a single database.

Starting the Oracle7 Server

There are three phases to database startup:

1. Start a new instance for the database.

2. Mount the database to the instance.

3. Open the mounted database.

You can start a database by using the Startup Database dialog box of Server Manager. (To use the Startup Database dialog box of Server Manager, you must connect to Oracle7 using a privileged administrative connection, as described in Chapter 9. To access this dialog box from the Administration Manager, select the Instance drawer, click on the Database folder tab, and then select Database ➤ Startup from the menu bar. Figure 7.1 shows the Startup Database dialog box.

The default settings of the Startup Database dialog box start a new instance and mount and open the database, all in one step. In most cases, this is just what you want to do, so you can simply select the OK button to start the database.

NOTE On UNIX systems, make sure that your operating system session variable ORACLE_SID is set for the target database and that the database's initialization file is: $ORACLE_HOME/dbs/initORACLE_SID.ora. This way, the default settings of the Startup Database dialog box will automatically start, mount, and open a new database when you select OK.

FIGURE 7.1:
Use Server Manager's Startup Database dialog box to start the Oracle7 database server and make the database available for use by applications and users.

Although the default settings for the Startup Database dialog box are the ones you will most commonly use, it is useful to understand all of its options in case there are special circumstances.

- The Startup Mode radio button list determines how many phases of database startup to perform: start a new instance and mount and open the database, start a new instance and mount the database, or just start a new instance. In most cases, the default selection Open is appropriate; select one of the other choices when a specific administrative operation calls for an incomplete database startup. For example, when you are preparing to issue a CREATE DATABASE statement for a new database, choose the Nomount option.

- The Parameter File entry field specifies the name of the initialization parameter file to use to start the database. Again, in most cases, you can leave this field blank because the default setting will specify the correct parameter file for database startup. However, you can override the default parameter filename by specifying a filename in this entry field. If you do not know the name of the database's parameter file, use the Find File button to locate the file on your computer.

- The Force check box shuts down any current instance before starting the new instance. Use this option only if the previous instance is still present and operating in an abnormal state (that is, it is hung).

- The Restrict check box limits access to those users, typically administrators, who have the RESTRICTED ACCESS system privilege. Use this option only when you want to limit access to database administrators.

After you start a new instance and mount and open the database, users can connect to the database using a client application and then perform work.

Special Considerations for Database Startup in Client/Server Environments

It is easiest to start up an Oracle7 database while directly connected to the database server itself, using a terminal or terminal emulator that creates a host session on the database server. However, there may be times when it is necessary to start up a database across a network using a remote client workstation.

Because Server Manager is running on the client workstation, a copy of the database's initialization parameter file must be on the client workstation. When distributing a copy of a database's initialization file, make sure the file copy accounts for any operating system differences between the client workstation and the host database server. For example, if the client workstation uses MS-DOS and the database server uses UNIX, the initialization parameter file must be translated correctly between the two operating systems. Operating systems such as SCO UNIX have programs such as dos2unix and unix2dos to convert simple text files between the MS-DOS and UNIX operating systems.

Stopping the Oracle7 Server

Just as with database startup, there are three phases to database shutdown:

1. Close the database.
2. Dismount the database from the instance.
3. Terminate the instance.

You can shut down a database easily using the Shutdown Database dialog box of Server Manager (to use this dialog box, you must connect to Oracle7 using a privileged administrative connection, as described in Chapter 9). To access this dialog box from the Administration Manager, select the Instance drawer, click on the Database folder tab, and then select Database ➤ Shutdown from the menu bar. The Shutdown Database dialog box is shown in Figure 7.2.

FIGURE 7.2:

Use Server Manager's Shutdown Database dialog box to stop the Oracle7 server, thus making the database unavailable for normal use.

The Shutdown Database dialog box has three options:

- The Normal option shuts down the database after all users disconnect from the database. Although the Normal option is user-friendly, you might not be able to shut down the database using this method on weekends or evenings, when users cannot be located so that they can end their sessions. Also, in a large company, where users are far removed from the database administrator and not easily contacted, a normal shutdown will rarely occur.

- As its name indicates, the Immediate option shuts down the database immediately after rolling back the effects of all current transactions.

- Use the Abort option only in special circumstances—for example, when a previous instance is hung and will not terminate any other way. The Abort option does not roll back current transactions before aborting the instance. Therefore, it may take some additional time to start up the database after aborting an instance because Oracle7 must perform crash recovery.

In most cases, you will want to choose the first or second option.

Special Considerations for Database Shutdown in Client/Server Environments

As with the database startup, it is easiest to shut down an Oracle7 database while directly connected to the database server itself, using a terminal or terminal emulator. However, you can shut down a database from a client workstation running Server Manager, provided that you can establish a remote privileged administrative session.

Taking Individual Tablespaces Online and Offline

With a database open, Oracle7 lets you control the availability of individual tablespaces within the database. The data in a tablespace is available when it is online and not available when it is offline.

In certain circumstances, you may want to temporarily take a tablespace offline. For example, if all of an application's data is in a single tablespace, you can effectively take the application offline by taking the corresponding tablespace offline.

You can control the availability of a tablespace using the Place Online and Take Offline options of the Tablespace menu in Server Manager. To access this menu from the Administration Manager, select the Storage drawer and then click on the Tablespaces folder tab to show a list of all of the database's tablespaces and their corresponding availability status. Figure 7.3 shows the Tablespaces folder of the Administration Manager. After you select the tablespace that you want to alter, select the Place Online or Take Offline option from the Tablespace menu.

FIGURE 7.3:
With the Tablespaces folder of Server Manager's Storage drawer open, use the Tablespace menu to alter the availability status of a target tablespace.

Tablespace	Status	Size (K)	Used (K)	Remain (K)	% Used
USERS	ONLINE	1,024	122	902	12
TEMP	ONLINE	1,624	6	1,618	0
RBS	ONLINE	3,072	504	2,568	16
TOOLS	ONLINE	5,120	2,772	2,348	54
DES2_I	ONLINE	10,240	7,862	2,378	77
DES2	ONLINE	22,528	9,168	13,360	41
SYSTEM	ONLINE	81,920	79,636	2,284	97

NOTE

To use the Place Online and Take Offline options of the Tablespace menu in Server Manager, you must have the ALTER TABLESPACE or MANAGE TABLESPACE system privilege. Furthermore, to take a tablespace offline, all rollback segments within the tablespace must currently be offline. See Chapter 10 if you need more information about rollback segments.

When you choose to take a tablespace offline, Server Manager presents a dialog box asking what offline mode to use when taking the tablespace offline. Choose the appropriate mode:

- When you use the default radio button, Normal, Oracle7 writes all modified data in memory back to the data files of the tablespace before taking the tablespace offline. You can use this option only when all data files of the tablespace can be written (that is, when there are no disk I/O problems).

- If you encounter a disk I/O problem, use the next available radio button, Temporary, to take the tablespace offline. When you use this option, Oracle7 writes modified data in memory to those files it can access and skips writing to files it cannot access.

- Use the last radio button, Immediate, only when the previous two buttons do not succeed.

After you have selected the offline mode, select the OK button to take the tablespace offline.

NOTE If you use either the Temporary or Immediate radio button when taking a tablespace offline and Oracle7 can't write to all data files of the tablespace, you will need to perform tablespace recovery when you want to bring the tablespace back online. See Chapter 11 for more information about tablespace recovery.

Extending a Database's Storage Capacity

Often, an Oracle7 database will outgrow its fixed storage capacity and require more space. For example, when you're installing a new client application on a database system, you might need to create new tables that will require more data storage space than is currently available to the database. The following sections explain how to extend the storage capacity for an Oracle7 database using several methods: creating new tablespaces, adding new data files to existing tablespaces, and extending the size of a tablespace's current data files.

Creating New Tablespaces

Several situations justify the creation of a new tablespace in an Oracle7 database:

- When you add a new client database application to your database system and the application uses data that is not already in your database, you will need to create the application's tables and indexes. In this case, it is best to logically and physically separate the new application's data into one or more of its own tablespaces. This way, you can manage all of the application's data easily by managing the application's tablespace.

- You can use individual tablespaces to separate different types of data and spread disk I/O across different disks. For example, you can create one tablespace to store all of an application's table data on one disk and another tablespace to store all of an application's index data on another disk. This way, Oracle7 can read or write table and index data in parallel and improve application performance.

You can create a new tablespace using the Create Tablespace dialog box of Server Manager. To access this dialog box from the Administration Manager, select the Storage drawer, click on the Tablespaces folder tab, and then select Tablespace ➤ Create from the menu bar. Figure 7.4 shows the Create Tablespace dialog box.

NOTE To use Server Manager's Create Tablespace dialog box, you must have the CREATE TABLESPACE system privilege and there must be at least two online rollback segments in the SYSTEM tablespace. See Chapter 10 for more information about rollback segments.

FIGURE 7.4:

Use Server Manager's Create Tablespace dialog box to create a new logical storage partition in an Oracle7 database, thus extending the database's storage capacity.

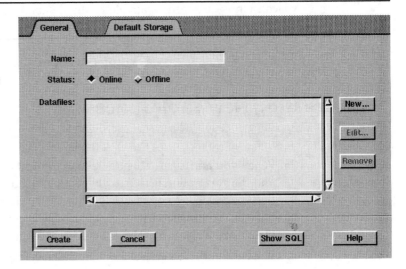

The Create Tablespace dialog box has two folders in which you can specify information for a new tablespace. In the General folder, enter the name for the new tablespace in the Name entry field and select one of the options in the Status radio button list to indicate whether you want to bring the new tablespace online or leave it offline after creation. Then specify one or more data files in the Datafiles list box.

To add, edit, and remove data file specifications from the Datafiles list box, use the adjacent New, Edit, and Remove buttons, respectively. For example, when you click on the New button, Server Manager presents a child dialog box that you can use to specify a new data file's name and size. When you dismiss the child dialog box, the new file specification appears in the Datafiles list box in the Create Tablespace dialog box. As you create the data files for a new tablespace, you can reduce tablespace data fragmentation on disk by creating fewer large data files rather than many small data files.

The Default Storage folder of the Create Tablespace dialog box allows you to enter the default extent storage parameters for objects that users create in the tablespace. These tablespace settings are optional. To learn more about tuning data storage with storage parameters, see Chapter 10.

After you complete the new tablespace specification, select the Create button to create the new tablespace. The operation may take some time because Oracle7 must allocate space for the data files on disk.

Adding Data Files to Tablespaces

When an Oracle7 tablespace uses fixed-sized data files that cannot grow dynamically, one way to extend the storage capacity for a tablespace is to add one or more data files to the tablespace.

You can add a new data file to a tablespace by using the Add Datafile dialog box of Server Manager. To access this dialog box from the Administration Manager, select the Storage drawer and then click on the Tablespaces folder tab to show a list of all of the database's tablespaces. After selecting the tablespace to which you want to add a new data file, select Tablespace ➤ Add Datafile from the menu bar. Figure 7.5 shows the Add Datafile dialog box.

NOTE   To use Server Manager's Add Datafile dialog box, you must have the ALTER TABLESPACE system privilege.

FIGURE 7.5:
Use Server Manager's Add Datafile dialog box to extend the storage capacity of a tablespace by adding a new data file.

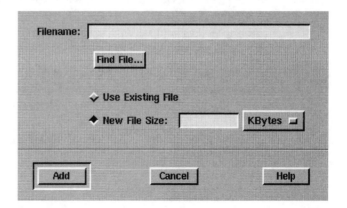

Enter a name for the new data file in the Add Datafile dialog box. You can reuse an existing data file that is already on disk (which will zero the file's information) or indicate the name of a new data file. When you specify a new file, make sure to indicate the file's size in kilobytes or megabytes. After completing the dialog box, select Add. Oracle7 extends the storage capacity of the selected tablespace by allocating the new data files. This operation can take a few minutes to complete.

Extending the Size of a Tablespace's Data Files

Another way to increase the storage capacity of a tablespace is to simply extend the size of a data file that is already part of the tablespace. However, keep in mind that when a data file dynamically allocates space after creation, it can become fragmented across a disk and reduce the performance of tablespace-related I/O operations.

One method for dynamically extending the size of a data file is to configure the data file to automatically extend when necessary. When the file and corresponding tablespace becomes full and more space is necessary, Oracle7 will automatically allocate a new chunk of disk space to the data file so that it has more storage capacity. Configuring a data file for automatic extension can eliminate crisis situations when a tablespace unexpectedly runs out of space during business operations, which would prevent application users from completing work.

You can configure a data file for automatic extension when you are creating a tablespace and its initial data files, when you are adding a new data file to a tablespace, or by altering the data file's specification after it already exists. For example, you can use an ALTER DATABASE statement to switch on the AUTOEXTEND setting for a data file:

```
ALTER DATABASE
   DATAFILE '/usr/oracle/dbs/patientsystem2.dbf'
      AUTOEXTEND ON NEXT 512K MAXSIZE 100M
```

Notice in this example that you can indicate the size of new allocations and the maximum size to which the file can grow when you are configuring a data file for automatic extension.

Another way to extend the size of a data file is to manually resize the file. The following example of an ALTER DATABASE statement increases the size of a data file that is currently 50 megabytes to 80 megabytes.

```
ALTER DATABASE
  DATAFILE '/usr/oracle/dbs/patientsystem2.dbf'
    RESIZE 80M
```

NOTE To alter a tablespace's data files using the ALTER DATABASE command, you must have the ALTER DATABASE system privilege.

Database Space Reduction

As an administrator, you can reduce the size of an Oracle7 database to reclaim valuable disk space for other uses. The next sections discuss several different methods for reducing the size of an Oracle7 database: resizing a tablespace's data files, archiving historical tablespaces, and dropping unwanted tablespaces.

Resizing a Tablespace's Datafiles

The previous section "Extending the Size of a Tablespace's Data Files" explains how you can resize a data file to increase the storage capacity of the encompassing tablespace. You can also use the same technique to reclaim an extraordinary amount of unused space in a data file. First, use the SPACEREPORT procedure shown later in the chapter (in Listing 7.2) to check for the amount of free space in a data file. After you have reviewed the report, use the ALTER DATABASE DATAFILE RESIZE statement to resize the file to a smaller size.

Archiving Historical Tablespaces to Free Disk Space

Databases often contain historical data that is almost never used but is too important to discard. If you correctly plan the storage of historical data, you can take advantage of Oracle7 tablespaces to safely archive the historical data and then reclaim the corresponding disk space. Follow these steps to make this plan work in your system:

1. Isolate all of the historical data into a tablespace specifically created for the purpose of archiving this data.
2. Take the historical tablespace offline.
3. Back up the data files of the offline historical tablespace.
4. Delete the data files of the historical tablespace from disk to reclaim the corresponding disk space. (Do *not* drop the historical tablespace; you may need to restore it from the archives.)

Step 1 requires some application-specific design decisions. For example, consider an order-entry application. After an order is filled and the customer pays for the order, the order information is rarely used. To archive old orders from the main orders and line items tables, a management component of the order-entry application can query those tables and copy the selected orders and line items to a historical copy of the table in another tablespace. The historical tablespace can be archived on a regular basis. Whatever archiving design you develop for your particular situation, be sure to test the strategy before going to production with your application.

To be sure you can bring the tablespace online again in the future, you must be able to write all of a tablespace's data files before archiving the tablespace indefinitely. When performing step 2, be sure to take the tablespace offline in normal mode.

To use the data in an archived historical tablespace at some point in the future, simply restore the tablespace's data files from the backup and bring the tablespace online.

TIP If you cannot restore a historical tablespace's data files in their original location because no space is available, use the Rename Datafile dialog box of Server Manager to indicate the tablespace's new filenames before bringing the tablespace online.

Dropping Unwanted Tablespaces

Many times, data in a specific tablespace is no longer of use. To reclaim the disk space associated with a defunct tablespace, you can drop the tablespace.

You can drop a tablespace using the Drop option of the Tablespace menu of Server Manager. To access this menu from the Administration Manager, select the Storage drawer and then click on the Tablespaces folder tab to show a list of all of the database's tablespaces. After selecting the tablespace that you want to drop, select Tablespace ➤ Drop from the menu bar.

NOTE To drop a tablespace, you must have the DROP TABLESPACE system privilege. Furthermore, all rollback segments within the tablespace must currently be offline. See Chapter 10 for more information about rollback segments.

When you choose to drop a tablespace that contains database objects, Server Manager will provide an appropriate warning that gives you one last chance to abort the operation. If you continue, Oracle automatically drops all of the tablespace's objects along with the tablespace, and also drops referential integrity constraints that depend on the objects that are being dropped.

When dropping a tablespace, Oracle7 does not actually delete the dropped tablespace's data files from disk. Therefore, after dropping a tablespace, you also need to use operating system commands to delete the dropped tablespace's data files.

NOTE On some operating systems (for example, UNIX), you must shut down the database server before you can delete the data files corresponding to a dropped tablespace. That's because Oracle7 specifically opens all data files of online tablespaces during instance startup and closes data files only when you take the corresponding tablespace offline or shut down the database server.

Viewing Database Structural Information

The Oracle7 data dictionary contains numerous views you can use to reveal availability and structural information about a database. Listing 7.1 contains a stored procedure you can use to print reports on all aspects of database structural information. Create the procedure in your database and use it whenever you want a quick report about your database's physical structure. The listing generates a report to show you information about the physical structure of a database, including tablespaces, data files, and the transaction log.

Listing 7.1: The DATABASEREPORT Procedure

```
CREATE or replace PROCEDURE databasereport AS
-- This procedure generates a report about the physical structure
-- of the database to which you are currently connected.
-- Run this script as an administrator such as SYSTEM that can
-- query the system-owned tables, and then grant the EXECUTE
-- privilege for the procedure to the desired users or roles.

-- variables to hold information returned by first query
var0 VARCHAR2(100);
var1 VARCHAR2(100);
var2 VARCHAR2(100);

-- cursor to display tablespace information
CURSOR tablespace IS
  SELECT tablespace_name, initial_extent, next_extent,
    min_extents, max_extents, pct_increase, status
    FROM sys.dba_tablespaces;

-- cursor to display data file information
CURSOR datafiles (tsname IN VARCHAR2) IS
  SELECT a.file_name, b.status
    FROM sys.dba_data_files a, v$datafile b
    WHERE a.tablespace_name = tsname
    AND a.file_name = b.name;
```

```
-- cursor to display transaction log group information
CURSOR loggroups IS
  SELECT group#, sequence#, bytes, members, archived
    FROM v$log;

-- cursor to display transaction log member information
CURSOR logmembers (groupnum IN NUMBER) IS
  SELECT member, DECODE(status,'INVALID','INACCESSIBLE',
    'STALE','INCOMPLETE','DELETED','DELETED','OK') memberstatus
    FROM v$logfile
    WHERE group# = groupnum;

BEGIN
-- print report header
  DBMS_OUTPUT.PUT_LINE('');
  DBMS_OUTPUT.PUT_LINE('Database Report '||SYSDATE);
  DBMS_OUTPUT.PUT_LINE('-------------------------------------------------');
  DBMS_OUTPUT.PUT_LINE('');

-- print general information about database
  SELECT name, created, DECODE(log_mode,'NOARCHIVELOG','NO','YES')
    INTO var0, var1, var2
    FROM v$database;
  DBMS_OUTPUT.PUT_LINE(' General Information');
  DBMS_OUTPUT.PUT_LINE(' ----------------------------------------------');
  DBMS_OUTPUT.PUT_LINE('  Database Name:  '||var0);
  DBMS_OUTPUT.PUT_LINE('  Creation Date:  '||var1);
  DBMS_OUTPUT.PUT_LINE('');

-- print information about tablespaces and corresponding data files
  DBMS_OUTPUT.PUT_LINE(' Tablespace and Data File Information '
    ||'for Database '||var0);
  DBMS_OUTPUT.PUT_LINE(' ----------------------------------------------');
  DBMS_OUTPUT.PUT_LINE('');
  FOR dbtablespace IN tablespace LOOP
    DBMS_OUTPUT.PUT_LINE('  Tablespace Name: '||dbtablespace.tablespace_name);
    DBMS_OUTPUT.PUT_LINE('  Availability:          '||dbtablespace.status);
    DBMS_OUTPUT.PUT_LINE('');
    DBMS_OUTPUT.PUT_LINE('  Default Storage Parameter Settings in Tablespace '
        ||dbtablespace.tablespace_name);
    DBMS_OUTPUT.PUT_LINE('');
```

```
      DBMS_OUTPUT.PUT_LINE('  Default Initial Extent Size:            '
            ||dbtablespace.initial_extent);
      DBMS_OUTPUT.PUT_LINE('  Default Subsequent Extent Size:  '
            ||dbtablespace.next_extent);
      DBMS_OUTPUT.PUT_LINE('  Default Minimum Object Extents:  '
            ||dbtablespace.min_extents);
      DBMS_OUTPUT.PUT_LINE('  Default Maximum Object Extents:  '
            ||dbtablespace.max_extents);
      DBMS_OUTPUT.PUT_LINE('  Default Extent Growth Size:           ',
            ||dbtablespace.pct_increase||'%');
      DBMS_OUTPUT.PUT_LINE('');
      DBMS_OUTPUT.PUT_LINE('  Data Files for Tablespace '
            ||dbtablespace.tablespace_name);
      DBMS_OUTPUT.PUT_LINE('');
      FOR dbdatafile IN datafiles(dbtablespace.tablespace_name) LOOP
            DBMS_OUTPUT.PUT_LINE('    Data File Name:
'||dbdatafile.file_name);
            DBMS_OUTPUT.PUT_LINE('    Availability:
'||dbdatafile.status);
            DBMS_OUTPUT.PUT_LINE('');
      END LOOP;
  END LOOP;

-- print information about transaction log groups and corresponding members
  DBMS_OUTPUT.PUT_LINE('');
  DBMS_OUTPUT.PUT_LINE(' Transaction Log Information for Database '||var0);
  DBMS_OUTPUT.PUT_LINE(' ----------------------------------------------------');
  DBMS_OUTPUT.PUT_LINE('');
  DBMS_OUTPUT.PUT_LINE('  Media Recovery Enabled?:  '||var2);
  DBMS_OUTPUT.PUT_LINE('');
  DBMS_OUTPUT.PUT_LINE('  Log Groups');
  DBMS_OUTPUT.PUT_LINE('');
  FOR dbloggroup IN loggroups LOOP
    DBMS_OUTPUT.PUT_LINE('   Group ID:                              '
          ||dbloggroup.group#);
    DBMS_OUTPUT.PUT_LINE('   Assigned Sequence Number:  '
          ||dbloggroup.sequence#);
    IF var2 = 'YES' THEN
          DBMS_OUTPUT.PUT_LINE('   Archived?:                           '
              ||dbloggroup.archived);
    END IF;
    DBMS_OUTPUT.PUT_LINE('   Size (Bytes):                        '
          ||dbloggroup.bytes);
```

```
   DBMS_OUTPUT.PUT_LINE('    Number of Members:              '
        ||dbloggroup.members);
   DBMS_OUTPUT.PUT_LINE('');
   DBMS_OUTPUT.PUT_LINE('    Member Information for Group '
        ||dbloggroup.group#);
   DBMS_OUTPUT.PUT_LINE('');
   FOR dblogmember IN logmembers(dbloggroup.group#) LOOP
        DBMS_OUTPUT.PUT_LINE('    Member File Name:  '||dblogmember.member);
        DBMS_OUTPUT.PUT_LINE('    Member Status:     '||dblogmember.memberstatus);
        DBMS_OUTPUT.PUT_LINE('');
   END LOOP;
 END LOOP;

END databasereport;
```

Use Listing 7.1 to create a copy of this procedure in your database. Then, using a Server Manager SQL worksheet, set server output on with a buffer size of 10,000 bytes and execute the procedure to get a detailed report of your database, as shown here:

```
SET SERVEROUTPUT ON SIZE 10000;

EXECUTE databasereport;

Database Report 16-NOV-96
-----------------------------------------------------


  General Information
              --------------------------------------------------
   Database Name:  SALES
   Creation Date:  10/06/96 08:40:47


  Tablespace and Data File Information for Database SALES
              --------------------------------------------------


   Tablespace Name:  SYSTEM
   Availability:     ONLINE

  Default Storage Parameter Settings for Tablespace SYSTEM

   Default Initial Extent Size:      10240
   Default Subsequent Extent Size:   10240
   Default Minimum Object Extents:   1
```

```
Default Maximum Object Extents:   121
Default Extent Growth Size:       50%
```

Data Files for Tablespace SYSTEM

```
    Data File Name:               /u/usr/oracle/dbs/systsales.dbf
    Availability:                 SYSTEM
```

```
Tablespace Name:   RBS
Availability:      ONLINE
```

Default Storage Parameter Settings for Tablespace RBS

```
Default Initial Extent Size:      131072
Default Subsequent Extent Size:   131072
Default Minimum Object Extents:   2
Default Maximum Object Extents:   121
Default Extent Growth Size:       0%
```

Data Files for Tablespace RBS

```
    Data File Name:               /u/usr/oracle/dbs/rbssales.dbf
    Availability:                 ONLINE
```

```
Tablespace Name:   TEMP
Availability:      ONLINE
```

Default Storage Parameter Settings for Tablespace TEMP

```
Default Initial Extent Size:      262144
Default Subsequent Extent Size:   262144
Default Minimum Object Extents:   1
Default Maximum Object Extents:   121
Default Extent Growth Size:       0%
```

Data Files for Tablespace TEMP

```
    Data File Name:               /u/usr/oracle/dbs/tempsales.dbf
    Availability:                 ONLINE
```

```
Tablespace Name:  TOOLS
Availability:     ONLINE

Default Storage Parameter Settings for Tablespace TOOLS

  Default Initial Extent Size:     10240
  Default Subsequent Extent Size:  10240
  Default Minimum Object Extents:  1
  Default Maximum Object Extents:  121
  Default Extent Growth Size:      50%

Data Files for Tablespace TOOLS

  Data File Name:          /u/usr/oracle/dbs/toolsales.dbf
  Availability:            ONLINE

Tablespace Name:  USERS
Availability:     ONLINE

Default Storage Parameter Settings for Tablespace USERS

  Default Initial Extent Size:     10240
  Default Subsequent Extent Size:  10240
  Default Minimum Object Extents:  1
  Default Maximum Object Extents:  121
  Default Extent Growth Size:      50%

Data Files for Tablespace USERS

  Data File Name:          /u/usr/oracle/dbs/usrsales.dbf
  Availability:            ONLINE


Transaction Log Information for Database SALES
-------------------------------------------------------

Media Recovery Enabled?:  YES

Log Groups
```

```
Group ID:                    1
Assigned Sequence Number:    376
Size (Bytes):                512000
Number of Members:           2

Member Information for Group 1

  Member File Name:   /u/usr/oracle/dbs/log1sales.dbf
  Member Status:      INCOMPLETE

  Member File Name:   /u2/usr/oracle/dbs/log1sales.dbf
  Member Status:      INCOMPLETE

Group ID:                    2
Assigned Sequence Number:    377
Size (Bytes):                512000
Number of Members:           2

Member Information for Group 2

  Member File Name:   /u/usr/oracle/dbs/log2sales.dbf
  Member Status:      OK

  Member File Name:   /u2/usr/oracle/dbs/log2sales.dbf
  Member Status:      OK

Group ID:                    3
Assigned Sequence Number:    378
Size (Bytes):                512000
Number of Members:           2

Member Information for Group 3

  Member File Name:   /u/usr/oracle/dbs/log3sales.dbf
  Member Status:      INCOMPLETE

  Member File Name:   /u2/usr/oracle/dbs/log3sales.dbf
  Member Status:      INCOMPLETE
```

Whenever you want a report about a database's physical structure, simply execute the DATABASEREPORT procedure.

> **TIP**
>
> Sometimes it's useful to save the output of a SQL worksheet session to a text file so you have it to refer to later. For example, you might want to save the output of the report produced by the DATABASE-REPORT procedure. To spool the output of a Server Manager SQL worksheet session to a text file, select Worksheet ➤ Spool to display the Spool dialog box. Then enter a filename to hold the output. After you select the OK button, Server Manager begins spooling output to the file. When you want to turn off spooling, select Worksheet ➤ Stop Spooling.

Another useful administrative procedure is the SPACEREPORT procedure shown in Listing 7.2. This procedure prints a report that shows useful information about the space usage in each tablespace of the database.

Listing 7.2: The SPACEREPORT procedure

```
CREATE or replace PROCEDURE spacereport AS
-- This procedure reports the total and free space sizes of
-- each data file in the database, by tablespace.
-- Run this script as an administrator such as SYSTEM that can
-- query the system-owned tables, and then grant the EXECUTE
-- privilege for the procedure to the desired users or roles.

CURSOR datafile1 IS
  SELECT tablespace_name, file_id, max(bytes) largeextent,
    sum(bytes) totalfreespace
    FROM sys.dba_free_space
    GROUP BY tablespace_name, file_id
    ORDER BY tablespace_name, file_id;

CURSOR datafile2 (fileid INTEGER) IS
  SELECT name, bytes
    FROM v$datafile
    WHERE file# = fileid;

dbname VARCHAR2(8);
```

```
BEGIN

SELECT name INTO dbname
  FROM v$database;
DBMS_OUTPUT.PUT_LINE('');
DBMS_OUTPUT.PUT_LINE('Space Report for Database '||dbname);
DBMS_OUTPUT.PUT_LINE('-----------------------------------');
DBMS_OUTPUT.PUT_LINE('');
FOR file IN datafile1 LOOP
  DBMS_OUTPUT.PUT_LINE('Tablespace Name:                 '||file.tablespace_name);
  DBMS_OUTPUT.PUT_LINE('');
  FOR filedata IN datafile2 (file.file_id) LOOP
    DBMS_OUTPUT.PUT_LINE('Data File Name:                        '
         ||filedata.name);
    DBMS_OUTPUT.PUT_LINE('Total File Size (KB):            '
         ||ROUND(filedata.bytes/1024,0));
    DBMS_OUTPUT.PUT_LINE('Free Space in File (KB): '
         ||ROUND(file.totalfreespace/1024,0));
    DBMS_OUTPUT.PUT_LINE('% Free Space in File:           '
         ||ROUND(((file.totalfreespace/filedata.bytes)*100),0)||'%');
    DBMS_OUTPUT.PUT_LINE('Largest Extent (KB):            '
         ||ROUND(file.largeextent/1024,0));
    DBMS_OUTPUT.PUT_LINE('');
  END LOOP;
END LOOP;

END spacereport;
```

After you create the SPACEREPORT procedure as shown in Listing 7.2, execute it with server output on to show a printout of space information in the database's tablespaces, like the one shown here:

```
Space Report for Database SALES
-----------------------------------

Tablespace Name:        RBS

Data File Name:         /u/usr/oracle/dbs/rbssales.dbf
Total File Size (KB):   6144
Free Space in File (KB): 32
% Free Space in File:   1%
Largest Extent (KB):    32

Tablespace Name:        SYSTEM
```

```
Data File Name:            /u/usr/oracle/dbs/systsales.dbf
Total File Size (KB):      25600
Free Space in File (KB):   6978
% Free Space in File:      27%
Largest Extent (KB):       5716

Tablespace Name:           TEMP

Data File Name:            /u/usr/oracle/dbs/tempsales.dbf
Total File Size (KB):      550
Free Space in File (KB):   548
% Free Space in File:      100%
Largest Extent (KB):       548

Tablespace Name:           TOOLS

Data File Name:            /u/usr/oracle/dbs/toolsales.dbf
Total File Size (KB):      15360
Free Space in File (KB):   10628
% Free Space in File:      69%
Largest Extent (KB):       8748

Tablespace Name:           USERS

Data File Name:            /u/usr/oracle/dbs/usrsales.dbf
Total File Size (KB):      1024
Free Space in File (KB):   738
% Free Space in File:      72%
Largest Extent (KB):       738
```

This chapter has introduced you to the most basic operations you'll need to perform as a database administrator, including the following:

- Configuring your operating system account settings for Oracle7 database administration

- Planning and creating a new Oracle7 database

- Starting up and shutting down the Oracle7 database server to control database availability

- Taking tablespaces online and offline to control the availability of specific data within a database

- Extending the storage capacity of an Oracle7 database by creating new tablespaces, adding new data files to existing tablespaces, and dynamically allocating more space for a data file

- Reducing the size of an Oracle7 database to reclaim disk space by resizing a tablespace's data files, archiving historical tablespaces, and dropping unwanted tablespaces

Now that you know how to create an Oracle7 database and get the server started, the next chapter explains how to configure the Oracle7 server for user connections.

CHAPTER

EIGHT

Configuring the Oracle7 Server for User Connections

- Oracle7 server process architectures: multithreaded server, dedicated server, and single-task server

- Multithreaded server configuration for client/server systems

- Remote client workstation connections to the Oracle7 server

Once you as an administrator create and start up an Oracle7 database, users of the client/server system will need to connect to it to be able to start work. Before users can connect to a database, you must configure the database instance's front-end servers for user connections. This chapter discusses the following issues:

- Different types of front-end server process configurations

- Configuring the Oracle7 server in a client/server system

- Connecting to Oracle7 from a remote client workstation

Types of Database Server Configurations

A highway architect in a populated metropolitan community has a tough job. The architect must design roadways that efficiently serve an ever-increasing number of people and cars on the road while keeping roadway construction projects within budgets and available land space. Like the highway architect, you must configure a database server so it efficiently serves all of the system's users without consuming an unnecessary amount of computer-system overhead.

Oracle7 can accommodate different types of computer systems and networks because it supports three different configurations for user connections and all types of network protocols:

- The multithreaded server, for most client/server connections

- The dedicated server, for administrative and batch operations in a client/server system

- The single-task server, for host-based system user connections

The following sections explain the different types of configurations and when it is appropriate to use each type.

The Multithreaded Server Architecture

Figure 8.1 shows the *multithreaded server architecture* used with client/server configurations. Notice that each client workstation uses a client process to run a client application. If the client is remote, it also uses SQL*Net to talk to Oracle7 across the network. Meanwhile, the database server uses a multithreaded server architecture—a combination of dispatcher, listener, and front-end server processes—to serve the requests of many clients with minimal process overhead on the database server. The Oracle7 server also has SQL*Net to communicate across the network.

FIGURE 8.1:

Oracle7 multithreaded server and dedicated server architectures are used by most client/server systems.

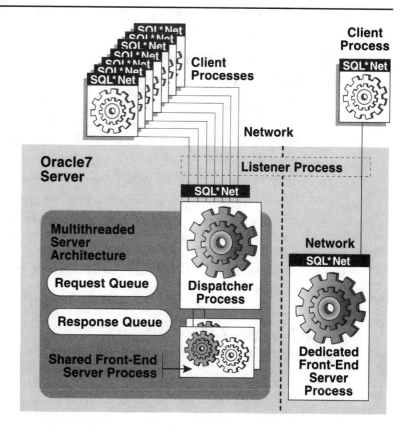

When a client application makes a network connection to Oracle7, the *listener process* gives the client the network address of a *dispatcher process*, to which the client then connects. Then, when the client makes a request of the database server, the dispatcher receives the request and places it in a *request queue*. As they become available, *shared front-end server processes* handle requests in the request queue on a first-in/first-out basis and return results to a *response queue*. From here, the dispatcher returns results to the proper client applications.

Oracle7's multithreaded server architecture is a cooperative processing architecture that results in minimal server process overhead for each connected client. If you plan to use Oracle7 in a client/server system, take the time to read the section "Configuring Oracle7 for Client/Server Systems" later in this chapter. It explains how to configure the processes and queues in the multithreaded server architecture.

The Dedicated Server Architecture

Figure 8.1 also shows the *dedicated server architecture,* an alternative process configuration that has a special use in client/server systems. Dedicated client/server connections are necessary only for special database administrative operations, including database startup and shutdown as well as database recovery, or for batch mode operations, such as running long reports.

When a client application connects to Oracle7, the listener process starts a *dedicated front-end server process* and connects the client directly to the dedicated server, bypassing the multithreaded server architecture. Because a dedicated server consumes a significant amount of database server memory for only a single user, dedicated servers should not be used for client application connections unless absolutely necessary.

The Single-Task Server Architecture

Figure 8.2 shows the Oracle7 *single-task* process configuration used for certain non-networked, host-based database server systems. In host-based database server systems, a user employs a dumb terminal or terminal emulator to establish a session on the host computer and run the client database application. SQL*Net is not required in the single-task architecture. The host computer runs the processes of both the applications and database server.

The Oracle7 single-task configuration is very efficient because it requires only one process to run both the client application code and the front-end server process code for each connected user. However, only certain host operating systems, including Digital's VAX VMS and IBM's MVS, support the Oracle7 single-task process configuration.

NOTE   Host-based UNIX systems, in which users connect directly to a host UNIX computer with terminals, cannot reliably separate application code and RDBMS code. For this reason, host-based UNIX systems typically use the Oracle7 multithreaded server process architecture to separate application code and RDBMS code into different processes.

FIGURE 8.2:

The Oracle7 single-task server process configuration is used only by certain host-based systems.

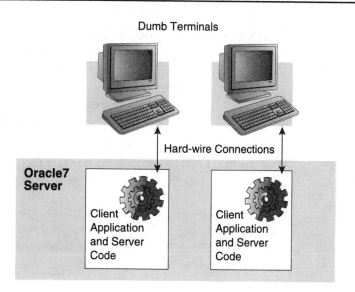

233

No matter which type of process architecture a database system uses, you must configure the system components so users can connect to the Oracle7 database. The next section explains how to configure Oracle7 instances for basic client/server systems.

Configuring Oracle7 for Client/Server Systems

Now that you understand the different types of process configurations that are available with Oracle7, let's concentrate on how to configure Oracle7 for client/server systems. Configuring Oracle7 for a client/server system includes several related steps:

1. Configure the Oracle client/server system's network. This step requires that you configure the SQL*Net listener process on the Oracle7 server, as well as configuring SQL*Net itself on both clients and configuring the server for remote server connections.

2. Start the listener process to listen for client connection requests across a network.

3. Set up the server processes used in a multithreaded server configuration. As the previous sections explain, the multithreaded server architecture is without a doubt the server process configuration you want to use when using Oracle7 in a client/server system for client application connections. To configure Oracle7 as a multithreaded server, you must configure dispatcher and shared-server processes before starting up the database server.

4. Tune the number of dispatcher and shared-server processes after database startup to deliver maximum performance to clients without using too much overhead on the database server.

To illustrate these procedures, the following sections explain each step while configuring a simple UNIX Oracle7 client/server system that uses a single network protocol, TCP/IP. The system that these sections configure is similar to the one shown in Figure 8.3.

FIGURE 8.3:

A simple Oracle7 client/server system configuration running on UNIX that uses the TCP/IP network protocol

Notice that the files and processes in Figure 8.3 clearly show the different components you need to configure for Oracle7 in a simple UNIX client/server system. Even if you use Oracle7 on another platform, with a different network protocol or with several network protocols, the information in the following sections is useful because it provides a solid foundation for understanding the SQL*Net configuration issues for all kinds of client/server systems.

NOTE

The remaining sections of this chapter assume that you already have configured and tested the network hardware and software on your system. In addition, Oracle's SQL*Net version 2.3 for the network's protocol must be installed correctly on both the clients and the database server in your system, as well as Oracle's Network Manager version 3 on at least one Microsoft Windows client.

Configuring SQL*Net for an Oracle7 Client/Server System

The first job in configuring an Oracle7 client/server system for user connections is the configuration of SQL*Net. SQL*Net is middleware that both Oracle clients and servers use to communicate across a network. The following sections explain network naming and SQL*Net configuration tasks.

Naming Networks

Before you start to configure your client/server network for SQL*Net, you'll need to understand how to name components in a network. Most client/server networks are part of larger networks and thus use a hierarchical domain naming scheme to uniquely identify individual networks. Perhaps the most common naming convention in use today is the Domain Naming Service that's used on the Internet. Regardless of the naming scheme that you choose to follow, there are some terms that you need to understand when devising a network naming scheme. The following are brief definitions of these terms.

Domain   A network *domain* is a logical area of organization in a network. Network domains can be broad or focused network classifications. For example, the broadest network domains on the Internet include com and edu. The com domain encompasses networks at all commercial institutions; edu includes all networks at educational institutions. Network domains underneath the broad com and edu Internet domains group more tightly related networks. For example, a company that has several networks typically has a high-level network domain that encapsulates all related networks under the control of the institution.

The breakdown of network domains within an institution can continue, depending on the number and organization of networks. For example, when a corporation has multiple office locations that in turn each have several networks, the company might design another level of network domain names that group networks at the various physical locations. Alternatively, a small business with one or just a few networks might decide that no further domain structures are necessary.

Community   A *community* is a network in which all networked computers communicate using the same communication protocol. A large client/server system might have many different communities that use different network protocols. For example, one community might be a LAN that uses the TCP/IP communication protocol, another community might be a different LAN that uses the IPX/SPX communication protocol, and so on. In the Internet, you identify a network community's exact name by listing the network domains that encompass the community. Network domains in a community's name proceed from the finest to the broadest domain levels, with each domain name separated by a dot (for example, sales.acme.com).

Node   Each computer in a network is a *node*. A node can be a client, a server, or both, depending on its role in the system. Each node in a network has a specific address and name so that other nodes can communicate with it. Specific nodes within a network, such as database or network file servers, are particularly important to identify because many other nodes commonly interact with these nodes.

Names Server   Many networks use special software to specifically keep track of network information such as node, service, and user names. Oracle Names is such software that is specifically designed to work in SQL*Net-based client/server systems.

Interchange   Client/server systems are often made up of several different communities that join to form one large network of clients and servers. Using a specific SQL*Net Multiprotocol Interchange adapter on a computer that is common to two different types of network communities, you can join the communities so they can work together and form one large distributed processing system. By using software (the SQL*Net Multiprotocol Interchange adapters) instead of expensive hardware (network routers and bridges), you create a client/server system that is more cost effective and more flexible to changes.

Creating the SQL*Net Configuration Files

With an understanding of your network and its components, it's relatively easy to configure SQL*Net because all you need to do is to create a few simple configuration files:

Configuration File	Description
listener.ora	Includes configuration parameters for the SQL*Net network listener process on the Oracle7 server. A SQL*Net network listener process is necessary in a client/server system to allow the server to listen for client application connection requests and route the connections to an available dispatcher process.
tnsnames.ora	Configures clients and servers so they can use SQL*Net to connect to remote servers across a network. This file includes SQL*Net aliases (named database server addresses) you can use when you start an application and want to connect to a remote server.
sqlnet.ora	Includes configuration parameters for SQL*Net clients.

Creating the different SQL*Net configuration files is painless with Oracle's Network Manager. Network Manager is a Microsoft Windows application you can use to enter information about your network and then automatically generate the necessary SQL*Net configuration files for both the clients and servers in your system. If Network Manager is not available, you must create the configuration files using a text editor.

The following sections provide instructions for using Network Manager to create the different SQL*Net configuration files. However, even if you can't use the Network Manager and must create configuration files manually, you can learn how to create the necessary configuration files by closely examining the examples of files produced with the Network Manager.

Getting Started with Network Manager

After you start Network Manager from the Windows 95 Taskbar or the Windows 3.1 Program Manager, Network Manager presents a blank window to reflect that a network configuration is not currently loaded. To get started and begin creating a new network configuration, click on the New button in the tool bar, as shown in Figure 8.4.

FIGURE 8.4:

To create a new network configuration with Network Manager, click on the New button in the tool bar.

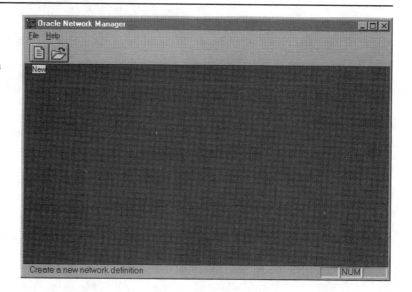

When you request to create a new network configuration, Network Manager asks whether you want to use a configuration wizard to step you through the process of creating the new network, or to configure the network by yourself. Not only does the configuration wizard walk you through the steps necessary to create a new network, but it also provides helpful information as you proceed. In this tutorial, we'll use the wizard to quickly configure our simple network.

Configuring a Network Description

After choosing to use the Network Manager's configuration wizard, the first step is to configure a description of the new network. Figure 8.5 shows the Network Description dialog box.

FIGURE 8.5:

The Network Description dialog box allows you to describe the primary characteristics of a new network.

The Network Description dialog box includes three groups of radio buttons:

Dialog Control	Description
Name Space button list	The type of network naming model you want to use for a network. Unless you are configuring a network that is isolated (one that will not interface with any other computer network), you'll always want to select the option Hierarchical Naming Space with domains. When you do so, the next series of dialog boxes will prompt you to identify the hierarchical domain structure of your network.
Protocols button list	Indicates whether a network will encompass one or more network communities. Our sample network includes only one TCP/IP community, so select the Single Protocol radio button and set the corresponding list box to TCP/IP.

Dialog Control	Description
Name Resolution button list	The method that you want to use to configure SQL*Net clients in the network. In this tutorial, we will use SQL*Net configuration files rather than Oracle Names to configure the clients in the system; therefore, choose the Addresses resolved via Configuration File option.

After you select the options in the Network Description dialog box, click on the OK button to continue configuring the network.

Configuring Network Domains

After you dismiss the Network Description dialog box, Network Manager's configuration wizard prompts you to identify the domain structure in the network using the Domain dialog box. Figure 8.6 shows the Domain dialog box with some configuration information for the outermost COM domain in our sample network.

FIGURE 8.6:
The Domain dialog box allows you to identify the hierarchical domain structure that encompasses an Oracle7 client/server network.

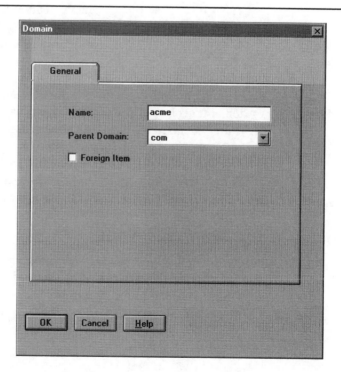

The General tab of the Domain dialog box has just three simple items to set:

Dialog Item	Description
Name entry field	The name of a domain that's present in the network structure. When creating a new network that contains several domain levels, always create parent domains before child domains. For example, to specify the domain structure ACME.COM, you would create the COM parent domain before the child ACME domain. Doing so allows you to indicate parent domains for each child domain as you proceed through network configuration.
Parent Domain list box	The parent domain of the domain you are creating. When you create the root domain of the system, select (root) from this list box.
Foreign Item check box	Controls administrative access to a domain when you are using Oracle Names to manage network naming. Since the sample network configuration in this tutorial does not use Oracle Names, leave this check box unselected.

The number of times you will use the Domain dialog box depends on the number of domain levels that the network contains. For example, to create the domain structure SALE.ACME, use the Domain dialog box to first create the parent domain COM, then again to create the child domain SALES. After you create each new domain, Network Manager prompts you to create another new domain or to continue. When you have created the entire domain structure of a network, move on to identify one or more nodes in the network.

Configuring a Node

The next step that Network Manager presents you with is the job of configuring the special nodes in the network using the Node dialog box. This dialog box has two tabs that allow you to specify information about a node: the General tab and the Communities tab. Figure 8.7 shows the General tab of the Node dialog box.

FIGURE 8.7:

The Node dialog box allows you to identify special nodes in a network.

The following list explains the items in the General tab:

Dialog Item	Description
Name entry field	The name of the node. For our example, we need to identify only a single node, named SALESSVR, that manages both Oracle7 and the listener process.
Domain list box	The domain that immediately encompasses the node. From the list box, you can select any domain in the network. For our example, select the ACME.COM domain.
Type list box	The type of computer for the node. For our example, select Unix Server from the list.

The Communities tab in the Node dialog box presents a group of related list boxes and action buttons. From the Available list box, you can select one or more communities in which the node is a member and move them to the Selected list box using the Add action button. For our example, select the lone TCP.ACME.COM community for the SALESSVR node. The client profile list box automatically shows the name of the client profile for the selected community.

After you complete the configuration for the SALESSVR node, dismiss the dialog box with the OK button and move on to configuring a listener process for the network.

Configuring a Listener

Every SQL*Net network must have a listener process that routes client connection requests to the database server. You can configure a listener process using Network Manager's Listener dialog box. Figure 8.8 shows the General tab of this dialog box.

FIGURE 8.8:

The many tabs and settings in the Listener dialog box let you configure a listener process.

The following list briefly explains the items in the General tab of the Listener dialog box:

Dialog Item	Description
Name entry field	The name of the listener process. The default name is LISTENER, but you can change this to any name you like. For our example, TCPLISTENER is a good choice.
Node list box	The name of the node on which the listener resides. Select the name of the node on which the listener process will run. For our example, select SALESVR.ACME.COM.
Password entry field	The password that limits who can perform administrative tasks with the listener process, such as starting and stopping the listener. A password is optional but does make the listener more secure.
Encrypt Password check box	When using a password for administrative control of the listener, select this check box to store the password in an encrypted format for more security. Otherwise, the listener's password is stored as plain text in the listener.ora configuration file.
Disable Dynamic Discovery Option check box	Indicates when to use an Oracle Names server to automatically configure a client requesting a connection. Since this quick tutorial shows how to use configuration files for SQL*Net configuration and does not use Oracle Names, select this check box.
Use Listener Check-point File check box	Determines when to use values in a listener's checkpoint file to override current values in the listener.ora configuration file. For our example, leave this check box unselected.

Dialog Item	Description
Startup Wait entry field	The amount of time in seconds to wait before starting up the listener when requested. The default of 0, adequate for most situations, starts the listener process immediately on request.
Connect Timeout entry field	The amount of time to wait for a valid connection request after a connection has been started. The default of 10 seconds is adequate for most situations.

The Addresses tab of the Listener dialog box, shown in Figure 8.9, allows you to indicate a service address for the listener process.

FIGURE 8.9:

The Addresses tab of the Listener dialog box indicates the service address for a listener process.

When configuring a new network using the Network Manager's configuration wizard, no addresses will be available in the Addresses list box. Therefore, you must choose the Create button to establish an address for the listener. After doing so, Network Manager presents the Service Address dialog box. By default, Network Manager fills in the items in this dialog box with defaults that should be fine for most installations. After you review the information in this dialog box, you can simply select the OK button to create the new service address and return to the Addresses tab of the Listener dialog box. You'll notice that Network Manager adds the new service address to the list box in this dialog box.

The Databases tab in the Listener dialog box, shown in Figure 8.10, allows you to indicate the databases to associate with the listener process.

No databases will be available as you configure a new network. Therefore, you need to select the Create button to identify a new database using the Oracle Database dialog box. Figure 8.11 shows the General tab of the Oracle Database dialog box.

FIGURE 8.10:

The Databases tab of the Listener dialog box identifies the Oracle databases to associate with a listener process.

FIGURE 8.11:

The many tabs of the Oracle Database dialog box allow you to identify an Oracle database's name, SID (system identifier), and other important database information.

In this tutorial, we'll focus on just the items in General tab of the Oracle Database dialog box. When you open the Oracle Database dialog box from the Listener dialog box, Network Manager automatically fills in the Node and Listener list boxes for you. All you need to do is enter information for the Name, SID, and Oracle Home entry fields.

Dialog Item	Description
Name	The name of the database. For our example, you can enter sales as the database name.
SID	The system identifier that uniquely identifies a specific database instance. For our example, you can enter sales as the SID.

Dialog Item	Description
Oracle Home	The operating system location of the database's home directory on the server computer. This location is the directory indicated by the environment variable $ORACLE_HOME. For our example, you can enter /usr/oracle as the home location of Oracle.

After you complete these entries in the General tab of the Oracle Database dialog box, choose the OK button to return to the Listener dialog box. You'll notice that the Selected list box of the Database tab now includes the new database.

The Logging tab of the Listener dialog box, shown in Figure 8.12, allows you to control the listener's logging options. When you enable logging, the listener keeps track of status information, such as startup information and connection requests, in a log file.

When you first configure a new network, it's a good idea to enable logging to help you troubleshoot any problems that might arise. To enable logging for the listener, select the Logging Enabled check box, and then enter a log filename and directory location on the server computer in the Log File Name and Log File Directory entry fields.

NOTE A listener can also provide you with very detailed information about its operation when you enable tracing from the Tracing tab of the Listener dialog box. However, tracing can create very large trace files, so its best to enable tracing only when investigating problem situations.

When you are satisfied with the configuration of the network listener, you can choose the OK button to create the new listener.

FIGURE 8.12:

The Logging tab of the Listener dialog box allows you to control a listener's logging options.

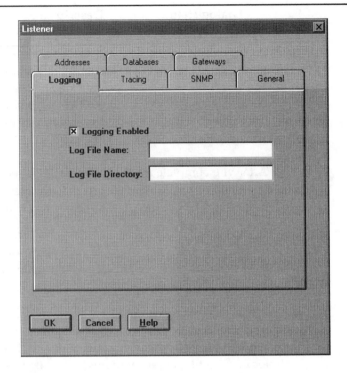

Saving Your Work

After you create the listener, your network configuration is complete. Network Manager's configuration wizard will then ask you to save your work.

Choose to save the network configuration as an operating system file in a directory on your Microsoft Windows client. Next, Network Manager will prompt you to export the network definition by generating the necessary configuration files. However, we need to make some adjustments to our network before we're ready to complete this step, so for now, you can cancel the export operation.

Editing a Network Configuration

After you complete the configuration of a network, Network Manager presents the network using two different windows. Figure 8.13 shows Network Manager's Tree View and Map View windows.

FIGURE 8.13:

Network Manager's Tree View and Map View windows provide different graphical representations of a network configuration.

The Tree View window provides a hierarchical representation of a network. The left pane of the Tree View window shows a tree or hierarchical diagram of the communities and nodes in the network and their relationships. The right pane of the Tree View window shows network objects associated with the selected object in the tree diagram in the left pane. For example, when you select the salessvr.acme.com node in the tree diagram, the right pane of the Tree View window shows the TCPLISTENER listener and sales.acme.com database that reside on the selected node.

The Map View window provides a graphical representation of all or just parts of a network. The lower pane of the Map View window shows all available network objects. You can drag objects from the lower pane to the upper pane to create a graphical diagram of the network configuration. Network Manager automatically shows the relationships among network objects with connecting lines.

The different Network Manager views provide for easy editing of a network configuration. For example, assume that we want to change the assigned name of the network community in our sample network, TCP.acme.com, to a more friendly name, such as sales.acme.com. To edit the community, just double-click on the community icon to display the Community dialog box. From there, simply change the name of the community to "sales" and then choose the OK button. Network Manager automatically updates the name of the community in both the Tree View and Map View windows. After editing a network definition, don't forget to save your work by choosing the Save button in the Network Manager tool bar.

TIP

To add a new network object, use the handy tools in the Network Object tool bar. Just drag and drop any network object from the tool bar onto an existing object in either the Tree View or Map View window. When you do so, Network Manager opens the appropriate dialog box for the new object and preconfigures several characteristics of the object relative to your drag-and-drop operation. For example, when you drag and drop a new database onto a network node, Network Manager shows the Oracle Database dialog box with the node information already included for the new database.

Generating the SQL*Net Configuration Files

After you've got your network configuration just right, you can automatically generate the necessary configuration files for SQL*Net clients and servers by selecting the Generate button in the Network Manager tool bar. Network Manager then prompts you for an output destination for the generated files. You must choose a folder or subdirectory that already exists on your Microsoft Windows client. Using the folder that you specify as a root directory, Network Manager will then create a directory structure to hold the client and server SQL*Net configuration files. The specific directory names depend on the names of the network configuration and objects within the network. For example, if you save the sample network configuration in a file called AL.NET and choose to generate the configuration files in the \ORAWIN\NETWORK directory, Network Manager will output the SQL*Net configuration files for the salessvr.acme.com server node in the folder \ORAWIN\NETWORK\AL\SALESSVR.

During the generation process, Network Manager automatically validates the proposed network configuration, checking for any naming inconsistencies and other problems. If you attempt to generate configuration files for a network definition that has problems, Network Manager informs you that an error occurred during file generation and allows you to examine a log of errors encountered during the generation process.

Examining the Generated SQL*Net Configuration Files

Network Manager generates all the configuration files necessary to configure SQL*Net on the different clients and servers in an Oracle7 client/server system. After you find the files, you can use a text editor to look at them. The following examples show three of the files Network Manager generates according to the information we used for the example in earlier sections.

```
################
# Filename......: listener.ora
# Name.........: salessvr.acme.com
# Date.........: 04-FEB-96 16:03:14
################
SQLNET.AUTHENTICATION_SERVICES = (NONE)
USE_CKPFILE_LISTENER = OFF
LISTENER =
  (ADDRESS_LIST =
        (ADDRESS=
          (PROTOCOL=IPC)
          (KEY= sales.acme.com)
        )
        (ADDRESS=
          (PROTOCOL=IPC)
          (KEY= sales)
        )
        (ADDRESS =
          (COMMUNITY = sales.acme.com)
          (PROTOCOL = TCP)
          (Host = salessvr.acme.com)
          (Port = 1526)
        )
  )
STARTUP_WAIT_TIME_LISTENER = 0
CONNECT_TIMEOUT_LISTENER = 10
TRACE_LEVEL_LISTENER = OFF
SID_LIST_LISTENER =
  (SID_LIST =
    (SID_DESC =
      (GLOBAL_DBNAME = sales.acme.com)
```

```
        (SID_NAME = sales)
        (ORACLE_HOME = /usr/oracle)
        (PRESPAWN_MAX = 10)
    )
  )


###############
# Filename......: tnsnames.ora
# Name.........: LOCAL_REGION.world
# Date.........: 04-FEB-96 16:03:14
###############
sales.acme.com =
  (DESCRIPTION =
    (ADDRESS_LIST =
        (ADDRESS =
           (COMMUNITY = sales.acme.com)
           (PROTOCOL = TCP)
           (Host = salessvr.acme.com)
           (Port = 1526)
         )
    )
    (CONNECT_DATA =
       (SID = sales)
       (GLOBAL_NAME = sales.acme.com)
    )
  )


###############
# Filename......: sqlnet.ora
# Name.........: salessvr.acme.com
# Date.........: 04-FEB-96 16:03:14
###############
AUTOMATIC_IPC = ON
TRACE_LEVEL_CLIENT = OFF
SQLNET.EXPIRE_TIME = 0
NAMES.DEFAULT_DOMAIN = acme.com
NAME.DEFAULT_ZONE = acme.com
SQLNET.CRYPTO_SEED = "742827846743480867"
SQLNET.AUTHENTICATION_SERVICES = (ALL)
```

The commented lines (those beginning with the # symbol) in each sample file clearly identify the name of each file and the type of machine (a client or a server) on which the file resides. Notice that each configuration file includes several parameters that allow you to configure the target component of SQL*Net on either a client or the server. Reviewing the different configuration items in Network Manager's different dialog boxes makes it easy to determine the correspondence between the items and the different configuration parameters in the preceding files. Many parameters can be parents to one or more child parameters to create hierarchical groups of parameters. When creating or editing any SQL*Net configuration file with a text editor, be careful with parentheses and indentation so that the parameter groupings are correct.

WARNING In most cases, you should not manually edit SQL*Net configuration files using a text editor. It's very easy to make a mistake while editing a configuration file, especially considering the countless number of confusing parameters and parentheses in almost every SQL*Net configuration file. Additionally, when you edit a configuration file using a text editor, the network configuration that you manage and document with Network Manager will not be in sync with the configuration files that you are using in your client/server network. Rather than manually edit SQL*Net configuration files, load the network definition into Network Manager and use the tool to make any necessary changes.

Distributing the SQL*Net Configuration Files

After creating the various SQL*Net configuration files, it's time to distribute them to their proper location on the clients and servers in the network. If you need to copy the text files among different operating systems (for example, UNIX to DOS), be sure to convert the text files properly.

The output directories that contain the generated configuration files tell you exactly which files need to go where in your network. For example, each client should have a copy of the sqlnet.ora, tnsnames.ora, and tnsnav.ora configuration files. The server should also have a copy of the these files (although they might be slightly different from the client versions), as well as a listener.ora file. On each computer, locate the configuration files in the path pointed to by the environment variable named TNS_ADMIN. For example, on a UNIX system, it's common to create an environment variable TNS_ADMIN that points to the /etc directory and then locate the SQL*Net configuration files there. On a Windows client PC, it's common to create a CONFIG variable TNS_ADMIN that points to the \orawin\network\admin directory and then locate the proper SQL*Net configuration files there.

Setting the Port Address on the Server Computer for the Listener Process

The final step for configuring SQL*Net is to set up a port address on the server computer that corresponds to the port address specified for the SQL*Net network listener process during the configuration steps. The way that you set up the port depends on the server's operating system. On UNIX systems, you configure a port by adding a line to the /etc/services file, which contains a service name, two spaces, and then a port address. Assuming that you are configuring a listener process for a TCP/IP communication protocol, the /etc/services file might contain a line such as:

```
tcplistener  1526/tcp
```

In this example, notice that the tcplistener is the service name that matches the name of the listener process configured earlier. Additionally, this service uses the port address 1526/tcp, the same port specified earlier when configuring the listener process service address.

> **NOTE** When you look at the /etc/services file, you will notice many other names and corresponding port addresses. Make sure that the name you choose for each listener process is unique among service names and that the address you assign to each listener is unique among port addresses.

Starting the Listener

After you complete the SQL*Net configuration, start the listener on the server using the lsnrctl program. This is a simple program with a command prompt that, among other things, allows you to start, stop, and check the status of the listener process(es) on your system. For example, the following commands start the lsnrctl program and the listener process named TCPLISTENER:

```
lsnrctl

Welcome to LSNRCTL, type 'help' for information.

LSNRCTL> start tcplistener
```

If you have configured everything correctly, the listener will start and lsnrctl will return a status report for the listener. Once the listener is running, you can exit LSNRCTL with the exit command:

```
LSNRCTL> exit
```

Configuring Dispatcher and Server Processes

The next step in setting up the multithreaded server is configuring the dispatcher and shared-server processes. You control the initial configuration of these processes with parameters in the initialization parameter file for the database. The parameters to adjust include the following:

Parameter	Description
MTS_LISTENER_ADDRESS	Identifies the address of the listener process for the database instance. Configure this initialization parameter using the same listener address parameters set in listener.ora.

Parameter	Description
MTS_SERVICE	Identifies the service name, or system identifier, of this database. Set the MTS_SERVICE parameter to match the value of SID_NAME in listener.ora.
MTS_DISPATCHERS	Configures the initial dispatchers that start with database startup. To set this parameter, specify one or more protocols ("tcp" for TCP/IP, "decnet" for DECnet, "osi4" for OSI4, "spx" for SPX/IPX, and "soc" for UNIX domain sockets). For each protocol, specify the number of dispatchers to start.
MTS_MAX_DISPATCHERS	Indicates the maximum number of dispatchers you can start for an instance. Initially, you might want to set this parameter high so you can experiment while tuning the server.
MTS_SERVERS	Indicates the initial number of shared servers that start with database startup. Shared servers are protocol-independent and can work with any available dispatcher. It is best to err on the low side when configuring the initial number of shared servers because Oracle7 automatically starts more servers if the system load is demanding.

Parameter	Description
MTS_MAX_SERVERS	Indicates the maximum number of shared-server processes you can start for an instance. Initially, you might want to set this parameter high so you can experiment while tuning the server.

An Example of Configuring the Initialization Parameters

Here is an example of configuring the initialization parameters for the multi-threaded server:

```
MTS_LISTENER_ADDRESS="(ADDRESS=(PROTO-
COL=tcp)(PORT=1526)(HOST=salessvr.acme.com"
MTS_SERVICES="sales"
MTS_DISPATCHERS="tcp,2","soc,1"
MTS_MAX_DISPATCHERS=5
MTS_SERVERS=5
MTS_MAX_SERVERS=20
```

When the Configuration Is Complete

After you configure the multithreaded server initialization parameters, start the database. The instance will start with the dispatchers and shared servers that are configured in the parameter file.

After startup, and after their client workstations are configured correctly, users can connect to the database using the multithreaded server. (See the section "Connecting to Oracle7 from Remote Client Workstations" later in this chapter.)

Monitoring and Tuning the Multithreaded Server

After you start an instance with the multithreaded server, you should monitor the configuration to see if it is meeting the demands of the system. Server Manager has several monitors for the multithreaded server. However, Server Manager monitors cannot record system activity information that would let you see how your configuration responds over time to fluctuating demands. To supplement the Server Manager monitors for the multithreaded server monitoring, the following sections present some listings of simple stored procedures that allow you to gather historical information about dispatcher and shared-server loads. They also include an explanation of how to use the stored procedures to effectively monitor a multithreaded server configuration.

Accessing the Server Manager Monitor for Dispatchers

To access the Server Manager monitor for dispatchers, select Monitor from the File menu of any Server Manager component (for example, the Administration Manager or a SQL worksheet), and then select Dispatcher from the list box that appears. Figure 8.14 shows an example of the Dispatcher monitor.

The key column on the Dispatcher monitor is Load. The load is expressed as a value from 0 to 1, with 1 representing a 100 percent load. If the load on a dispatcher process of an instance is consistently high, it is likely that the dispatcher for that protocol is a bottleneck in serving the requests of system users.

FIGURE 8.14:

Server Manager's Dispatcher monitor allows you to view cumulative information about the loads placed on dispatchers during their lives.

To generate historical load information for dispatchers over time, use the table and administrative stored procedure in Listing 8.1.

Listing 8.1: CAPTUREDISPATCHERLOADS Stored Procedure

```
CREATE TABLE dispatcherhistory (
  timepoint DATE,
  name VARCHAR2(10),
  network VARCHAR2(10),
  cumulativebusy REAL,
  cumulativeidle REAL,
  intervalload REAL)


CREATE PROCEDURE capturedispatcherloads
  (interval INTEGER, timepoints INTEGER) AS
-- This procedure wakes up at the given interval (specified in
-- minutes) and records the load placed on each dispatcher that
-- occurred during that interval. Load information is placed
-- in the dispatcher history table. You can then use the data
-- in the dispatcher history table to see the fluctuation in
-- dispatcher loads over time on the different dispatchers in your
-- system and make appropriate modifications in your multithreaded
-- server configuration.

counter INTEGER := 0;
previousbusy REAL;
previousidle REAL;
intervalbusy REAL;
intervalidle REAL;
load REAL;
CURSOR dispatch IS
  SELECT name, network, busy, idle
    FROM v$dispatcher;
BEGIN
  WHILE counter <= timepoints LOOP
    FOR status IN dispatch LOOP
-- special case the first datapoints in a session with a NULL load
      IF counter = 0 THEN
        INSERT INTO dispatcherhistory
        VALUES(SYSDATE,status.name,status.network,status.busy,status.idle,null);
      ELSE
```

```
    SELECT cumulativebusy, cumulativeidle INTO previousbusy, previousidle
      FROM dispatcherhistory
      WHERE name = status.name
      AND timepoint = (SELECT MAX(timepoint)
                         FROM dispatcherhistory
                         WHERE name = status.name);
      intervalbusy := status.busy-previousbusy;
      intervalidle := status.idle-previousidle;
-- special case when busy time is negative or zero to avoid divide-by-0 errors
      IF intervalbusy <= 0 THEN
        intervalbusy := 0.001;
      END IF;
      load := (intervalbusy/(intervalbusy+intervalidle))*100;
      INSERT INTO dispatcherhistory
      VALUES(SYSDATE,status.name,status.network,status.busy,status.idle,load);
    END IF;
  END LOOP;
  COMMIT;
  dbms_lock.sleep(interval*60);  -- convert interval from seconds to minutes
  counter := counter + 1;
  END LOOP;
END capturedispatcherloads;
```

Gathering Dispatcher Load Information

To start gathering dispatcher load information, establish a connection to the database server using a Server Manager SQL worksheet. Then create and execute the CAPTUREDISPATCHERLOADS procedure (Listing 8.1). For example, this statement gathers dispatcher information every 15 minutes for 8 hours (32 times):

```
    EXECUTE capturedispatcherloads(15, 32);
```

The CAPTUREDISPATCHERLOADS procedure sleeps most of the time. It wakes at the specified interval to get dispatcher load information and then goes back to sleep. For this reason, you will need to dedicate a connection to gathering dispatcher load information and should use a dedicated server connection. (See the section "Connecting to Oracle7 Using a Dedicated Server Connection" later in this chapter.)

Once you have used the CAPTUREDISPATCHERLOADS procedure to get some history of the load on a multithreaded server configuration's dispatchers, you can query the DISPATCHERHISTORY table at any time. The output information will look something like this:

```
SELECT * FROM dispatcherhistory
```

TIMEPOINT	NAME	NETWORK	CUMULATIVEBUSY	CUMULATIVEIDLE	INTERVALLOAD
02-DEC-96	D000	tcp	212344	507403	
02-DEC-96	D001	soc	46754	672993	
02-DEC-96	D000	tcp	487220	642911	67.0
02-DEC-96	D001	soc	105356	1024775	14.3
02-DEC-96	D000	tcp	667296	763882	59.8
02-DEC-96	D001	soc	148722	1263917	15.4
02-DEC-96	D000	tcp	893753	827610	78.0
02-DEC-96	D001	soc	190670	1548799	12.8

.
.
.

As you can see from this sample output, the load on the TCP/IP dispatcher is consistently high for every interval. Therefore, it might be wise to add another dispatcher for the TCP/IP protocol.

Modifying the Configuration

You can modify the configuration of the instance's multithreaded server by adding one or more dispatchers for any overloaded protocol. Alternatively, if the load on a dispatcher is consistently low and there is more than one dispatcher for a protocol, you can reduce process overhead on the server by terminating one or more of the dispatchers for that protocol.

NOTE
To use the ALTER SYSTEM command, you must have the ALTER SYSTEM system privilege.

If you find it necessary to modify the configuration of dispatchers for a database instance, you can do so without shutting down the instance. To modify the configuration of dispatchers, use the SQL command ALTER SYSTEM with the SET MTS_DISPATCHERS clause. For example, the following ALTER SYSTEM statement establishes two TCP/IP dispatchers for a server.

```
ALTER SYSTEM SET MTS_DISPATCHERS = 'TCP,2'
```

TIP

If you determine that the initial configuration for an instance's dispatcher processes is incorrect for normal system processing and then dynamically adjust the configuration, duplicate the configuration change in the MTS_DISPATCHERS initialization parameter. This way, the next time you start the database's instance, the configuration will be correct.

Accessing the Monitor for Shared Servers

To access the Server Manager monitor for shared servers, select Monitor from the File menu of any Server Manager component and then select Shared Server from the list box that appears. Figure 8.15 shows Server Manager's Shared Server monitor.

Normally, you will not need to make any configuration modifications for an instance's shared servers because Oracle7 dynamically adjusts the number of shared servers based on the system load. However, as Oracle7 dynamically adjusts the number of shared servers, it never terminates shared servers below the current minimum set for the instance. Therefore, if you set MTS_SERVERS so that the minimum number of shared servers is too low or too high, there can be negative consequences:

- If the minimum number of shared servers is too high, the loads on the shared servers will be consistently low, resulting in wasted process overhead on the server.

- If the minimum number of shared servers is too low, Oracle7 will frequently start and stop shared servers during periods of fluctuating system load, resulting in spikes on system performance.

FIGURE 8.15:

The Shared Server monitor of Server Manager allows you to view cumulative information about the loads placed on servers during their lives.

Recording the Statistics

To record statistics on how Oracle7 manages the shared servers of a multithreaded server configuration during a time period, you can use the table and administrative stored procedure in Listing 8.2.

Listing 8.2: CAPTURESERVERCOUNTS Stored Procedure

```
CREATE TABLE sharedserverhistory
(
  timepoint DATE,
  servercount INTEGER
)

CREATE PROCEDURE captureservercounts
  (interval INTEGER, timepoints INTEGER) AS
-- This procedure wakes up at the given intervals and records
-- how many servers are in use into a history table.
-- You can then use the data in the server history table to
-- see how ORACLE7 starts and stops servers over time in your
-- system and make appropriate modifications to MTS_SERVERS
-- in your multithreaded server configuration.

counter INTEGER := 0;
CURSOR server IS
  SELECT count(*) servers FROM v$shared_server;
```

265

```
BEGIN
  WHILE counter <= timepoints LOOP
    counter := counter + 1;
    dbms_lock.sleep(interval*60);
    FOR status IN server LOOP
      INSERT INTO sharedserverhistory
        VALUES (SYSDATE, status.servers);
    END LOOP;
    COMMIT;
  END LOOP;
END captureservercounts;
```

Like the administrative stored procedure for recording dispatcher information, the CAPTURESERVERCOUNTS stored procedure sleeps most of the time, waking at the specified interval to get the server process count and then going back to sleep. For this reason, you will need to dedicate a connection to gathering shared-server information.

TIP

If you want to gather both dispatcher and shared-server information at the same interval for the same amount of time, you can combine the logic of the two tables and procedures (Listings 8.1 and 8.2). This way, you will need to dedicate only one session to gather all multithreaded server monitoring information.

After you have used the CAPTURESERVERCOUNTS stored procedure to determine trends for shared-server counts in a multithreaded server configuration, you can query the SHAREDSERVERHISTORY table at any time. The output information will look something like this:

```
SELECT * FROM sharedserverhistory

TIMEPOINT SERVERCOUNT
--------- -----------
15-JUL-96           2
15-JUL-96           8
15-JUL-96           9
15-JUL-96           7
15-JUL-96           3
```

```
15-JUL-96          8
15-JUL-96          9
15-JUL-96          8
    .
    .
    .
```

> **NOTE**
>
> If you haven't set the MTS_SERVERS and MTS_MAX_SERVERS parameters low and high enough, respectively, you won't see the true load fluctuation that normal processing places on the multithreaded server configuration. If results from the CAPTURESERVERCOUNTS procedure (Listing 8.2) show server counts that either bottom out or top out according to the present limits, consider changing the limits to allow more fluctuation and then regathering server information.

Adjusting the Number of Shared Servers

If you notice a trend in the number of servers typically used over a time period, you should adjust MTS_SERVERS to a number that matches this trend. You can adjust the minimum number of shared servers using the SQL command ALTER SYSTEM with the SET MTS_SERVERS clause. For example, the following ALTER SYSTEM statement establishes eight shared servers for an Oracle7 instance:

```
ALTER SYSTEM SET MTS_SERVERS = 8
```

> **NOTE**
>
> To use the ALTER SYSTEM command, you must have the ALTER SYSTEM system privilege.

Based on the number of shared servers that you indicate in an ALTER SYSTEM statement and the current number of shared servers for an instance, Oracle7 either terminates or starts shared servers to alter the minimum to the new number.

To summarize, configuring the dispatchers and servers for a multithreaded server configuration requires patience and some trial and error. However, with the help of the stored procedures listed in this chapter, you can get a better feel for the requirements of a system over time and quickly get an Oracle7 server working at its best.

Connecting to Oracle7 from Remote Client Workstations

Once the multithreaded server is up and running and both clients and servers are configured with SQL*Net, a user can start a client application and establish a remote connection to the Oracle7 server. When starting the application, the user must specify a username and password, along with a database alias listed in the client's tnsnames.ora file. For example, the following operating system command starts SQL*Plus on the local workstation and establishes a remote connection to the SALES database:

```
sqlplus username/password@sales
```

Different tools use different methods for specifying the database alias, or *connection string*. However, in most cases, a user's username/password combination is followed by the @ symbol to indicate a remote connection and then the alias name specified in the client's tnsnames.ora file.

Connecting to Oracle7 Using a Dedicated Server Connection

As an administrator, you will occasionally need to establish the remote connection using a dedicated server connection. For example, you need a dedicated server connection when you want to remotely start up or shut down an Oracle7 database, and you should use a dedicated server connection when using the procedures shown in Listings 8.1 and 8.2. To specifically establish a dedicated server connection to Oracle7 when the multithreaded server is present, preceed a connect string with *d_* (which stands for dedicated):

```
sqlplus username/password@d_sales
```

This chapter has explained all aspects of configuring and using Oracle7 in a client/server system, including the following:

- Using Network Manager to configure SQL*Net for all clients and servers in an Oracle7 client/server system

- Starting the SQL*Net network listener process to accept and route remote client connections to the Oracle7 server

- Configuring and tuning the Oracle7 server as a multithreaded server to efficiently service remote client connections in a client/server system

- Connecting to Oracle7 from a remote client

Now that client workstations can create remote connections to the Oracle7 database server, it's time to learn how to create database users and make the database secure using Oracle7's security features, as described in the next chapter.

CHAPTER

9

NINE

Securing an Oracle7 Database

- Oracle7 database user account creation and management

- Database system security management using Oracle7 system privileges and roles

- Control of database system resource usage with tablespace quotas and resource limit profiles

Security is one of the most important jobs of a database administrator. Without adequate security controls, anyone would be able to access a database and query or change the data it contained. This chapter explains how you as an administrator can control access to a database and to a server's system resources using the security features provided by Oracle7. The chapter discusses these issues:

- Database users and user authentication

- Database access privileges and roles

- Resource limitation and user profiles

Controlling Database Access with User Accounts

Almost every business today has a voice-mail system, in which each employee has a mailbox to record incoming messages. To hear these messages, the employee must call the voice-mail system and then type his or her phone extension and password, using the phone's touch-tone keypad. After passing the system's security check, the employee can listen to the messages or administer his or her voice-mail box (change the greeting, change the password, and so on). A similar system is used to control who can connect to a database. After the database administrator registers users by creating database user accounts, those users can access the database and administer their own accounts. The following sections explain how to manage user accounts in an Oracle7 database.

Creating Users

As with a voice-mail system, to connect to an Oracle7 database, the user must have a database *username* and *password* or a *user account*. As the database administrator, you can create user accounts in a database system using the Create User dialog box of Server Manager. To access this dialog box from the Administration Manager, select the Security drawer and then click on the Users folder tab. Next, select User ➤ Create from the menu bar. Figure 9.1 shows the General tab of the Create User dialog box.

FIGURE 9.1:

Server Manager's Create User dialog box allows you to create a new database user and set the user's many account settings.

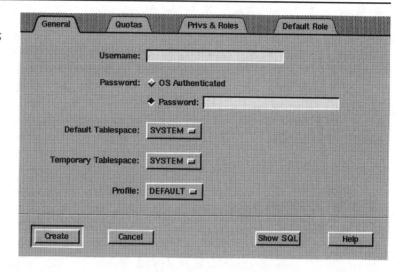

To use the Create User dialog box in Server Manager, you must have the CREATE USER system privilege.

To create a new user account, first specify the new user's name in the Username entry field. The next step is to choose an authentication method from the Password radio button list.

Password Authentication versus Operating System Authentication

When a user attempts to connect to a database or to enable a role, Oracle7 ensures system security by *authenticating* the operation; that is, Oracle7 makes sure the user is a valid database user or has the right to enable the role. You can choose to handle authorization using either a password or an external service, such as the server computer's operating system. When a database uses passwords for authentication, Oracle7 asks users for a password when they want to create a new database session or enable a role. Alternatively, when a database uses operating system authentication, Oracle7 looks at who the user is according to the user's operating system session information and allows or disallows the user to connect or enable a role based on the information.

Each authentication method has advantages and disadvantages. The primary advantage of operating system authentication is that it centralizes all security in the operating system. Therefore, when using operating system authentication for database users and roles, the administrator does not need to manage passwords for operating system user accounts and database user accounts and database privilege roles.

> **WARNING** Do not use operating system authentication when running Oracle7 in a client/server environment!

The big disadvantage of using operating system authentication when running Oracle7 in a client/server environment is that it opens up a large security hole. Any remote machine can try to establish a session with Oracle7 across a network, and many client workstations, such as personal UNIX workstations, are private machines that allow users to manage their own user accounts on the client. This makes it easy for a person on a client workstation to impersonate a real database user and break into an Oracle7 database system. Only when your network has a secure network authentication service should you employ an external authentication facility for database users and roles. If you are using Oracle7 in a network client/server system, it is much more secure to use authentication by passwords.

Identifying Account Characteristics for the User

After you choose an authentication method for a new user, the next step is to identify some important account characteristics for the user. Complete the following fields in the General tab of the Create User dialog box:

- The user's *default tablespace* is the tablespace where Oracle7 creates the user's objects (for example, tables and indexes) when no tablespace is explicitly specified in a CREATE statement. If you do not explicitly pick a default tablespace for the user, the default is the SYSTEM tablespace.

- The user's *temporary tablespace* is the tablespace where Oracle7 allocates temporary work space for completing complicated statements (for example, sorts and joins) on behalf of the user. If you do not explicitly pick a temporary tablespace for the user, the default is the SYSTEM tablespace.

- The user's *profile* is a set of system resource limits (for example, CPU processing time and idle time allowed). For more information, see the section "Limiting Other System Resources Using Resource Limit Profiles" later in this chapter.

To avoid problems, it is important to carefully plan these user account characteristics before creating each new user. For example, users with unlimited access to system resources can potentially run large, complicated queries that can adversely affect the performance of the system for all users. The remainder of this chapter will help you plan the characteristics for each new user in the system.

Setting a User's Tablespace Quotas

The Quotas tab of the Create User dialog box allows you to establish the initial tablespace quotas for a new user. A user's *tablespace quotas* control how much space the user's objects can consume in specific tablespaces of the database. Tablespace quotas are a way to limit user access to disk space in a database. For more information, see the section "Setting Space Quotas for Users" later in this chapter.

Setting a User's Initial Privileges and Roles

When you create a new database user, no one can use the account to connect to Oracle7 unless you grant the account the privilege to connect to the system. This ability is controlled by the CREATE SESSION Oracle7 system privilege. Furthermore, after connecting to the system, a user cannot perform any database operations unless the account has other access privileges.

The Privs & Roles tab of the Create User dialog box allows you to grant some initial privileges and roles to a new user. For more information about privilege management for Oracle7 database users, see the section "Privilege Management" later in this chapter.

Setting a User's Default Roles

The Create User dialog box allows you to set a user's *default role*. When a user establishes a new session in a database, Oracle7 automatically enables all of the user's default roles to establish the user's initial privilege domain. To set the default role list for a user, use the Default Roles tab in the Alter User dialog box. For more information about setting a user's default role list correctly, see the section "Privilege Management" later in this chapter.

Changing Oracle7 Database Passwords

All Oracle7 users should regularly change their account's password to prevent security leaks. Without any special privileges, any user can change his or her password using the SQL command ALTER USER in any Oracle interactive query tool. For example, if a user is Abe Lincoln, the following statement changes Abe Lincoln's password to yertqw:

```
ALTER USER alincoln IDENTIFIED BY yertqw
```

As the database administrator, it is your responsibility to determine how often users should change their passwords and then make sure they know how to change them using the ALTER USER command.

Altering User Accounts

You may need to change the characteristics for one or more users. For example, you may want to change a user's tablespace quotas to give the user more space or change a user's profile if the user changes jobs.

After creating a user account, you can modify any of the account's characteristics using Server Manager's Alter User dialog box. To access this dialog box from the Administration Manager, select the Security drawer and then click on the Users folder tab to display a list of all current users. To modify a particular user's account, just double-click on the user record in the folder tab display. You can then change any of the selected account's characteristics using the dialog box tabs and controls, as in the Create User dialog box. Figure 9.2 shows the Alter User dialog box.

FIGURE 9.2:

Server Manager's Alter User dialog box allows you to change the account settings of any Oracle7 database user.

NOTE To use the Alter User dialog box in Server Manager, you must have the ALTER USER system privilege.

Dropping Users

A user account may become unnecessary because a user transfers to a different division in a company or leaves the company altogether. In this case, you will want to delete unnecessary user accounts to keep a database's user account table current.

You can delete a user account using Server Manager. To drop a user when using the Administration Manager window, select the Security drawer and then click on the Users folder tab to display a list of all current users. After selecting the user to drop from the folder tab display, select User ➤ Drop from the menu bar.

NOTE To drop a user, you must have the DROP USER system privilege.

When you want to drop a user that owns any database objects (for example, tables or views), Server Manager will warn you of this condition and ask if you still want to drop the user. When you drop a user that owns objects, Oracle7 also drops the user's objects.

Using Encryption to Secure Remote Connections in a Client/Server Environment

Many networks in the client/server world are not secure. In other words, it is easy for a malicious user to figure out database passwords in a network client/server database system by using some special software that can "sniff" the network for *unencrypted* packets of information. A persistent bandit can eventually get network packets containing users' connection requests, which include database usernames and passwords. At this point, access to the database system is as easy as walking through an unlocked door.

To avoid this security hole, you can configure an Oracle7 client to *encrypt* the username and password before sending it across the network. To do this, you set the ORA_ENCRYPT_LOGIN operating system session variable on the client to TRUE. (The name of this session variable may be different on different operating systems.)

Privilege Management

After a person connects to a voice-mail system, the system restricts the person to working only within his or her own voice-mail box; for example, the system prevents anyone from hearing other people's voice-mail or changing someone else's greeting. Similarly, after a user connects to a database, Oracle7 controls the user's capabilities according to the user's database system privileges and database object privileges. To simplify privilege management in an Oracle7 database system, the administrator uses roles to control a user's privilege domain.

The privileges of a database user should always correspond to the application the user is currently running. The sections that follow provide general information about privilege management for different types of users in a database system. For more information, see Chapter 18.

Managing Privileges for Database Administrators

Database administrators perform important system operations—database startup and shutdown, database backup and recovery, security management, and instance configuration, just to name a few—that affect all users of the database. The ability to perform each different administrative operation is protected by a database system privilege. For example, to create users, an administrator must have the CREATE USER system privilege; to drop tables, an administrator must have the DROP ANY TABLE system privilege; and to alter triggers, an administrator must have the ALTER ANY TRIGGER system privilege. These are just a few examples of the many different powerful system privileges an administrator might require to complete the job.

WARNING   Never risk the security of a database system by granting a powerful system privilege to a database user other than a database administrator or, in certain cases, an application developer. See the section "Managing Privileges for Application Developers" later in this chapter for more information about setting privileges for developers.

Protecting Database Availability

Oracle7 allows an administrator to start up or shut down a database only when using a *privileged administrative connection*. Since database startup and shutdown are extremely powerful operations, only a very few individuals should have the ability to create privileged administrative connections.

When using Oracle7 release 7.0, the only way to establish a privileged administrative connection is by using the special administrator account INTERNAL. For example, after starting Server Manager and connecting to Oracle7 as INTERNAL, you can start up the server's database with the Startup Database dialog box.

All server sessions that connect to the server as INTERNAL actually use the SYS account, but with special privileges to manage the server. On many platforms (UNIX platforms are a notable exception), Oracle Server cannot authenticate privileged connections as INTERNAL using a password, and must therefore rely on external authentication, which might not always be secure. Additionally, when multiple administrators all use a central account such as the INTERNAL account, there is no accountability as to who actually performs powerful administrative operations using the account.

The later releases of Oracle7 (7.1, 7.2, and 7.3) have features that provide more secure remote administration for privileged administrative operations. The following steps are necessary to secure remote privileged administrative connections:

1. Create a password file using the ORAPWD utility.

2. Grant the SYSOPER and SYSDBA roles to administrative users.

3. Set the REMOTE_LOGIN_PASSWORDFILE server parameter and restart the server.

To secure administrative connections for an Oracle7 database server, you first must use the ORAPWD utility on the server to create a *password file*. The syntax of the command-line ORAPWD utility is:

```
orapwd FILE=filename PASSWORD=password [ENTRIES=integer]
```

The FILE parameter indicates the operating system filename for a password file. The name and location of a password file are important.

- When a server manages a single database, create a corresponding *local password file* in the home of the database (for example, $ORACLE_HOME/dbs on UNIX installations).

- When a server manages more than one database, you can conveniently create and manage a single, shared *global* password file for all databases in a central directory location on the server (for example, /etc on a UNIX box). However, you must create individual local password files in the home of each database (for example, $ORACLE_HOME/dbs) when you want exact accountability for privileged administration connections to the server (see later in this section).

The PASSWORD parameter specifies the password to authenticate all remote administrative connections. The optional ENTRIES parameter allows you to limit the entries in the password file, which limits how many database users you can register as administrators. A higher value for ENTRIES also increases the size of the password file, but not to the extent that it should raise any concerns about space utilization.

The following example shows the use of the ORAPWD utility on a UNIX server to create a local password file for the TEST database with 50 entries:

```
orapwd FILE=$ORACLE_HOME/dbs/orapwdTEST PASSWORD=yertw
ENTRIES=50
```

A password file is an encrypted file that the server computer's operating system manages. Even though Oracle encrypts the information in a password file, make sure to restrict operating system access to protect the file against unauthorized users.

After creating a password file for a database server, you must grant database administrators the access rights to perform privileged administrative functions, such as server startup and shutdown and database backup and recovery. You can control access to powerful administrator privileges using the SYSOPER and SYSDBA system privileges, as follows:

- Database users with the SYSOPER privilege can start up and shut down the database server; mount, open, close, back up, and recover the database; and manage the database's transaction log.

- Database users with the SYSDBA privilege are "all powerful" because SYSDBA provides access to all system privileges with the ability to in turn grant system privileges to other users.

You can grant SYSOPER and SYSDBA privileges as you would any other type of system privilege to a user account—by using the SQL command GRANT:

```
GRANT SYSOPER TO gwashington
GRANT SYSDBA TO alincoln
```

When you grant a user the SYSOPER or SYSDBA system privilege, Oracle Server includes the user's privilege as an entry in the external password file. Later in this section, you will see how grantees of the SYSOPER and SYSDBA privileges can use them to establish a privileged connection to Oracle Server.

After creating a password file, set the REMOTE_LOGIN_PASSWORDFILE server initialization parameter, and then restart the server, if necessary. This parameter determines how the server will use the password file. The following are the different options for the REMOTE_LOGIN_PASSWORDFILE server initialization parameter:

- The default setting is NONE. With this setting, Oracle Server does not use the password file and does not allow secure remote administrative connections across a network.

- When set to SHARED, Oracle Server allows only privileged administrative connections using the SYS account, even when other grantees of the SYSOPER and SYSDBA privileges exist in the password file. Since all privileged administrative connections funnel through the SYS account, there is no user accountability for such connections. Consider using SHARED only as a convenience when you use a global password file for multiple databases on the same server, but understand the sacrifices necessary for a little added convenience.

- The most secure setting is EXCLUSIVE. Oracle Server allows individual grantees of the SYOPER and SYSDBA privileges to establish secure, privileged administrative connections using their accounts.

To summarize, you can achieve the tightest security for remote administrative connections by creating a password file for each database and setting the server initialization parameter REMOTE_LOGIN_PASSWORDFILE to EXCLUSIVE.

Assuming that you follow the above recommendations, a grantee of the SYSOPER or SYSDBA privilege can establish a secure, privileged, client/server connection through Server Manager's Connect dialog box by choosing SYSOPER or SYSDBA from the Connect As pick list.

NOTE Maintenance releases of Oracle Server continue to support the INTERNAL administration account for backward compatibility with earlier releases. However, you should use the password file facility to authenticate privileged administrative connections and gain the benefits of security and accountability.

Using Roles to Manage Database Administration System Privileges

With more than 70 different system privileges, it is important to use roles to simplify privilege management. With each Oracle7 database, there is a default database administration role named DBA. Initially, the DBA role has every system privilege, so a user with the DBA role can do anything within the database.

While the DBA role may be adequate for smaller systems where only one administrator is present, medium-sized and large Oracle7 systems will have multiple administrators, each with a specific job. To make sure no one administrator has more power than is necessary to accomplish that administrator's job, several specialized administrative roles are necessary. To create new roles, use Server Manager's Create Role dialog box. To access the Create Role dialog box from the Administration Manager, select the Security drawer and then click on the Roles folder tab. Next, select Role ➤ Create from the menu bar. Figure 9.3 shows the General tab of the Create Role dialog box.

FIGURE 9.3:
Using Server Manager's Create Role dialog box, you can create a new role, determine its authentication method, and establish its privilege domain.

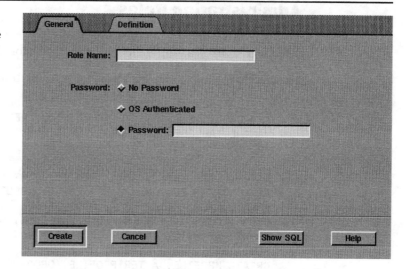

NOTE To use the Create Role dialog box in Server Manager, you must have the CREATE ROLE system privilege. To grant roles and system privileges successfully using the Definition tab of the Create Role dialog box, you must have the role or system privilege with the ADMIN option, or you must have the GRANT ANY ROLE system privilege or the GRANT ANY PRIVILEGE system privilege.

To create a new role, use the items in the General tab in this dialog box. First, give the role a name in the Role Name entry field, and then decide which authentication method you want to use for the role. As with user accounts, you can use either passwords or the operating system to protect the use of a role. For client/server systems, always choose to use passwords rather than the operating system to close network security holes. You can also craft the role's privilege domain by granting system and object privileges and other roles to it using the Definition tab of the Create Role dialog box.

An Example of Database Administration Roles

Listing 9.1 shows several sample statements that suggest how to create specialized administrative roles for the different administration duties in a system.

Listing 9.1: Custom Roles for Database Administrators

```
CREATE ROLE backupadmin IDENTIFIED BY password
GRANT CREATE SESSION, ALTER SESSION, RESTRICTED SESSION,
  MANAGE TABLESPACE, BACKUP ANY TABLE
  TO backupadmin

CREATE ROLE securityadmin IDENTIFIED BY password
GRANT CREATE SESSION, ALTER SESSION, RESTRICTED SESSION,
  CREATE USER, ALTER USER, DROP USER,
  CREATE ROLE, ALTER ANY ROLE, DROP ANY ROLE, GRANT ANY ROLE,
  GRANT ANY PRIVILEGE,
  AUDIT ANY, AUDIT SYSTEM,
  CREATE PROFILE, ALTER PROFILE, DROP PROFILE,
  ALTER RESOURCE COST,
```

```
CREATE PUBLIC SYNONYM, DROP PUBLIC SYNONYM,
CREATE ANY SYNONYM, DROP ANY SYNONYM
TO securityadmin WITH ADMIN OPTION

CREATE ROLE spaceadmin IDENTIFIED BY password
GRANT CREATE SESSION, ALTER SESSION, RESTRICTED SESSION,
  ALTER DATABASE,
  CREATE ROLLBACK SEGMENT, ALTER ROLLBACK SEGMENT,
  DROP ROLLBACK SEGMENT,
  CREATE TABLESPACE, ALTER TABLESPACE, DROP TABLESPACE
  TO spaceadmin

CREATE ROLE objectadmin IDENTIFIED BY password
GRANT CREATE SESSION, ALTER SESSION, RESTRICTED SESSION,
  ANALYZE ANY,
  CREATE ANY CLUSTER, ALTER ANY CLUSTER, DROP ANY CLUSTER,
  CREATE ANY INDEX, ALTER ANY INDEX, DROP ANY INDEX,
  CREATE ANY PROCEDURE, ALTER ANY PROCEDURE,
  DROP ANY PROCEDURE,
  CREATE ANY SEQUENCE, ALTER ANY SEQUENCE,
  DROP ANY SEQUENCE,
  CREATE ANY TABLE, ALTER ANY TABLE, DROP ANY TABLE,
  LOCK ANY TABLE, COMMENT ANY TABLE,
  CREATE ANY TRIGGER, ALTER ANY TRIGGER, DROP ANY TRIGGER,
  CREATE ANY VIEW, DROP ANY VIEW
  TO  objectadmin
  .
  .
  .
```

Notice how each of the preceding roles has only specific privileges that allow assigned users to perform a specific administration task: the BACKUPADMIN role has only the privileges necessary to connect to the server and perform database backup, the SECURITYADMIN role has only the privileges necessary to connect to the server and administer database security (such as creating users or roles), and so on.

NOTE Notice that every administrative role has the RESTRICTED SESSION privilege. This ensures that any type of administrator can connect to a database started in restricted mode.

As you can see, Oracle7's many system privileges offer very precise control over almost every system operation. For a complete list of the different Oracle7 system privileges, see Appendix A.

Managing Privileges for Application Developers

Application developers, like database administrators, need some powerful system privileges to complete their jobs. For example, an application developer needs to create database objects, such as tables, indexes, stored procedures, and triggers. It is important for the security administrator to carefully plan a security policy for application developers.

Privilege management techniques for an application developer may vary, depending on the environment in which the application developer works:

- If the application developer works in a test database environment (as opposed to a production database environment), privilege management for the developer can be somewhat relaxed. Because the data in a test database is not real, it is not important to real users of the system. To remove unnecessary barriers to productive application development, a developer in a test database is usually given many system privileges, including those normally reserved for database administrators.

- If the application developer works in a production database environment, privilege management should be very tight so the developer does not unnecessarily affect the productivity of other users. For example, an application developer should not be able to start up and shut down a production database system.

Using Roles to Manage Developer System Privileges

By default, every Oracle7 database has a role intended for application developers: the RESOURCE role. However, the RESOURCE role is present primarily for backward compatibility with previous versions of Oracle. Even smaller systems may find that the system privileges granted to RESOURCE are inadequate for productive application development. Consequently, you need to create custom application development roles for the application developers in an Oracle7 system. You can do this through Server Manager's Create Role dialog box, using the techniques presented in the previous section, "Using Roles to Manage Database Administration System Privileges."

To create database objects necessary for applications, developers are normally given space quotas for one or more tablespaces in a database. When developers work in a test database, you can give them unlimited quotas on all tablespaces in the database using the UNLIMITED TABLESPACE system privilege. However, when developers work in a production database, use specific tablespace quotas to restrict them to only the tablespaces they need to perform their job. See the section "Resource Limitation" later in this chapter for more information.

NOTE Strangely enough, even though Oracle7 stores all procedures, functions, packages, and triggers in the data blocks of the SYSTEM tablespace, no quota is necessary to create stored procedures. All an application developer needs is the necessary privilege to create the PL/SQL program.

Examples of Accounts and Roles for Application Developers

Listing 9.2 shows several sample statements that suggest how to create application development user accounts and a custom role for application developers in a production database system.

Listing 9.2: Custom Application Developer Accounts and Roles

```
CREATE USER applicationdeveloper IDENTIFIED BY password
  DEFAULT TABLESPACE testapplications
  TEMPORARY TABLESPACE testapplications
  QUOTA UNLIMITED ON testapplications
  PROFILE developerprofile

CREATE ROLE productiondbdeveloper IDENTIFIED BY password

GRANT CREATE SESSION, ALTER SESSION,
  CREATE TABLE, CREATE CLUSTER, CREATE VIEW,
  CREATE SEQUENCE, CREATE PROCEDURE, CREATE TRIGGER,
  CREATE ROLE, CREATE SYNONYM
  TO productiondbdeveloper
```

Managing Privileges for Application End Users

In general, application users need object privileges only to access the objects associated with an application. Chapter 18 explains how application developers can plan and create roles for applications that dynamically manage the privilege domains of end users as they switch between different applications.

Application users should never have more than a select few system privileges. For example, every database user needs the CREATE SESSION system privilege to establish a connection to the Oracle7 database. The CONNECT role, present in every Oracle7 database, is intended for typical end users. However, this role includes some system privileges you might not want typical end users to have, such as the CREATE TABLE system privilege. Therefore, you might want to create your own default connection role for end users of your database system, including at least the CREATE SESSION privilege.

Resource Limitation

After you have created users and given them access to a database, the next thing to consider when designing a good security policy is limiting their use of system resources within the database system. For example, if user sessions can remain idle for only 30 minutes before being terminated by Oracle7, unused sessions cannot stick around forever, wasting valuable resources on the database server that active sessions could be using. The following sections explain how to limit the consumption of valuable system resources using the built-in resource limitation features of Oracle7: space quotas and resource limit profiles.

Setting Space Quotas for Users

One of the most valuable system resources to control in a database system is disk space for data storage. If you give a user the privilege to create database objects such as tables, the user's objects will consume disk space. If you allow the user unlimited access to any tablespace in the database, the user's objects can potentially hoard too much of the disk space allocated to the database.

To control the disk space consumption per user, Oracle7 uses *tablespace quotas*. You set space quotas to a user using Server Manager's Create User or Alter User dialog box. Within each dialog box, there is a tab that allows you to build a list of tablespace quotas for the user. As Figure 9.4 shows, you can give a user a finite or an infinite quota for a tablespace.

FIGURE 9.4:
Both the Create User and Alter User dialog boxes in Server Manager permit you to control a user's access to disk space with tablespace quotas.

In most cases, it is not necessary for a user to have any space quotas at all, because typical users normally cannot create database objects that consume disk space (for example, tables and indexes). Even if you give a user the privilege to create objects such as views and synonyms, the user does not need any tablespace quotas because those types of database objects make simple entries in the data dictionary. End users do not even need a tablespace quota for their temporary tablespace; Oracle7 does not consider tablespace quotas for temporary statement work space.

Application developers and administrators are the users you should be concerned with when setting tablespace quotas. If an administrator or application developer is working in a test environment, it is relatively common to give the user unlimited access to every tablespace in the system, as described in the following section. Alternatively, if an application developer works in a production environment, the developer will likely need a quota for any tablespaces that hold application objects.

Space and object administrators in a production environment are generally the only administrators who need access to all tablespaces in a system.

Using The UNLIMITED TABLESPACE System Privilege

To grant unlimited access to all tablespaces in a database, use the UNLIMITED TABLESPACE system privilege instead of explicitly assigning quotas for all tablespaces in the system. Oracle7 ignores any explicitly specified tablespace quotas for a user when the user has the UNLIMITED TABLESPACE system privilege. Use this powerful system privilege only for application developers in a test database or for administrators who perform space and database object management.

NOTE The UNLIMITED TABLESPACE system privilege is unique because Oracle7 does not allow you to grant the system privilege to a role. The only way to grant a user this powerful system privilege is by directly granting the user the privilege.

Limiting Other System Resources Using Resource Limit Profiles

To control the consumption of other types of system resources, use Oracle7 system resource limits. *Resource limits* control the following:

- A user's CPU usage and disk I/Os, both on per-statement and per-session intervals

- The number of sessions per user

- The maximum connect time and idle time per session

- The memory used by a multithreaded server session

You can manage all of these resource limits easily by first creating profiles that describe different types of user needs and then assigning the profiles to the appropriate users.

NOTE

Oracle7 resource limits wisely pay attention to logical disk I/Os, not physical disk I/Os. *Logical I/Os* occur when Oracle7 reads or writes a data block in memory. *Physical I/Os* occur when Oracle7 reads or writes a block from disk into memory. Since Oracle7 caches large amounts of data in shared memory and must perform both a physical and logical I/O when reading new data from disk into shared memory, Oracle7 counts the number of logical I/Os to get an accurate account of a user's operation.

The DEFAULT Profile

Every Oracle7 database has a default profile, appropriately named DEFAULT. Oracle7 automatically limits the operations of all users not assigned to a specific profile in accordance with the limits specified in the DEFAULT profile. Other profiles can also defer to the settings in the DEFAULT profile for specific limits. Initially, all resource limits in the DEFAULT profile are set to unlimited; therefore, it is important that you alter the settings for the DEFAULT profile after you create a database.

Creating New Profiles for Users

To create a new resource limit profile, use Server Manager's Create Profile dialog box. To access the Create Profile dialog box from the Administration Manager, select the Security drawer and then click on the Profiles folder tab. Next, select Profile ➤ Create from the menu bar. Figure 9.5 shows the Create Profile dialog box.

NOTE

To use the Create Profile dialog box in Server Manager, you must have the CREATE PROFILE system privilege.

The tabs of the Create Profile dialog box allow you to shape the new profile and then assign it to database users. As you work through these tabs, notice that for each resource limit, you can specify a specific limit, specify an unlimited setting, or defer to the setting in the DEFAULT profile. The settings for CPU time limits are in hundredths of a second, connect and idle time limits are in elapsed minutes, and private

FIGURE 9.5:

Using the Create Profile dialog box in Server Manager, you can create different resource limit profiles to control user consumption of server resources.

memory per session is in bytes (although you can specify K for kilobytes and M for megabytes).

> **NOTE**
>
> Oracle7 doesn't actually perform resource limit checking unless the server is started with the initialization parameter RESOURCE_LIMIT set to TRUE. This initialization parameter can be useful in tuning server performance because, as you might guess, the Oracle7 server incurs additional processing overhead to perform resource limit checking for all user sessions and requests.

Altering Profiles

To alter a resource limit profile, use Server Manager's Alter Profile dialog box. To access this dialog box from the Administration Manager, select the Security drawer and then click on the Profiles folder tab to display a list of all resource limit profiles. To change a profile, double-click on the profile's record in the folder tab display. You can then alter any of the selected profile's resource limit settings using the dialog box tabs and controls, as with the Create Profile dialog box. Figure 9.6 shows the Alter Profile dialog box.

FIGURE 9.6:

You can change a resource limit profile's setting with the Alter Profile dialog box in Server Manager.

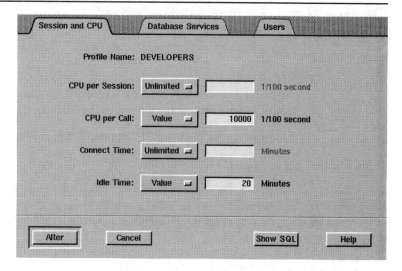

> **NOTE**
> To use the Alter Profile dialog box in Server Manager, you must have the ALTER PROFILE system privilege.

Dropping Unwanted Profiles

If you find that a profile is no longer necessary in a database, you can drop the profile using Server Manager's Administration Manager. To drop a profile, select the Security drawer and then click on the Profiles folder tab to display a list of all profiles. After selecting the profile to drop from the folder tab display, select Profile ➤ Drop from the menu bar.

> **NOTE**
> To drop a profile, you must have the DROP PROFILE system privilege.

When you drop a profile that is assigned to users of the database, Oracle7 automatically assigns those users to the DEFAULT profile. Be sure to review those users assigned to the DEFAULT profile and assign them to another profile if necessary.

Reporting Security Settings for Users

The data dictionary of every Oracle7 database has several views that reveal the security settings for all users in a database. Listing 9.3 shows a stored procedure you can use to generate a report of the security settings for a user in a database.

Listing 9.3: SECURITYREPORT Stored Procedure

```
CREATE PROCEDURE securityreport (user VARCHAR2) AS
-- This procedure generates a security report for the specified
-- user. The report shows the user's default and temporary
-- tablespaces, resource limit profile, tablespace quotas,
-- directly granted system privileges, directly granted object
-- privileges, and roles.

-- variables to hold account information
var0 VARCHAR2(100);
var1 VARCHAR2(100);
var2 VARCHAR2(100);

-- cursor to hold tablespace quota information
CURSOR quotas IS
  SELECT tablespace_name, bytes,
    DECODE(max_bytes,-1,'Unlimited Space',TO_CHAR(max_bytes)) quota
    FROM sys.dba_ts_quotas
    WHERE username = UPPER(user);

-- cursor to hold system privilege information
CURSOR sysprivs IS
  SELECT privilege, admin_option
    FROM sys.dba_sys_privs
    WHERE grantee = UPPER(user);

-- cursor to hold object privilege information
CURSOR objprivs IS
  SELECT owner, table_name, privilege, grantable
    FROM sys.dba_tab_privs
    WHERE grantee = UPPER(user);
```

```
-- cursor to hold role information
CURSOR roles IS
  SELECT granted_role, admin_option, default_role
    FROM sys.dba_role_privs
    WHERE grantee = UPPER(user);

BEGIN
-- Gather account information about user for first part of report.
-- If the specified user does not exist, return an error message.

  SELECT default_tablespace, temporary_tablespace, profile
    INTO var0, var1, var2
    FROM sys.dba_users
    WHERE username = UPPER(user);

-- print report header
DBMS_OUTPUT.PUT_LINE('');
DBMS_OUTPUT.PUT_LINE('Security Report for User: '||UPPER(user));
DBMS_OUTPUT.PUT_LINE('----------------------------------------');

-- print user's account settings
DBMS_OUTPUT.PUT_LINE('');
DBMS_OUTPUT.PUT_LINE(' '||UPPER(user)||' Account Settings');
DBMS_OUTPUT.PUT_LINE(' ---------------------------------------');
DBMS_OUTPUT.PUT_LINE('  Default Tablespace:      '||var0);
DBMS_OUTPUT.PUT_LINE('  Temporary Tablespace:    '||var1);
DBMS_OUTPUT.PUT_LINE('  Resource Limit Profile:  '||var2);

-- print user's tablespace quotas, if any
DBMS_OUTPUT.PUT_LINE('');
DBMS_OUTPUT.PUT_LINE(' '||UPPER(user)||' Tablespace Quotas');
DBMS_OUTPUT.PUT_LINE(' ---------------------------------------');
FOR userquota IN quotas LOOP
  DBMS_OUTPUT.PUT_LINE('  Tablespace:     '||userquota.tablespace_name);
  DBMS_OUTPUT.PUT_LINE('  Bytes Used:     '||userquota.bytes);
  DBMS_OUTPUT.PUT_LINE('  Quota (Bytes):  '||userquota.quota);
  DBMS_OUTPUT.PUT_LINE('');
END LOOP;
```

```
-- print user's system privileges, if any
DBMS_OUTPUT.PUT_LINE('');
DBMS_OUTPUT.PUT_LINE(' '||UPPER(user)||' Directly Granted System Privileges');
DBMS_OUTPUT.PUT_LINE(' ------------------------------------');
FOR usersyspriv IN sysprivs LOOP
  DBMS_OUTPUT.PUT_LINE('  Privilege:        '||usersyspriv.privilege);
  DBMS_OUTPUT.PUT_LINE('  Admin Option?:  '||usersyspriv.admin_option);
  DBMS_OUTPUT.PUT_LINE('');
END LOOP;

-- print user's object privileges, if any
DBMS_OUTPUT.PUT_LINE('');
DBMS_OUTPUT.PUT_LINE(' '||UPPER(user)||' Directly Granted Object Privileges');
DBMS_OUTPUT.PUT_LINE(' ------------------------------------');
FOR userobjpriv IN objprivs LOOP
  DBMS_OUTPUT.PUT_LINE('  Object Name:      '||userobjpriv.owner||'.'
    ||userobjpriv.table_name);
  DBMS_OUTPUT.PUT_LINE('  Privilege:        '||userobjpriv.privilege);
  DBMS_OUTPUT.PUT_LINE('  Grant Option?:  '||userobjpriv.grantable);
  DBMS_OUTPUT.PUT_LINE('');
END LOOP;

-- print user's roles, if any, indicating which are default roles
DBMS_OUTPUT.PUT_LINE('');
DBMS_OUTPUT.PUT_LINE(' '||UPPER(user)||' Roles');
DBMS_OUTPUT.PUT_LINE(' ------------------------------------');
FOR userroles IN roles LOOP
  IF userroles.default_role = 'YES' THEN
    DBMS_OUTPUT.PUT_LINE('  Default Role:  '||userroles.granted_role);
  ELSE
    DBMS_OUTPUT.PUT_LINE('  Role:           '||userroles.granted_role);
   END IF;
  DBMS_OUTPUT.PUT_LINE('  Admin Option?: '||userroles.admin_option);
  DBMS_OUTPUT.PUT_LINE('');  END LOOP;

EXCEPTION
-- if user does not exist, raise user-defined error message
  WHEN NO_DATA_FOUND THEN
    raise_application_error(-20000, UPPER(user)||' is not a valid database
user.');
END securityreport;
```

After creating the SECURITYREPORT procedure, you can use it in a Server Manager SQL worksheet or SQL*Plus by setting server output on and then executing the procedure with a specific user's name:

```
SET SERVEROUTPUT ON SIZE 10000

EXECUTE securityreport('alincoln')

Security Report for User: ALINCOLN
-----------------------------------------------------------

ALINCOLN Account Settings
-----------------------------------------------------------
  Default Tablespace:     TEST
  Temporary Tablespace:   TEST
  Resource Limit Profile: DEVELOPERS

ALINCOLN Tablespace Quotas
-----------------------------------------------------------
  Tablespace:      TEST
  Bytes Used:      0
  Quota (Bytes):   Unlimited Space

  Tablespace:      SYSTEM
  Bytes Used:      10452
  Quota (Bytes):   204800

ALINCOLN Directly Granted System Privileges
-----------------------------------------------------------
  Privilege:     CREATE SESSION
  Admin Option?: NO

ALINCOLN Directly Granted Object Privileges
-----------------------------------------------------------
  Object Name:   SALES.CUSTOMERS
  Privilege:     SELECT
  Grant Option?: NO

ALINCOLN Roles
-----------------------------------------------------------
  Default Role: APPDEVELOPER
  Admin Option?: NO
  Role:         MINIDBA
  Admin Option?: NO
```

This chapter has explained the aspects of database system security that are important for an administrator to consider, including the following:

- Enrolling new users for an Oracle7 database and configuring their account settings

- Altering user account settings, including changing a user password

- Managing the system privileges required by different types of Oracle7 users using roles

- Controlling the consumption of important system resources, such as disk space, processing time, and disk I/Os

After reading this chapter and the previous chapters in this part of the book, you should have a clear understanding that there are many important tasks for which an Oracle7 administrator is responsible. The next chapter discusses the many administrative jobs related to supporting client applications.

CHAPTER

TEN

Database Administration on Behalf of Applications

- Application schema setting fine-tuning

- Application security settings

- Rollback segment creation and management for applications

- Optimizer statistics for an application schema

As a client/server database system takes shape, part of your job as the administrator is to be closely involved with the application developers' efforts. This is important because when a new application is ready for use in the production database environment, you must perform a number of jobs to get the application installed and running. This chapter explains the tasks an administrator must perform on behalf of client database applications, including the following:

- Reviewing, editing, and running an application's DDL script to create the application schema

- Creating and managing rollback segments to handle application transactions

- Generating and maintaining optimizer statistics for the objects in application schemas

Creating the Application Schema

Let's assume that a new application has passed all of the rigorous trials in a test database environment and everything is now ready to move to the production database. As the database administrator, some or all of a database application's installation will be your responsibility. The following sections explain the part of application installation that always falls into the database administrator's lap: running the application's DDL script to create the tables, views, and other database objects on behalf of the application.

What Is an Application's DDL Script?

When a developer creates a new database application, part of the job is to design the *application schema*—the tables, views, procedures, triggers, and other database objects that are part of the application. When the application is finished and ready for implementation, the developer must hand off the application's source code and executable file to the database administrator, along with a script file that includes the DDL SQL statements for creating the application schema.

Developers can generate an application's DDL script using several approaches. If the developer has CASE or database design tools, such as Oracle's Designer/2000, the developer diagrams the entities and relationships in the database, and the CASE tool automatically creates the corresponding DDL script. Even when using a sophisticated CASE or database design tool, the developer might write part of an application's DDL script by hand. In the absence of a CASE tool, the developer must write all of an application's DDL script by hand.

A developer who generates an application's DDL script typically does not pay much attention to low-level storage considerations for an application's database objects—considerations that can affect the performance of the application and storage requirements on the database server. Such storage considerations are the responsibility of the database administrator. The next two sections explain the different storage parameters for database objects and how to set these parameters appropriately within an application's DDL script.

Setting Object Tablespace Placement

The primary storage characteristic to consider for database objects is where to store them. You can manage the physical location of many database objects, including tables, indexes, and clusters, using tablespaces. For example, if you store the ACCOUNTSREC table in the ACCOUNTING tablespace, Oracle7 physically stores the table's data in one or more of the data files that make up the tablespace.

```
CREATE TABLE accountsrec
( ... column specifications ... )
TABLESPACE accounting
 .
 .
 .
```

Note that Oracle7 stores other objects, such as procedures, functions, packages, and database triggers, within the SYSTEM tablespace and offers no option to physically locate them elsewhere. Therefore, it is important to plan enough space for objects that Oracle7 stores in the SYSTEM tablespace. See the section "Estimating Space Requirements for Application Database Objects" later in this chapter for more information.

Setting Object Storage Parameters

To control how Oracle7 uses the space with the data blocks of a table, index, or cluster, Oracle7 has several types of *storage parameters:*

- INITIAL, NEXT, MINEXTENTS, MAXEXTENTS, and PCTINCREASE

- PCTFREE and PCTUSED

- INITRANS and MAXTRANS

Different types of storage parameters have different purposes. The following sections describe each class of storage parameters based on their functions.

NOTE   As you read the following sections, keep in mind that all of the storage parameters in Oracle7 are options you can specify when you create a table, index, or cluster; Oracle7 does not require you to specify any storage parameters because there are default values for each. However, when you want to squeeze out every last bit of performance related to disk I/O while at the same time use every last byte of available disk space, you will need to learn how to set the Oracle7 storage parameters correctly.

Controlling Space Allocation with Extent Storage Parameters

Much as Oracle7 preallocates contiguous disk space for tablespaces using data files, Oracle7 preallocates contiguous space within the data files of a tablespace for tables, indexes, and clusters using extents. An *extent* is nothing more than a number of contiguous data blocks that Oracle7 allocates for an object when more space is necessary for the object's data. The group of all of the extents for an object is called a *segment*.

The single preallocation of many data blocks as an extent delivers a tremendous performance advantage for applications; otherwise, Oracle7 would need to allocate blocks every time a user inserts new data into an object. Figure 10.1 shows how Oracle7 allocates data blocks for an object using extents.

When you create a table, index, or cluster, Oracle7 allocates one or more extents to hold the object's initial data. As users insert data into the object, Oracle7 automatically allocates additional extents, as needed, to hold data that does not fit the current set of extents for the object.

FIGURE 10.1:

Oracle7 allocates data blocks for an object in clusters of data blocks called extents.

There are several storage parameters that allow you to control how Oracle7 allocates extents for tables, indexes, and clusters. In general, the Oracle7 extent storage parameters are available so you can force all of an object's data within a small number of extents, thereby reducing data fragmentation and increasing performance with respect to disk I/O. The following list explains each extent storage parameter and its purpose:

Parameter	Description
INITIAL	Determines the size, in bytes, of an object's initial extent. You can use INITIAL to preallocate all or a large majority of the space you ever expect an object to require. This way, all or most of the object's data resides in a contiguous set of data blocks. To set INITIAL accurately, you must estimate an object's size. (See the section "Estimating Space Requirements for Application Database Objects" later in this chapter.)
NEXT	Determines the size, in bytes, of the next extent Oracle7 will allocate, if necessary, for the object. You can explicitly set the size for the second extent of an object using NEXT, but the value of NEXT may grow, depending on the value for PCTINCREASE.
MINEXTENTS	Determines how many extents to preallocate when creating a table, index, or cluster. For example, if you create a table and specify MINEXTENTS as 2, Oracle7 immediately allocates two extents for the table.

Parameter	Description
MAXEXTENTS	Determines the maximum number of extents Oracle7 can ever allocate for a table, index, or cluster. You use MAXEXTENTS to effectively control the maximum size of an object. When you do not want to limit the size of an object, you can set MAXEXTENTS to UNLIMITED. However, for releases of Oracle7 prior to release 7.3, there is an operating system-dependent upper bound when setting MAXEXTENTS.
PCTINCREASE	Determines the growth factor as Oracle7 allocates new extents to a table, index, or cluster. For example, if you set a table's NEXT to 200K and PCTINCREASE to 50, the second extent will be 200K, the third extent will be 300K, the fourth extent will be 450K, and so on. You can use PCTINCREASE to increase the size of subsequent extents and try to reduce data fragmentation within an object.

Figure 10.2 demonstrates how Oracle7 uses the extent storage parameter settings for a table as the table grows.

When setting extent storage parameters for a table, index, or cluster, consider these issues:

- If you specify a size for INITIAL and NEXT that is not a multiple of the database's data block size, Oracle7 rounds the number up.

- You can change the value for NEXT to explicitly set the size of an object's next extent. If you change PCTINCREASE, the new value does not take effect until Oracle7 allocates the extent subsequent to the very next extent.

- Changing the setting for an object's INITIAL or MINEXTENTS parameter has no effect since the initial number of extents has already been allocated for the object.

- In general, concentrate on sizing object extents correctly so you can set PCTINCREASE to 0.

FIGURE 10.2:

Storage parameters determine the size and growth characteristics of a segment's extents.

```
CREATE TABLE...
  (...column definitions)
STORAGE
  (INITIAL 200K, NEXT 200K,
  MINEXTENTS 2,
  MAX-EXTENTS 4,
  PCTINCREASE 50)
```

Extent 1   Extent 2
(200K)   (200K)

Extent 1   Extent 2   Extent 3
(200K)   (200K)   (300K)

Extents 1 and 2 are full,
allocating extent 3

Extent 1   Extent 2   Extent 3   Extent 4
(200K)   (200K)   (300K)   (450K)

Extents 1, 2, and 3 are full,
allocating extent 4.

Extent 1   Extent 2   Extent 3   Extent 4
(200K)   (200K)   (300K)   (450K)

Extents 1, 2, 3, and 4 are full,
but cannot allocate extent 5
because MAXEXTENTS is 4   X

To set extent storage parameters for an object, use the STORAGE clause of several CREATE and ALTER commands. For example, this statement shows the STORAGE clause that sets the extent storage parameters for the ACCOUNTSREC table:

```
CREATE TABLE accountsrec
( ... column specifications ... )
STORAGE  (INITIAL 100K
          NEXT 100K
          MINEXTENTS 2
          MAXEXTENTS 10
          PCTINCREASE 0)
  .
  .
  .
```

The STORAGE clause is available for many commands, including CREATE TABLE, ALTER TABLE, CREATE INDEX, ALTER INDEX, CREATE CLUSTER, ALTER CLUSTER, CREATE ROLLBACK SEGMENT, and ALTER ROLLBACK SEGMENT.

Each tablespace in an Oracle7 database has a set of *default extent storage parameters.* When a user creates an object in a tablespace and chooses not to set storage parameters for the object, the object's storage parameters take the values set for the tablespace's default extent storage parameters. Setting a tablespace's default storage parameters can make space administration easier when you have determined that many objects in a tablespace should have the same extent storage parameter settings.

To set a tablespace's default extent storage parameters, specify the storage parameters in Server Manager's Create Tablespace or Alter Tablespace dialog box. For example, Figure 10.3 shows the Default Storage tab in the Create Tablespace dialog box.

FIGURE 10.3:
The Default Storage tab in Server Manager's Create Tablespace dialog box lets you indicate the default extent storage parameters for a tablespace.

Controlling Row Chaining Using PCTFREE

When you are managing the health of a database, it is important to avoid row chaining in tables if at all possible. A *row chain* occurs when Oracle7 does not store all of a row's data within the same data block but instead is forced to break the row into *row pieces* and store them in different data blocks. In other words, the row is fragmented among multiple data blocks. To return all of a row's data for a query, Oracle7 must piece the row back together by traversing the row's chain of data blocks. As with other types of data fragmentation on disk, significant amounts of row chaining within a table can degrade disk I/O performance because Oracle7 must read more data blocks to read rows in the table. Figure 10.4 shows a row chain in an Oracle7 table.

FIGURE 10.4:

Row chaining can occur when an Oracle7 table's rows are too large to fit in a single data block.

Data Blocks

In most circumstances, Oracle7 chooses to store an entire row within the same block. However, there are two situations in which Oracle7 cannot avoid chaining rows:

- If a row has more data than can fit inside a single data block. For example, when you have a table with a LONG RAW column that stores large images, each row will probably require several data blocks. Unfortunately, there is nothing you can do to avoid this type of row chaining.

- If a user updates a row to make it longer than the original version. If the data block that holds the row does not have ample space for the additional bytes of information for the new version of the row, Oracle7 must fragment the row among multiple data blocks.

PCTFREE is a storage parameter you can use to minimize row chaining resulting from the second situation. PCTFREE controls how much of the space in a block is reserved for statements that update existing rows in the object. For example, if a table's PCTFREE is set to its default value of 10, Oracle7 will allow users to insert rows into a data block of the table until 10 percent of the free space remains in the block. Oracle7 reserves the remaining 10 percent of free space in the block for updates that might make the table's existing rows grow in size.

The guidelines for setting PCTFREE are relatively straightforward. If a table is one in which users will update original rows to make them grow, set the table's PCTFREE storage parameter to a higher number to reserve more space for updates to the table. For example, if a table's rows are much smaller than the database block size and they grow by a factor of x, you might set PCTFREE for the table to $(1/x)*100$ (plus a little bit extra). Alternatively, if the table rarely experiences updates or updates that make rows larger, set the table's PCTFREE storage parameter to a lower number to make more data block space available for row inserts.

The next section explains the mechanical procedure for setting an object's PCTFREE storage parameter.

Controlling Data Block Free Space Availability with PCTUSED

When you and a friend go to a restaurant for dinner, the first person you see is the maitre d'. The maitre d' has a list of available tables and takes you and your friend to a table when one is ready. Similarly, when a user inserts a row into a table, Oracle7 must choose a data block to store the new row. To make block selection for row inserts fast and easy, Oracle7 keeps one or more *free space lists* for each table—lists that state which data blocks have available free space for new rows.

Oracle7 decides which data blocks appear on free space lists using the PCTFREE and PCTUSED storage parameters. When users insert new rows into a data block that cause the PCTFREE threshold to be reached, as described in the preceding section, Oracle7 takes the data block off the table's free space lists.

After reaching PCTFREE, Oracle7 does not return a data block to the table's free lists until another threshold, PCTUSED, is reached. PCTUSED is a percentage of used space in a data block that triggers the data block to return to the table's free space list. As users delete rows from a table, Oracle7 frees space in the table's data blocks. When there are enough deletes to cause PCTUSED to be reached, Oracle7 returns the data block to the table's free space lists. For example, when a table's PCTUSED is set to its default value of 40, Oracle7 will not return a block to the table's free space lists until users delete enough rows so that only 39 percent of the space in the block is used. After returning the block to the table's free space lists, Oracle7 uses the block for new row inserts until the block again fills to PCTFREE. Figure 10.5 illustrates the cycle described above where PCTFREE and PCTUSED govern a data block's status in the free space lists of a table.

The guidelines for setting PCTUSED affect both storage utilization and system performance. Higher PCTUSED settings make sure that Oracle7 keeps data blocks

FIGURE 10.5:

A data block's movement on and off free space lists is determined by PCTFREE and PCTUSED.

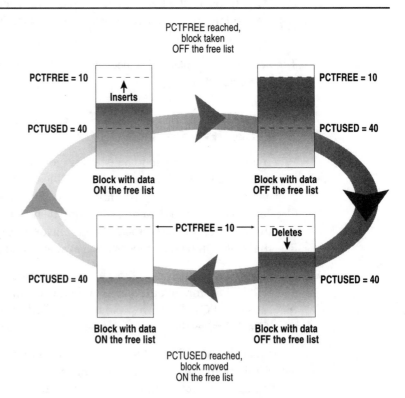

relatively full, but these settings can also degrade system performance as Oracle7 constantly moves blocks on and off free space lists. Alternatively, lower PCTUSED settings can lead to pockets of wasted storage space when users often delete rows. You need to look at the characteristics of your application and set PCTUSED to obtain an acceptable compromise between performance and space usage.

To set an object's PCTFREE and PCTUSED storage parameters, simply specify each option and an integer indicating the setting. For example, this statement creates the ACCOUNTSREC table with PCTFREE set to 15 and PCTUSED set to 60:

```
CREATE TABLE accountsrec
( ... column specifications ... )
PCTFREE 15
PCTUSED 60
  .
  .
  .
  .
```

NOTE The sum of PCTFREE and PCTUSED cannot be greater than 100. Additionally, avoid setting PCTFREE to 0, since this can create block space allocation problems for other internal operations.

After creating an object, you can always change the settings for PCTFREE and PCTUSED. However, the new settings will apply only to new data blocks added to the object as part of a subsequent extent allocation.

Controlling Transaction Access to Data Blocks with INITRANS and MAXTRANS

As a transaction touches data in an object, Oracle7 must allocate small amounts of space in the corresponding data blocks of the object to hold internal processing information until the transaction commits or rolls back. Oracle7 has two storage parameters, INITRANS and MAXTRANS, that allow you to tune performance with respect to this internal processing mechanism on behalf of transactions.

Parameter	Description
INITRANS	Preallocates space for a specified number of *transaction entries* in each data block of an object. This way, Oracle7 does not need to dynamically allocate space for transaction entries as they enter data blocks. The default value is 1.
MAXTRANS	Limits the number of transactions that can concurrently enter a data block and thus the amount of space that transaction entries can consume in a block at any given time. If MAXTRANS number of transactions are using a block at the same time, the next transaction to request information in the block must wait until another transaction using the block either commits or rolls back.

The guidelines for setting INITRANS and MAXTRANS correspond to table characteristics and application behavior. For example, if many application users concurrently need access to a small lookup table, set the table's INITRANS and MAXTRANS parameters to higher numbers for better performance and no waiting among application users. Alternatively, large tables reduce the likelihood of several users touching the same data blocks at the same time; therefore, you can make more data block space available to actual data by using a smaller setting for INITRANS.

To set an object's INITRANS and MAXTRANS storage parameters, simply specify each option and an integer indicating the setting. For example, this statement creates the ACCOUNTSREC table with INITRANS set to 4 and MAXTRANS set to 20:

```
CREATE TABLE accountsrec
( ... column specifications ... )
INITRANS 4
MAXTRANS 20
  .
  .
  .
```

Estimating Space Requirements for Application Database Objects

To set certain extent storage parameters correctly for tables and indexes in an application's DDL script (as described in the section "Setting Object Storage Parameters" earlier in this chapter), it is useful to get an estimate of the space a table and associated indexes will require in the production database. Specifically, size estimates help you set the values for INITIAL and MINEXTENTS to preallocate all or much of a table's and index's storage space. Similarly, it is useful to estimate the sizes of other application objects, like packages and triggers, so you can make sure the SYSTEM tablespace contains enough free space to support the new application when you run the application's DDL script. The following sections show how to easily estimate the space requirements for all types of application objects.

Estimating Space for Tables and Indexes

Space estimates for tables and indexes are useful if you want to plan disk storage requirements and preallocate all of the space a table and its indexes will ever need. For example, after estimating a table's size, you can use this information to set the INITIAL and MINEXTENTS storage parameters in the table's CREATE TABLE statement.

Correctly estimating the size of a table and associated indexes is relatively simple if you perform the following steps:

1. Create a prototype of the table and indexes in either the production or test database. When creating the table and indexes, be sure to set PCTFREE as you plan to have it when the application is in production.

2. Insert approximately 1000 representative rows into the prototype table.

3. Gather statistics on the prototype table and its indexes.

4. Estimate the maximum number of rows you think the table will store.

5. Create and execute the ESTIMATETABLESIZE procedure given in Listing 10.1 a little later in this chapter.

Step 1, creating a prototype table and its indexes, is simple to accomplish because the application's DDL script already has the CREATE statements for the table and its indexes. All you need to do is add the PCTFREE parameter and run these statements.

Step 2, inserting approximately 1000 representative rows into the table, is also easy to accomplish with a simple anonymous PL/SQL block; for example:

```
DECLARE
x DATE := SYSDATE;
y NUMBER := 10000.12;
BEGIN
  FOR counter IN 1 .. 1000 LOOP
    INSERT INTO prototypetable
      VALUES ( ... x, y, other column values ... );
    x := x + 1;
    y := y + 4;
  END LOOP;
END;
```

Notice that this sample block inserts a representative range of index key values into the table and its indexes by using variables in the anonymous PL/SQL block that change with each iteration through the insertion loop. This trick makes the rows in the prototype table and its indexes more representative of the production table and indexes.

For step 3, use the ANALYZE command to gather some statistics about the prototype table and its indexes:

```
ANALYZE TABLE prototypetable COMPUTE STATISTICS
```

The ESTIMATETABLESIZE procedure will need these statistics later. (If you are not familiar with the ANALYZE command, see the section "Generating Optimizer Statistics" later in this chapter.)

Step 4 is up to you; only you know your data and can reasonably estimate the maximum number of rows the table will ever hold.

Step 5 is the fun part. The ESTIMATETABLESIZE procedure in Listing 10.1 simplifies what would otherwise be the laborious process of estimating space requirements for a table and its indexes. Comments in the code explain the procedure's functionality.

Listing 10.1: ESTIMATETABLESIZE Procedure

```
CREATE PROCEDURE estimatetablesize (tableowner IN VARCHAR2,
  tablename IN VARCHAR2, rowestimate IN INTEGER) AS
-- This procedure estimates the size of a table and its indexes.
-- This procedure requires that you first create a prototype
-- table and any indexes, insert representative rows, and then
-- use the ANALYZE command to gather statistics about the table
-- and indexes.

-- variables to hold various numbers necessary for calculations
blocksize INTEGER;
reservedblockspace INTEGER;
averagerowlength INTEGER;
numberofrows INTEGER;
tablesizeestimate NUMBER;
indexsizeestimate NUMBER;

-- cursor to retrieve statistics for the table's indexes
CURSOR indexdata (own IN VARCHAR2, tab IN VARCHAR2) IS
  SELECT index_name, leaf_blocks
  FROM sys.dba_indexes
  WHERE table_owner = own AND table_name = tab;

BEGIN
-- query to capture statistics about the table
SELECT avg_space, avg_row_len, num_rows
  INTO reservedblockspace, averagerowlength, numberofrows
  FROM sys.dba_tables
  WHERE owner=UPPER(tableowner) AND table_name=UPPER(tablename);

-- query to get the database's block size
SELECT value INTO blocksize
  FROM v$parameter
  WHERE name='db_block_size';

-- calculation for table size estimate
tablesizeestimate := CEIL(rowestimate/FLOOR((blocksize-reservedblockspace)/
averagerowlength)) ;

-- print report header
DBMS_OUTPUT.PUT_LINE('');
```

```
DBMS_OUTPUT.PUT_LINE('Size Estimates for Table:'||UPPER(tableowner)||'.'||UPPER
(tablename));
DBMS_OUTPUT.PUT_LINE('----------------------------------------');
DBMS_OUTPUT.PUT_LINE('');

-- print table size estimate in bytes
DBMS_OUTPUT.PUT_LINE('Size in KBytes:    '
||ROUND((tablesizeestimate*blocksize)/1000,0)||'K');
DBMS_OUTPUT.PUT_LINE('');

 -- header for index size estimates, if any
DBMS_OUTPUT.PUT_LINE('  Associated Index Size Estimates');
DBMS_OUTPUT.PUT_LINE('');
-- print index size estimates, if any
FOR tableindexes IN indexdata(UPPER(tableowner), UPPER(tablename)) LOOP
  DBMS_OUTPUT.PUT_LINE('  Index Name:      '||tableindexes.index_name);

-- calculation for index size estimate
  indexsizeestimate := tableindexes.leaf_blocks*(rowestimate/numberofrows);
  DBMS_OUTPUT.PUT_LINE('  Size in KBytes:  '
||ROUND((indexsizeestimate*blocksize)/1000,0)||'K');
  DBMS_OUTPUT.PUT_LINE('');
END LOOP;
END estimatetablesize;
```

Create the ESTIMATETABLESIZE procedure in your database and use it to estimate table and index space requirements for applications. Before executing the
ESTIMATETABLESIZE procedure using a Server Manager SQL worksheet or
SQL*Plus, be sure to set server output on with a buffer of at least 10,000 bytes. When
you execute the ESTIMATETABLESIZE procedure, you will see a report something
like this:

```
EXECUTE estimatetablesize('ACCOUNTING','SAVINGS',10000)

Size Estimates for Table: ACCOUNTING.SAVINGS
----------------------------------------------
Size in KBytes:   172K

Associated Index Size Estimates

    Index Name:       ACCTNUM
    Size in KBytes:   23K
```

```
Index Name:        CUSTOMERNUM
Size in KBytes:    20K
```

Use the report's size estimates to preallocate all of a table's space in a single extent, such as the following:

```
CREATE TABLE accounts.savings
(ACCTNUM INTEGER
  PRIMARY KEY USING INDEX STORAGE (INITIAL 30K),
  ... other column specifications ... )
STORAGE (INITIAL 180K)
   .
   .
   .
```

NOTE   The ESTIMATETABLESIZE procedure generates reasonably accurate size estimates for "average" tables (and their associated indexes). With tables that are minuscule or that have particularly long rows (such that row chaining is unavoidable), the ESTIMATETABLESIZE procedure's results might not be particularly accurate.

Estimating Space for Procedures, Functions, Packages, and Triggers

Unfortunately, the CREATE commands for procedures, functions, packages, and database triggers do not allow you to specify a tablespace location; Oracle7 stores all procedures, functions, packages, and triggers in the SYSTEM tablespace. Since stored PL/SQL programs can consume significant amounts of space, it is important to plan adequate space in the SYSTEM tablespace for applications that create many procedures, functions, packages, and triggers.

To investigate the amount of space PL/SQL programs such as procedures, functions, packages, and triggers consume in the SYSTEM tablespace, use the REPORT-PROCEDURESIZE stored procedure shown in Listing 10.2 to return the information you need.

Listing 10.2: REPORTPROCEDURESIZE Procedure

```
CREATE PROCEDURE reportproceduresize (objowner IN VARCHAR2) AS
-- This procedure prints a size report of all procedures, functions, package
-- specifications, and package bodies in the specified schema.

-- cursor to select storage space required by different parts of a procedure
CURSOR objectsize (own IN VARCHAR2) IS
  SELECT owner, name, type, source_size,
    (source_size+parsed_size+code_size+error_size) total_size,
    ROUND((source_size + parsed_size+code_size + error_size) /
source_size,1) storage_factor
    FROM sys.dba_object_size
    WHERE owner = own
    AND type IN ('PROCEDURE','FUNCTION','PACKAGE','PACKAGE BODY','TRIGGER');

BEGIN
-- print report header
DBMS_OUTPUT.PUT_LINE('');
DBMS_OUTPUT.PUT_LINE('Object Size Report '||SYSDATE);
DBMS_OUTPUT.PUT_LINE('----------------------------------------------');
DBMS_OUTPUT.PUT_LINE('');
-- print individual object size reports
FOR dbobjectsize IN objectsize (UPPER(objowner)) LOOP
  DBMS_OUTPUT.PUT_LINE('Object Name:              '||dbobjectsize.name);
  DBMS_OUTPUT.PUT_LINE('Object Type:              '||dbobjectsize.type);
  DBMS_OUTPUT.PUT_LINE('Object Source Size:       '||dbobjectsize.source_size);
  DBMS_OUTPUT.PUT_LINE('Object Total Size:        '||dbobjectsize.total_size);
  DBMS_OUTPUT.PUT_LINE('Source-to-Total Storage Factor:  '
  ||dbobjectsize.storage_factor);
  DBMS_OUTPUT.PUT_LINE('');
END LOOP;
END reportproceduresize;
```

As with the other report-generating procedures in this book, make sure server output is on in a Server Manager SQL worksheet or SQL*Plus with a buffer size of at least 10,000 bytes. Connect to the development test database and execute the REPORTPROCEDURESIZE procedure by specifying the application's schema name. The procedure prints a simple report of all the schema's procedures, functions, packages, and corresponding size information, such as the following:

```
EXECUTE reportproceduresize('SYS')

Object Size Report 21-JUL-96
```

```
-------------------------------------------------
Object Name:                      STANDARD
Object Type:                      PACKAGE
Object Source Size:               31225
Object Total Size:                153076
Source-to-Total Storage Factor:   4.9

Object Name:                      STANDARD
Object Type:                      PACKAGE BODY
Object Source Size:               20986
Object Total Size:                140756
Source-to-Total Storage Factor:   6.7

Object Name:                      DBMS_STANDARD
Object Type:                      PACKAGE
Object Source Size:               1368
Object Total Size:                6027
Source-to-Total Storage Factor:   4.4
  .
  .
  .
```

Perhaps the most interesting field in the report is the Source-to-Total Storage Factor field. As you use this reporting procedure, you may notice trends in the Source-to-Total Storage Factor field, revealing how much total space is required to corresponding bytes of source code. If you discover a trend like this, it can be useful in predicting the amount of disk space required to hold all of an application's PL/SQL programs.

NOTE Releases 7.0, 7.1, and 7.2 of Oracle7 do not store database triggers in a compiled form inside the database. Instead, these earlier releases of the server store only the source code for a database trigger and compile it the first time that a statement fires the trigger. Therefore, to estimate the space required for an application's database triggers, check the byte count of the script that creates all of an application's triggers.

Monitoring Table and Index Storage Capacities

After you create an application's objects and people work with the application for a while, the tables and indexes of the application normally begin to enter application data that consumes the space preallocated for the objects. As described earlier, if a table or index requires more space than it already has been preallocated, Oracle7 automatically extends the object's storage capacity by allocating one or more new extents for the underlying segment. But as you know, object space extension can continue only up to a limit because the MAXEXTENTS storage parameter controls how many extents an object can ultimately have. When Oracle7 tries to allocate another extent for an object that has reached MAXEXTENTS, Oracle7 returns an error.

The preset limit that MAXEXTENTS imposes often causes the error condition described above. In fact, the "max # extents..." type errors are among the most common problems an administrator must address when managing space in an Oracle7 database. These error conditions are particularly frustrating for application users because they attempt to insert or update application data, but Oracle7 simply refuses to cooperate.

Given that these error conditions can dramatically affect the productivity of an entire team of application users, it is important that you, as an administrator, frequently monitor the current number of extents that each application's objects contain. Specifically, you need to look for any objects with an extent count that is dangerously approaching the limit set by the MAXEXTENTS storage parameter. You can look for these conditions using a simple query on the DBA_SEGMENTS data dictionary view:

```
SELECT owner, segment_name, segment_type, extents, max_extents
  FROM sys.dba_segments
  WHERE max_extents-extents <= 2
```

This query returns the names of those objects (actually, segments) that can extend only 0, 1, or 2 more times. If you want to be more cautious, simply change the query to ask for those segments that can extend 3 or fewer more times, and so on.

When you find that an object is coming close to its extent limit, you can avoid its reaching the limit using several different approaches:

- Increase the value of the object's MAXEXTENTS storage parameter to allow the object to extend more times.

- Increase the value for the object's NEXT storage parameter so that when the object does extend, its subsequent extents are larger than they were before. This may avoid the object's needing to extend again in the future.

- Archive and/or delete data from the object to free space in the current extents of the object.

Checking Row Datatypes for an Application's Tables

When a developer delivers an application's DDL script, don't assume that each table's definition is absolutely correct. Often, the developer hasn't used the best datatypes possible when defining an application's tables but has instead simply used datatypes that work. Specifically, a developer might have an opportunity to choose between two different datatypes that will both work for a particular column but for some reason chooses the datatype that stores the column's data using more database space than the other datatype would have required. Such errors in datatype choice can have significant implications when it comes to the amount of database space necessary to support the application as a whole, especially if the application has very large tables.

The most common datatype choice error arises with the character datatypes, specifically when a developer uses the CHAR datatype when the VARCHAR2 datatype would be more appropriate. Recall that Oracle7 stores data in a VARCHAR2 column very efficiently; it stores only the characters given for the column and nothing more. This contrasts with a CHAR column, where Oracle7 pads all values shorter than the maximum with blanks, and storing blanks requires database space. Consequently, improper use of the CHAR datatype can result in significant amounts of wasted database space. For example, can you figure out how much space would be wasted in a million-row table that has a CHAR(255) column with an average column value length of 55? The answer is 200 million bytes, or 20180 megabytes!

Incorrect datatype choices are not always the result of developers being unfamiliar with the space requirements for the different Oracle7 datatypes. For example, older versions of Oracle's CASE tools that generate application DDL scripts might not support newer Oracle7 datatypes, such as the VARCHAR2 datatype. As a result, the tool uses the older CHAR datatype for tables with character columns, and the developer might miss correcting for this situation before turning in the application's DDL script for installation. In conclusion, know your Oracle7 datatypes and pay close attention to DDL scripts for incorrect datatype usage.

Naming Integrity Constraints to Identify Them Easily

When a developer hands off a new application's DDL script to you for installation, look specifically at the declaration of the integrity constraints in the application schema. In most cases, you'll want to take advantage of Oracle7's ability to name integrity constraints so you can easily identify the different constraints in the data dictionary after you create the application's tables.

For example, an application's script might have the following excerpt, which creates a new table:

```
CREATE TABLE items
( id NUMBER(5,0),
  orderid NUMBER(5,0),
  partid NUMBER(5,0) NOT NULL,
  quantity NUMBER(5,0) NOT NULL,
  total NUMBER(10,2),
  PRIMARY KEY (id, orderid),
  FOREIGN KEY (orderid) REFERENCES orders ON DELETE CASCADE,
  FOREIGN KEY (partid) REFERENCES parts )
```

Notice that in this CREATE TABLE statement, none of the integrity constraints have names. To name the constraints, simply include the CONSTRAINT clause in each integrity constraint's declaration in the CREATE TABLE statement:

```
CREATE TABLE items
( id NUMBER(5,0),
  orderid NUMBER(5,0),
  partid NUMBER(5,0) CONSTRAINT itemspartid_nn NOT NULL,
  quantity NUMBER(5,0) CONSTRAINT itemsquantity_nn NOT NULL,
  total NUMBER(10,2),
  CONSTRAINT items_pk PRIMARY KEY (id, orderid),
  CONSTRAINT itemsorderid_fk FOREIGN KEY (orderid)
    REFERENCES orders ON DELETE CASCADE,
  CONSTRAINT itemspartid_fk FOREIGN KEY (partid)
    REFERENCES parts )
```

When naming constraints, be sure to set up and follow naming conventions that give all constraints logical and easily identifiable names. If the developer has already named the application's integrity constraints, simply make sure that the constraint names comply with your database system's integrity constraint naming guidelines.

Checking Application Security Settings

When developing an application, the application developer usually takes the first crack at designing the security settings for the application. The application developer must code certain statements within an application (for example, SET ROLE) so the application can take advantage of Oracle7 roles for dynamic privilege management. However, the database security administrator is ultimately responsible for reviewing an application's final DDL script to check that the proposed security settings are satisfactory.

Checking an application's security settings takes several steps. First, look at the proposed roles for the application and ask yourself these questions:

- Does the application's role grant more privileges than are necessary to run the application? For example, if application users only need to insert and retrieve rows from a specific table, the application's role should have only the INSERT and SELECT object privileges for the table, and not have the UPDATE and DELETE privileges.

- Are any of the application role's privileges too powerful? For example, an application's role should never have the SELECT ANY TABLE system privilege but rather the SELECT privilege for the specific tables used by the application.

- Could the application make use of more than one role? For example, some application users should have read-only access to the application's tables to generate reports, while other users should have full access to the application's tables for inserts, updates, and deletes. Such situations justify two different roles for the application.

- Is the application's role protected by authentication? If not, it should be, to prevent unauthorized users from running the application. If so, is the role's authentication method correct for your type of system? As described in

Chapter 9, roles should always use password authentication in client/server systems.

After you've worked out the details of an application's security settings, the next step is fitting the application's security into the grand scheme of things. For example, assume you are installing a new accounting application on a database system for a large company with many users in different divisions. You are probably already using roles to make privilege management easier for the different types of company users—workers in the sales department all have the SALESDEPT role, and workers in the accounting department all have the ACCOUNTINGDEPT role. Therefore, when you install the new accounting application, you should grant the new application's role(s) to the ACCOUNTINGDEPT role. Figure 10.6 illustrates a hierarchical group of roles that can appear in a corporate database system.

This simple example of role hierarchy can stimulate your creativity for designing a security policy for the big picture—the entire database system, which has many different types of users and several applications.

FIGURE 10.6:
It's likely that you'll want to create a hierarchy of roles in a corporate database's security system.

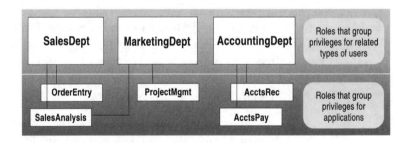

Managing Rollback Segments on Behalf of Applications

As mentioned earlier, as a user's transaction changes data in the database, Oracle7 keeps "undo" information in a rollback segment in case the user decides to roll back rather than commit the transaction. Oracle7 also uses rollback segment data to create read-consistent snapshots of data for queries throughout the system. When you as a database administrator install a new application, it is important to design and create the rollback segments necessary to support the transactions users will generate using the application. The following sections explain how to plan, create, and manage rollback segments on behalf of applications.

Planning Rollback Segments for Applications

Planning rollback segments for an application and, in a larger sense, a database is a tricky job. There are many factors to consider, including the following:

- OLTP applications that issue small update transactions will experience better performance if they use smaller rollback segments. That's because when a rollback segment is small, Oracle7 can probably keep all of the segment in shared memory, thereby reducing or eliminating disk I/O on behalf of transactions that generate rollback information.

- Decision support and reporting applications that issue large or complicated queries can sometimes run across an infamous ORACLE error message: "Snapshot too old." When a query receives this error message, it means that when Oracle7 tried to create a read-consistent snapshot for the query, certain blocks necessary to generate the snapshot had since been overwritten by another transaction and were no longer available. Larger rollback segments tend to reduce the likelihood of such errors because it takes longer for Oracle7 to wrap around and overwrite older rollback segment information.

- Large data loads, all part of a single transaction, can generate large amounts of transaction rollback information. If you do not want to break up a large load into smaller transactions, the database needs a large rollback segment to handle the load.

- Applications can design transactions to use specific rollback segments based on the types of transactions and current application requirements.

With all of these considerations and features to think about, planning rollback segments for an Oracle7 database might seem intimidating. However, Oracle7 provides features that allow you to implement a good rollback segment strategy. The following sections will help you get started with designing rollback segments for applications.

The SYSTEM Rollback Segment

Every Oracle7 database has a rollback segment named SYSTEM. During database creation, the initial database rollback segment is created in the SYSTEM tablespace.

The SYSTEM rollback segment is adequate for initial administrative operations after database creation. However, very soon after database creation, you should begin planning the other rollback segments for the database. For example, to create and use another tablespace (besides the SYSTEM tablespace) in a database, you must create a second rollback segment in the SYSTEM tablespace.

Creating New Rollback Segments

Once you have planned the rollback segments for an application or a database, you can create them using Server Manager's Create Rollback Segment dialog box. To access this dialog box from the Administration Manager, select the Storage drawer, click on the Rollback folder tab, then select Rollback ➤ Create from the menu bar. Figure 10.7 shows the Create Rollback Segment dialog box.

NOTE To use the Create Rollback Segment dialog box in Server Manager, you need the CREATE ROLLBACK SEGMENT system privilege.

To create the new rollback segment, enter some basic information in the General tab of the Create Rollback Segment dialog box. First, enter a name for the new rollback segment in the Rollback Segment entry field. Then select a tablespace to store the new rollback segment from the pick list of available tablespaces—make sure to see the next section for guidance on selecting a tablespace for rollback segments. Next, indicate whether or not to automatically bring the new rollback segment online after creation. A rollback segment is not available to transactions unless it is online. (See the section "Controlling Rollback Segment Availability" later in this chapter.)

Finally, you can use the Storage tab of the Create Rollback Segment dialog box to specify the new rollback segment's extent storage parameters. (See the section "Setting Rollback Segment Extent Storage Parameters" a little later in this chapter.) Once you are satisfied with the settings for the new rollback segment, select the OK button, and Oracle7 creates the new segment.

FIGURE 10.7:

Use Server Manager's Create Rollback Segment dialog box to create a new rollback segment and set its storage parameters.

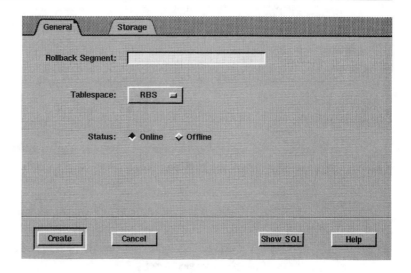

Public versus Private Rollback Segments

It's important to note that Server Manager's Create Rollback Segment dialog box does not reveal that Oracle7 can create two different types of rollback segments: public and private rollback segments. At database server startup, Oracle7 automatically acquires access to and brings online all public rollback segments in the database. Conversely, Oracle7 acquires access to and brings online only those private rollback segments that you explicitly list in the ROLLBACK_SEGMENTS parameter of the server's initialization parameter file. Private rollback segments are useful only when you use Oracle7 with the Parallel Server option and want different instances of the same database to explicitly acquire a mutually exclusive set of the database's rollback segments.

Because of the extra steps necessary to configure private rollback segments, they are more difficult to manage than public rollback segments. And unless you have the Oracle7 Parallel Server option, there is no advantage to using private rollback segments. Therefore, most administrators should choose to use public rollback segments.

Now the bad news. The Create Rollback Segment dialog box in Server Manager can only create private rollback segments. To create a public rollback segment, you must use the SQL command CREATE ROLLBACK using a Server Manager SQL worksheet.

```
CREATE PUBLIC ROLLBACK SEGMENT rbs_pub_3 ...
```

To automatically make Oracle7 bring online a private rollback segment during database startup, make sure to include the rollback segment's name in the setting for the server's ROLLBACK_SEGMENTS initialization parameter.

```
ROLLBACK_SEGMENTS (rbs1, rbs2, rbs3)
```

After database startup, you can see which rollback segments are online by using the Rollback folder of the Storage drawer in the Administration Manager.

Which Tablespace Should Store New Rollback Segments?

As with tables and indexes, you can store rollback segments in any tablespace of a database. It is common for an Oracle7 database to have a "rollback segment tablespace" used exclusively to store rollback segments. For example, the default initial database installed on Oracle7 for UNIX platforms has a tablespace named RBS that stores several rollback segments.

Keeping rollback segments separated in their own tablespace from other types of data makes database administration easier. For example, when you want to take a tablespace offline or drop it, you cannot do so until all of the rollback segments in the tablespace are offline. Once the tablespace is unavailable, the rollback segments within are also unavailable, which is a waste of allocated disk space. You can avoid these problems by creating and using a tablespace specifically for rollback segments.

Setting Rollback Segment Extent Storage Parameters

Just as with tables and indexes, when you create a rollback segment you can set extent storage parameters to control how the extent uses space. However, rollback segments have an additional extent storage parameter, its *optimal size*, that other types of segments do not have. To understand how to set rollback segment storage parameters, it is helpful to know more about how Oracle7 writes data to rollback segments.

Figure 10.8 shows how Oracle7 writes undo information to a rollback segment.

FIGURE 10.8:

How Oracle7 circularly writes transaction rollback information to the extents of a rollback segment and allocates additional extents if necessary.

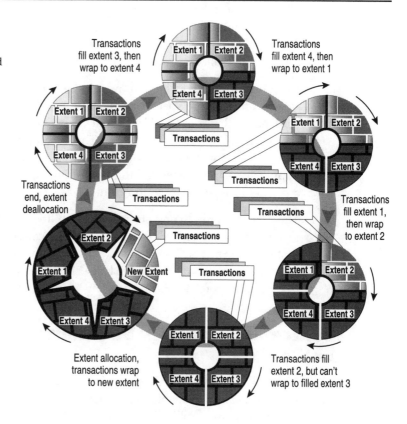

You can think of a rollback segment as a circle because of the method Oracle7 uses to write data to the extents of a rollback segment: Oracle7 assigns transactions on a round-robin basis to available rollback segments. As a new transaction begins, Oracle7 assigns the transaction to an available rollback segment. When a transaction generates rollback data, Oracle7 writes the data to an extent. As the transaction and others assigned to the same rollback segment fill the current extent, they can continue writing by "wrapping" to the next extent in the rollback segment. When transactions happen to fill the last extent of a rollback segment, they can continue writing undo information by wrapping to the first extent in the segment.

Transactions often generate more rollback data than the current extents of a rollback segment can hold. For example, what happens when transactions wrap around to the first rollback segment extent and continue writing until they eventually reach the extent in which they started writing? To allow transactions to be as long as they want and prevent transactions from writing over their own rollback data, Oracle7 extends rollback segments as needed. Therefore, rollback segments can grow and allocate more space to accommodate large transactions.

What happens when a large transaction is finished and now an extended rollback segment has all that space? Fortunately, a rollback segment can also shrink in accordance with its "optimal" size. When you create or alter a rollback segment, you can specify its optimal size, in bytes. This determines the number of extents Oracle7 tries to keep for the rollback segment on a regular basis. When Oracle7 needs to wrap extents in an extended rollback segment, it checks to see if it can deallocate any extents to get closer to its optimal size.

The dynamic growth and shrinking capabilities of Oracle7 rollback segments can lead to on-the-fly disk allocations and deallocations that degrade application and system performance. You can avoid this problem by setting rollback segment extent storage parameters carefully. See the section "Monitoring and Altering Extent Storage Parameters for Rollback Segments" later in this chapter for more information.

Controlling Rollback Segment Availability

Much like tablespaces, rollback segments can be either online or offline. *Online rollback segments* are available to transactions in the system; *offline rollback segments* are not. In most cases, rollback segments should be online so transactions can use them. However, when you want to take offline a tablespace that contains an online rollback segment or when you want to drop a rollback segment, you must take the rollback segment offline first.

To bring an offline rollback segment online, you can use the Place Online menu option in Server Manager. To access this menu option from the Administration Manager, select the Storage drawer and click on the Rollback folder tab to display a list of the database's rollback segments. After you select a target offline rollback segment, select Rollback ➤ Place Online from the menu bar.

To bring a rollback segment online or take a rollback segment offline, you need the ALTER ROLLBACK SEGMENT system privilege.

To take an online rollback segment offline, you can use the Take Offline menu option in Server Manager. To access this menu option from the Administration Manager, select the Storage drawer and click on the Rollback folder tab to display a list of the database's rollback segments. After you select a target online rollback segment, select Rollback ➤ Take Offline from the menu bar. When you request Server Manager to take an online rollback segment offline, Oracle7 will take the rollback segment offline after all transactions currently using the rollback segment commit or roll back.

Monitoring and Altering Extent Storage Parameters for Rollback Segments

After you have created a rollback segment for an application and a database, you should investigate how the settings for the rollback segment's extent storage parameters are working. To monitor rollback segments, you can use Server Manager's Rollback monitor. To access the monitor for rollback segments, select Monitor from the File menu of any Server Manager component (for example, the Administration Manager or a SQL worksheet), and then select Rollback from the list box that appears. Figure 10.9 shows the Rollback monitor of Server Manager.

It is important to look at the Shrinks column in the Rollback monitor. This column shows how many times Oracle7 has dynamically shrunk a rollback segment since the current instance started. If the number is high for a rollback segment, Oracle7 is wasting resources by dynamically expanding and shrinking the rollback segment. To remedy the situation, increase the setting for the rollback segment's OPTIMAL extent storage parameter. Then monitor the rollback segment again to see if the number of shrinks holds steady.

FIGURE 10.9:

Use Server Manager's Rollback monitor to check whether a rollback segment's optimal size is correct.

> **NOTE**
>
> At the expense of consuming additional space for a larger rollback segment, raising a rollback segment's OPTIMAL storage parameter setting serves to reduce the likelihood of users experiencing "snapshot too old" errors when transactions need to use older transaction undo information in the rollback segment. That's because the rollback segment is larger, so it will take longer for new transactions to overwrite older rollback segment information.

To alter a rollback segment's storage parameters, you can use the Storage tab in the Alter Rollback Segment dialog box in Server Manager. To access this dialog box from the Administration Manager, select the Storage drawer and then click on the Rollback folder tab to display a list of the database's rollback segments. Next, double-click on the rollback segment that you want to alter. Figure 10.10 shows the Storage tab of the Alter Rollback Segment dialog box.

Dropping Rollback Segments

If you need to drop a rollback segment, you can use Server Manager. To drop a rollback segment using the Administration Manager, select the Storage drawer and

FIGURE 10.10:

You can alter a rollback segment's storage parameters with Server Manager's Alter Rollback Segment dialog box.

then click on the Rollback folder tab to display a list of the database's rollback segments. You can only drop a rollback segment that is offline. After you pick an offline rollback segment from the Rollback folder tab display, select Rollback ➤ Drop from the menu bar.

 To drop a rollback segment, you need the DROP ROLLBACK SEGMENT system privilege.

Generating Optimizer Statistics

When you are planning a long road trip to get to a vacation spot, you usually sit down with some road maps to determine the fastest possible route to the trip's destination. Similarly, when you issue a SQL statement to Oracle7, you want Oracle7 to perform the statement and return the results as quickly as possible so you can be more productive in your work. To make sure SQL statements execute as quickly as possible, all applications rely heavily on the *cost-based optimizer* of Oracle7. For each statement, the optimizer's job is to figure out a good *execution plan*—the best way to execute each SQL statement.

To determine good query execution plans, the Oracle7 optimizer uses statistics about a database's data. For example, Oracle7 can generate statistics that indicate how many rows are in a table, how many data blocks are being used to store the table's data, and how many chained rows are in the table. Oracle7 keeps similar statistics for indexes. When a user issues a SQL statement, Oracle7 reads the pertinent statistics in the data dictionary to determine the *costs* of different execution plans. To execute the statement as quickly as possible, Oracle7 uses the execution plan with the lowest cost.

To avoid affecting performance, Oracle7 updates the statistics for objects only when you, as the database administrator, tell it to. You can gather statistics for a table, index, or cluster using the SQL command ANALYZE. The ANALYZE command has several options that let you describe how to gather statistics. This syntax diagram shows some of the most frequently used options of the ANALYZE command:

```
ANALYZE
   TABLE¦INDEX¦CLUSTER objectname
   [COMPUTE¦ESTIMATE[SAMPLE integer [ROWS¦PERCENT]]] STATISTICS
```

Notice that the ANALYZE command allows you to either compute or estimate statistics for an object. *Computing statistics* gathers exact statistics for the object but can take a long time to complete when the object is large. Alternatively, *estimating statistics* gathers reasonably accurate statistics from a representative sampling of the object's data and proceeds much more quickly than computing statistics.

This statement estimates statistics for the CUSTOMERS table using a random 15 percent of the table's data:

```
ANALYZE TABLE customers ESTIMATE STATISTICS SAMPLE 15 PERCENT
```

To make statistic-gathering easier, Oracle7 also includes a special stored procedure, DBMS_UTILITY.ANALYZE_SCHEMA, that can analyze all of the objects in a schema with a single procedure call. For example, this procedure call (issued in a Server Manager SQL worksheet) gathers statistics for all of the objects in the SALES schema in an Oracle7 database:

```
EXECUTE dbms_utility.analyze_schema('SALES');
```

Analyzing an application's schema objects is an important ongoing maintenance task that ensures maximum application performance. Without regularly updating the statistics for an application schema, the Oracle7 optimizer might not be using data statistics that reflect the current application data.

This chapter has explained many of the key administration tasks necessary on behalf of client database applications, including the following:

- Estimating application object sizes

- Setting application object storage parameters appropriately

- Reviewing a new application's security settings and incorporating them into a database system that supports many applications

- Gathering optimizer statistics for an application's data so the optimizer works the best it can for the application's transactions

At this point, applications are presumably working with your Oracle7 server. Now let's learn how to safeguard important application data from catastrophes with the protective features of Oracle7. The next chapter explains how to back up and recover an Oracle7 database system.

### ELEVEN

Protecting Work and Data

- Configuration of database transaction log groups and members

- Media recovery enabling and automatic log archiving

- Oracle7 database backup

- Databases recovery—offline and online

- Parallel recovery configuration for Oracle7

- Standby database configuration

Computer systems are not reliable a hundred percent of the time; sometimes things go wrong. After you have spent lots of time creating and configuring a database for client applications, it would be a tragedy to lose all that work if someone tripped over a power cord or, even worse, a disk crashed on the server. Problems like these are the driving force behind the comprehensive and sophisticated data-protection mechanisms built into the Oracle7 database server. This chapter explores Oracle7's protective features, including the following:

- The transaction log—how to configure and manage it to safeguard the work of ongoing transaction processing

- Database backups—the different kinds, how to make them, how to automate the backup process, and how to test a backup strategy to protect data from inevitable disk failures

- Database recovery—the different types of recovery and how to complete database recovery to get a system up and running after a failure

- A standby database—a unique database configuration for sites with extreme high-availability requirements

Transaction Logging

A database's transaction log (also called the redo log) is a vital component in Oracle7's protective mechanisms. Its job is to immediately record the changes made by ongoing application transactions in a database so that, in the event of an unforeseen failure, all committed work is protected and fully recoverable. Database recovery operations rely on the data in the transaction log to rebuild, or redo, the committed changes from lost transactions.

Because of its importance in the grand scheme of database protection, you as the database administrator must carefully consider the design of the transaction log to make sure its structure adequately and efficiently safeguards ongoing transaction processing. The following sections explain how to manage the structure of the transaction log and configure the database server to automatically back up the transaction log's data.

Adding Log Groups to a Database's Transaction Log

Each Oracle7 database's transaction log requires at least two fixed-size log groups. While writing to one log group, the server archives the transaction entries in the other group. (See the section "Configuring Transaction Log Archiving" later in this chapter.) Once the current log group fills with new data, a *log switch* occurs, and the server continues writing new transaction entries to the other group. The filled group can then be archived (backed up), after which it is again available when the next log switch is necessary. The cyclical process of writing to and archiving transaction log groups allows Oracle7 to efficiently use a small amount of static disk space to log the changes made by ongoing transactions.

How many log groups should a database have? The answer depends on the demands of a database system. In general, the fewer the number of log groups in the transaction log, the easier it is to manage. However, too few log groups in a transaction log can hamper database performance if log switches must wait each time for Oracle7 to finish archiving a log group.

Determining the number of log groups for a database is a trial-and-error process. After configuring a transaction log, monitor it closely to see how it is doing. See the section "Monitoring the Transaction Log" later in this chapter for more information.

If Oracle7 must wait for a transaction log group to be archived before it can continue transaction logging, add one or more log groups to the database's transaction log; this will help ensure that there are more free log groups in the database's transaction log. Likewise, if Oracle7 archives filled log groups well before they are needed for reuse, the current log configuration might be wasting space. It might be appropriate to drop one or more log groups to obtain a more efficient transaction log configuration.

When you create a new database, you configure the initial transaction log groups in a database. However, you can always add new groups to a database's transaction log using the Add Redo Logfile Group dialog box in Server Manager. To access this dialog box from the Administration Manager, select the Recovery drawer, click on the Redo Logs folder tab, then select Redo ➤ Add Logfile Group from the menu bar. Figure 11.1 shows the Add Redo Logfile Group dialog box.

FIGURE 11.1:

Use Server Manager's Add Redo Logfile Group dialog box to add one or more log groups to a database's transaction log.

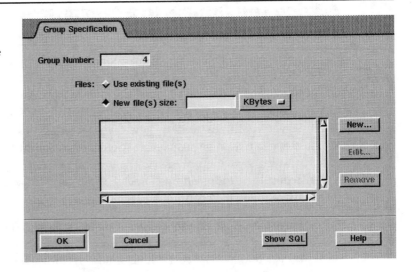

NOTE To use the Add Redo Logfile Group dialog box in Server Manager, you must have the ALTER DATABASE system privilege.

The Group Number entry field permits you to determine the number of the new log group in the database's transaction log. In most cases, it is best not to change the default group number that Server Manager picks for you when you open the Add Redo Logfile Group dialog box.

The Files radio button list allows you to specify the log members for the new group. These two options allow you to reuse existing operating system files (for example, old log files that are no longer members in a log group) or to create new files as members of the new log group. When you create a list of existing operating system files, all files must be the same size, and Oracle7 clears the blocks of the files when establishing the new log group. When you create a list of new filenames to use as members for the new log group, it is best to make the file sizes for all database log groups consistent; there is no advantage to having log groups of different sizes. If you do not want to specify a member size, do not check the box in front of the field. This way, Oracle7 uses the default file size for log members, which is machine-dependent.

The number of log groups you can create is limited by two different factors:

- The MAXLOGFILES parameter of the CREATE DATABASE command used to create a database limits the number of log groups that can be created for the database.

- The LOG_FILES initialization parameter limits the number of log groups that can be opened for the current instance. If LOG_FILES is less than MAXLOGFILES, the limit set by LOG_FILES is in effect; if LOG_FILES is greater than MAXLOGFILES, the limit set by MAXLOGFILES has precedence. It is atypical to set LOG_FILES below MAXLOGFILES.

> **NOTE**   Some UNIX systems limit the possible sizes of raw devices, so you might be forced to make different log groups with different file sizes.

Planning Log Group Member File Placement

Disk drives, like all other types of machinery, are not immune to Murphy's Law, which states that whatever can go wrong will go wrong. They die from old age, they occasionally lose bits of magnetic media, disk arms and controllers fail, and formats go awry. To insulate the Oracle7 transaction log from such potential disk failures, it is important to consider the placement of different log members within the log groups in a database's transaction log.

Using Multiple Members to Mirror Files

Oracle7 permits multiple members in the transaction log's groups so you can mirror the files in the transaction log; this protects the log from isolated disk failures, or single-points of failure. For example, assume that a log group has two members, one on disk A and another on disk B. When Oracle7 uses the log group, it writes to both members in parallel. If disk B crashes, Oracle7 can continue logging ongoing transactions without problems because the log member on disk A is still available. Figure 11.2 illustrates this example.

FIGURE 11.2:

A mirrored transaction log can protect an Oracle7 database system from single points of failure.

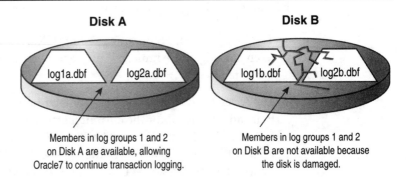

Members in log groups 1 and 2 on Disk A are available, allowing Oracle7 to continue transaction logging.

Members in log groups 1 and 2 on Disk B are not available because the disk is damaged.

The example illustrates the cardinal rule for configuring the members in a database's log groups: Wisely use the disk drives of the database server so log groups are protected from single points of failure. The more disk drives available to the database server, the more levels of mirroring you can create in a database's transaction log. However, don't get carried away; two to three levels of file mirroring are adequate for most systems.

Performance Considerations

Although protection of the transaction log is the primary consideration when configuring a database's transaction log groups and members, there are also performance considerations. If your database server has a handful of disk drives, there are file structure designs that can minimize disk I/O contention and eke out more performance for the database server:

- Place data files and log files on different disks whenever possible. This way, transaction logging, log archiving, and database reads and writes do not contend with each other for disk access time.

- If all log members throughout a database's transaction log are on different disks, transaction logging and log archiving never contend for the same files.

The degree to which you spread out different database files depends on the number of disks available to the database server. The more disks you are willing to buy, the greater the number of options available to your configuration and the greater the amount of database protection you can have.

> **WARNING** Never put a data file on the same disk that stores the archived log files or an unmirrored log group. If you do, you are vulnerable to a single point of failure and, thus, an unrecoverable situation.

Adding Log Members

When you add a new disk drive to a database server, you might want to use the new disk to add another protection layer for the transaction log by mirroring one or more log groups on the new disk with additional members. To add a new member to a database's transaction log group, you can use the Add Redo Logfile Member dialog box in Server Manager. To access this dialog box from the Administration Manager, select the Recovery drawer, click on the Redo Logs folder tab, and then select Redo ➤ Add Logfile Member from the menu bar. Figure 11.3 shows the Add Redo Logfile Member dialog box.

FIGURE 11.3:
Server Manager's Add Redo Logfile Member dialog box allows you to add members to a log group and thus increase the degree of mirroring in the group.

NOTE To use the Add Redo Logfile Member dialog box in Server Manager, you must have the ALTER DATABASE system privilege.

To add a new member to a log group, first decide if you want to use an existing operating system file or create a new file to serve as the log member. When you want to reuse an existing file, select the Use Existing File radio button and use the Find File button to locate the file on disk. When you want to create a new log file, select the New File radio button and enter the name for the new file in the Filename entry field. Finally, select the group to which you want to add the new log member from the Group list box. If you do not know which group number to select, see the DATA-BASEREPORT procedure (Listing 7.2 in Chapter 7) to help you decide.

NOTE The number of log members per group is limited by the setting for the MAXLOGFILES parameter of the CREATE DATABASE command used to create a database. If you try to add more members to a group than this limit allows, Oracle7 returns an error.

Dropping Log Members

Just as there are situations that justify adding new members to a log group, there are other situations that call for dropping one or more members from a group. For example, if a disk fails and it will not be replaced, you need to drop the log members on the disk to eliminate the constant error reporting that Oracle7 performs for the damaged file. To drop a log member from a group, you can use the Drop Logfile Member menu option in Server Manager. To access this menu option from the Administration Manager, select the Recovery drawer, and then click on the Redo Logs folder tab to display a list of all log members. After you select the log member that you want to drop from the folder display, select Redo ➤ Drop Logfile Member from the menu bar.

NOTE To drop a log member, you must have the ALTER DATABASE system privilege.

There are several considerations to keep in mind when dropping a log group member. First, Oracle7 does not allow you to drop the last member of a group; in effect, this would drop the group. Second, Oracle7 will not drop a log member if that member is in the currently active log group or a log group that has not yet been archived.

After you drop a log member from the database, the physical operating system file still exists on disk. To release the space the dropped log member occupies on disk, use your operating system to drop the corresponding file.

Dropping Log Groups

If you find that a database's transaction log has too many log groups and may be wasting space, you can drop one or more log groups to reduce the size of the transaction log. To drop a log group, you can use the Drop Logfile Group menu option in Server Manager. To access this menu option from the Administration Manager, select the Recovery drawer, and then click on the Redo Logs folder tab to display a list of all log members. After you select a log member that is member in the group that you want to drop, select Redo ➤ Drop Logfile Group from the menu bar.

NOTE To drop a log group, you must have the ALTER DATABASE system privilege.

Oracle7 will not allow you to drop a log group if it will leave the transaction log with fewer than two groups, if it is the current log group, or if the log group remains to be archived. As when dropping individual transaction log members, after you drop a log group from the database's transaction log, the physical operating system files still exist on disk. To release the space the dropped log members occupy on disk, use your operating system to drop the corresponding files.

Configuring Transaction Log Archiving

As described earlier in this chapter, Oracle7 cyclically writes to the groups in a database's transaction log, allowing it to continuously log transactions in a contained, fixed amount of disk space. The cyclical writing process to transaction log groups causes the information in each log group to be overwritten every time Oracle7 cycles through the log. Therefore, to preserve older transaction entries in a database's transaction log, Oracle7 automatically archives, or backs up, filled log groups after each log switch. Oracle7 notes whether a transaction log group has been archived before allowing itself to overwrite the log group's transaction entries.

Archiving log groups as they become filled creates what is called an *archived* or *offline transaction redo log*. A database's archived log consists of a sequence of backup files that correspond to the transaction log groups as they filled during database processing. Figure 11.4 illustrates a database's archived transaction log.

FIGURE 11.4:
The archived log of an Oracle7 database is a sequenced compilation of all the log groups as they filled throughout database processing.

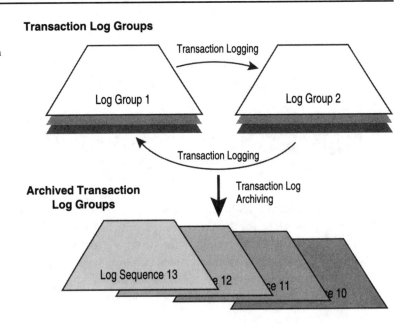

The archived log is the enabling component for complete database recovery from a media failure. For example, when a disk fails and causes the loss of a data file, the database administrator recovers the database by replacing the disk and then restoring the damaged data file from the most recent backup. However, at this point, the restored version of the data file is out of date—it is missing all the changes made since the last backup of the data file. Therefore, the next step in database recovery is application of the transaction log to the restored data file to recover the lost transactions. In most cases, recovery requires transaction entries in both the archived transaction log and the current log groups in the transaction log. See the section "Database Recovery" later in this chapter for more information.

The next few sections explain how to configure Oracle7 to archive transaction log groups as they fill.

Enabling and Disabling Media Recovery

When Oracle7 requires log groups to be archived before they can be reused, *media recovery* is enabled because Oracle7 can use backup data files, the archived transaction log, and the current transaction log groups to completely recover all committed transactions from a disk media failure. You also have the option of disabling media recovery. This means that Oracle7 does not archive the transaction log.

However, disabling media recovery is not a recommended mode of operation. No matter how good the configuration of a database's transaction log and backup strategy, the database is vulnerable to any type of disk failure. Therefore, after creating a database, make sure media recovery is enabled and always leave it this way. You can use the DATABASEREPORT procedure (Listing 7.2 in Chapter 7) to determine whether or not media recovery is enabled for a database.

> **NOTE**
> When media recovery is enabled for a database, the database is said to be running in ARCHIVELOG mode. When media recovery is disabled, the database is said to be running in NOARCHIVELOG mode. These clumsy terms come from the options of the ALTER DATABASE command that enable and disable media recovery for a database.

After you create a database, media recovery is disabled. For this reason, one of the first post-database creation steps is to enable media recovery. You can do so using the ARCHIVELOG option of the SQL command ALTER DATABASE, as shown here:

```
ALTER DATABASE ARCHIVELOG
```

Although you should almost never use it, the NOARCHIVELOG option of the ALTER DATABASE command disables media recovery:

```
ALTER DATABASE NOARCHIVELOG
```

NOTE To enable or disable media recovery using the ALTER DATABASE command, you must have the ALTER DATABASE system privilege, and the database must be mounted but not open. Therefore, this is one particular case where you need to use a different startup procedure—starting up an instance and mounting the database but not opening it.

Before enabling media recovery, you can save yourself a step by configuring the instance for automatic archiving of transaction log groups as they fill. The next section explains how to accomplish this.

Configuring a Database Server for Automatic Log Archiving

After you enable media recovery for a database, Oracle7 does not overwrite a filled transaction log group unless the group has been successfully archived. Consequently, the database server can hit a brick wall if the next group slated for writing in the transaction log has not been archived. In this situation, Oracle7 simply suspends all database operations until the log is freed as a result of being archived.

To make sure a database never hits the brick wall, you can configure an Oracle7 database instance to automatically archive log groups as they fill. The initialization parameters to consider are listed here:

Parameter	Description
LOG_ARCHIVE _START	Determines whether or not Oracle7 automatically archives transaction log groups as they fill. A setting of TRUE enables automatic archiving; a setting of FALSE disables automatic archiving. In most cases, set LOG_ARCHIVE_START to TRUE when media recovery is enabled. Otherwise, you must constantly monitor the transaction log and manually archive log files as they fill.
LOG_ARCHIVE _DEST	Determines the location in which Oracle7 creates the archived transaction log. In a few cases, Oracle7 running on some operating systems can archive log groups directly to tape, which means you can specify a tape drive for this parameter. However, many Oracle7 systems do not support direct tape archiving. Therefore, the setting for LOG_ARCHIVE _DEST should be a directory location on disk. After Oracle7 archives log groups to disk, you can use operating system commands or a special backup utility to compress and move the archived transaction log to offline tape storage, thus freeing up disk space in the archive log location.

Parameter	Description
LOG_ARCHIVE _FORMAT	Determines the filename format of the files in the archived transaction log. In most cases, it is not necessary to specifically set this parameter; the default value clearly indicates the sequence numbers of the log groups in the filenames. If you want to set this parameter yourself, be sure to decide on a filename format and then stick with it for the life of the database. With this kind of foresight you can make a complicated administrative operation, database recovery, a little bit easier.

The following example is an excerpt from an initialization parameter file for a database using Oracle7 on a UNIX platform. The example shows how to set two of the three parameters listed above (the LOG_ARCHIVE_FORMAT parameter uses the default value, as recommended):

```
LOG_ARCHIVE_START=TRUE
LOG_ARCHIVE_DEST=/usr/oracle/dbs/arch
```

If your version of Oracle7 does not support direct archiving of log groups to tape, at first you might consider this a problem—another thing to deal with when administering an Oracle7 database system. However, you can also look at this as a positive. That's because you can save offline tape storage space by using operating system commands or a backup utility to compress the archived log before copying it to tape. To make the tape storage of the archived log convenient, integrate the compression and backup commands into the automated backup process you use for the computer that runs Oracle7.

Monitoring the Transaction Log

After configuring a database's transaction log, be sure to monitor it while the database is running in normal operation to see how it is serving database processing.

Assuming that the transaction log is mirrored, media recovery is enabled, and automatic archiving is enabled, it's important to monitor that the current structure of the transaction log is not adversely affecting the performance of the database server. For example, if transaction log groups are too small or there are not enough transaction log groups, Oracle7 might need to wait for a transaction log group to be archived before it can continue transaction logging. Consequently, database users may need to wait until Oracle7 catches up with the necessary log archiving.

The easiest way to get some valuable information about a database's transaction log is to take a look at the Redo Logs folder display in Server Manager. To access this display from the Administration Manager, select the Recovery drawer, and then click on the Redo Logs folder tab to display the most important information about the log members in the database's transaction log. Figure 11.5 shows the Redo Logs folder display in Server Manager.

FIGURE 11.5:

Server Manager's Redo Logs folder display shows valuable information about the log members in an Oracle database.

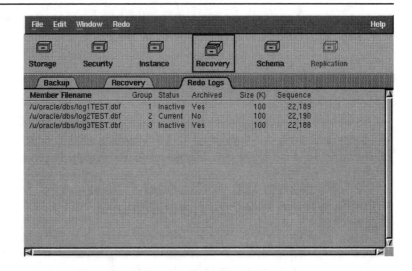

Notice that the Redo Logs folder display lists lots of information about the groups and members in the transaction log. For example, you can quickly see which log groups are inactive but remain to be archived. If ongoing transaction logging fills all log groups before Oracle7 can finish archiving one, users will need to wait until archiving of a log group is finished. This situation might warrant a change to the transaction log's structure, such as an additional log group.

Database Backup

The same types of disk failures that can damage a database's transaction log can also damage other types of database files, including the database's data files, control file, and initialization parameter files. Oracle7 does not contain file-mirroring and/or automated-backup features for any database files other than the files in the transaction log. Therefore, as a database administrator, it is crucial to develop a sound backup strategy to protect a database's files from disk failures.

Considering Oracle7's configuration options, there are many acceptable ways to back up a database. For example, if a database runs with media recovery enabled, you can back up data files when the database is open or when it is closed; you can back up all of the data files or just some of them; you can back up a database's control file when you back up data files; or you can do it whenever you please. As you can see, planning an Oracle7 database backup strategy can quickly become confusing.

The next sections explains the two basic approaches most administrators use to back up an Oracle7 database system:

- Online database backups
- Offline database backups

Both database backup methods consider backups of a database's data files, control files, and initialization parameter files.

Backing Up a Closed Database: Offline Database Backups

One way to back up a database is to shut down the database before backing up its files. This type of database backup is called an *offline database backup*. Follow these steps to complete an offline database backup:

1. Shut down the current instance of the database, if necessary. When shutting down a database in preparation for an offline database backup, make sure you use the Normal or Immediate option in the Server Manager Shutdown

Database dialog box. Furthermore, make sure the database shutdown completes normally. If you need to abort an instance to complete database shutdown, reopen and shut down the database to make sure the database closes normally before backup.

2. Back up the database's data files, control file, and initialization parameter file using operating system commands or a backup utility.

3. You can also back up a database's transaction log when the database is closed. However, backups of the transaction log files are useful only if media recovery is disabled for the database. Otherwise, skip backing up the database's transaction log.

4. After completing all file backups, start up the database to make it available for application use.

After you have completed an offline database backup, you are left with a complete set of the files that make up the database with respect to an instant in time (when the database was shut down). Fittingly, some call an offline database backup a *consistent database backup*.

NOTE Offline database backups are the only option available to databases with media recovery disabled. If media recovery is disabled, offline database backups must always include backups of the database's transaction log.

Backing Up an Open Database: Online Database Backups

Many database systems cannot afford to frequently shut down a database to make backups. For example, Oracle7 might support a mission-critical application that needs to run 24 hours a day. In this type of situation, an *online database backup* is necessary—a backup taken while the database is open and in use.

> **NOTE** Only databases that operate with media recovery enabled can make online database backups.

Online database backups are a bit more involved than offline backups. Here is a quick list of the necessary steps:

1. Back up the data files of each tablespace, one tablespace at a time.

2. Back up the database's control file.

3. Back up the database's initialization parameter files.

The next few sections explain how to complete each of these steps.

Backing Up Data Files of an Open Database

To back up the data files of an online database, you should back up the data files in each tablespace, one tablespace at a time. To identify each tablespace, its availability status (online or offline), and the corresponding data files, use the DATABASEREPORT procedure given in Listing 7.2 in Chapter 7.

If there are any offline tablespaces in the online database, back up the corresponding data files first. To back up the data files of an offline tablespace, use operating system commands or a backup utility that compresses and then safely backs up the data files to offline storage.

To back up the data files of an online tablespace, you must first mark the online tablespace for backup using the Start Online Backup menu option in Server Manager. To access this menu option from the Administration Manager, select the Recovery drawer, and then click on the Backup drawer to display a list of the database's tablespaces. After you select an online tablespace to back up from the folder list, select Backup ➤ Start Online Backup.

NOTE To use the Start and End Online Backup menu options in Server Manager, you must have the ALTER TABLESPACE or MANAGE TABLESPACE system privilege.

After you mark an online tablespace for back up, use operating system commands or a backup utility to compress and back up the data files in the tablespace. When data file backup is complete, remove the online tablespace from backup mode using the End Online Backup menu option in Server Manager. To access this menu option from the Administration Manager, select the Recovery drawer, and then click on the Backup drawer to display a list of the database's tablespaces. After you select the online tablespace that is in backup mode from the folder list, select Backup ➤ End Online Backup.

WARNING The first and final steps in making an online tablespace backup are extremely important. If an online tablespace is not marked for backup before taking data file backups, the backups are useless. If an online tablespace is not removed from backup mode after data file backup is complete, the database can become damaged if the server runs for several days with this condition, and the server crashes.

Backing Up the Control File of an Open Database

To back up the control file of an online database, use the BACKUP CONTROLFILE option of the ALTER DATABASE command. For example, this statement backs up a database's control file on a UNIX system:

```
ALTER DATABASE
   BACKUP CONTROLFILE TO '/dbbackup/ctrlsalesbkup.ctl'
```

NOTE To use the ALTER DATABASE command to back up a database's control file, you must have the ALTER DATABASE system privilege.

Backing Up the Initialization Parameter Files of an Open Database

Initialization parameter files are not actively used during database processing. The only time Oracle7 uses a database's initialization parameter file is during database startup. Therefore, to back up the initialization parameter files of an online database, use operating system commands or a backup utility.

Other Files to Consider When Backing Up a Database

Even though they are not part of an Oracle7 database, other files on the database server related to Oracle7 are important to back up. For example, consider backing up the following types of files when making a database backup:

- Application-specific files such as executables, source code, configuration files, and so on

- The configuration files for Oracle SQL*Net, including TNSNAMES.ORA, LISTENER.ORA, and so on

- Any special command script files that administrators and other types of users have created

Documenting Database Backups

It is a good idea to keep some type of documentation with each database backup. Simple things like the date of the backup, the database name, and so on can make finding the right backup easier when the pressure is on because of a database failure. Also note the highest log sequence number in the transaction log. You can do this before shutdown using the DATABASEREPORT procedure given in Listing 7.2. If you know the current log sequence number that corresponds to a database backup, you will know which archived transaction log groups to restore if recovery from a disk failure is necessary using the backup.

Automating Database Backups

As the preceding sections demonstrate, performing a database backup includes several steps, some of which are extremely important. Given this and the fact that database backups are one of the most frequently performed database administration operations, most Oracle7 administrators integrate database backup into a system backup procedure or write command scripts to automate the database backup process.

Listing 11.1 shows one command script a database administrator could run from within a Server Manager (line mode version only) to perform an online database backup of a simple database and its supporting files running on Oracle7 for a UNIX system.

Listing 11.1: A Script that Performs an Online Database Backup

```
-- This is a command script to perform an online
-- backup of the SALES database. Before running
-- this script, use line mode Server Manager to
-- connect to the database with an account
-- that has the following system privileges:
-- ALTER DATABASE, MANAGE TABLESPACE.
-- In addition, the person running the script must
-- have the file permissions for the specified files
-- and directories.

-- clear any old backup files in the backup directory
host rm /dbbackup/*

-- back up SYSTEM tablespace
ALTER TABLESPACE system BEGIN BACKUP;
host cp $ORACLE_HOME/dbs/systsales.dbf /dbbackup/systsales.dbf
ALTER TABLESPACE system END BACKUP;

-- back up RBS tablespace
ALTER TABLESPACE rbs BEGIN BACKUP;
host cp $ORACLE_HOME/dbs/rbssales.dbf /dbbackup/rbssales.dbf
ALTER TABLESPACE rbs END BACKUP;

-- back up TEMP tablespace
ALTER TABLESPACE temp BEGIN BACKUP;
```

```
host cp $ORACLE_HOME/dbs/tempsales.dbf /dbbackup/tempsales.dbf
TABLESPACE temp END BACKUP;

-- back up TOOLS tablespace
ALTER TABLESPACE tools BEGIN BACKUP;
host cp $ORACLE_HOME/dbs/toolsales.dbf /dbbackup/toolsales.dbf
ALTER TABLESPACE tools END BACKUP;

-- back up USERS tablespace
ALTER TABLESPACE users BEGIN BACKUP;
host cp $ORACLE_HOME/dbs/usrsales.dbf /dbbackup/usrsales.dbf
ALTER TABLESPACE users END BACKUP;

-- back up the database's control file
ALTER DATABASE BACKUP CONTROLFILE TO '/dbbackup/ctrlsales.ctl'

-- back up the database's initialization parameter files
host cp $ORACLE_HOME/dbs/*.ora /dbbackup
-- back up the SQL*Net V2 configuration files on the server
host cp /etc/*.ora /dbbackup

-- back up the special admin scripts
host cp $ORACLE_HOME/rdbms/admin/~*.sql /dbbackup

-- archive and compress the files in the backup directory
host tar -cvf /dbbackup/dbbackup.tar /dbbackup/*
host compress /dbbackup/dbbackup.tar

-- clear all temporary backup files from the backup directory,
-- except the compressed backup file
host rm /dbbackup/*.dbf
host rm /dbbackup/*.ctl
host rm /dbbackup/*.ora
host rm /dbbackup/*.sql
```

Scripts are a simple way of automating the backup process. There are other more complicated but powerful approaches to automating the database backup process. For example, you can create a Pro*C program that interactively queries and records the names of all database files and then uses menus to interactively guide and customize a database backup. You can also use operating system facilities, such as UNIX's *cron*, to automatically execute a shell script that performs a database backup at a specified interval. The possibilities for automated database backup are limited only by your imagination. Whatever method you choose, be sure to automate the Oracle7 database backup process somehow to make it easy and more reliable.

Planning a Database Backup Strategy

Now that you understand how to back up an Oracle7 database, the remaining questions are:

- When should you make database backups?

- How often should you make database backups?

- How long should you keep older database backups?

Like many other administrative operations, database backup strategies vary with each database and installation, depending on things like transaction throughput and database size. However, there are a few standard rules every backup strategy should follow:

- Back up a database frequently. The longer you wait between database backups, the longer it will take to complete a database recovery process. That's because more transaction log groups must be applied to older versions of data files during the roll-forward recovery process.

- Back up a database regularly. No matter whether you back up the database nightly, every other day, or once a week, you are more likely to not forget about or put off database backup if your backup strategy is executed on a regular basis.

- Back up a database after making structural modifications. For example, if you add a new tablespace or data file to the database, alter your backup script to address the new tablespace, and then back up the database that day so the most recent database backup includes the new data files added to the database. It is important to back up a database after database creation, after creating or dropping a tablespace, after adding or renaming data files, and after modifying the configuration of the database's transaction log.

- Hold onto at least the two most recent database backups. This simple rule reduces the likelihood that you will be left empty-handed if the most recent database backup has some sort of problem.

Testing Database Backups to Ensure Success

Imagine the horror when you lose a disk and attempt a database recovery, only to find that for weeks your tape drive has been working incorrectly and your most recent database backups are useless. What do you do now? Situations like these can easily be avoided if you perform regular test database recoveries to guarantee the soundness of a database backup strategy and all of the involved hardware components.

To test a database backup strategy, pick a time when you can shut down the database system for an extended period of time (perhaps on a weekend or overnight). First, copy all of the production database's files (data files, transaction log files, and control file) to a temporary backup location using operating system commands, and verify that the file copies are intact and valid. This step is important to protect the production database in case your database backups have a problem. Next, restore the database from your most recent backup. After restoring the database, perform a database recovery to see if everything works okay.

If everything goes well, you can sleep better at night knowing that your database is safe and sound. And you will now be experienced at performing database recovery, so surprises will be less likely when the heat is on during a real database failure situation.

If database recovery does not succeed, it's time to play Sherlock Holmes to determine what is going wrong. After you correct the problem, test a database recovery again and make sure you fixed what you thought you did.

Verifying the Integrity of Backup Files

In rare circumstances, the physical integrity of an Oracle7 database can be compromised by corrupted data blocks in one or more data files. It's often difficult to pinpoint why such problems occur, but common sources are faulty disk media and inevitable software bugs. To investigate the physical integrity of an Oracle7 database's data files, you can use the DBVERIFY utility. DBVERIFY can verify both data files and data file backups.

The DBVERIFY utility is a simple command-line utility that accepts a few parameters to control its behavior. For example, the following DBVERIFY command verifies the physical integrity of a backup data file:

```
DBVERIFY FILE =  '/dbbackup/systsales.dbf'
```

By default, the DBVERIFY utility prints its log to the terminal from which you execute it. If the output from a DBVERIFY command identifies any integrity errors on the current data files of an Oracle database, contact Oracle Corporation's technical support staff for aid in correcting your problem. When DBVERIFY identifies integrity errors in a data file backup, the backup media, rather than the data file itself, might be faulty. Immediately make a new data file backup and reverify the data file.

Mirroring Data Files Using Hardware Mirroring

File mirroring is especially important for database systems that require high availability—those that cannot afford to tolerate even a few seconds of downtime resulting from hardware-related problems. The mirroring capability of Oracle7's transaction log is an important feature for high-availability systems because the database system can continue to operate without interruption, even when an isolated disk failure damages members in the transaction log.

Unfortunately, Oracle7 does not also support file mirroring for its data files. Does this mean that Oracle7 is not available when a disk crash occurs? Not necessarily. In most cases, when a disk failure causes the loss of a data file, the Oracle7 database system continues to operate. However, the data in the damaged data file is unavailable to users, while the intact data files remain open for use. If Oracle7 supported software file mirroring of a database's data files, the entire set of data files would continue to remain available, even when an isolated disk failure occurs, just as with the transaction log.

> **NOTE**
>
> The only time an Oracle7 database must go offline because of a damaged data file is when the damaged data file is part of the SYSTEM tablespace. That's because the data files of the SYSTEM tablespace store the database's data dictionary information, which is absolutely necessary for Oracle7 to operate.

For sites that require the high level of availability assurance that file mirroring delivers, there is a solution: *hardware disk mirroring*. Disk mirroring can provide the same level of fault tolerance as software file mirroring, but by redundantly writing all files on an entire disk instead of just selected files. And hardware disk mirroring is more efficient than software mirroring because of the way disk arms on mirrored disks move together. You need to buy special hardware and install it, but disk mirroring is well worth the trouble if you need the extra fault tolerance it provides.

Database Recovery

System and database backup are jobs administrators must perform frequently, but with luck, an administrator will never need to perform database recovery for real. It is stressful when something goes wrong and the productivity of many workers depends solely on how quickly system and/or database administrators can recover the damaged system.

The following sections explain how Oracle7 can recover from different types of failures.

Database Recovery Basics

Before you can perform a database recovery, it is best to know something about the recovery process so you can understand what is going on and make intelligent decisions when you need to. Figure 11.6 illustrates Oracle7 database recovery.

Figure 11.6 shows the key process in database recovery, which is called *roll-forward recovery*. During roll-forward recovery, the transaction log is applied to the database's data files to redo all changes that have been lost because of a failure. All types of database recovery include this essential step for restoring lost work.

FIGURE 11.6:

The roll-forward phase of database recovery applies changes made by transactions to data files.

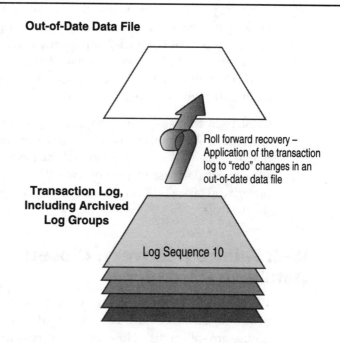

Out-of-Date Data File

Roll forward recovery –
Application of the transaction log to "redo" changes in an out-of-date data file

Transaction Log, Including Archived Log Groups

Log Sequence 10

The next few sections explain the two most basic types of failures and their respective database-recovery procedures.

Crash Recovery

At any given time, a multi-user Oracle7 database server is processing the transactions of many different application users. But suppose the power unexpectedly goes out. Transactions in process are left in limbo, and some committed data in shared memory may not yet have been written to the database's data files. How are you going to recover the database from this mess?

This type of failure is appropriately called a *system crash* or *instance failure*. Building on this terminology, database recovery from a system crash is called *crash recovery*. As bad as it might seem, database recovery from a crash is simple because no one needs to do anything; Oracle7 does all the work for you.

After the power is back on and the computer used for the database server is running again, Oracle7 automatically performs crash recovery during the next database startup. That is, Oracle7 applies any necessary changes in the transaction log to the intact data files, thereby rolling them forward and recovering all committed work. Once the database is open, users can employ an application to connect normally and begin working.

Crash recovery transparently happens during the database startup that occurs after any type of abnormal database shutdown, including power failures and aborting a database instance. After an abnormal database shutdown occurs, don't worry if the subsequent database startup operation takes a little longer than normal to complete; it can take a little time for Oracle7 to complete crash recovery before opening the database.

Disk Failure Recovery: Closed Database Recovery

With Oracle7, all of the necessary components to complete crash recovery are in place—no data files have been damaged and all of the necessary transaction log groups are still on disk. However, recovery of lost work from a disk failure is not as easy. *Disk failure recovery*, sometimes called media recovery, requires help from the database administrator and includes steps:

1. Repair any hardware problems (for example, replace a damaged disk).

2. Using the most recent database backup, restore any lost or damaged files.

3. Restore any necessary archived transaction log groups on tape to a disk location.

4. Establish a privileged administrative connection to Oracle7 using Server Manager.

5. Start up an instance and mount the database; do not open the database.

6. Start the database recovery process from a Server Manager SQL worksheet.

7. Clean up when database recovery is successful.

How do you know for sure when you have a problem that requires disk failure recovery? For one, Server Manager will alert you to database file problems when you attempt to start up and open a database. For example, Figure 11.7 shows an alert message indicating a problem with a particular data file.

Server Manager warns you when a database requires disk-failure recovery.

> MGR-02163: an error occurred while executing a menu action
> ORA-01113: file 3 needs media recovery
> ORA-01110: data file 3: '/u/oracle/dbs/tempTEST.dbf'
>
> OK

The next few sections explain more about each of the steps necessary to recover a damaged database.

> **NOTE** The following sections explain how to recover from a disk failure with the database closed. As a result, some refer to the following procedure as *closed database recovery*.

Repairing Hardware Problems

If you need to perform disk-failure recovery, the root of the problem is obviously the first thing to fix. If a disk fails, you can fix it, reformat it, or replace it—whatever it takes to get the disk back in operation. After you fix the disk problem, the next step is to regenerate the original file directory structure. One way to do this is by using the most recent system backup.

Restoring Any Damaged Files

If you fix or replace a damaged disk to get up and running, the restoration process is fairly simple: Restore all the database files that were lost because of the disk failure, including data files, transaction log files, copies of the database control file, and any initialization parameter files. What source should you use to restore the different types of files? Depending on the type of file, the answer is different:

- Restore all damaged data files from the most recent database backup. If you are not absolutely sure which data files are damaged, use the information displayed by Server Manager alerts (see Figure 11.7) to assemble a list of damaged data files. Be sure to restore the files to their original location if at all possible.

- If you are following the recommendations put forth in this book, the database's transaction log and control file are mirrored. Therefore, you can restore a damaged member in the transaction log or a copy of the database control file by copying an intact version of the file.

- If you lost any other files, such as initialization parameter files or SQL*Net configuration files, restore them from the most recent database backup.

NOTE   If you unwisely chose to not mirror a database's transaction log or control file, or even worse, to run a database with media recovery disabled, the database recovery process is the simple restoration of *all* (intact and damaged) database files from the most recent database backup. This means, however, that all work performed since the most recent backup is lost.

Extracting Necessary Archived Log Groups from Tape Archives

If you have good notes with each database backup, you have a good idea which archived transaction log groups the database-recovery process will need. If you restore the necessary archived transaction log groups before beginning the database-recovery process, database recovery is literally automatic. The only trick is to restore all archived transaction log groups to the location specified by the LOG_ARCHIVE _DEST initialization parameter.

If you do not know which archived transaction log groups will be necessary for the database recovery, don't worry—the Oracle7 recovery procedure will prompt for archived transaction log groups that it cannot find, by log sequence number. Using another operating system session, you can restore necessary archived transaction logs after database recovery begins.

Commencing Database Recovery

After completing all of the preparatory steps, it is time to start the actual database recovery process. As with database backup, there are several options available for database recovery. To avoid confusion, this section sticks to an approach that will work for almost every type of database recovery. (For more advanced recovery operations, see the section "Advanced Types of Database Recovery" later in this chapter.)

If you have restored all damaged files to their original locations and you have already restored all the necessary archived transaction log groups to the location pointed to by LOG_ARCHIVE_DEST, database recovery is easy. After establishing a privileged administrative connection using Server Manager, start up the database, mount it, but do not open it. Next, open a SQL worksheet and use the special Server Manager RECOVER command to recover the closed database:

```
RECOVER
```

A simple RECOVER statement without any of the command's many options indicates to Oracle7 that the server can expect to find all of the necessary archived transaction log groups in LOG_ARCHIVE_DEST, so the server can suggest and apply the transaction log without prompting for log files.

NOTE If you did not restore archived transaction log files to the location specified by LOG_ARCHIVE_DEST, Server Manager prompts for log files, one at a time, by their log sequence number. When prompted, specify the complete filename or use the Find File button to locate the requested log file.

Database recovery can take a little time to complete as Oracle7 applies the transaction log to the restored data files. If you suspect that database recovery will take an extraordinary amount of time to complete because there are many archived log groups to apply, you can speed the recovery operation by recovering different data files in parallel. See the section "Configuring a Database for Parallel Recovery" later in this chapter for more information.

After database recovery is complete, the recovered database now contains all committed work that happened before the disk failure. Next, you must open the database so that users can again connect to the server and accomplish work. From the Administration Manager in Server Manager, you can open a closed but mounted database using the Open menu option. To access this menu option, select the Instance drawer, open the Database folder tab, and then select Instance ➤ Open from the menu bar.

Cleaning Up after Database Recovery

When database recovery is complete, you can have many archived transaction log groups somewhere on disk that you will not need to use again unless another disk failure occurs in the near future. Therefore, to free some disk space on the database server, use operating system commands to remove the files from disk. However, before doing so, make sure you are not erasing your only copies of these important files—you never know when another disk failure will occur that requires these older log groups to complete database recovery from a disk failure.

Advanced Types of Database Recovery

The preceding sections have offered a simple approach to recovering an Oracle7 database damaged from a disk failure. However, there are other situations where you can benefit from knowing some of the more advanced database-recovery operations Oracle7 supports. The following sections briefly explain two different types of advanced Oracle7 database recovery features: parallel recovery and online database recovery.

Configuring a Database for Parallel Recovery

Recovery of a database system can never happen too quickly. When a database system is not available because of a failure, users cannot run applications and be productive workers. Depending on the type of business the database supports, this can translate to lots of lost revenue.

To speed the database recovery process, releases 7.1, 7.2, and 7.3 of Oracle7 allow you to configure an instance for *parallel recovery*. When you start database recovery and an instance is configured for parallel recovery, Oracle7 automatically starts multiple recovery processes at the same time. Multiple data files undergo the roll-forward recovery at the same time, which dramatically reduces the time necessary to recover the database. Figure 11.8 illustrates parallel database recovery.

FIGURE 11.8:

The database recovery process is quicker with parallel recovery.

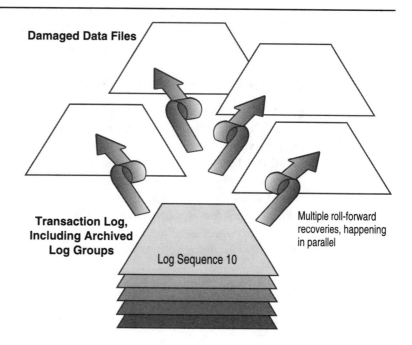

Damaged Data Files

Transaction Log, Including Archived Log Groups

Log Sequence 10

Multiple roll-forward recoveries, happening in parallel

The easiest way to configure an instance for parallel database recovery is to set a initialization parameter, RECOVERY_PARALLELISM. This parameter determines the number of operating system processes Oracle7 uses when performing database recovery from instance or disk failure. Set this parameter to the number of disks the database server uses to store the different data files for the database but no more than two times the number of CPUS in the system. For example, assume that a database server uses five disks to store the different data files of a database. Here is an excerpt from the database's initialization parameter file:

```
        .
        .
        .
RECOVERY_PARALLELISM=5
        .
        .
        .
```

When you start database recovery, Oracle7 automatically uses the value for the RECOVERY_PARALLELISM initialization parameter to start multiple recovery processes and make the roll-forward recovery process happen more quickly.

Online Database Recovery

Money is time, and downtime is lost money. Therefore, Oracle7 supports *online database recovery* to help reduce or eliminate lost productivity caused by localized failures. Online database recovery is the recovery of damaged tablespaces or data files in an online database. For example, assume that only the data files of a single tablespace are damaged in a disk failure. In this case, Oracle7 can continue running uninterrupted while the damaged tablespace is offline and being recovered. Of course, as with all offline tablespaces, the data in the damaged tablespace is not available until the recovery process completes and you bring the recovered tablespace back online. Similarly, you can perform online recovery for individual data files that are damaged.

Two conditions are necessary for online database recovery:

- The database must be running with media recovery enabled.

- All data files of the SYSTEM tablespace must be intact.

NOTE If you follow the configuration guidelines in this book and place all rollback segments in their own tablespace, the preceding condition list is complete. However, if you have one or more online rollback segments in a damaged, offline tablespace, you should also take the rollback segments offline before attempting online database recovery of the tablespace. This extra step ensures that transactions will not attempt to use the rollback segment(s) in the damaged tablespace during recovery operations.

If your situation meets these conditions, online database recovery is one possibility for solving your problem. Here are the steps for achieving online database recovery from the loss of one or more data files:

1. Identify the damaged tablespaces and take them offline.

2. Repair any hardware problems. (For example, replace a damaged disk.)

3. Using the most recent database backup, restore any lost or damaged files.

4. Restore any necessary archived transaction log groups on tape to a disk location.

5. Establish a privileged administrative connection to Oracle7 using Server Manager.

6. Start the database-recovery process from a Server Manager SQL worksheet.

7. Clean up when database recovery is successful.

Steps 1 through 5 and step 7 in this procedure should be familiar to you by now; they were discussed in earlier sections of this book.

If you have restored all damaged files to their original locations and you have already restored all the necessary archived transaction log groups to the location pointed to by LOG_ARCHIVE_DEST, establish a privileged administrative connection to Oracle7 from a Server Manager SQL worksheet. Then you can begin online database recovery using a RECOVER command.

```
RECOVER TABLESPACE tablespace_name ...

RECOVER DATAFILE data_file_name ...
```

The first statement above shows how to use the TABLESPACE option of the RECOVER command to recover all data files in a tablespace, in which case Oracle7 automatically applies the transaction log to any damaged data files in the offline tablespace. The second statement above shows how to use the DATAFILE option of the RECOVER command to recover only a specific data file of an offline tablespace. In any case, if you configure Oracle7 for parallel recovery, Oracle7 automatically starts a number of multiple recovery processes, as determined by the RECOVERY_PARALLELISM initialization parameter, to carry out the online database recovery more quickly. After recovery is complete, you can bring the offline tablespace back online so it is available for normal application processing.

Configuring a Standby Database for High Availability

Companies or institutions that "bet their business" on client/server database systems often have extreme high-availability requirements that dictate very short periods of downtime for recovery from any problem situation. Additionally, such environments often require database server configurations that provide for quick recovery from even the most damaging of failure situations, such as a complete site disaster, natural or otherwise (for example, fires, earthquakes, and floods). Fortunately, Oracle7 can address the needs of sites with extreme high-availability requirements with its standby database feature. Figure 11.9 illustrates an Oracle7 standby database architecture.

Available only with release 7.3 of Oracle7, a *standby database* is an offline database that exactly mirrors its *primary database* that is online and in use with applications. To protect the database's availability from site disasters, the primary database and standby database must operate on physically different machines at physically different locations. Both databases must operate with media recovery enabled. As the primary database archives filled log groups, a mechanism must transfer the logs and apply them to the offline standby database. By doing so, this keeps the standby database current with the changes that have been made to the primary database. If a disaster happens that will make the primary database unavailable for an unacceptable period of time, you can activate the standby database and bring it online to support applications.

FIGURE 11.9:

A remote standby database protects the work done to its primary database.

Primary Database

Open and in Use
by Applications

**Archived
Log Groups**

Standby Database

Transfer of
Archived Log Groups

Closed and in Standby
Recovery Mode

NOTE To a large degree, the different servers that manage the primary and standby databases must match. For example, each server must use identical versions of the server operating system and Oracle7. Although Oracle can support standby database configurations that use server computers with different but similar hardware configurations, such variations can create problems.

The following sections explain how to create, manage, and use a standby database.

Creating a Standby Database

To create a standby database, you need to perform the following steps at the primary database:

1. Back up all data files of the primary database.

2. Create a standby database control file.

3. Force a log switch and archive the current log groups of the primary database.

4. Transfer the files created in steps 1 through 3 to the remote standby database site.

> **NOTE** You can perform steps 1, 2, and 3 with the primary database open or closed.

Earlier sections of this chapter explain how to back up the data files of an Oracle7 database. Make sure to create backups of all the database's data files, including those data files that are in offline tablespaces.

To create a standby database control file, you must use the SQL command ALTER DATABASE with the special CREATE STANDBY CONTROLFILE clause. For example, from a Server Manager SQL worksheet that's connected to the primary database server, you might issue the following statement to create a standby database control file:

```
ALTER DATABASE
   CREATE STANDBY CONTROLFILE AS 'filename'
```

To force a log switch and archive the current log group of the primary database, you can use the SQL command ALTER SYSTEM with the ARCHIVE LOG CURRENT option:

```
ALTER SYSTEM
   ARCHIVE LOG CURRENT
```

After collecting the backup data files, standby database control file, and archived log files, you must transfer them to the remote database site. For example, if a network connects the primary and standby database sites, you might copy the files using a file-transfer mechanism (for example, FTP with TCP/IP networks).

TIP   To make the configuration of the standby database painless, make sure to mirror the file directory structure of the primary database when you create the standby database. This recommendation includes the mirrored structure of the database's transaction log groups and control file. Otherwise, you'll need to use a lot of ALTER DATABASE ... RENAME FILE statements to identify the different file layout of the standby database.

Besides transferring the database files that form the standby database, you'll also want to collect and transfer many other supporting files from the primary database site to the standby database site. For example, you might want to include initialization parameter files, important command scripts, and application-specific files.

Managing the Standby Database

After the structure of a standby database is in place, you can put the database into standby mode by performing the following steps:

1. Mount the standby database to an instance.

2. Place the mounted standby database in standby-recovery mode.

A special series of steps is necessary to start a new instance and mount the standby database. To start up a new instance for the standby database, you can use the Startup Database dialog box in Server Manager. Make sure to select the Nomount button from the Startup Mode radio button list. Next, you can use a Server Manager SQL worksheet to issue an ALTER DATABASE command that will mount the standby database to the new instance:

```
ALTER DATABASE
  MOUNT STANDBY DATABASE
```

After you mount the standby database, you can then place the standby database into standby-recovery mode using the Server Manager RECOVER command:

```
RECOVER STANDBY DATABASE
```

When the standby database is in standby-recover mode, its server constantly works to apply archived log files to the standby database that you supply it from the primary database.

Moving Logs from the Primary Database to the Standby Database

One goal of using a standby database system is to bring the database back online as soon as possible after a site disaster. Therefore, you must strive to keep the standby database as current as possible with the primary database. The easiest and most reliable method of accomplishing this task is to put in place an automated mechanism that frequently checks for newly archived log groups at the primary database site. When these groups are found, the mechanism must quickly transfer the archived log groups to the standby database site and apply them in a timely fashion. Unfortunately, Oracle7 itself has no such mechanism to support standby database configurations. Depending on your environment, you might choose to use operating system facilities, such as the UNIX cron facility, that can schedule the execution of shell scripts to do the work for you.

Configuring Log Groups with Sudden Disasters in Mind

It is the goal of any database recovery to lose absolutely no work as a result of a problem that damages the database. However, when a sudden catastrophic failure destroys a primary database site, there most likely will be some amount of work that cannot be recovered—the work of committed transactions that is present in the current log group at the time the disaster suddenly destroys the primary database site. In fact, the work in the primary database's current log group is always vulnerable to a sudden site disaster until a log switch occurs, Oracle7 archives the log group, and transfers the archived log group to the remote standby database.

In light of Oracle7's transaction-logging mechanism and standby database architecture, it is important to consider the size of the log groups in a database's transaction log. You can use the size of the log groups in a transaction log to help you limit the amount of lost work after a sudden site disaster. For example, compare how much work would be lost in a sudden site disaster if a database's transaction log has ten log groups with each group's member size at 200K versus a transaction log that has two groups with each group's member size at 1M. If the site disaster happens just before completely filling the current log group, the first configuration loses just under 200K worth of work; the latter configuration loses just under 1M worth of work.

Activating a Standby Database

Hopefully, a catastrophe never strikes your world. However, if a disaster makes your primary database site unavailable, it's time to consider switching activity from the primary database site to the standby database site. This section explains the steps necessary to move activity from the primary database to the standby database:

1. If possible, archive the current log group of the primary database.
2. If possible, transfer all archived log groups to the standby database.
3. Apply all available archived logs to the standby database.
4. Activate the standby database and open it for application use.

Before taking the leap to activate a standby database, it's important to capture as much work as possible that has been done with the primary database. If possible, archive the current log group of the primary database (see the previous section that explains this operation). Next, transfer all archived log groups from the primary database that have not been moved and applied to the standby database site.

After you are absolutely sure that you have applied all available archived logs to the standby database, you can activate the standby database using the SQL command ALTER DATABASE:

```
ALTER DATABASE
   ACTIVATE STANDBY DATABASE

ALTER DATABASE OPEN
```

After you activate a standby database, it essentially becomes the primary database.

> **WARNING** After you activate a standby database, you can no longer apply archived log groups that originate from the primary database. Therefore, make sure that you apply all available primary database archived logs to the standby database before activating the standby database.

Redirecting Applications to the Standby Database

When you use a standby database configuration, you must plan for a switchover in the event of a failure. For one thing, applications that normally connect to the original primary database site must now be able to connect to the new primary database. To account for a possible database switchover, configure the system's SQL*Net network to include both the primary and standby databases. This way, application users can simply specify the new database connect string at application startup.

Testing, Testing, and More Testing

Just as with Oracle7's database backup and recovery mechanisms, it's very important to test an Oracle7 standby database configuration to make sure that it will work as planned. Given the complexity of configuring and maintaining a standby database architecture, you'll most certainly want to put together a test primary/standby database system that allows you to become familiar with creating, managing, and switching over to the standby database. Such testing will no doubt uncover flaws that you would not want to discover when a real tragedy strikes your production database system.

This chapter has described the key features in Oracle7 that permit the database administrator to protect and recover a database from all types of failures that can damage a database. The chapter has covered the following topics:

- How to configure the structure of an Oracle7 database's transaction log

- How to configure the transaction log for automatic archiving

- How to monitor a database's transaction log for problems

- How to make offline and online backups of an Oracle7 database

- How to increase protection of database availability by mirroring an Oracle7 database's data files with hardware mirroring

- How to recover an Oracle7 database from disk failures using offline and on-line recovery techniques

- How to configure Oracle7 for quicker parallel recovery operations

- How to use a standby database to protect a database from site disasters

CHAPTER

TWELVE

Monitoring and Tuning Database Server Performance

- Tuning an operating system for Oracle7

- Tuning the Oracle7 memory caches

- Eliminating disk I/O contention in an Oracle7 server

- Reducing the performance impact of temporary segments

- Tuning the size of rollback segments

- Tuning an Oracle7 multithreaded server

- Reducing performance hits caused by checkpoints

After you've driven a car for a while, the car's engine can begin to run poorly. The engine's spark plugs can get old and caked with oil grit, and the contacts in the distributor cap can become worn. To keep a car running like new, it is important to regularly tune up the car's engine. The Oracle7 database server is another type of engine that needs an occasional tune-up to keep things running smoothly.

Oracle7 has an intimidating number of knobs and dials that the administrator can adjust to affect the performance of the database server. To make server performance tuning easier to understand, this chapter discusses several important tuning tips that can noticeably affect the performance of the Oracle7 server:

- Tuning an operating system for the Oracle7 database server

- Reducing disk I/O by adjusting the sizes of the Oracle7 memory caches

- Eliminating disk contention for files and data in an Oracle7 database

- Reducing the negative performance effects of temporary segments

- Sizing rollback segments correctly to reduce dynamic space allocations and deallocations

- Tuning the number of processes in the Oracle7 multithreaded server

- Reducing the performance hits that checkpoints can create

As your database system evolves, keep in mind the tuning tips in this chapter and others so that the tuning process is less involved.

Tuning Tip 1: Tune the Operating System for Oracle7

Oracle7 clearly depends heavily on the multi-user operating system used to run the database server. If the database server's operating system does not deliver maximum performance, then no matter how well you tune Oracle7, the database server will not perform as well as it could. Therefore, it makes sense to tune the operating system with the Oracle7 database server in mind.

The following sections discuss three of the most important considerations when tuning an operating system for Oracle7.

Planning System Resources for Oracle7

First, you need to plan how much of the server computer's resources you want to dedicate to the Oracle7 database server. This is an important factor that can significantly affect the performance of Oracle7. For example, if you reserve a lot of memory for Oracle7, it can cache more database data in memory, which reduces disk I/Os to deliver more performance. If you allow Oracle7 to access multiple processors on a multiprocessor computer, Oracle7 can perform work in parallel to reduce wait times for user requests. In summary, first determine what resources are available on the server computer, and then determine how much of the resources you want Oracle7 to use.

In many client/server systems, it is reasonable to dedicate all resources of a server computer to run Oracle7. This is especially the case when the server machine is a small, inexpensive microcomputer or workstation, such as a microcomputer running SCO UNIX or Windows NT or a Novell NetWare file server. If you decide to dedicate a computer to Oracle7, the primary job is to make sure the server computer has ample resources to run Oracle7.

In contrast, demanding client/server systems can use a large multiprocessor minicomputer at the center of a corporate network. Larger systems such as these are less likely to dedicate all of the server computer's resources to the database system. It is necessary to reserve some system resources for other tasks, such as print queues and electronic-mail systems. Determining which resources different applications use and require on larger systems can be a challenge. To make your job easier, consider the use of special system administration utilities that are available to help tune operating system operation. However, many times tuning the operating system on larger systems is a try-and-see process that takes a significant amount of expertise and time.

Tuning Operating System Virtual Memory Settings

Most operating systems use virtual memory to simulate the presence of more real memory on a computer. *Real memory* is the random-access memory that memory chips in the computer supply for software operation. *Virtual memory* is a reserved area of disk space, often called a *swap space,* that the operating system uses to page information into and out of real memory when there is not enough real memory to handle software requests. Therefore, virtual memory can make it appear as though a computer has more real memory than it actually does.

At reasonable levels, paging using virtual memory is beneficial because it provides more memory in which a computer's application programs can work. However, if a computer's memory supply is significantly overloaded, paging can become more of a problem than a benefit. For example, a serious condition known as *thrashing* occurs when a computer's processor spends more time paging information into and out of memory than it does performing useful work on behalf of applications and users. When such a condition occurs, it significantly slows server performance for all applications.

To avoid the performance degradation associated with disadvantageous virtual memory usage, system and Oracle7 administrators should closely monitor swapping activity and aim to reduce or altogether eliminate swapping for the server system. To reduce or eliminate swapping, the only real solution is to purchase and install more memory in the server.

NOTE Most operating systems have utilities or operating system commands you can use to monitor swapping activity on a computer. For example, many UNIX systems support the command "sar", which displays a short report of system swapping activity.

Setting Operating System Process Priorities for Oracle7

Many operating systems allow you to tune their functions by selectively prioritizing the actions of operating system processes. An administrator can give more priority to more important tasks and less priority to less important tasks. The result is that the most demanding tasks complete more quickly than the less demanding tasks, which usually satisfies the majority of system users.

Although setting operating system process priorities can be helpful for some applications, it can hurt the performance of the Oracle7 database server. In an Oracle7 database system, all background and foreground database server processes perform equally important actions and need to run with the same priority. Therefore, make sure that when you install Oracle7, all server processes run using the default process priority of the server computer.

Tuning Tip 2: Reduce Disk I/O in Oracle7

Disk access is a very slow operation that can hurt the performance of any computer system. The less disk I/O, the better the performance of the computer. Software applications that use large amounts of data use memory caches to reduce disk I/O and improve overall performance.

Using Memory Caches

A *memory cache* is a preallocated memory area that Oracle7 specifically reserves to hold frequently requested pages or blocks of information. By holding frequently used data blocks in memory, Oracle7 eliminates the need for costly disk I/Os that would otherwise hurt database server performance for all client applications. Before focusing on ways to tune the sizes of the different memory caches that Oracle7 uses to reduce disk I/Os, let's learn some of the basic terminology related to memory caches:

Term	Meaning
Caching algorithms	Most memory caches are static, preallocated areas in memory. Therefore, there is a limit to how much data a cache can hold. To intelligently decide which data pages to keep in memory caches, software programs use a *caching algorithm* or caching strategy. A common caching algorithm is a *most-recently used/least-recently used caching algorithm*. With this strategy, a program keeps a data page in a memory cache according to how long it has been since the last request for the page. Consequently, the most recently requested pages will stay in memory longer, while the least recently requested pages are *aged out* of the cache to make room for new pages that are not already in the cache.
Cache hit	When an application requests some information that is already in a memory cache, the program gets the information from memory rather than disk. This is called a *cache hit* or a *cache get*.
Cache miss	When an application requests some information that is not in memory, the program gets the information from disk. This is called a *cache miss* or a *cache getmiss*.
Cache reload	When an application requests some information that used to be in the memory cache but has since been aged out, the porgram reloads the information from disk. This is called a *cache reload*.

Figure 12.1 illustrates the basic concepts of memory caches.

Now let's see how Oracle7 caches data in memory. Oracle7 has three primary memory caches for different types of data: the library cache, the dictionary cache, and the buffer cache.

FIGURE 12.1:

Caching algorithms and cache hits, misses, and reloads

Cache	Description
Library cache	When a user issues a SQL statement, calls a database procedure, or fires a trigger, Oracle7 uses memory to parse and determine execution plans for the statement or procedure. To save memory when many users all execute the same SQL statements and procedures of a compiled application, the *library cache* stores and shares SQL statements and PL/SQL procedures in memory. Shared SQL can also improve application performance because Oracle7 does not need to redetermine a statement's execution plan if it is already in memory.
Dictionary cache	During system processing, Oracle7 constantly uses information in a database's data dictionary for almost every operation. To reduce disk I/Os associated with data dictionary tables and indexes, the *dictionary cache* holds dictionary information in memory.

Cache	Description
Buffer cache	The *buffer cache* reduces disk I/O by storing data that transactions have recently requested. It is also the in-memory work area for transaction processing. For example, when a transaction includes a statement to update a row in a table, Oracle7 finds the data block on disk that contains the requested row. Then Oracle7 reads the block from disk into the buffer cache and updates the row. If another transaction wants to update the same row or another row in the same data block, no disk access is necessary; the row is already in memory.

Together, the library and dictionary caches make up the *shared pool*. The shared pool combined with the buffer cache make up the *system global area*, or the *SGA*. Figure 12.2 shows the different memory caches Oracle7 uses.

FIGURE 12.2:

Library, dictionary, and buffer caches in an Oracle7 database server

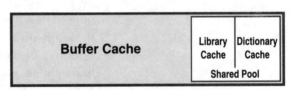

System Global Area (SGA)

To tune an Oracle7 database server's SGA, you must gather some information about the ratio of misses or reloads to hits in the different caches of the SGA. Once you know how the caches are serving application requests, you can tune server performance by increasing or decreasing the sizes of the different caches.

An easy and effective way to monitor the percentage of misses in the library, dictionary, and buffer caches is to use the table and procedure in Listing 12.1.

Listing 12.1: The GATHERSGASTATS Procedure and SGASTATSHISTORY Table

```
CREATE TABLE sgastatshistory (
timepoint DATE,
```

```
-- columns for cumulative stats
cumlibraryreloads REAL,
cumlibrarypins REAL,
cumdictionarygetmisses REAL,
cumdictionarygets REAL,
cumsgablockgets REAL,
cumsgaconsistentgets REAL,
cumsgadiskgets REAL,
-- columns for interval percentages
intlibraryreloadpercentage REAL,
intdictionarymisspercentage REAL,
intbuffermisspercentage REAL);

CREATE PROCEDURE gathersgastats (interval INTEGER, timepoints INTEGER) AS
-- This procedure gathers data points at the specified interval (in minutes)
-- for the given number of timepoints to track the percentage of misses to
-- gets in the library, dictionary, and buffer caches. Low percentages are
-- good; high percentages mean that the cache sizes need tuning.

counter INTEGER := 0;
-- variables for current cumulative stats
curlibraryreloads REAL;
curlibrarypins REAL;
curdictionarygetmisses REAL;
curdictionarygets REAL;
cursgablockgets REAL;
cursgaconsistentgets REAL;
cursgadiskgets REAL;
-- variables for previous cumulative stats
prevlibraryreloads REAL;
prevlibrarypins REAL;
prevdictionarygetmisses REAL;
prevdictionarygets REAL;
prevsgablockgets REAL;
prevsgaconsistentgets REAL;
prevsgadiskgets REAL;
-- variables for interval stats
intlibraryreloads REAL;
intlibrarypins REAL;
intdictionarygetmisses REAL;
intdictionarygets REAL;
intsgablockgets REAL;
intsgaconsistentgets REAL;
intsgadiskgets REAL;
-- variables for interval percentages
```

```
libraryreloadpercentage REAL;
dictionarymisspercentage REAL;
buffermisspercentage REAL;

-- cursor to fetch SGA buffer cache stats
CURSOR bufferdata IS
SELECT name, value
FROM v$sysstat
WHERE name IN ('db block gets','consistent gets','physical reads');

BEGIN

-- set loop for wake/sleep gathering of data points
WHILE counter < timepoints LOOP

-- query to gather library cache stats
SELECT SUM(reloads), SUM(pins)
INTO curlibraryreloads, curlibrarypins
FROM v$librarycache;
-- query to gather dictionary cache stats
SELECT SUM(getmisses), SUM(gets)
INTO curdictionarygetmisses, curdictionarygets
FROM v$rowcache;
-- open cursor to gather SGA buffer cache stats
FOR buffercache IN bufferdata LOOP
IF buffercache.name = 'db block gets' THEN
cursgablockgets := buffercache.value;
ELSIF buffercache.name = 'consistent gets' THEN
cursgaconsistentgets := buffercache.value;
ELSE
cursgadiskgets := buffercache.value;
END IF;
END LOOP;

-- Calculate library reload percentage, dictionary miss percentage,
-- and buffer cache miss percentage. Special case first datapoint
-- in a session with NULL percentages.
IF counter != 0 THEN

-- first, gather previous cumulative stats from SGASTATHISTORY
SELECT cumlibraryreloads, cumlibrarypins,
cumdictionarygetmisses, cumdictionarygets,
cumsgablockgets, cumsgaconsistentgets, cumsgadiskgets
INTO prevlibraryreloads, prevlibrarypins,
prevdictionarygetmisses, prevdictionarygets,
```

```
prevsgablockgets, prevsgaconsistentgets, prevsgadiskgets
FROM sgastatshistory
WHERE timepoint = (SELECT MAX(timepoint)
FROM sgastatshistory);

-- calculate library reload percentage
intlibraryreloads := curlibraryreloads - prevlibraryreloads;
intlibrarypins := curlibrarypins - prevlibrarypins;
libraryreloadpercentage :=
ROUND((intlibraryreloads/(intlibraryreloads + intlibrarypins))*100,2);

-- calculate dictionary miss percentage
intdictionarygetmisses := curdictionarygetmisses - prevdictionarygetmisses;
intdictionarygets := curdictionarygets - prevdictionarygets;
dictionarymisspercentage :=
ROUND((intdictionarygetmisses/(intdictionarygetmisses +
intdictionarygets))*100,2);

-- calculate buffer cache miss percentage
intsgablockgets := cursgablockgets - prevsgablockgets;
intsgaconsistentgets := cursgaconsistentgets - prevsgaconsistentgets;
intsgadiskgets := cursgadiskgets - prevsgadiskgets; buffermisspercentage :=
ROUND((intsgadiskgets/(intsgablockgets + intsgaconsistentgets))*100,2);
ELSE
libraryreloadpercentage := NULL;
dictionarymisspercentage := NULL;
buffermisspercentage := NULL;
END IF;

-- insert datapoint into SGASTATSHISTORY table
INSERT INTO sgastatshistory
VALUES (SYSDATE, curlibraryreloads, curlibrarypins, curdictionarygetmisses,
curdictionarygets, cursgablockgets, cursgaconsistentgets, cursgadiskgets,
libraryreloadpercentage, dictionarymisspercentage, buffermisspercentage);

counter := counter + 1;
dbms_lock.sleep(interval*60);
END LOOP;

END gathersgastats;
```

To gather performance statistics for each of a database server's SGA memory caches, run the GATHERSGASTATS procedure. Notice that this administrative procedure is a wake-and-sleep procedure, like several other procedures given in this book. Therefore, you will need to dedicate the Server Manager SQL worksheet or SQL*Plus session you use to run this procedure.

The GATHERSGASTATS procedure lets you specify two arguments: the interval (in minutes) to wake up and gather data, and the total number of data points to gather. A good strategy is to run the procedure for the duration of a normal day to see how the SGA cache settings work as the load on the database server fluctuates during a normal day. If you start an instance at the beginning of the day, there will be a high number of misses early on because the caches in the SGA are empty. As applications load data, the miss percentages in the different caches should stabilize and give you a good idea of how the instance configuration is working.

After gathering enough data points, you can query the SGASTATSHISTORY table to see the percentages of misses to total gets throughout the statistic-gathering interval. The following statements execute the GATHERSGASTATS procedure every 30 minutes for 8 hours and query the SGASTATSHISTORY table to show how the miss percentages fluctuate in a well-tuned database server's SGA throughout a normal day:

```
SELECT intlibraryreloadpercentage, intdictionarymisspercentage,
  intbuffermisspercentage
  FROM sgastatshistory
```

INTLIBRARYRELOADPERCENTAGE	INTDICTIONARYMISSPERCENTAGE	INTBUFFERMISSPERCENTAGE
1.23	21.61	40.82
.98	17.56	35.91
.77	10.42	28.23
.68	9.97	27.89
.61	8.53	40.13
.55	8.37	36.36
.54	8.32	32.42
.54	10.28	31.51
.54	10.61	30.05
.53	10.21	30.12
.52	11.02	30.87
.54	10.93	29.14
.55	10.54	30.01
.54	9.77	29.88
.54	10.08	29.91

In general, cache misses in the library and dictionary caches are more expensive than misses in the buffer cache. Therefore, you should try to tune the percentage of misses or reloads in the library, dictionary, and buffer caches to less than 1 percent, 15 percent, and 40 percent, respectively.

The next three sections explain the initialization parameters you can use to tune the size of the different caches in an Oracle7 database server's SGA.

Tuning the Library and Data Dictionary Caches

If the average percentage of reloads in the library cache is greater than 1 percent or the average percentage of misses in the dictionary cache is greater than 15 percent, you should increase the amount of memory dedicated to the shared pool. (Try using a query with the AVG SQL function to see these values.) Alternatively, if the miss percentages are lower than the targets, you may be able to maintain good performance and free some memory for other operating system services by reducing the size of the shared pool.

To adjust the amount of memory allocated to the shared pool, use the SHARED _POOL_SIZE initialization parameter. Set the amount of memory for the shared pool in bytes. This example sets the shared pool size to 4 megabytes:

```
SHARED_POOL_SIZE=4194304
```

After altering the setting for the SHARED_POOL_SIZE parameter in a database's initialization parameter file, you need to shut down and restart the database server for the new setting to take effect.

NOTE   Keep in mind that when you increase the size of the shared pool, you can reduce the amount of memory that is available for other uses, such as the SGA's buffer cache, or increase the amount of operating system paging, which is bad. Therefore, be sure you consider the big picture when setting the size of a database server's shared pool.

Tuning the Buffer Cache

If the average percentage of misses in the buffer cache is greater than 40 percent, you should increase the size of the buffer cache. Alternatively, if the average percentage of misses in the buffer cache is less than 40 percent, you may be able to maintain performance and free memory for other resources by decreasing the size of the buffer cache.

To adjust the amount of memory allocated to the buffer cache, use the DB _BLOCK_BUFFERS initialization parameter. Set DB_BLOCK_BUFFERS to the number of data blocks you want the buffer cache to hold. This example sets the buffer cache size to 500 data blocks:

```
DB_BLOCK_BUFFERS=500
```

The size of a data block buffer corresponds to the setting for the DB_BLOCK_SIZE initialization parameter. To reveal the data block size for a database in bytes, you can query the V$PARAMETER table:

```
SELECT name, value
  FROM v$parameter
  WHERE name = 'db_block_size'

NAME                                 VALUE
--------------------------------     -------------
db_block_size                        2048
```

When you know a database's data block size, you can determine the buffer cache's total size in bytes by multiplying the database's data block size by the number of data block buffers allocated to the buffer cache. For example, 512 2K block buffers result in a 1 megabyte buffer cache.

As with other initialization parameters, after you change the value for the DB _BLOCK_BUFFERS parameter in a database's initialization parameter file, you need to shut down and restart the database server for the new setting to take effect.

NOTE After database creation, it is impossible to change the database block size. Therefore, changing the value for DB_BLOCK_SIZE after database creation has no effect.

Tuning Tip 3: Reduce Disk Contention

Consider what happens when two different processes make a request to read or write data that resides on the same disk. The disk has only one disk head and, as a result, can serve the disk access request of only one process at a time. This is an example of two processes contending for data on the same disk, or *disk contention*. Disk contention reduces system performance because some processes must wait while other processes get their disk access requests filled. Disk contention is no stranger to an Oracle7 database system. This tip focuses on ways to reduce disk contention within an Oracle7 database system.

Reducing Disk Contention by Separating Files

When creating new files for an Oracle7 database, whether they are data files for a tablespace or log files for the database's transaction log, carefully consider the disk resources available on the database server. If the server has multiple disks, you can significantly improve database server performance by spreading out files among available disks to reduce contention among a database's data files and transaction log files.

The basic rule for database file separation is to store data files separately from transaction log files. This way, ongoing transaction-processing disk access is not hampered by the disk access necessary for corresponding transaction logging.

If a server has a great many disks, the possibilities for file separation can be more imaginative. For example, suppose that two demanding applications use an Oracle7 database server and each application has a distinct set of data. You can eliminate inter-application disk contention by creating two different tablespaces, one for each application's data. Store the data files for the first application's tablespace on one disk drive and the data files for the second application's tablespace on another disk drive. This strategy physically separates the storage for each application's data, eliminating the possibility of any disk contention between the two applications.

If you have many disks to work with, you can also eliminate a source of disk contention in a database's transaction log. By placing each member of the transaction log on a different disk drive, you can eliminate disk contention when Oracle7 concurrently writes new transaction log records to one log group and reads another filled log group for archiving.

These are just a few of the ways you can improve database server performance if the server computer has many different disks and you use them wisely to spread out file I/O.

Reducing Disk Contention between Tables and Indexes

Almost all tables in an Oracle7 database have indexes to speed the performance of applications by reducing disk I/O for user requests. Internally, Oracle7 stores table data separately from corresponding index data. Therefore, when a user's transaction requests a row in a table, Oracle7 scans the data blocks in the index to find the row and its address, and then the server reads the data block in the table that contains the row.

When many concurrent SQL statements request rows from the same table and index and both the table and index are on the same disk, there is disk contention—Oracle7 can read only table data or only index data at any given time.

To reduce disk contention between table and index data, separate an application's table data from its index data on different physical disks. For example, store an application's table data in a tablespace on one disk and the corresponding index data in a different tablespace on another disk. As a result, you eliminate disk contention, and Oracle7 can read table and index data in parallel on behalf of SQL requests.

TIP

Oracle7 automatically creates a unique index to enforce both PRIMARY KEY and UNIQUE integrity constraints. You can control the tablespace placement and storage parameters of an integrity constraint's index with the USING INDEX clause of a constraint declaration in a CREATE TABLE or an ALTER TABLE statement.

Tuning Tip 4: Configure Temporary Segment Settings

A *temporary segment* is allocation of data blocks in a tablespace that provides temporary work space for the intermediate processing steps of a specific SQL statement. Temporary segments are commonly referred to as *sort segments* because SQL statements that include sort operations typically require temporary segments. For example, a query of a large table that includes an ORDER BY clause or a CREATE INDEX statement for a large table would most likely require a temporary segment.

```
SELECT *
  FROM largetable
  ORDER BY col_a

CREATE INDEX index_z
  ON largetable (col_b, col_c)
  ASC
```

Oracle7 automatically creates a temporary segment only when it is necessary to complete processing for a SQL statement, and it drops the temporary segment after the statement completes execution. Because the constant allocation and deallocation of temporary segments generates disk I/O, temporary segments can significantly degrade the performance of a database application. The following sections explain the tuning features that Oracle7 provides to help reduce the performance hits that temporary segments can introduce.

Setting the SORT_AREA_SIZE Server Parameter

Oracle7 automatically creates a temporary segment on behalf of a SQL statement only when the server cannot complete statement processing in server memory. The server initialization parameter SORT_AREA_SIZE determines the size, in bytes, of each user session's temporary work area in server memory. When application's commonly require a temporary segment to process a small amount of information, you might be able to reduce the allocation of temporary segments by slightly increasing the size of the server's SORT_AREA_SIZE initialization parameter.

WARNING When you increase the setting for the SORT_AREA_SIZE server parameter, make sure to do so with the entire system in mind. By increasing the setting for SORT_AREA_SIZE, remember that you are setting aside more memory on the database server for every user session's temporary sort space. At the same time, you are reducing the amount of server memory that is available for other important functions, both internal and external to the database server.

Setting a User's Temporary Segment Tablespace

When Oracle7 must create a temporary segment to complete processing for a user's SQL statement, the server allocates the segment from the tablespace indicated by the user's TEMPORARY TABLESPACE setting. Unfortunately, when you create a new user account, the default setting for the user's temporary tablespace is the SYSTEM tablespace. If you allow users to create temporary segments in the SYSTEM tablespace, the temporary segments will contend with internal system operations for disk I/O, contend with internal system tables for free space, and can significantly fragment the free extents of the SYSTEM tablespace. To avoid such problems, make sure to create a specific tablespace in a database as a target for temporary segments and then set every user's temporary tablespace setting to the tablespace.

Configuring a Temporary Tablespace

With Oracle7 release 7.3, you can further reduce the negative performance effects of temporary segments by using a special type of tablespace for temporary work space: a *temporary tablespace*. A temporary tablespace is a essentially one large temporary sort segment that all user sessions can concurrently target for temporary work space. A temporary tablespace improves the performance of SQL statement processing by reducing the amount of disk I/O that's necessary to simply obtain a segment of temporary work space for a statement. Rather than create and drop individual temporary segments on demand within a normal tablespace, Oracle7 can quickly dole out temporary work space in a temporary tablespace by inserting and deleting small entries in the tablespace's sort segment table.

To create a new tablespace as a temporary tablespace, include the TEMPORARY keyword in the CREATE TABLESPACE statement:

```
CREATE TABLESPACE temp TEMPORARY ...
```

You can also convert an existing tablespace into a temporary tablespace using the TEMPORARY keyword in an ALTER TABLESPACE statement:

```
ALTER TABLESPACE temp TEMPORARY ...
```

Before converting an existing tablespace into a temporary tablespace, make sure that the tablespace does not contain database objects. A temporary tablespace is a unique structure designed specifically for temporary work space, and it cannot serve as a storage area for other types of database objects such as tables and indexes. If you want to convert a temporary tablespace back to a normal permanent tablespace so that it can support other types of database objects, use the keyword PERMANENT in an ALTER TABLESPACE statement:

```
ALTER TABLESPACE temp PERMANENT ...
```

Tuning Tip 5: Size Rollback Segments Correctly

Rollback segments can dynamically grow and shrink to handle fluctuating transaction sizes. However, the dynamic allocation and deallocation of extents in a rollback segment creates hits of disk I/O that can contribute to poor system performance. The solution to this problem is to tune the storage parameters for each rollback segment so they do not dynamically grow and shrink.

To keep a rollback segment's size relatively static for the average transaction size without wasting database space, it is necessary to set the rollback segment's OPTIMAL storage parameter correctly. Chapter 10 explains when Oracle7 allocates and deallocates extents for a rollback segment, how to monitor the number of growths and shrinks in a rollback segment, and how to adjust the setting of a rollback segment's OPTIMAL extent storage parameter. Use the information in Chapter 10 to reduce the likelihood of a rollback segment changing in size.

Tuning Tip 6: Tune the Oracle7 Multithreaded Server

Most Oracle7 client/server systems use a multithreaded server configuration to reduce the amount of process overhead on the server. If the number of processes in a multithreaded server is not correct for the transaction load, it can degrade system performance. To solve the problem, you can monitor and tune the configuration of the Oracle7 multithreaded server in a client/server database system.

There are two key areas to tune for the multithreaded server configuration: the number of dispatchers per network protocol and the number of shared servers.

- If there are many clients for a network protocol and there are too few dispatcher processes for the network protocol, the dispatchers can be a performance bottleneck in accepting and fulfilling the requests of transactions.

- Oracle7 can dynamically start and stop shared server processes based on the load in a database system. If the minimum number of shared server processes is too low, system performance can be hurt because Oracle7 wastes resources to frequently start and stop shared server processes as transaction loads fluctuate. If the maximum number of shared servers is too low, system performance can be hurt because Oracle7 will not allow enough servers to handle heavy loads.

Chapter 8 includes all the information you need to configure, monitor, and tune an Oracle7 multithreaded server configuration. Follow the instructions in Chapter 8 to make sure your multithreaded server is not unnecessarily degrading system performance.

Tuning Tip 7: Reduce the Performance Hits of Checkpoints

Checkpoints are mileposts that regularly occur to write all modified data in memory back to a database's data files. Checkpoints serve several purposes. For one, they make sure that frequently modified data blocks, which Oracle7 will cache in memory for long periods of time, are regularly written back to the database's data files. Checkpoints also indicate to Oracle7 how much of the transaction log to apply to the data files if crash recovery is necessary.

Because a checkpoint writes data to disk, the disk I/Os that correspond to the checkpoint can degrade database server performance. The next two sections explain how to reduce the performance hits associated with checkpoints.

Tuning the Number of Checkpoints

One way to reduce the performance degradation of checkpoints is to make sure checkpoints occur only when necessary.

A database checkpoint always occurs when Oracle7 switches writing from one transaction log group to another. You can also force checkpoints to occur between transaction log group switches by setting the LOG_CHECKPOINT_INTERVAL and LOG_CHECKPOINT_TIMEOUT initialization parameters. However, there are not many situations that justify the performance hits associated with forcing additional checkpoints between log switches. Therefore, you should set the values of these initialization parameters so database checkpoints occur only at log switches.

The LOG_CHECKPOINT_INTERVAL initialization parameter indicates how often Oracle7 should perform checkpoints, based on the number of blocks written to the transaction log. To eliminate additional checkpoints between log switches, set the parameter so that the block threshold is larger than the number of blocks in the members of the database's transaction log.

The LOG_CHECKPOINT_INTERVAL initialization parameter is tricky to set because you specify the threshold as a number of operating system blocks, not data blocks. Therefore, you need to perform a bit of math in order to set the threshold above the size of the transaction log groups.

For example, many UNIX systems use a block size of 512 bytes, and the default log member size for Oracle7 on most UNIX systems is 512K. Therefore, if you use Oracle7 on UNIX and use transaction log members with a size of 512K, there are 1024 operating system blocks for each transaction log member. To eliminate checkpoints between log switches on this type of system, set LOG_CHECKPOINT_INTERVAL to a number greater than 1024:

```
LOG_CHECKPOINT_INTERVAL=1100
```

> **NOTE** All members in a database's transaction log should be the same size; there is no advantage to varying the size of log groups. However, if a database's transaction log has members of varying size, set the LOG_CHECKPOINT_INTERVAL parameter higher than the size of the largest transaction log member.

The LOG_CHECKPOINT_TIMEOUT parameter indicates how often Oracle7 should perform checkpoints based on the number of seconds that have passed since the last checkpoint. Simply set this parameter's value to 0 so additional checkpoints do not occur between log switches:

```
LOG_CHECKPOINT_TIMEOUT=0
```

Tuning the Performance of Database Checkpoints

When a checkpoint occurs, three different operations take place. First, the DBWR process writes all modified data blocks in the SGA back to the appropriate data files of the database. Second, the LGWR background process updates the database's control file to indicate when the last checkpoint occurred. Finally, the LGWR background process updates the headers in all the data files to indicate when the last checkpoint occurred. The second and third steps are necessary to allow Oracle7 to determine how much of the transaction log to apply to the data files if crash recovery is necessary.

If you follow the recommendations in this book, you will use a small number of data files in a database. However, as a database grows and you add more and more data files, checkpoints can begin to create noticeable hits on system performance. This is primarily because LGWR must update many data file headers while

still performing transaction logging for ongoing transactions. To improve performance, tune the Oracle7 database server to more efficiently complete checkpoints so
they do not degrade transaction logging performance.

To relieve the burden on LGWR during checkpoints, you can start the optional
CKPT background process. When CKPT is present for an Oracle7 database server,
it updates the headers of data files during checkpoints rather than LGWR. Therefore, LGWR can concentrate on its transaction logging duties and serve ongoing
transaction processing more effectively.

To use the CKPT background process, modify the database's parameter file to set
the CHECKPOINT_PROCESS initialization parameter to TRUE:

```
CHECKPOINT_PROCESS=TRUE
```

Then restart the database server using the updated parameter file.

Once the CKPT background process has started, checkpoints will proceed without
negatively affecting ongoing transaction logging. As a result, the Oracle7 database
server will perform better during checkpoint operations.

Other Ways to Improve Performance

Suppose you carefully tune an Oracle7 database server using the performance tuning tips described in this chapter, but application performance is still inadequate.
What should do you do next?

There are other areas of the Oracle7 database server you can tweak to tune its performance. However, it is unlikely that these fine-tuning techniques will make a significant difference in improving the performance of the server's applications. It is
more productive to shift your tuning efforts to the application itself.

Tuning the Application

There are many things in an application design that can degrade system performance. For example, if a client application always issues SQL statements across a network rather than using stored procedures when possible, the excessive network

I/O in the system can be a significant factor for poor application performance. There are many ways to improve application performance. Chapters 15 and 16 concentrate on application-tuning techniques.

Tuning the System's Hardware Configuration

If after tuning the database server and tuning the application, your client/server system still delivers inadequate performance, the next step is to look at your system's hardware configuration. The problem might be that you are trying to make a demanding application perform in a client/server system that is not suited for the job. If this is the case, the next step might be substituting a more powerful server machine for the current server computer to gain additional database server performance. For example, by replacing a uniprocessor server with a multiprocessor computer, you can use the Oracle7 Parallel Query option. By parallelizing server operations across multiple processors, you can dramatically improve the performance of several types of applications, most notably decision-support applications. (For more information about using the Oracle7 Parallel Query option to improve database server performance, see Appendix B.)

Performance-Monitoring Techniques

The only way to know if an Oracle7 database server is performing well is to closely monitor its activities. Monitoring system status and performance is a big job, and the database administrator must pay close attention.

What is the most effective way to monitor an Oracle7 database server? There are two answers to this question, depending on the situation:

- If the database server is running relatively smoothly and you want to make sure it is working as well as it can, it is useful to do general maintenance monitoring that records statistics related to server performance. By studying such statistics, you can make adjustments to fine-tune system performance.

- If there is a critical problem, you need to do emergency monitoring to pinpoint the problem quickly. You will want to make immediate changes in the server to fix the critical problem.

Server Manager does not include any features for performing general monitoring for the Oracle7 server. However, an easy way to do so is to use the many different administrative stored procedures given in the listings in this book. For example, the CAPTUREDISPATCHERLOADS procedure given in Listing 8.1 (in Chapter 8) is an effective way to gather performance-related information for tuning a multi-threaded server configuration. Listing 12.1 (earlier in this chapter) is another example of a simple stored procedure and table you can use to gather tuning information for the memory caches in an Oracle7 database server. As long as you know what areas of the database server to focus on, you can create an entire set of administrative stored procedures like the ones in this book to help you tune the server's performance.

If are not sure which areas to monitor or you do not want to create stored procedures to help monitor server performance, another option is to use one of several third-party administrative tools that include built-in monitoring and alerting features. If you are serious about getting the best performance out of your database server, these administrative utilities are well worth the additional cost.

If you have a critical problem, the monitors built into Server Manager can help reveal the root of the problem. Chapters 8 and 10 discussed how to use several of the different Server Manager monitors to firefight problems that need immediate attention.

By no means has this chapter discussed the hundreds of tuning knobs and dials you can adjust for the Oracle7 database server. However, this chapter has focused on the major techniques for making noticeable improvements when tuning an Oracle7 database server:

- Tuning the operating system with the Oracle7 server in mind

- Reducing disk I/O by adjusting the sizes of the Oracle7 memory caches

- Eliminating disk I/O contention for Oracle7 database files and data

- Configuring a temporary tablespace for temporary segments

- Sizing rollback segments correctly to reduce dynamic space allocations and deallocations

- Tuning the number of processes in an Oracle7 multithreaded server

- Reducing performance hits caused by checkpoints

This chapter concludes Part II of the book, which has covered database administration. The chapters in Part III explain what to consider when developing client applications for an Oracle7 client/server database system.

PART III

Application Development
in an Oracle7 System

The database server is the central component in a client/server system. However, users can't accomplish any work unless there are client applications that interface with the database server. Chapters 13 through 19 concentrate on the features of Oracle7 that application developers must understand when developing client applications, as well as on other Oracle products developers can use to create client applications.

CHAPTER

THIRTEEN

Application Development for Oracle7

- Defining an application's purpose and logic

- Planning an application's schema

- Determining what goes into a client application

- Using the Oracle7 database server to reduce network I/O

This chapter discusses general topics for application development, including the following:

- The responsibilities of the application developer

- A quick guide to distributing the components in a client/server application: which belong in client-side applications and which belong in the Oracle7 database server

What Does an Application Developer Do?

The person who develops client applications for an Oracle7 database system is the application developer. Like the database administrator, the application developer has a distinct set of responsibilities to consider when developing database applications. The next few sections explain the different types of jobs you need to perform as an application developer.

Defining an Application's Purpose

Before you tackle any type of complicated job, whether it is landscaping a yard, designing a new office building, or developing a client/server database application, it is important to set clear goals for the project. This makes it easy to determine if you have actually accomplished your purpose.

What are the goals when developing a new client database application? The purpose of an application varies, depending on the needs of the users who will eventually use the application to interact with the database information.

For example, suppose a company wants to use Oracle7 to run its business, including everything from sales orders to inventory management. When you sit down to develop custom applications for the company, the first question to ask is, "What are the needs of the application users?" In a typical business setting, you'll find requirements like these:

- Many salespeople need a quick way to input a large number of sales orders.

- The marketing folks need to analyze information about sales revenues and product sales.

- The people running the company warehouse need to generate shipping labels and manage product inventory.

This first look at various user needs reveals some early application development goals:

- To provide the sales department with an OLTP application for sales order input

- To provide the marketing department with a decision-support application to permit canned and ad hoc queries for various types of database information

- To provide the shipping department with a set of standard reports for product inventory and shipping labels

From this point, you can refine the application development goals into more focused objectives, which will help you make a few more important decisions. For example, members of the sales department are used to filling out paper forms to enter sales information. You might decide to use Oracle Forms to create a client application that mimics the familiar paper form. And executives in the marketing department probably want some standard reports to analyze product sales and sales revenues. You might use Oracle Reports and Oracle Graphics (or other third-party tools) to create some predefined reports and graphs for the marketing department.

As this simple business case demonstrates, you will learn more and more about the application development process as you drill down further into your application goals. You can tell what users really need to be productive in their work, and you can determine which application tools you need to build the enabling client applications.

Defining an Application's Logic

Once you know what you want an application to do, it is time to get on with the job of building the application. Using the application development tool of your choice, you must define the presentation and the internal *logic* of the application.

When defining an application's logic, there are a number of factors to consider. One primary development objective is to present an intuitive user interface that application users can employ to accomplish work with ease. Prudent use of common graphical user interface elements, such as menus, buttons, check boxes, radio button lists, list boxes, and pop-up menus, make working with an application easy to learn, less prone to errors, and consequently very productive.

If you use a 3GL application development approach—for example, with a C compiler and Oracle's Pro*C precompiler—you need to know how to manually create a user interface in the source code of the application. Many language compilers can take advantage of standard windowing libraries to make user interface development somewhat easier, but 3GL user interface development is still a job best suited for experienced programmers.

Putting together a good user interface can be relatively simple when you use a 4GL application development tool, even if you have no programming experience. That's because most 4GL environments have easy-to-use screen painting and visual layout capabilities.

Behind the covers of an application's user interface, the application must have the necessary program code to perform the operations of the application, including any SQL or PL/SQL to interact with the database. When you create an application using a 3GL development tool, not only do you need to write the source code for the user interface, you must also write the source code for the internal application logic and database access calls. The disadvantage of the 3GL approach is that you must be experienced in working with a 3GL to get the job done swiftly. The advantage is that once you know what you are doing, 3GLs offer a great deal of flexibility and power that you can tap into when developing an application.

On the other hand, 4GL tools automatically generate most of the internal application program from the elements you create for a database application. Most 4GLs even have features that will create the necessary SQL to access database information, although they also allow you to write your own SQL. While the 4GL approach to application development can make complicated programming tasks much easier to accomplish, they generally take away some level of the flexibility and power that 3GLs can deliver.

As with any application development process, it is important to create the application so it performs well. However, because application processing is distributed across a network in a client/server database system, it is also important to design client database applications so they do not place an excessive burden on either the central database server or the network. For example, a poorly designed client application might not take advantage of database stored procedures to minimize network access. As a result, the application performs an excessive amount of network I/O, which saturates the network and degrades the performance of the entire database system for all users. This simple example shows that developers must have a clear understanding of the application development tool and the Oracle7 database server features that are available to create well-behaved client database applications. (The section "Distributing the Application between the Client and the Server" later in this chapter describes the different features in Oracle7 to consider when developing applications for client/server systems.)

Planning an Application's Schema

Part of developing a client database application is defining the application's schema, or the set of database objects necessary to support the application. For example, every application works with a set of database tables and views that hold information of interest. In addition, other types of database objects may be necessary to support the application, such as table indexes, synonyms, and sequences. Since the developer must create and test the functionality of the application, the developer is the appropriate person to design the application's schema.

There are several ways a developer can design a new application's schema. The easiest approach is using a CASE or database design tool to model the entities and relationships within the application schema. When a design is finished, most CASE tools generate a DDL script that the developer can then use to automatically create the new schema. Most CASE tools also store the definition of the schema in a repository, where entity and relationship information is available to other tools for automatic application generation. If a CASE or database design tool is not available to help automate the creation of an application schema, the developer must accomplish the job manually, using SQL commands.

After trying a new database application in a test environment, developers usually hand off the new application to the database administrator for installation into a production database environment. Part of this hand-off is a script that includes the DDL commands for creating the new application's schema.

Distributing the Application between the Client and the Server

Recall that a client/server database application is a fancy term for distributed application processing. In other words, application processing in a client/server environment is distributed between the client application and the database server. To develop sound applications for client/server systems, you need to understand how to distribute the parts of the application between components of the system. The next sections provide some guidelines for what goes where in a client/server database application.

What's in the Client Application?

The preceding sections have already given you a good idea of what should be in the client application. Client-side applications should focus primarily on presenting and/or analyzing data in a way that is useful for its audience.

Network traffic is one of the most important areas to focus on when developing client applications. Pay close attention to how an application sends information to or receives information from the database server and how much data it sends or receives. In general, network I/O tends to be a bottleneck for application performance in client/server systems. The less network I/O an application generates, the better the application and the entire system will perform.

The key to eliminating unnecessary network traffic from a client application is understanding and taking advantage of Oracle SQL and other features in the Oracle7 database server. For example, consider a reporting application that wants to display total dollars for all of the line items in each sales order. This calculation involves two steps: multiplying the quantity of each line item by the item's unit price, and then totaling the amount for all line items for each order. One way the application can accomplish this operation is to request the values for each column, a row at a time, and then perform the calculations inside the application using local variables:

```
SELECT orderid, quantity, unitprice
  FROM items, parts
  WHERE items.partid=parts.id
  ORDER BY orderid

ORDERID    QUANTITY    UNITPRICE
--------   --------    ---------
       1          1         6.03
       1          4         21.4
       1          2        87.12
       2          2         8.97
       2          3         21.4
     .
     .
     .
-- other application logic
```

This query sends order ID, quantity, and unit prices for all the line items in the ITEMS table. This can be a lot of data if your company is doing a brisk business and the ITEMS table has many rows for sales orders.

A more efficient way of performing the same operation with less network I/O would be to have the database server perform the calculations and then ship only the results across the network:

```
SELECT orderid, SUM(quantity*unitprice)
  FROM items, parts
  WHERE items.partid=parts.id
  GROUP BY orderid
  ORDER BY orderid

ORDERID  SUM(QUANTITY*UNITPRICE)
-------  -----------------------
      1                   265.87
      2                    82.14
    .
    .
    .
```

As you can see, the second query is much more efficient than the first option because it uses a combination of SQL, an Oracle7 SQL function (SUM), and a GROUP BY clause to have the Oracle7 server do the calculations and send less data across the network.

This simple example illustrates how you can use SQL and SQL functions to reduce the amount of network traffic in a client/server environment. It illustrates that developers must be intimately familiar with SQL to create good client database applications. For more information about SQL and SQL functions, see Chapter 5 and Appendix A.

What's in the Database Server?

Earlier releases of the Oracle database server supported client connections across a network using SQL*Net. However, Oracle7 is the first version release of the Oracle server that has the essential features for client/server work—features to reduce network I/O between client applications and servers. The following sections examine the features of Oracle7 that developers should take advantage of in a client/server system.

Integrity Constraints

All client applications must adhere to a set of predefined data integrity rules and business rules to make sure all of a database's data is valid. (Chapter 2 discussed domain, entity, and referential integrity and business rules.) There are two ways an application developer can enforce a simple integrity rule:

- Letting the application perform the integrity check

- Using Oracle7 integrity constraints

Letting the Application Perform the Integrity Check   For example, assume you want to make sure all transactions insert new sales orders such that the customer ID in each sales order matches a valid customer ID in the CUSTOMERS table. This is simple referential integrity. One way to enforce the referential integrity rule is to have the application perform the integrity check itself. First, an application transaction can query the database to make sure the customer exists in the CUSTOMERS table. If the query finds the customer, it must then lock the corresponding row for the duration of the transaction to make sure no one deletes the customer before the transaction inserts the new sales order. Finally, the transaction can safely insert a new row using the validated customer ID and then commit the transaction to release the lock on the CUSTOMERS table. Here is an anonymous PL/SQL block that demonstrates client-side application code to enforce referential integrity:

```
DECLARE
  flag INTEGER;
BEGIN
SELECT id INTO flag
  FROM customers
  WHERE id = 3
  FOR UPDATE OF id;

IF SQL%FOUND THEN
  INSERT INTO orders
    VALUES (5, 3, SYSDATE, null, null, 'F');

-- other application logic
COMMIT;

END IF;
END;
```

This process is just one method you can use to enforce the referential integrity rule inside an application. In any event, you can see that the application spends lots of time requesting and sending data across the network just to enforce a simple integrity rule.

Using Oracle7 Integrity Constraints   For several reasons, a better way to enforce simple integrity rules such as referential integrity is to use Oracle7 integrity constraints. For one, you can easily create integrity constraints along with a table definition. Developers can be more productive because they do not need to create, test, and debug complicated data integrity logic to enforce simple integrity rules. Second, an integrity constraint is a centralized method for enforcing an integrity rule. Therefore, Oracle7 forces all applications to adhere to the same integrity rule. (If the application performs the integrity check, developers need to work hard to create, test, and debug the same data integrity logic in each application.) Finally, because Oracle7 enforces integrity constraints without creating any network I/O, client/server systems do not suffer from performance penalties caused by network access. To learn more about data integrity and integrity constraints, see

Chapter 2, which introduces integrity constraints, and Chapter 14, which explains how to create integrity constraints for the tables in an Oracle7 database.

Database Triggers

Applications often need to enforce complex business rules that you cannot express using integrity constraints. Rather than revert to enforcing a complex integrity rule inside an application, you can use database triggers to make Oracle7 enforce the rule. By using database triggers to enforce complex business rules, you gain the advantages of ease of creation, centralized rule enforcement, and elimination of unnecessary network I/O that simple integrity rules also provide.

You can use database triggers to centralize and automate other types of application logic too. For example, consider the TOTAL column of the ITEMS table. The value in the TOTAL column is the quantity of parts ordered, multiplied by the unit price of the part. The part's unit price is in the PARTS table. How does an application figure out a value for the TOTAL column when inserting a new line item? One way would be to let the application perform the operation using SQL statements:

```
DECLARE
partprice REAL;
BEGIN
SELECT unitprice INTO partprice
  FROM parts
  WHERE id = 4

-- other application logic for calculation

INSERT INTO items VALUES (...)
END;
```

Notice that the application makes a request across the network for the unit price of a part and then inserts the row with a total for the line item. Keep in mind that the application also must include similar logic to account for situations in which users update the quantity of a line item in the ITEMS table. Additionally, many users may be placing and updating orders at the same time. In short, this method for calculating the TOTAL column can create lots of network traffic in a client/server system.

Alternatively, you could use a database trigger to derive the TOTAL value for a line item automatically and without any network access when users insert new rows or update the QUANTITY column in the ITEMS table. Here is an example:

```
CREATE TRIGGER linetotal
BEFORE INSERT OR UPDATE OF quantity, partid ON items
FOR EACH ROW
DECLARE
  itemprice REAL;
BEGIN
  SELECT unitprice INTO itemprice
    FROM parts WHERE id = :new.partid;
  :new.total := :new.quantity * itemprice;
END linetotal;
```

After creating the LINETOTAL trigger, application developers don't need to consider the problem of keeping the TOTAL column current when programming applications. Furthermore, all clients in the network database system benefit from fewer network I/Os.

This is just one example of how developers can take advantage of database triggers in an Oracle7 system. Chapter 2 introduced database triggers, and Chapter 17 explains how to create database triggers for an application schema.

Procedures and Packages

The preceding sections explained how you can reduce network I/O in an Oracle7 client/server database system: by moving application logic to the database server in the form of integrity constraints and database triggers. You can reduce client/ server application network I/O even more by distributing other types of application logic to the database server, using stored procedures. Then, instead of using multiple network-intensive SQL statements to perform database server operations, applications make simple, efficient calls to stored procedures. Packages are a way to encapsulate a number of related procedures inside the database.

Stored Procedures   To illustrate the difference between using SQL and using stored procedures, let's assume you want to insert a new order with some line items. Here's how an application could do this using SQL statements:

```
INSERT INTO orders VALUES (...)
INSERT INTO items VALUES (1, ...)
UPDATE parts SET onhand = ...
INSERT INTO items VALUES (2, ...)
UPDATE parts SET onhand = ...
```

```
INSERT INTO items VALUES (3, ...)
UPDATE parts SET onhand = ...
COMMIT;
```

To create a new sales order and insert three line items for the sales order, the application must issue seven different SQL statements, each of which sends data across the network. To reduce all the network traffic these SQL statements generate in a client/server system, you could create two simple procedures to insert orders and line items:

```
CREATE PROCEDURE placeorder (custid IN INTEGER) AS
BEGIN
  INSERT INTO orders
    VALUES (orderseq.NEXTVAL, custid, SYSDATE, null, null, 'F');
END placeorder;

CREATE PROCEDURE placeitem
  (itemid IN INTEGER, stockid IN INTEGER, quan IN INTEGER) AS
BEGIN
  INSERT INTO items (id, orderid, partid, quantity)
    VALUES (itemid, orderseq.CURRVAL, stockid, quan);
  UPDATE parts
    SET onhand = onhand - quan
    WHERE id = stockid;
END placeitem;
```

Now, instead of issuing SQL statements to insert a new order and line items, the application can simply call the procedures:

```
placeorder(3)
placeitem(1,3,2);
placeitem(2,8,1);
placeitem(3,9,3);
```

Notice that when an application calls a stored procedure, the only data it sends across the network is the procedure call and the data values for the arguments of the stored procedure.

Packages   Packages are an extension of simple stored procedures, and developers can use them when developing applications. Packages are a way to organize and encapsulate related procedures and functions into a single database program unit on behalf of an application. To learn more about procedures and packages, see Chapter 17.

Database Alerts

Database users often need to be alerted when certain things happen in the database so they can take the appropriate actions. For example, if you are an inventory manager, it is important to know when the quantity of any part in stock falls below its reorder point. That way, you can order more inventory for the part before it goes out of stock.

Good application designs will include logic to account for alert conditions; this way, the application automatically notifies interested application users of alert conditions. For example, when developing an inventory management application, you can program an alert to check for parts that have fallen below their reorder points. One way to accomplish this would be to have the inventory management application regularly issue a SQL query for parts that have fallen below their reorder points:

```
-- every 5 minutes poll for stock problems ...
SELECT id FROM parts
  WHERE onhand < reorder

-- other application code to handle the alert
```

This method of checking for alert conditions has a significant problem in client/server systems: the constant polling to check for alert conditions creates excessive amounts of network I/O, especially when lots of users poll for lots of alert conditions at the same time. A better way to poll for alert conditions is to use Oracle7 *database alerts*. Database alerts automatically signal interested users when a named event occurs. Using simple procedure calls, applications can register and wait for named alert conditions. To learn more about Oracle7 database alerts, see Chapter 17.

This chapter has laid the groundwork for understanding the application development process in an Oracle7 client/server database system. You should have a clear understanding of what the application developer does and what types of things go into a client-side database application. The next chapter introduces the Oracle tools and how to use them to develop a simple application.

CHAPTER

FOURTEEN

Designing an Application's Schema

- Planning the tables and integrity constraints for an application schema

- Using views and synonyms in application schemas

- Managing tables, views, and synonyms for an application

A building is only as good as the foundation upon which it is built. Likewise, you can develop a quality database application only if the application uses well-designed data structures. This chapter describes how to create an application schema—the collection of database objects an application uses—including the following:

- Planning the database tables in an application schema

- Setting integrity rules and defining table relationships in an application schema

- Using views effectively for an application

- Creating and managing tables and views

Designing an Application Schema

For the database administrator, planning the physical structure of a database is crucial before creating a new Oracle7 database. Similarly, the application developer must carefully plan and create an application's database objects before diving into application development. This approach ensures a sound application development foundation from the start, one that can save lots of application development work in the long run.

The concept of normalization and database design techniques is a complicated one. The following sections discuss the key topics to consider when planning the tables, integrity constraints, and views in an application's schema and present a few examples to give you an idea of the possibilities.

Designing Tables and Normalization

The theory of *normalization* is a key element of database design when putting together an application schema. In simple terms, normalization is the process of decomposing and arranging the attributes in a schema, which results in a set of tables with very simple structures. The purpose of normalization is to make tables as simple as possible.

You can quickly understand one aspect of the normalization process by studying a simple example involving the CUSTOMERS table. Figure 14.1 shows two ways you could create the CUSTOMERS table. Notice that the first version has the attribute NAME, which holds concatenated values of a customer's first and last name. You can normalize the CUSTOMERS table to a degree, as shown in the second version, by splitting the NAME column, which contains a relation in itself, into a simpler structure—one with a column for the LASTNAME and FIRSTNAME of each customer.

FIGURE 14.1:

Denormalized and more normalized versions of the CUSTOMERS table

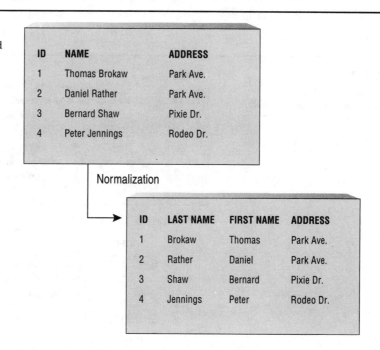

Clearly, normalization can directly affect the functionality and performance of an application. For example, using the denormalized version of the CUSTOMERS table, it is difficult to develop a reporting application that prints customer records in order of the last names of customers. The more normalized version of the CUSTOMER table makes this common reporting requirement a trivial task using this query:

```
SELECT ... FROM customers
  ORDER BY lastname
```

A key focus of normalization is reducing the redundancy of information within a database. For example, consider the two options for storing sales order information shown in Figure 14.2.

The first method for storing sales orders is inefficient because of the redundant information represented in each order; for each order line item, the ORDERS table stores the order number, order, ship and paid dates, and order status. The second method for storing sales orders is much more efficient; the ORDERS table stores all order information just once and the ITEMS table stores related order line item information.

FIGURE 14.2:

Two options for storing sales data, showing how to reduce redundancy of information

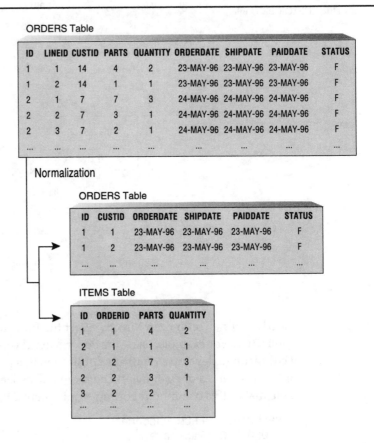

ORDERS Table

ID	LINEID	CUSTID	PARTS	QUANTITY	ORDERDATE	SHIPDATE	PAIDDATE	STATUS
1	1	14	4	2	23-MAY-96	23-MAY-96	23-MAY-96	F
1	2	14	1	1	23-MAY-96	23-MAY-96	23-MAY-96	F
2	1	7	7	3	24-MAY-96	24-MAY-96	24-MAY-96	F
2	2	7	3	1	24-MAY-96	24-MAY-96	24-MAY-96	F
2	3	7	2	1	24-MAY-96	24-MAY-96	24-MAY-96	F
...	...	...	...	...	...	...	...	...

Normalization

ORDERS Table

ID	CUSTID	ORDERDATE	SHIPDATE	PAIDDATE	STATUS
1	1	23-MAY-96	23-MAY-96	23-MAY-96	F
1	2	23-MAY-96	23-MAY-96	23-MAY-96	F
...	...	...	...	...	...

ITEMS Table

ID	ORDERID	PARTS	QUANTITY
1	1	4	2
2	1	1	1
1	2	7	3
2	2	3	1
3	2	2	1
...	...	...	...

TIP

In most situations, you should strive to eliminate data redundancy within a database design. However, in some situations, you can improve the performance of applications noticeably by creating data redundancy on purpose. That's because by lumping attributes together in the same table (as in the first version of the ORDERS table in Figure 14.2), the database design eliminates the need for applications to perform join operations across related but separately stored tables. This can improve application performance, but the drawback is wasted storage space. When designing a schema, carefully consider the trade-offs between data redundancy and normalized tables.

Another focus of normalization is determining the relationships that exist between different attributes in a schema. For example, the ORDERS and ITEMS tables in Figure 14.3 are related by the ID of each order. Furthermore, the relationship is a one-to-many relationship because there can be more than one line item for each order. The process of clearly identifying table relationships is the basis for determining the primary keys and referential integrity rules in a database.

Relationship determination in a schema can be represented using simple diagrams. Figure 14.3 shows an *entity-relation diagram* of the database used in this book.

Diagrams like the one in Figure 14.3 are the foundation for CASE and database design methodologies used by tools such as Oracle's Designer/2000 suite of CASE tools. The different shapes in the diagram indicate different parts of the schema (tables are rectangles, relationships are lines, and so on). For more information about entity-relation diagramming and CASE tools, see Chapter 19.

Choosing Keys and Determining Integrity Rules

As you design the tables in an application schema, it is important to determine the keys in the tables and the relationships you want between tables. You can then enforce the integrity rules identified by your analysis using Oracle7 integrity constraints such as PRIMARY KEY, UNIQUE, and FOREIGN KEY. Let's take a quick

FIGURE 14.3:

An entity-relation diagram graphically represents the data and relationships in an application schema.

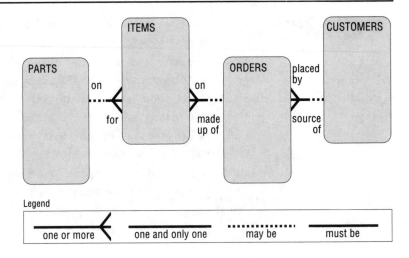

look at some important issues to consider when planning the integrity rules for a schema.

Choosing Primary Keys

Every table in a database should have a primary key—a column or set of columns whose values uniquely identify each row in the table. When you create a new table, it is important to correctly set the table's primary key; otherwise, applications that use the table might not work as planned.

Primary keys for tables have three qualities: they are unique, they remain static, and they are concise.

Uniqueness   By definition, a table's primary key cannot contain any duplicate values; if it did, you would not be able to use it to uniquely identify each row in the table. Implicit in the quality of uniqueness is the fact that a primary key cannot contain any NULLs, because it is impossible to distinguish between two NULLs. Schema designs commonly have tables with ID columns that serve as primary keys to uniquely identify each row in the database. However, in certain tables, this may not be necessary. For example, an employee table might use each employee's social security number as the primary key for employee records.

A Static State   Primary keys are columns that do not undergo frequent changes. After you assign a row's primary key, the primary key should be static for the life of the row; otherwise, the primary key has no meaning. For example, it is unlikely that there will ever be any real need to change a customer's arbitrarily assigned ID number.

Conciseness   In terms of primary keys, the shorter they are, the better, especially since most applications look for rows using primary key values. The best type of primary key is a single column that contains integers, such as the ID type of primary key seen throughout the sample tables in this book. Keep this recommendation in mind as you read Chapter 15. That chapter shows how to tune application performance using another Oracle7 feature, sequences, which an application can use to automatically generate unique integer values for primary keys.

Follow the preceding guidelines when selecting primary keys for the tables in a new application schema. But keep in mind that in some situations you cannot follow all of the recommendations. For example, it is appropriate for the ITEMS table to use a *composite primary key*—one made up of more than one column. Although Oracle7 supports composite primary key specifications, avoid them whenever possible to make application development an easier process in the long run.

After you determine the primary keys in an application schema, you can enforce the associated integrity rule of guaranteed uniqueness using Oracle7 PRIMARY KEY integrity constraints. See the section "Managing Tables and Integrity Constraints" later in this chapter for more information about specifying integrity constraints when creating tables.

Identifying Alternate Keys and Columns to Index

When determining the primary keys for the tables in a schema, you should also look for any alternate keys in a table. In fact, you might need to choose a table's primary key from two or more candidate keys. Alternate keys contain unique values that applications commonly use to find rows in a database. For example, the CUSTOMERS table shown in earlier examples in this book has an alternate key; applications might commonly query customer records by customer name instead of customer ID.

To find the alternate keys in a schema, simply identify those columns an application will commonly use to query rows. Once you find the alternate keys, you can use the analysis to identify the columns in unique keys when creating tables for the new schema.

When looking for alternate keys, you might also find columns that applications commonly query but that do not necessarily contain unique values. These columns, although not primary or alternate keys, are important to flag for later work when tuning application performance with indexes. Chapter 15 explains how you can create indexes on columns of a table to improve application performance.

Identifying and Enforcing Relationships in a Schema

As you normalize tables in a schema, you break apart large, complicated tables into smaller, simple tables that have relationships. During this process, you must clearly map out the table relationships so you can enforce associated data integrity rules using referential integrity constraints. Let's take a look at some of the issues to consider when identifying relationships in an application schema.

You can classify a relationship in a schema as one of three varieties: one-to-one, one-to-many, and many-to-many. Understanding a relationship's type helps you determine the different types of integrity constraints that are required to enforce necessary integrity rules.

One-to-many relationships are common in most application schemas. For example, review the entity-relation diagram shown earlier in Figure 14.3. The ORDERS and ITEMS tables relate by the IDs for each sales order. In this relationship, there should be unique order numbers, but there can be many different line items for an individual order. Therefore, a one-to-many relationship exists between an order and its line items. To enforce the one-to-many relationship rule, make the ID column of the ORDERS table a primary key with a PRIMARY KEY integrity constraint, and make the ORDERID column of the ITEMS table a foreign key with a referential integrity constraint.

Similarly, you can use Oracle7 integrity constraints to enforce one-to-one relationships. For example, one-to-one relationships occur when you partition a table into vertical sections. You can make sure there is a one-to-one relationship between vertical table partitions by simply making the primary key in the secondary partition a foreign key to the primary partition of the table. Figure 14.4 illustrates how to enforce a one-to-one relationship between partitions of a modified version of the CUSTOMERS table.

FIGURE 14.4:

Modified version of the CUSTOMERS table, showing how to vertically partition row data and establish a one-to-one relationship between the partitions

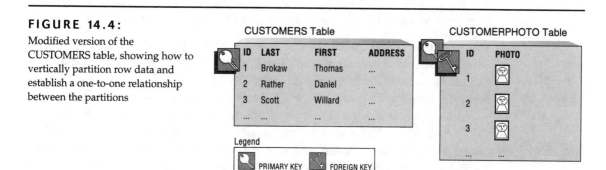

After identifying different relationships in a schema, analyze the referential integrity rules even further to understand the referential actions you want to enforce. Referential actions tell Oracle7 how to maintain referential integrity when users want to modify or delete parent key values that have dependent foreign key values. For example, how do you want Oracle7 to maintain referential integrity when a user tries to delete a sales order in the ORDERS table but the order has dependent line items in the ITEMS table?

Oracle7 referential integrity constraints support two different types of referential actions:

- The update/delete restrict action restricts anyone from updating a parent key value or deleting a parent table row when the parent key value has at least one dependent foreign key value.

- The delete cascade action cascades the deletion of a parent table row to all child rows that depend on the parent key in the deleted parent table row. (Note that Oracle7 enforces update restrict when you specify delete cascade.)

The referential integrity constraints in the ITEMS table clearly demonstrate both types of referential actions. One foreign key references the ORDERS table with the delete cascade referential action (as shown in the section "Using Integrity Constraints to Enforce Standard Data Integrity Rules" in Chapter 2). Therefore, when someone deletes a sales order from the ORDERS table, Oracle7 automatically cascades the delete by removing all corresponding order line items in the ITEMS table. The other foreign key in the ITEMS table uses the update/delete restrict referential action, which restricts all operations on a parent key that has dependent child rows. Therefore, Oracle7 prohibits a user from updating a part number or deleting a part from the PARTS table if the part has dependent order line items.

The relational model includes other types of referential actions not enforced by Oracle7 integrity constraints, including update cascade (cascade the update of a parent key value to any dependent foreign key values), update/delete set null (set dependent foreign key values to NULL when someone updates a parent key value or deletes a parent row), and update/delete set default (set dependent foreign key values to a default value when someone updates a parent key value or deletes a parent row). Although Oracle7 cannot enforce these other referential actions automatically using simple referential integrity constraints, it is possible to use database triggers to enforce many of these rules. See Chapter 17 for more information about using database triggers in an application schema.

To learn more about creating and managing tables and integrity constraints in an application schema, see the section "Managing Tables and Integrity Constraints" later in this chapter.

Using Views Effectively in a Schema Design

Chapter 2 introduced the use of views for several purposes: to add more levels of security, to show table data with a different perspective, and to hide complex queries. Here, we'll delve more deeply into the subject of how and when to use views within an application schema design.

Isolating Application Logic

One of the best reasons to use views in an application schema is to isolate application logic from direct dependence on table structure. For example, assume that an application directly references a database table by name using SQL commands. It is not hard to predict what would happen to the application if at some point you changed the name of the table—you would need to modify the source code of the application to adjust all SQL references to the old table name and then recompile the application. Alternatively, if you use a view on top of the table, you can hide the renaming of the table from the application by simply replacing the definition of the view. The application still references the view, but everything continues to work fine because the view now refers to the new table name. Figure 14.5 illustrates this advantage of using views.

FIGURE 14.5:

Views can eliminate an application's direct dependency on tables.

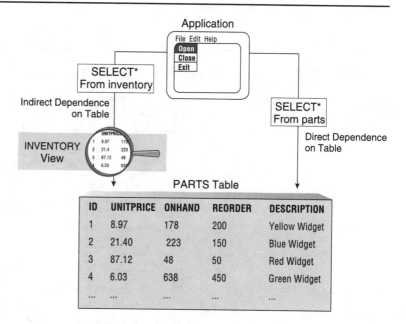

NOTE   Using views is just one way you can isolate applications from directly referencing tables; you can use synonyms or stored procedures as well. See the section "Using Synonyms Effectively in a Schema Design" later in this chapter for information about synonyms, and see Chapter 17 for more information about stored procedures.

Eliminating SQL Commands

Another reason to use views is to eliminate complicated SQL commands from application code, which improves the productivity of application development. For example, applications can use complicated SQL queries that join data from multiple tables or use simple queries on views that perform the same joins. In the latter case, you need to code and test a complicated join query only once when creating a view, as opposed to the former case, where you must work with complicated queries every time the application needs to join table data. Figure 14.6 illustrates this benefit of using views.

FIGURE 14.6:

Use views to hide complicated queries and improve application development productivity.

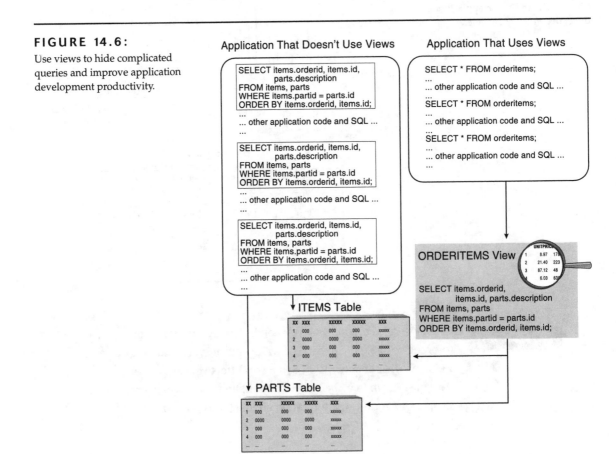

Improving Security

Security is another reason you might use views in an application schema. For example, if a client/server system supports ad hoc query tools for end users, you might want those end users to query table information indirectly through views to hide certain pieces of information. The following view's defining query uses the SQL function USER to allow a user to query employment information about himself or herself but not about other users:

```
CREATE VIEW myinformation AS
   SELECT * FROM emp WHERE ename = USER
```

To learn more about creating and managing views in an application schema, refer to the section "Managing Views" later in this chapter.

Using Synonyms Effectively in a Schema Design

In the previous section, you learned how it can be beneficial to use views to isolate application logic from direct dependence on tables; specifically, if an application references a view and the name of the view's base table changes, the application can continue to work without modification by simply redefining the view to address the new table name. Similarly, you can use another Oracle7 feature, synonyms, to accomplish the same goal, but on a broader scale.

A *synonym* is simply an alias (an alternative name) for an Oracle7 table, view, sequence, stored procedure, function, package, or another synonym. Use synonyms when you want to remove an application's direct dependence on these types of objects. For example, the following statements show how the INVENTORY synonym functions to hide the real name of the PARTS table from application code:

```
CREATE SYNONYM inventory FOR parts

INSERT INTO inventory VALUES (...)

DELETE FROM inventory WHERE id = 5
```

> **NOTE**
>
> Synonyms play an important role in distributed database systems, where applications can reference both local and remote database objects to accomplish work. In a distributed database, you can make application code simpler and more flexible to changes by using synonyms to hide the location of data structures from applications and create what is called *location transparency*.

To learn more about how to create and manage synonyms for an application schema, see the section "Managing Synonyms" later in this chapter.

Managing Tables and Integrity Constraints

If you do not have the luxury of using a CASE or database design tool to help create an application's schema, you need to manually plan and diagram the schema on paper and then create an application's tables and views using SQL commands. Even when you use a CASE tool for schema design and creation, it is nice to know how to use the various DDL commands of SQL that create, alter, and drop tables and views in case you ever need to use them. The following sections describe how to use several DDL commands to create and manage tables and their integrity constraints. Later sections in this chapter describe the same operations for views. Also see Chapter 15, which discusses other schema objects, such as indexes and sequences, you can use to improve an application's performance.

Creating Tables

When you want to create a new table for an application, use the SQL command CREATE TABLE. Here's a statement that creates a new table to store sales order information:

```
CREATE TABLE sales.orders
( id INTEGER PRIMARY KEY,
  customerid INTEGER NOT NULL REFERENCES customers,
  orderdate DATE DEFAULT SYSDATE NOT NULL,
```

```
shipdate DATE DEFAULT SYSDATE,
paiddate DATE DEFAULT SYSDATE,
status CHAR(1) DEFAULT 'F' CHECK (status IN ('F','B'))  )
```

When you name a table, you can specify the schema that will contain the new table. Simply precede the table name with the schema name and a dot. The preceding example creates the ORDERS table in the schema SALES. If you omit a schema name, Oracle7 assumes you want to create the table in your schema.

NOTE To use the CREATE TABLE command, you must have the CREATE TABLE system privilege to create tables in your schema and the CREATE ANY TABLE system privilege to create tables in another schema.

A table's name can be any literal up to 30 characters (or bytes) in length. However, the table's name must begin with an alphabetic character, and it cannot conflict with an Oracle reserved word. For example, you could not name the table in the preceding example ORDER because ORDER is an Oracle reserved word—Oracle7 uses the word ORDER in the ORDER BY clause of SQL.

If you really want to, you can name a table (or any other database object) using an Oracle reserved word by delimiting the table name with double quotation marks in the CREATE TABLE statement:

```
CREATE TABLE "order"
    .
    .
    .
```

However, most programmers avoid using Oracle reserved words for object names because it makes work difficult when using SQL; all references to a table named with an Oracle7 reserved word must also include quotation marks:

```
SELECT * FROM "order"
INSERT INTO "order" ...
```

You can save yourself some headaches by not using Oracle reserved words for table and other object names.

Finally, make sure a table's name is a unique object name within the target schema. For example, there cannot be two ORDERS tables in the SALES schema.

As the preceding example shows, the CREATE TABLE command offers several options for customizing the structure of a new table. The options of concern to an application developer include those for specifying columns and establishing integrity constraints. The next few sections explain more about these two important options for the CREATE TABLE command.

Specifying Columns and Datatypes

The first thing to consider when creating a new table is the table's columns. The columns define the structure for the rows of data that the table can hold. The sample CREATE TABLE statement in the preceding section showed how to specify the different parts of a column specification.

To specify a table's columns in the CREATE TABLE command, you include a comma-separated list of *column specifications*. Each column specification can consist of several parts. At the very least, a column specification requires a column name and a column datatype. A column's name can be any literal up to 30 characters (or bytes) in length that begins with an alphabetic character and does not conflict with any Oracle reserved words. A column's datatype can be any Oracle datatype, including CHAR, VARCHAR2, NUMBER, DATE, LONG, RAW, LONG RAW, and ROWID. (See Table 2.1 in Chapter 2 for more information about Oracle datatypes.)

TIP

For convenience, you can also specify a column's datatype using most ANSI, IBM DB2, or IBM SQL/DS datatypes. The CREATE TABLE example earlier in this chapter uses the INTEGER datatype for the ID and CUSTOMERID columns. If you choose to specify a column's datatype using a datatype external to Oracle7, Oracle7 automatically converts the external datatype specification to an equivalent Oracle datatype specification. In the example, Oracle7 automatically converts the ANSI INTEGER datatype specification to the ORACLE NUMBER(38) datatype.

Optionally, a column specification in a CREATE TABLE statement can include a default column expression and integrity constraints for the column. (See the next section for information about integrity constraints inside a column specification.) A column's *default expression* is a convenient SQL feature that indicates the value to supply for an INSERT statement that does not specify a value for the column. You can specify any default column expression that does not include reference to another column or a sequence. A default column expression can also be an Oracle7 SQL function, such as SYSDATE or USER. All the date columns in the ORDERS table of the previous example use the SQL function SYSDATE to fill in a date if INSERT statements do not specify order, ship, and paid dates. If you do not specify a default column expression for a column, Oracle7 supplies NULL for missing column values in INSERT statements (assuming that the column permits NULLs).

Specifying Integrity Constraints

Chapters 2 and 17 explain the significant advantages that integrity constraints can provide in a client/server database system. When you plan a new table, be sure to also plan its integrity constraints. Then, when you create a new table, you can create its integrity constraints at the same time.

SQL lets you create a new table's integrity constraints both inside and outside column specifications. The CREATE TABLE example earlier in this chapter demonstrates several integrity constraints within column specifications.

If Oracle7 allows you to specify integrity constraints both inside and outside column specifications of the CREATE TABLE statement, how do you decide which option to use? In most cases, the choice is yours, because it is no more than a syntactic option of SQL. There are only two situations that call for a specific method of integrity constraint specification:

- You must specify NOT NULL integrity constraints inside the respective column specification.

- When an integrity constraint involves more than one column, you must specify the integrity constraint outside any one column specification. For example, you might want to create a composite primary or unique key on multiple columns.

To demonstrate these considerations, the following CREATE TABLE statement shows how to create several NOT NULL constraints within column specifications and a composite PRIMARY KEY constraint outside any one column specification:

```
CREATE TABLE items
( id INTEGER,
  orderid INTEGER REFERENCES orders ON DELETE CASCADE,
  partid INTEGER NOT NULL REFERENCES parts,
  quantity INTEGER NOT NULL,
  total DECIMAL(10,2),
  PRIMARY KEY (id, orderid) )
```

Notice that including integrity constraint specifications inside a column specification when possible clearly shows the integrity rules that apply to each column.

TIP   Don't spend a lot of time debating which syntactic option to use. Get the job done and move on to more important issues.

Other Options

If you look at a complete syntax diagram of the Oracle7 CREATE TABLE command, you will see that there are many other options. For example, Chapter 10 explains how to specify various storage parameters for a new table with the TABLESPACE and STORAGE clauses of the CREATE TABLE command. If you are an application developer working in a test environment, the other options of the CREATE TABLE command will rarely be of interest to you because your tables are just prototypes that contain very little data. However, if you are creating tables for a production database, these other options are important. Usually, the administrator addresses the complicated storage considerations for a new table when installing a new application to ensure that the correct amount of space is allocated for each table. For more information about setting storage options for tables, see Chapter 10.

Modifying Tables

How many times have you created a masterpiece only to find that later on you need to change something about it? When you are involved in the complicated process of creating new tables for an application, you will often discover something new and want to modify the structure of a table. Oracle7 includes the SQL command ALTER

TABLE so you can change a table without needing to drop the old version and start again.

The ALTER TABLE command is also convenient when you need to alter a table while an application is using the table in a production database. Instead of suspending or shutting down the application for maintenance operations, Oracle7's ALTER TABLE command lets you modify the table without affecting the availability of the application.

> **NOTE** To alter a table with the ALTER TABLE command, you must own the table, have the ALTER object privilege for the table, or have the ALTER ANY TABLE system privilege.

Adding and Modifying Columns

One way to alter a table is to modify an existing column or add another column that you originally forgot to include. The ADD and MODIFY clauses of the ALTER TABLE command let you change the structure of an existing table easily. Here are some examples that show how to use the ALTER TABLE command to add and change the definition of columns:

```
ALTER TABLE customers ADD (fax VARCHAR2(10))

ALTER TABLE customers MODIFY (fax VARCHAR2(20))

ALTER TABLE sales.orders MODIFY (status CHAR(1) DEFAULT NULL)
```

The first statement adds a new column to the CUSTOMERS table for the customer's fax number. The second statement modifies the new FAX column to expand its maximum length. The third statement changes the default column expression for the STATUS column in the ORDERS table.

> **NOTE** You can also use the MODIFY clause to decrease a column's size or change its datatype. However, Oracle7 allows you to perform these operations only when all column values are NULL.

Adding and Modifying Integrity Constraints

Rules are rules, but rules can change. If you decide you need to change the integrity rules tied to a table, you can use the ADD, MODIFY, and DROP clauses of the ALTER TABLE command. To add and drop integrity constraints using the ALTER TABLE command, you must learn a few keywords in the Oracle SQL syntax:

- To add a new integrity constraint separately from a new column definition in the ADD clause, you can use the PRIMARY KEY, UNIQUE, FOREIGN KEY, and CHECK clauses, just as with the CREATE TABLE command.

- To drop an integrity constraint in the DROP clause, you can use the keywords PRIMARY KEY and UNIQUE to drop a primary or unique key and use CONSTRAINT to drop FOREIGN KEY and CHECK constraints by their constraint names.

The following statements show how you can use these different clauses to modify a table's integrity constraints:

```
ALTER TABLE customers ADD (fax VARCHAR2(20) NOT NULL)

ALTER TABLE customers MODIFY (fax VARCHAR2(20) NULL)

ALTER TABLE customers ADD (PRIMARY KEY (id))

ALTER TABLE customers DROP UNIQUE (lastname, firstname)

ALTER TABLE customers DROP PRIMARY KEY CASCADE

ALTER TABLE customers DROP CONSTRAINT sysc0991
```

The first statement is somewhat of a repeat of a previous example; however, this example shows that you can add a new column to a table simultaneously with a new integrity constraint in a column definition. The second example shows how to remove a NOT NULL integrity constraint from a column definition. The third example demonstrates how to add a PRIMARY KEY integrity constraint, and the remaining examples show how to remove specific integrity constraints. Notice the statement that drops the primary key in the CUSTOMERS table; it also includes the keyword CASCADE, which cascades the drop of the primary key to all dependent foreign keys.

Determining Names for Integrity Constraints

To determine the names for the different integrity constraints in a database, you can query the DBA_CONSTRAINTS or USER_CONSTRAINTS data dictionary view. For example, the following query returns the names of all constraints on the ITEMS table:

```
SELECT constraint_name, constraint_type, search_condition
  FROM sys.dba_constraints
  WHERE owner = 'SALES'
  AND table_name = 'ITEMS';
```

```
CONSTRAINT_NAME         C SEARCH_CONDITION
----------------        - --------------------
SYS_C00436              C PARTID IS NOT NULL
SYS_C00437              C QUANTITY IS NOT NULL
SYS_C00438              P
SYS_C00439              R
SYS_C00440              R
```

Notice that the CONSTRAINT_TYPE column (shown in the printout with the heading "C") reveals the different types of constraints: *P* stands for PRIMARY KEY constraint, *U* stands for UNIQUE constraint, *R* stands for referential constraint, and *C* stands for CHECK constraint as well as NOT NULL constraints. You can distinguish between CHECK constraints and NOT NULL constraints by looking at the SEARCH_CONDITION column.

Dropping Columns

Because Oracle7's ALTER TABLE command does not include an option to drop a column of a table, all the benefits that the ALTER TABLE command provides (such as application availability) are not there when you want to drop a column in a table. Consider the side effects (loss of data availability and a lot of extra work), and if you still want to drop a column in a table, follow these steps:

1. If you are working in a production database that is currently available to application users, shut down the applications that need to access the table.

2. Use a CREATE TABLE … AS SELECT … statement to create a new copy of the table, making sure not to include the columns you want to drop. Use a temporary name for the new version of the table.

```
CREATE TABLE newtable AS SELECT col1, col2, col3 FROM oldtable
```

3. Create the necessary integrity constraints and indexes for the new copy of the old table. A CREATE TABLE … AS SELECT … statement does not search the Oracle7 data dictionary to duplicate the constraints and indexes of the old table. Therefore, you must manually search the data dictionary and duplicate these supporting table structures yourself.

4. Rename the old and new versions of the table:

```
RENAME oldtable TO oldtabletemporary
RENAME newtable TO oldtable
```

5. Grant the same access privileges for the new version of the table that exist for the old version of the table.

6. Re-create any views and procedures that depended on the dropped column. If views and procedures did not explicitly refer to the dropped column, they will use the new version of the table without problems.

You can eventually drop the old version of the table to reclaim its disk space after you verify that the applications using the new version of the table still function correctly and that you did not make a mistake in the process.

NOTE A CREATE TABLE … AS SELECT statement is a convenient way to create a copy of all or part of an existing table. When you are copying a large table and want to reduce the time necessary to make the copy, use the UNRECOVERABLE option of the STORAGE clause to disable transaction logging for the CREATE TABLE statement. When you create a table with transaction logging disabled, the new table and its data are vulnerable to a disk failure until after you back up the tablespace that contains the table.

Dropping Tables

If you want to completely remove a table from an application's schema, you can drop the table using the SQL command DROP TABLE. The following statements demonstrate how to use this command:

```
DROP TABLE items
```

```
DROP TABLE orders CASCADE CONSTRAINTS
```

The first statement shows how to drop a table that does not contain a primary or unique key to which other tables refer. The second statement shows how to drop a table that has a primary or unique key to which other tables refer. By using the CASCADE CONSTRAINTS option, Oracle7 automatically drops the foreign keys that depend on the primary key in the table being dropped.

NOTE To drop a table with the DROP TABLE command, you must own the table or have the DROP ANY TABLE system privilege.

Managing Views

After you have finished crafting the tables in an application's schema, the next thing you might do is create different views on top of the application's tables. You can use views in an application schema for many reasons (see the section "Using Views Effectively in a Schema Design" earlier in this chapter). The following sections explain the procedural details of creating and managing views for an application schema.

Creating Views

To create a new view for an application, use the SQL command CREATE VIEW. The rules for naming a view are identical to those for naming tables. See the section "Creating Tables" earlier in this chapter for more information about naming rules for tables.

You can specify many options in the CREATE VIEW command to create a new view, including the following:

- The defining query of a view
- Column aliases for the column names in a view
- Integrity constraints for a view

The next few sections explain each of these options.

NOTE   To create a view, you must have the CREATE VIEW or CREATE ANY VIEW system privilege.

Specifying a View's Query

The primary consideration when creating a new view is the view's defining query. A view's query describes exactly what table data the view will represent. A view's query can be simple, such as this one, which creates the view to mask the name of a table:

```
CREATE VIEW inventory AS
  SELECT * FROM parts
```

When users use the INVENTORY view, it will look exactly the same as when they work with the PARTS table. The following examples show how SELECT and INSERT statements work identically for both the INVENTORY view and PARTS table:

```
SELECT * FROM inventory

ID         UNITPRICE  ONHAND    REORDER   DESCRIPTION
---------  ---------  --------  -------   ----------------
        1       8.97       178      200   Yellow Widget
        2       21.4       223      150   Blue Widget
        3      87.12        48       50   Red Widget
        4       6.03       638      450   Green Widget
        .
        .
        .
```

```
SELECT * FROM parts

ID          UNITPRICE  ONHAND    REORDER   DESCRIPTION
---------   ---------  --------  -------   ----------------
        1        8.97       178       200  Yellow Widget
        2        21.4       223       150  Blue Widget
        3       87.12        48        50  Red Widget
        4        6.03       638       450  Green Widget
  .
  .
  .
```

```
INSERT INTO inventory VALUES (5, 7.93, 600, 250, 'Orange Widget')
```

```
INSERT INTO parts VALUES (6, 23.52, 300, 150, 'Black Widget')
```

A more restrictive view query creates a view that corresponds to only selected table columns and/or rows:

```
CREATE VIEW reorder AS
   SELECT id, onhand, reorder FROM parts
   WHERE onhand < reorder
```

The REORDER view is an example of a view that corresponds to very specific table data based on particular columns and row values in the PARTS table:

```
SELECT * FROM reorder

ID          ONHAND    REORDER
---------   -------   --------
        1       178        200
        3        48         50
  .
  .
  .
```

Another example of a view that targets specific data is one that includes a join query:

```
CREATE VIEW orderreport AS
   SELECT orders.id order_id, orders.orderdate,
     items.id line_id, item.partid
   FROM orders, items
   WHERE items.orderid=orders.id
```

When users query the ORDERREPORT view, Oracle7 joins the related row data from the ORDERS and ITEMS tables:

```
SELECT * FROM orderreport

ORDER_ID    ORDERDATE  LINE_ID    PARTID
--------    ---------  -------    -------
       1    23-MAY-96        1          4
       1    23-MAY-96        2          2
       1    23-MAY-96        3          3
       2    23-MAY-96        1          1
       2    23-MAY-96        2          2
       .
       .
       .
```

The query you use for a view directly affects the functionality of the resulting view. For example, users can use simple views like the INVENTORY view—ones that reference only a single base table in their defining query—for all DML operations, including SELECT, INSERT, UPDATE, and DELETE operations. However, users cannot use complex views for INSERT, UPDATE, and DELETE statements since it is unclear how Oracle7 should map such statements to the base tables. In this particular context, you can consider complex views those views that include set or DISTINCT operators, group functions, and GROUP BY, CONNECT BY, or START WITH clauses. Additionally, the next section discusses when Oracle7 supports INSERT, UPDATE, and DELETE operations in views that contain join operations.

Updatable Join Views   Releases 7.0, 7.1, and 7.2 of Oracle7 do not allow applications to update any view that contains a join operation. However, release 7.3 of Oracle7 supports *updatable join views*, with several important restrictions. Before discussing what types of join views are updatable, it's necessary to understand some terminology used to discuss join views.

Term	Definition
Updatable join view	A join view with a defining query that does not include set or DISTINCT operators, group functions, and GROUP BY, CONNECT BY, or START WITH clauses.
Join column	A column present in the WHERE clause of a join view's defining query.

Term	Definition
Key-preserved table	A base table of an updatable join view that projects its primary key and all of its alternate keys in the view.
Materialized view principle	The update of a view will have the same effects as when the database server materializes the view into a table, which it then updates.

Oracle7 allows INSERT, UPDATE, and DELETE operations through a join view so long as the server can uphold the materialized view principle. Specifically, this translates into the following restrictions:

- An INSERT, UPDATE, or DELETE statement can target only one base table of a join view per statement.

- INSERT and UPDATE statements can target only key-preserved tables.

- DELETE statements can delete rows through a join view only when the view contains just one key-preserved table.

Considering the definition of the ORDERREPORT view earlier, the following DML statements are valid. The comments above each statement explain why.

```
-- Inserts a row into the key-preserved ORDERS table
INSERT INTO orderreport (order_id, orderdate)
  VALUES (23, SYSDATE)

-- Updates a column of the key-preserved ORDERS table
UPDATE orderreport
  SET orderdate = SYSDATE
  WHERE order_id = 22
```

In contrast, the following DML statements are not valid considering the earlier definition of the ORDERREPORT view.

```
-- Attempts to insert a row in more than one table of the view
INSERT INTO orderreport
  VALUES (23, SYSDATE, 1, 12)

-- Attempts to update a base table that is not key-preserved
UPDATE orderreport
```

```
SET line_id = 10
WHERE order_id = 22 AND line_id = 9
```

Significant additional restrictions apply to join views with a defining queries that contain a WITH CHECK OPTION. For more information about these restrictions, see the section "Creating Integrity Constraints for Views" later in this chapter.

TIP

There are significant performance trade-offs to consider before designing database applications to make extensive use of updatable join views for data modification operations. In order to support DML operations that target join views, Oracle7 must perform extra semantic checking to ensure that the integrity of a join view's underlying base table data is preserved. Consequently, transaction-processing applications will generally perform better when they modify base table data directly, or indirectly using synonyms or simple views.

View Functionality

View functionality can be tricky to understand if you create a view in one schema that is based on tables or views from another schema. In this case, the view owner's object privileges for the base tables determine the functionality of a view. This way, Oracle7 prevents a simple view definition from bypassing the internal security controls for object access.

For example, assume that you create the INVENTORY view (shown earlier in this chapter) for the PARTS table, which is in another user's schema, and that you have only the SELECT privilege for the PARTS table. Consequently, you can use the INVENTORY view for SELECT statements only, not for INSERT, UPDATE, or DELETE statements. Additionally, you cannot use any object privileges obtained from roles (as opposed to being granted the object privileges directly) to create a view.

These caveats should not concern you when you are creating an application schema that contains all the objects necessary for an application. That's because the owner of (or schema that contains) all application objects, including views and underlying base tables, is one and the same—you will never need to consider these tricky privilege requirements.

Using Column Aliases to Name the Columns in a View

In many cases, you might want to use alternate names for a view's columns instead of those that correspond to the underlying table column names. For example, when creating a view that joins two different tables, it is important to clearly distinguish columns with identical names that originate from different tables. The ORDERREPORT view shown earlier in this chapter illustrates one way of specifying view column aliases: by indicating individual column aliases just as you do in a SELECT statement. CREATE VIEW, as shown in the next example, also allows you to specify a comma-separated list of column aliases before a view's defining query. If you use this method, the number of column aliases must match the number of columns in the defining query.

```
CREATE VIEW orderreport (order_id, order_date, line_item_id, part_id) AS
   SELECT orders.id, orders.orderdate, items.id, items.partid
     FROM orders, items
     WHERE items.orderid = orders.id
```

Creating Integrity Constraints for Views

A table's integrity constraints enforce integrity rules from all points of access, including any work done on the table through a view of the table. Oracle7 does not permit anyone to bypass a table's integrity rules by creating and using a view.

If you create a view for an application that users will employ to insert or update table data, consider using a special integrity constraint that you can create for the view. If you specify the CHECK option of the CREATE VIEW command when creating a view, Oracle7 permits users to insert and update through the view only those rows that the view in turn can select. For example, this statement defines a view to show only those customers in the state of California:

```
CREATE VIEW california AS
   SELECT companyname, lastname, firstname, city FROM customers
   WHERE state = 'CA'
   WITH CHECK OPTION
```

Now, see if you can predict which of the following two UPDATE statements Oracle7 disallows because of the CALIFORNIA view's integrity constraint:

```
UPDATE california
  SET city = 'SOUTH LAKE TAHOE'
  WHERE id = 7593

UPDATE california
  SET state = 'WA'
  WHERE id = 7593
```

If you picked the second statement, you're right. Oracle7 does not permit the second statement because it would result in a row that the CALIFORNIA view could not select—a record for a customer located in the state of Washington.

Additional Restrictions for Updatable Join Views   When you plan to use a join view to support DML operations and the view's defining query includes a WITH CHECK OPTION, there are several additional restrictions that apply to DML operations:

- INSERT statements are not supported.

- UPDATE statements cannot update any join column or column of a key-preserved table that is repeated in the join view (for example, a base table involved in a self-join).

- DELETE statements cannot target a key-preserved table that is repeated in the join view.

Replacing Views

Sometimes it is necessary to replace the current version of a view with a new definition. For example, if you add a new column to a table, you might want to change the definition of an associated view to show the new column.

One way to replace a view with a new version is by dropping the current view and then re-creating the view with the new definition. However, when you replace a view by dropping it and then re-creating it, you also remove all privilege grants made for the view. You would then need to regrant the necessary privileges for the new version of the view to get an application back in business. To avoid this problem, Oracle7 provides an option to replace the current version of a view with a newer version, the REPLACE option of the CREATE VIEW command:

```
CREATE OR REPLACE VIEW ...
```

TIP Like the ALTER TABLE command, the REPLACE option of the CREATE VIEW command is convenient when you need to replace the definition of a view while an application is online in a production database environment. Instead of suspending or shutting down the application for maintenance operations, you can simply replace the view without affecting the availability of the application.

Dropping Views

If you find that a view is no longer needed, it is best to drop the view to clean up the application's schema and the database's data dictionary. To drop a view, use the SQL command DROP VIEW:

```
DROP VIEW reorder
```

NOTE You can always drop a view that you own. To drop a view in another schema with the DROP VIEW command, you must have the DROP ANY VIEW system privilege.

Managing Synonyms

When you are finished creating the tables and views for an application schema, the next step might be to consider creating synonyms for the database objects that the application will reference to accomplish work. This way, you eliminate any direct dependence the application would otherwise have on database objects (see the discussions about this topic earlier in this chapter). The following sections explain how to create and manage the synonyms in an application schema.

Creating Public and Private Synonyms

Before creating a synonym, you must consider whether or not you want the synonym to be publicly accessible or private to the containing schema. A *public synonym* is available to all users in the database. When you create a public synonym, you provide a name that all users can reference (although users still need privileges for the underlying database object). A *private synonym* is available only to the user who creates the private synonym and the users who have access to the private synonym's base object. For more information about the considerations of security privileges for both public and private synonyms, see Chapter 18.

Once you decide which type of synonym is appropriate, you can create a synonym for a table, view, sequence, stored procedure, function, package, or another synonym with the SQL command CREATE SYNONYM. The following examples illustrate the creation of both public and private synonyms:

```
CREATE SYNONYM sales.inventory FOR sales.parts;

CREATE PUBLIC SYNONYM parts FOR sales.parts;
```

> **NOTE** To create a public synonym, you must have the CREATE PUBLIC SYNONYM system privilege; to create a private synonym in your schema, you must have the CREATE SYNONYM system privilege; and to create a private synonym in another user's schema, you must have the CREATE ANY SYNONYM system privilege.

Using Synonyms

After you create a public or private synonym, application developers can reference the synonym in application code to accomplish work. For example, application code could equivalently reference either the PARTS table or its private synonym INVENTORY:

```
INSERT INTO parts VALUES ( ... )
UPDATE parts ...
DELETE FROM parts WHERE ...

INSERT INTO inventory VALUES ( ... )
UPDATE inventory ...
DELETE FROM inventory WHERE ...
```

As when referencing database objects directly, the application user must have the appropriate privileges for a synonym's base object to successfully complete the request performed by a SQL statement.

Dropping Synonyms

If you drop a synonym's base object for good or decide that you no longer need a synonym, it's best to drop the synonym to clean up the database's data dictionary. You can drop a synonym using the DROP SYNONYM command. When dropping a public synonym, be sure to include the PUBLIC keyword.

```
DROP SYNONYM sales.inventory

DROP PUBLIC SYNONYM parts
```

NOTE To drop a private synonym, you must own the synonym or have the DROP ANY SYNONYM system privilege. To drop a public synonym, you must have the DROP PUBLIC SYNONYM system privilege.

This chapter has discussed the essential database objects of an application's schema, including the following:

- Planning tables with regard to normalization and choosing keys

- Identifying and enforcing domain, entity, and referential integrity rules using Oracle7 integrity constraints

- Using views to eliminate application code from directly depending on schema tables, improve application security, and make complicated SQL coding much easier

- Using synonyms to avoid having application code depend directly on schema tables

- Creating, altering, and dropping tables, views, and synonyms

The next chapter builds on the information in this chapter by beginning a discussion of how to tune client/server application performance using a variety of other Oracle7 schema objects, including indexes, data clusters, and sequences.

CHAPTER

FIFTEEN

Tuning Applications with Database Structures

- Using indexes to speed up data retrieval times

- Using data clusters to improve application performance

- Using sequences to automatically generate primary keys

After you have an application schema's tables and views in place, you can develop and run the application. However, soon after you begin using it, you might find that the application does not perform as well as you might like. Now begins the tuning phase of the application development process.

This chapter explains the first phase in the application tuning process. It describes how to create and use supplementary database objects to tune the use of an application's tables and views, including the following:

- Using indexes and data clusters to speed the retrieval of specific rows in a table

- Using sequences to automatically create unique primary keys for tables without contention among concurrent users who are inserting new rows

Using Indexes to Speed Applications

To find the pages in a book that discuss a very specific subject, you would use the book's index. But assume that the book is terrible and that there is no index. Now it is a bit tougher to find the pages you want. Your next step might be to use the table of contents, but it is unlikely that this very specific subject will appear there. Your only remaining option would be to read every word on every page. And if the book is large, it would take you a lot of time to find what you are looking for. After this, you would probably make sure that the next book you use has an index.

Database management systems such as Oracle7 also use indexes to find specific pieces of table data without requiring complete table scans. Furthermore, an Oracle7 table's index works the same way as the index in a book. Figure 15.1 shows what an index looks like in an Oracle7 database and how it speeds the retrieval of certain rows.

Notice in Figure 15.1 that an Oracle7 index is an ordered tree of data blocks or nodes. When Oracle7 uses an index to find an index value, it descends from the root node to the branch nodes and then to the leaf nodes, searching for the requested index value. Each read of a node results in a disk I/O unless the corresponding data block is currently cached in the database server's buffer cache. In each leaf node of

FIGURE 15.1:

An index for a table allows Oracle7 to quickly find rows by their index values with minimal disk I/O.

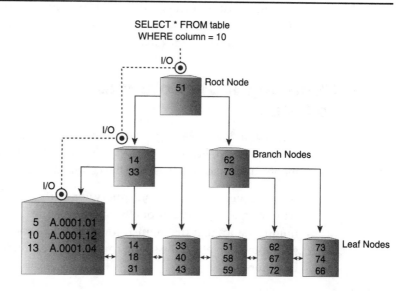

an index, there are index values along with their corresponding physical addresses. When Oracle7 finds the requested index value, it reads the physical address of the corresponding table's row so it can immediately access the row.

Indexes are supplementary, optional database structures that you can add to an application's tables to make access to the table much faster. When you do not have an index on a table, Oracle7 can still find the rows that an application user requests, but it takes longer because the server must scan all of the rows in the table. If the user requests only a handful of rows in a large table, the database server ends up performing a lot of unnecessary disk I/Os to find the requested rows. Alternatively, if the server can use an index to find rows in a table, the server can access only the specifically requested rows without very much disk access.

When a table has an index, Oracle7 automatically uses the index if it finds that using it will improve the performance of a statement. Oracle7 transparently uses indexes for all types of SQL statements, including SELECT statements with WHERE clauses and subqueries for UPDATE and DELETE statements (WHERE clauses). If a statement updates an indexed value in a row, Oracle7 automatically updates the value in the index along with the value in the table's row.

Although indexes can speed the performance of applications, they are not appropriate for every column in a table. The following section explains how to choose the correct columns to index in a table.

Choosing Table Columns to Index

When you develop an application and its schema, it is important to note all of the columns an application's SQL statements use in the WHERE clauses of SQL statements. In most cases, these are the columns that should have an index.

Most frequently, applications query for particular table rows by asking for rows with specific primary key or alternate key values. That's because a table's keys hold unique values that distinguish rows from one another. For example, this query is guaranteed to return the single row that corresponds to the customer identified by ID number 3:

```
SELECT *
  FROM customers
  WHERE id = 3
```

There is no need for you to create an index on a primary key or an alternate key that is already declared for the table; Oracle7 automatically creates unique indexes behind the PRIMARY KEY and UNIQUE integrity constraints for a table.

Table columns without PRIMARY KEY or UNIQUE integrity constraints are not guaranteed to have unique column values. However, applications often use some of these columns to find specific table rows. For example, an application might want to find all of the backlogged sales orders using the following query:

```
SELECT id
  FROM orders
  WHERE status = 'B'
```

In this case, it might improve the performance of the order-entry application if you created an index on the STATUS column of the ORDERS table. That way, Oracle7 could find all of the rows in the index with a backlog status.

When you identify a non-key column as a candidate for indexing, consider these factors to determine if an index will actually improve application performance:

- The table you want to index should not be too small. If Oracle7 can store all of a table's rows in a just a few data blocks, there is no point in creating an index; it will not reduce the amount of disk I/O to access rows in the table.

- Index the columns that statements use to join related tables. Most often, statements join tables by their primary key/foreign key relationships. Since a table's primary key already has an index, all you need to do is index the foreign key. Although following this suggestion can improve the performance of retrieval operations involving related tables, it also slows down the performance of update operations on the columns of the foreign key. Carefully consider the number of retrieval operations versus the number of update operations to determine whether or not it is appropriate to index the foreign key.

- Queries and subqueries for UPDATE and DELETE statements should regularly search for less than 20 percent of the table's rows. Statements that search for more than 20 percent will probably receive no performance gain from using an index because Oracle7 performs an equivalent or larger amount of disk I/O to access both the index's data blocks and the table's data blocks.

- Queries and subqueries that point to indexes with NOT NULL searches do not use indexes. That's because Oracle7 does not store NULLs in an index.

- The only limiting factor that determines the number of possible indexes for a table is the number of column combinations possible for an index. Otherwise there is no limit to the number of indexes per table. However, also consider that the more indexes you add to a table, the more indexes Oracle7 needs to maintain when users modify index values in the table. If a table is in a decision-support database where DML activity is rare, then having more indexes per table is reasonable to improve the performance of different types of queries. However, when a table is in an OLTP database where DML activity is high, many indexes per table will no doubt slow down application response time.

- If an application requests many table lookups on a set of columns and none of the individual columns are themselves highly specific, but the entire set of columns together is, consider building a composite index of multiple columns. Composite indexes can contain up to 16 columns in the same table, assuming that the amount of data for each index entry is less than the database's data block size (minus some overhead).

- You cannot index LONG and LONG RAW columns.

For example, do you think that indexing the CUSTOMERS table's STATE column is justifiable? If applications frequently query rows in the CUSTOMERS table by a customer's state, the table has quite a few customer records, and customers are spread out among many different states, the STATE column would be a prime candidate for an index. However, if most customers are all in the same state, creating an index for the STATE column might be a waste.

What about indexing the QUANTITY column of the ITEMS table? Considering that most sales order line items are for one, two, or three parts, an index on the QUANTITY column probably will not make much of a difference for queries that select line items by the quantity ordered.

Creating Indexes for Table Columns

Now that you have some understanding of which columns to index, it is time to learn how to create an index for a table. To do so, you use the SQL command CREATE INDEX. For example, this statement creates a new index for the STATE column of the CUSTOMERS table:

```
CREATE INDEX sales.stateindex ON customers (state)
```

NOTE To use the CREATE INDEX command, you must own the table you are trying to index, or you must have the CREATE ANY INDEX system privilege or have been granted the INDEX object privilege for the table.

The preceding index is for a single column in a table. You can also create *composite indexes* to index the concatenated values of more than one table column. This statement creates a composite index:

```
CREATE INDEX index ON table (column1, column2, ...)
```

When you create a composite index, it is critical that you order the columns in the index with some thought; if you don't, some queries might not be able to use the index at all. The leading columns in a composite index's column list should be the columns that most queries use to find table rows.

Rebuilding Indexes

If a table experiences a good deal of update and delete activity, the table's indexes can get out of balance, uncondensed, and as a result, somewhat ineffective in maximizing lookup performance. The telltale sign is when users notice that operations involving the index gradually slow down over time.

If your client/server application modifies a table's index values frequently and application performance with respect to that index gradually slows down over time, a problem with the index might be the reason. The first thing you can do is use the ANALYZE command to make sure the statistics corresponding to the index are current in the data dictionary. If statistics are not current with the data in the index, the optimizer might not be making intelligent decisions. If you are not familiar with analyzing tables and indexes, see Chapter 10.

If reanalyzing application data fails to improve application performance with respect to a specific index, the next step is to assume that the index has become unbalanced and uncondensed. In this case, the only solution is to rebuild the index. The best time to rebuild an index is when the corresponding application(s) is offline or under a light load.

With releases 7.0, 7.1, and 7.2 of Oracle7, rebuilding an index means that you need to drop and re-create the index. However, starting with release 7.3 of Oracle7, you can use the REBUILD clause of the SQL command ALTER INDEX to quickly rebuild an index. For example, the following statement rebuilds the index for the STATE column of the CUSTOMERS table:

```
ALTER INDEX sales.stateindex
  REBUILD UNRECOVERABLE
```

Similar to a CREATE TABLE … AS SELECT statement (see Chapter 14), the REBUILD clause of the ALTER INDEX command allows you to rebuild the index with transaction logging disabled to reduce the time necessary to build the index. When you rebuild an index with transaction logging disabled, the new index and its data are vulnerable to a disk failure until after you back up the tablespace that contains the index.

How often should you rebuild indexes that applications frequently modify? As you might expect, the answer is specific to your particular situation. For example, you might find it necessary to rebuild an index every few months or just once a year. Be sure to consider how quickly an index becomes unbalanced as a result of user activity and how much performance gain user operations experience from rebuilding the index.

TIP

Prior to release 7.3 of Oracle7, you can rebuild the indexes behind PRIMARY KEY and UNIQUE integrity constraints by simply disabling and enabling the constraints. Oracle7 automatically drops a constraint's index when you disable the constraint and re-creates the index when you enable the constraint. (See Chapter 6 for more information about disabling and enabling integrity constraints.) When using release 7.3 of Oracle7, use an ALTER INDEX … REBUILD statement to rebuild the index behind an integrity constraint. The name of an index behind a PRIMARY KEY or UNIQUE key constraint is the same name as the constraint.

Dropping Indexes

If after you create an index you find that the index does not improve performance or if you are in the process of rebuilding an index, you need to know how to drop an index. To drop a table's index, you use the SQL command DROP INDEX. This statement drops the STATEINDEX index of the CUSTOMERS table:

```
DROP INDEX sales.stateindex
```

After you drop an index, Oracle7 frees the space used by the index for other objects. Applications can still access the table as before, but the index is no longer available to help process statements.

Note that when you drop a table, Oracle7 automatically drops any associated indexes. This means that you do not need to waste time dropping a table's indexes before dropping the table.

To use the DROP INDEX command, you must own the index or have the DROP ANY INDEX system privilege.

Using Data Clusters

When you go to the registration area at a big trade conference, there are usually several registration booths that correspond to several ranges of attendees' last names. For example, there might be one booth for attendees with last names that begin with the letters A through E, another booth for F through K, and so on. The idea is to improve the efficiency of registering many attendees by organizing different booths to separate and clump together conference badges, conference materials, and so on for each range of attendees by last name.

Using the same idea as the conference registration booths, Oracle7's *data clusters* can physically store related rows together to improve the performance of certain operations. For example, if a reporting application regularly generates reports of customer information according to the state in which a customer lives, it might be beneficial to the reporting application if you cluster all of the rows in the CUSTOMERS table by the STATE column. This way, when you generate a report of customers from the state of New York, Oracle7 needs to read only the one data block (or a small number of blocks) that contains all of the customer records from New York.

In an unclustered table, Oracle7 stores a new row in whatever data block can hold the row. Therefore, if a statement wants to retrieve all of the rows that have a specific column value, it is likely that Oracle7 will need to read many data blocks to retrieve all of the rows. For example, if you want to retrieve all of the records from an unclustered CUSTOMERS table for customers who live in the state of New York, Oracle7 will probably need to read several data blocks. Figure 15.2 illustrates the difference between a clustered and an unclustered table.

FIGURE 15.2:

Clustered and unclustered versions
of the CUSTOMERS table

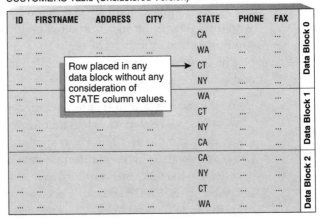

CUSTOMERS Table (Clustered Version)

CUSTOMERS Table (Unclustered Version)

Oracle7 supports two different types of data clusters: indexed data clusters and
hash data clusters. In an *indexed data cluster*, Oracle7 physically stores rows by the
key values in the data cluster's index. In a *hash data cluster*, Oracle7 physically stores
rows by the result of a hash function that is applied to each row's key value. The
next section explains more about the different types of data clusters and when to
use them to improve the performance of an application's SQL statements.

Deciding When to Use Data Clusters

If your application is working more slowly than you think it should, when do you consider using data clusters to help performance? And should you use indexed data clusters or hash data clusters?

Indexed Data Clusters

As the example in the preceding section illustrates, the idea of using an indexed data cluster to physically locate and cluster rows by their key values seems like a promising approach to improve the performance of certain operations. Oracle7 even allows you to have *multi-table data clusters,* in which related rows of master and detail tables are physically prejoined on disk in the same data blocks.

It would seem that prejoining tables on disk would improve the performance of join queries. However, indexed data clusters have been available in several versions of Oracle leading up to Oracle7, and in that time, Oracle users consistently report minimal gains, if any, from using indexed data clusters. In certain situations, Oracle7's indexed data clusters can improve the performance of limited read operations, but they degrade the performance of insert, update, and delete operations. Without a doubt, there are some cases where the use of an indexed data cluster can make a noticeable improvement. In general, though, you should avoid using indexed data clusters and use tables with indexes, hash data clusters, or both.

Hash Data Clusters

Hash data clusters can significantly improve application performance when an application continuously issues exact-match queries on a lookup table. (This type of operation is common in most relational database schemas.) *Exact-match queries* are those that ask for a row by a specific value:

```
SELECT description
  FROM parts
  WHERE id = 4
```

Hash data clusters are a good idea for exact-match queries because Oracle7 can find the data block that holds the requested row with a single disk I/O. Oracle7 applies a hash function to the value in the WHERE clause of the query, which automatically tells Oracle7 which data block stores the requested row. The idea of using hash clusters is not so much to physically clump together many related rows (as with indexed data clusters), but to physically locate rows so Oracle7 can find them with only one disk I/O.

Right now, you are probably thinking of many Oracle7 tables that you might want to store in a hash data cluster to tune application performance. But before you get to work, also consider that a table in a hash cluster should also be relatively static. In other words, applications should use a table in a hash cluster primarily for queries, not for INSERT, UPDATE, and DELETE statements. Oracle7 physically preallocates space when creating a hash cluster so it can locate the rows within. Consequently, a volatile table can quickly unorganize the physical layout of the hash cluster, taking with it the performance benefits.

Unclustered Tables with Indexes versus Hash Clusters

When should you use hash data clusters and when should you use unclustered tables with indexes to improve the performance of your application? To make your decision, answer two simple questions:

- Is the table static or volatile?

- Do applications use equality or range searches on the table's key?

Figure 15.3 shows a flow diagram that illustrates the decision-making process.

Notice that the flow diagram in Figure 15.3 can lead to three different results. First, if a table is volatile rather than static, you should always use an unclustered table with indexes, as explained in the preceding section.

FIGURE 15.3:

How to decide between unclustered tables with indexes and hash data clusters

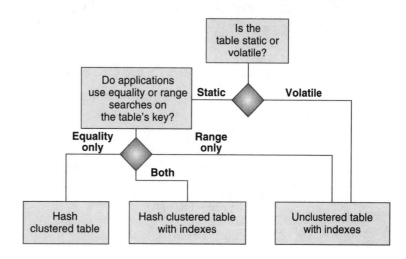

The second question attempts to determine the types of queries an application issues on a static table. In general, you cannot go wrong with an unclustered table with indexes; they are very good at improving the performance of all queries because they reduce the disk I/O necessary to complete both range and equality queries.

If you want the very best performance for equality queries on a static table, hash clusters are the way to go; they require only one disk I/O to find the rows requested by an equality search. However, hash clusters are very bad for range searches; Oracle7 needs to perform a full table scan to find the rows requested by a range query when only a hash cluster is present.

A third possibility arises when applications issue both range and equality searches on a static table. In this case, it is appropriate to both cluster the table and have supplementary indexes on the keys of the table. Oracle7 automatically takes care of this for you when you declare the primary key and alternate keys for a table, whether or not you create the table in a hash cluster. When an application issues a query, the Oracle7 optimizer will choose the hash approach to find rows requested by equality searches and choose the index approach to find rows requested by range searches. Therefore, you have both cases covered if you combine the two approaches.

The next section describes how to create and use hash data clusters. As explained earlier, in general, you should avoid using indexed data clusters.

Creating and Using Hash Data Clusters

To create a hash data cluster, you use the SQL command CREATE CLUSTER. For example, this statement creates a hash cluster in preparation for the PARTS table:

```
CREATE CLUSTER partcluster (id INTEGER)
   SIZE 40
   HASH IS id
   HASHKEYS 1000
```

To place a table in a hash cluster, you specify the cluster when you create the table:

```
CREATE TABLE parts
( id INTEGER PRIMARY KEY,
   ... other columns ... )
CLUSTER partcluster (id)
```

NOTE To create a cluster, you must have the CREATE CLUSTER or CREATE ANY CLUSTER system privilege. To create a table in a hash cluster, you must own the cluster and have the CREATE TABLE system privilege or the CREATE ANY TABLE system privilege.

Notice that when you create a hash cluster, you must specify the key for the cluster. In most cases, you will want the key for a clustered table to be one of the table's keys: primary, alternate, or foreign; after all, most queries will attempt to identify rows by a key value.

Also notice that the CREATE CLUSTER command has a few special clauses that allow you to determine the physical layout of a hash cluster's storage. Since the developer knows the application behavior, it is up to the developer to set these parameters correctly:

- The optional SIZE clause allows you to specify the size of the rows in the hash cluster. SIZE is specified in bytes. For example, the SIZE specification for the PARTCLUSTER is 40, meaning that the average size of a row in the PARTS table is approximately 40 bytes. Oracle7 uses this parameter to determine how many unique hash values it can map to each data block. If you omit the SIZE clause, Oracle7 stores only one hash key value in each data block, which can lead to a tremendous amount of wasted space. Therefore, use the techniques shown in Chapter 10 to determine the average table row size, and use this value to set a hash cluster's SIZE parameter correctly.

- The HASH IS clause is optional. Use this clause of the CREATE CLUSTER command only when the cluster's key is a single, numeric column and the key contains uniformly distributed positive integers. For example, the key for the PARTCLUSTER is the ID column of the PARTS table. Since the ID column is the primary key of the PARTS table (all values must be unique), the values in the cluster key are uniformly distributed.

- The HASHKEYS clause is required. It specifies the number of unique keys you think will ever be in the table in the cluster. For example, the setting shown earlier in this section means that the PARTS table will contain, at most, 1000 unique parts.

NOTE If you are using release 7.2 or 7.3 of Oracle7, you can use the HASH IS clause to specify a SQL expression as the hash function. Use this option when a cluster's single column key does not contain uniformly distributed positive integers. The expression that declares the hash function must always evaluate to positive values and can include only numeric columns with a scale of zero. Additionally, the expression that declares the hash function can reference only columns in the same cluster; should not always evaluate to the same value; and cannot contain a subquery, reference to a user-defined PL/SQL function, or use the SYSDATE, USERENV, TO_DATE, UID, USER, LEVEL, or ROWNUM SQL functions.

Dropping Clusters

If you try a cluster and decide that it is not helping application performance or if you want to drop the table in the cluster for another reason, you can drop the cluster and any tables within by using the SQL command DROP CLUSTER. This statement drops the PARTCLUSTER cluster:

```
DROP CLUSTER partcluster
```

If you want to drop a cluster that currently contains one or more tables, you can drop the cluster and the tables all in one operation by using the INCLUDING TABLES option of the DROP CLUSTER command:

```
DROP CLUSTER partcluster
   INCLUDING TABLES
      CASCADE CONSTRAINTS
```

If you want to keep the table data but remove it from a cluster, you need to create a new version of the table and copy the old table's data to the new version before dropping the cluster:

```
CREATE TABLE newparts
(id INTEGER PRIMARY KEY,
 ... other columns and constraints ... )

INSERT INTO newparts SELECT * FROM parts

DROP CLUSTER partcluster
```

After creating the new, unclustered version of the table and dropping the old version, rename the new table and then grant the same privileges that existed for the clustered version of the table.

The CASCADE CONSTRAINTS option is just like the same option of the DROP TABLE command. Specify this option only if you are dropping a table that contains a primary key referenced by a foreign key in another table. Otherwise, you must manually drop the dependent foreign keys before dropping the clustered table with the primary key.

Using Sequences

OLTP applications are characterized by many small insert and update transactions. OLTP environments usually demand high performance because the productivity of many workers hinges on the database server's ability to quickly complete a high number of transactions.

Most OLTP applications are specifically insert-intensive. For example, a sales order application that services many different sales representatives can bombard the database server with new sales orders, especially when business is good. Inherent in inserting new records into a table is the requirement that each row have a unique primary key value. Imagine the logic a developer would need to code into a multi-user client/server sales order application to make sure every new sales order had a unique ID, much less to make it efficient enough that it does not saturate the network with database requests and slow down the productivity of sales representatives. Fortunately, application developers do not need to consider such problems when working with Oracle7 because of an OLTP feature called the *sequence generator*.

The Oracle7 sequence generator generates sequences of unique integers that applications can use as primary key values for insert-intensive applications. The following sections explain how to create and use sequences for the tables in an application schema to improve the performance of the application.

Creating Sequences

To create a new sequence of numbers, you use the SQL command CREATE SEQUENCE. For example, these statements create sequences for a couple of tables in an application schema:

```
CREATE SEQUENCE sales.customersequence
   START WITH 1
   INCREMENT BY 1
   NOMINVALUE
   NOMAXVALUE
   NOCYCLE
   NOCACHE

CREATE SEQUENCE sales.ordersequence
   START WITH 1
   INCREMENT BY 1
   NOMAXVALUE
   NOCYCLE
   CACHE 5
```

> **NOTE**
> To create a sequence you must have the CREATE SEQUENCE or CREATE ANY SEQUENCE system privilege.

There are several parameters you can set when creating a new sequence of integers. For example, you can determine the starting integer for the sequence and how to increment the sequence (negative integers indicate descending-sequence integer generation), as well as minimum and maximum sequence integers.

You can also indicate whether or not you want the sequence to cycle. An ascending sequence cycles upon reaching its maximum value; a descending sequence cycles upon reaching its minimum value.

Finally, the CACHE parameter lets you pregenerate and cache a number of integers all at one time to reduce the disk I/O when applications use the sequence. (Disk I/O is necessary because Oracle7 needs to keep track of a sequence's current number in the data dictionary.)

> **NOTE**
> If you cache sequence numbers, some sequence numbers may be lost, for example, when the database server shuts down. However, primary keys should have no particular meaning other than to uniquely identify rows in a table. Therefore, if you lose some sequence numbers, this should have no effect on the readability of a table.

Using Sequences in Applications

Now that you know how to create a sequence of numbers, this section shows how you can use sequences to improve the performance of an application.

Typically, INSERT statements use a sequence to generate a unique primary key for the new row. To reference a sequence and generate a new sequence number, reference the sequence with the pseudo-column NEXTVAL:

```
INSERT INTO customers
  VALUES (customersequence.NEXTVAL, ... )
```

> **NOTE** To use a sequence, you must have the SELECT object privilege for the sequence or the SELECT ANY SEQUENCE system privilege.

The preceding INSERT statement generates the next unique sequence integer for the CUSTOMERSEQUENCE and assigns this value to the user session that generated the value. Once an application user generates a sequence number, no other sessions can use the same value.

After generating a new sequence number, the same session can reuse the current sequence number by referencing the sequence with the CURRVAL pseudo-column. This is primarily useful when inserting detail records along with a master record. For example, this transaction inserts a new sales order and three line items for the same order, using the ORDERSEQUENCE to generate and reuse a unique sales order ID:

```
INSERT INTO orders
  VALUES (ordersequence.NEXTVAL, ... )
INSERT INTO items
  VALUES (1, ordersequence.CURRVAL, ...)
INSERT INTO items
  VALUES (2, ordersequence.CURRVAL, ...)
INSERT INTO items
  VALUES (3, ordersequence.CURRVAL, ...)
COMMIT
   .
   .
   .
```

This example uses the ORDERSEQUENCE for both the ORDERS and ITEMS tables, revealing that sequences are not tied in any way to specific database tables in the Oracle7 data dictionary. Users can use any sequence to generate unique numbers for any table.

Altering Sequences

If you find that you would like to adjust one of the parameters for a sequence in an application schema, you can alter the sequence using the SQL command ALTER SEQUENCE. For example, suppose that sales orders are entered more quickly than you thought. To reduce disk I/O on behalf of the sequence, you decide to increase the number of sequence numbers to cache for the ORDERSEQUENCE:

```
ALTER SEQUENCE ordersequence
    CACHE 50
```

NOTE
To alter a sequence, you must own the sequence, or you must have the ALTER object privilege for the sequence or the ALTER ANY SEQUENCE system privilege.

Dropping Sequences

Although a sequence is not directly linked by Oracle7 to specific database tables, applications do associate a sequence for use with specific tables. Therefore, if you drop a table, you should determine whether or not sequences related to the table have any more use in the database. If not, then you should also drop the sequences to clean up the data dictionary.

To drop a sequence, you use the SQL command DROP SEQUENCE. For example, the following statement drops the CUSTOMERSEQUENCE:

```
DROP SEQUENCE sales.customersequence
```

NOTE
To drop a sequence, you must own the sequence or have the DROP ANY SEQUENCE system privilege.

This chapter has shown you the most basic ways you can tune an ORACLE7 application's performance—by using supplementary database structures like indexes, clusters, and sequences. You have learned the following:

- How indexes, indexed data clusters, and hash data clusters can reduce disk I/O for SQL operations and thus improve performance for corresponding applications

- How to decide when indexes or data clusters can indeed help application performance

- How to decide which columns to index

- How to create and manage indexes and data clusters

- How the Oracle7 sequence generator can improve the performance of OLTP applications by automatically generating unique primary keys without contention in a multi-user database system

- How to create, use, and manage sequences

The next chapter continues the discussion of Oracle7 application tuning but focuses on tuning an application's logic, including SQL statement tuning, transaction design, and manual locking strategies.

CHAPTER

SIXTEEN

Tuning Application Logic

- **Using EXPLAIN PLAN and Oracle7 hints to tune SQL statements**

- **Designing transactions for maximum performance**

- **Overriding default locking mechanisms and using SET TRANSACTION**

- **Pinning an application's code in server memory**

- **Using array processing to reduce network traffic**

Once you have done all you can to tune an application with indexes, clusters, and sequences, you still might find that it is not delivering the performance you expect or require. This leads you to the next phase of application tuning: tuning the logic within the application itself. This chapter explains several areas to focus on when trying to tune the logic of an Oracle7 client application, including the following:

- Designing SQL statements to take advantage of available indexes and hash clusters

- Examining and tuning SQL statement execution

- Tuning transaction behavior for maximum performance

- Using all available Oracle7 client/server features to reduce network traffic between clients and the database server

Tuning SQL Statements

One of the first places to look when tuning an application's logic is the SQL statements the application issues to the database server. If your statements are not well designed or if the server is not executing them efficiently, you need to make some changes. The following sections explain techniques for tuning SQL statements:

- How to design SQL statements intelligently

- How to display the Oracle7 server's execution plan for a SQL statement

- What to look for when tuning SQL statements for a client/server environment

- How to influence SQL execution with Oracle7 hints

Designing Statements for Optimal Performance

Chapter 15 focused on using supplemental Oracle7 features, such as indexes and hash clusters, to improve the performance of SQL statements. But the mere fact that a table has an index or is in a hash cluster does not mean Oracle7 can improve the performance of every statement that uses the table. Only by designing SQL statements intelligently to take advantage of indexes and clusters can you produce significant performance gains.

For example, consider this query:

```
SELECT * FROM items
   WHERE orderid = 3
```

Recall that the ITEMS table has a composite primary key of the ID and ORDERID columns. Since the ITEMS.ORDERID column is indexed, you might expect Oracle7 to use the index to complete the query. However, Oracle7 cannot use the index behind the primary key because the query does not refer to the leading portion of the concatenated index values—the ID of the line items.

To get the query to return the same results but use the available index, you need to reference the leading portion of the index. This rewrite of the query shows one way to do it:

```
SELECT * FROM items
   WHERE id < 1000
   AND orderid = 3
```

The second query includes a reference to all line items with an ID of less than 1000 (there should not be any orders with more than a few line items, so 1000 is a safe bet) and an ORDERID of 3. With this simple rewrite of the original query, Oracle7 now uses the index that includes the ORDERID column.

This example is just one of many possible situations in which poor SQL statement design leads to less than optimal behavior. The next section explains the EXPLAIN PLAN feature of Oracle7, a tool you can use to reveal the execution plans for SQL statements.

Explaining Statement Execution to Diagnose Tuning Problems

Once an application's SQL statements are designed to use all available indexes, hash clusters, and sequences, you can turn your attention to tuning the execution of the SQL statements within the application. In most cases, you do not need to worry about the internals of statement execution. That's because Oracle7's cost-based optimizer can make intelligent decisions in order to execute all SQL statements the fastest way possible. However, there are situations when the optimizer can be doing the wrong thing. Before exploring these situations, let's learn a little about diagnosing problem statements.

The first trick is identifying statements you suspect might need some tuning. You might be able to identify those statements by reviewing an application's code. For example, a simple INSERT statement is less likely to need tuning than a query that joins and sorts information from three different tables. This simple type of code analysis can target some initial statements to analyze for tuning improvements.

Examining the application's code helps you identify the easy cases. But in many other cases, it may not be apparent that a statement is executing more slowly than it should. To help you pinpoint problematic SQL statements that might benefit from analysis and tuning, rely on the feedback from application users.

After you have targeted a SQL statement to analyze for tuning, you can use the SQL command EXPLAIN PLAN to find out how Oracle7 is executing it. But before you attempt to use this command, you must create a table to store its output. To create an EXPLAIN PLAN table, run the UTLXPLAN.SQL script that comes with Oracle7. This script creates a table called PLAN_TABLE that can receive the output of an EXPLAIN PLAN statement. The UTLXPLAN.SQL script's location is system dependent; for example, on UNIX systems the UTLXPLAN.SQL script is in the $ORACLE _HOME/rdbms/admin directory, and on Novell NetWare systems, the script is in the ORACLE_HOME\rdbms\admin directory.

After you have created the PLAN_TABLE table, you can run EXPLAIN PLAN statements to diagnose tuning problems for SQL statements. For example, the following statement checks how the Oracle7 server executes a statement and places this information in the PLAN_TABLE table:

```
EXPLAIN PLAN
  SET STATEMENT_ID 'NY Customers1'
  INTO plan_table
  FOR
    SELECT lastname, firstname
    FROM customers
    WHERE state = 'NY'
```

To check the statement execution output from this EXPLAIN PLAN statement, issue a simple query on PLAN_TABLE:

```
SELECT statement_id, operation, options, cost
  FROM plan_table
```

```
STATEMENT_ID        OPERATION           OPTIONS       COST
--------------      ----------------    ----------    ----
NY Customers1       SELECT STATEMENT                    9
NY Customers1       TABLE ACCESS        FULL ACCESS    16
```

Notice that the EXPLAIN PLAN statement shows that Oracle7 found the customers in New York by doing a full table scan (in the OPTIONS column). The cost of each step in the statement's execution is revealed by the COST column in the first row for a statement in the PLAN_TABLE table. The numeric value of a statement's cost is an arbitrary measurement—it does not correspond to anything real (for example, milliseconds or logical I/Os). Therefore, analyze the costs that you gather with the EXPLAIN PLAN command using a comparative method rather than a quantitative method.

NOTE With releases 7.0, 7.1, and 7.2 of Oracle7, the EXPLAIN PLAN statement/PLAN_TABLE table does not include a COST column output. Instead, the POSITION field in the first row of statement output reveals the cumulative cost to execute the statement.

Remember that the CUSTOMERS table has an index on the STATE column. But then why didn't Oracle7 use this index? In this case, there might be a very simple answer: the administrator has not analyzed the STATEINDEX index recently created for the CUSTOMERS table.

After you analyze the CUSTOMERS table (or just the STATEINDEX index), the same EXPLAIN PLAN statement produces the expected results:

```
ANALYZE TABLE customers COMPUTE STATISTICS

EXPLAIN PLAN
  SET STATEMENT_ID 'NY Customers2'
  INTO plan_table
  FOR
    SELECT lastname, firstname
    FROM customers
    WHERE state = 'NY'
```

```
SELECT statement_id, operation, options, cost
  FROM plan_table

STATEMENT_ID        OPERATION           OPTIONS        COST
------------        ----------------    ----------     ----
NY Customers1       SELECT STATEMENT                   9
NY Customers1       TABLE ACCESS        FULL ACCESS    16
NY Customers2       SELECT STATEMENT                   3
NY Customers2       TABLE ACCESS        BY ROWID       0
NY Customers2       INDEX               RANGE SCAN     1
```

NOTE The EXPLAIN PLAN command of Oracle7 uses the current statistics in the data dictionary to do its best to return an accurate execution plan and corresponding cost of executing a statement. However, if statistics are not up-to-date, then, of course, the EXPLAIN PLAN command might not return an accurate execution plan and cost.

The next section examines some of the more common situations to look for when troubleshooting unexpected statement executions revealed by the EXPLAIN PLAN feature of Oracle7.

Troubleshooting Unexpected Statement Execution Plans

Neglecting to analyze a table or its indexes can cause the Oracle7 optimizer to pick less-than-optimal SQL statement execution plans. Here is a list of other common problems to check for when EXPLAIN PLAN reveals what you feel are incorrect statement execution plans made by the Oracle7 optimizer:

- Oracle7 makes all of its decisions based on the statistics for objects in the data dictionary. If an object experiences a lot of DML activity, older statistics may no longer represent the object's actual data. Therefore, Oracle7 is making the correct choice based on the object's statistics; but this turns out to be the wrong choice because the statistics are incorrect. To remedy the situation, the database administrator should frequently and regularly analyze an application schema to keep all statistics current.

- If Oracle7 is not using an index you believe it should be using and the index's statistics are current, the index might be unbalanced and undercompressed because of a lot of DML activity. To remedy this situation, rebuild the index (as described in Chapter 15).

- If Oracle7 is not using a hash cluster for a table search, it could be that the table has experienced enough DML activity that the hash cluster layout is no longer effective. In this case, the Oracle7 optimizer is making the right decision because the hash cluster is in such bad shape. This problem is hard to fix because it appears that you have made a bad choice by putting a volatile table in a cluster.

Using Histograms to Improve Column Selectivity

Complicated queries can test a cost-based optimizer's design because they present more choices for the optimizer. The sample query in the previous sections is extremely simple and demonstrates some basic optimizer functionality. Now let's consider a slightly more complicated query, one with two predicates in the WHERE clause:

```
SELECT * FROM customers
  WHERE city = 'Springfield' AND state = 'NY'
```

The above query requests all the customer records for customers that live in Springfield, New York. Assuming that both the CITY and STATE columns have indexes, the optimizer might choose two different execution plans for the statement:

- Find all of the customers that live in a city named Springfield, and from the result set, find all the customers that live in the state of New York.

- Find all of the customers that live in the state of New York, and from the result set, find all the customers that live in the city of Springfield.

Which of the above execution plans is optimal? The better execution plan will be the one that uses the more selective WHERE clause predicate in the first step of statement execution. Using this plan, Oracle7 will return the smallest number of rows to evaluate in the second step of statement execution, and thus minimize the cost of the second step in statement execution. The more selective predicate in this example is not constant, but varies depending on the characteristics of the data. For example, if 100,000 customers live in the state of New York, but only 100 live in a city named Springfield, the CITY column is much more selective. On the other hand, if only 5 customers live in the state of New York and 100 live in a city named Springfield, the STATE column is more selective.

A cost-based optimizer cannot compare the selectivity of different table columns without statistics about each column's data. With all releases of Oracle7, the SQL command ANALYZE gathers basic statistics that can help to reveal a column's selectivity (and a corresponding index's), including the number of distinct values in the column as well as the range of values in the column. Such basic statistics can accurately reveal a column's selectivity, as long as the column contains a uniformly distributed set of values. For example, consider a CUSTOMERS table with 100,000 customer records such that the CITY column contains 1000 distinct city values. In this case, the optimizer could conclude that the average number of customer records per city is 100 and use this conclusion as a relative measure of the column's selectivity.

Unfortunately, the basic statistics that the ANALYZE command generates for columns and indexes cannot convey the selectivity of columns that contain an irregular distribution of values. For example, consider again the previous example of the CUSTOMERS table. What if half of the customers live in the city of New York, and the remaining customers are evenly split among the remaining 999 suburb towns and cities? In this case, the optimizer's conclusion of 100 customers per city would be inaccurate. To reveal the selectivity of columns with uneven distributions of data, you must provide Oracle7's cost-based optimizer with additional statistics.

The ANALYZE command in release 7.3 of Oracle7 allows you to generate histograms for columns in a database. A *histogram* is a representation, often graphical, of a frequency distribution. For example, Figure 16.1 shows a height-balanced histogram for the CITY column of the CUSTOMERS table.

In a height-balanced histogram, all buckets contain the same number of values. The range of values that each bucket contains reveals the density of values in each

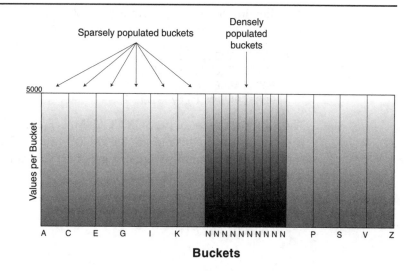

FIGURE 16.1:

A histogram can reveal the frequency of specific values contained in a data set with an irregular distribution of values.

bucket. An analysis of the histogram in Figure 16.1 shows that there are approximately 5000 cities that begin with the letters A…C, C…E, and so on, and 50,000 cities that begin with the letter N. Therefore, this histogram reveals the irregular distribution of city names in the CITY column of the CUSTOMERS table.

When to Use Histograms

Histograms can take quite some time for Oracle7 to generate. Therefore, you should not use histograms where they cannot substantially help application performance. In general, you should only generate histograms for columns that queries commonly reference in WHERE clauses, and columns that contain an irregular distribution of data. Additionally, when the irregular distribution of values in a column shifts as application users update the encompassing table, you must regenerate the histogram for the column so that the histogram accurately represents the column's data distribution.

Generating Histograms

To generate a histogram for a table's columns, you use the special FOR clause of the ANALYZE command (available only with release 7.3 of Oracle7). For example, the following statement generates table statistics for the CUSTOMERS table as well as column statistics (a histogram) for the CITY column:

```
ANALYZE TABLE customers
   COMPUTE STATISTICS
   FOR TABLE
   FOR COLUMN city SIZE 20
```

The SIZE parameter of the FOR COLUMN clause indicates the number of buckets to create within the histogram; the default value is 75. When a column already has statistics that you simply want to regenerate, you can use the FOR COLUMN clause without a SIZE parameter, as in:

```
ANALYZE TABLE customers
   COMPUTE STATISTICS
   FOR COLUMN city
```

Dynamically Controlling Oracle7's Optimizer for Interactive and Batch Mode Applications

Client applications can vary the types of SQL statements they issue. For example, consider two different types of queries an application might issue. The first is a batch mode operation, a query with an aggregate function, such as this:

```
SELECT SUM(total)
   FROM items
   WHERE orderid < 1000
```

In this situation, it's best to have Oracle7 execute the entire query for maximum throughput because the query returns only one row as an answer—the total amount of income from all sales orders with an ID of less than 1000.

Now consider an interactive mode operation, a query for a cursor in a PL/SQL block:

```
DECLARE
   CURSOR ordercursor IS
      SELECT orderid, SUM(total)
         FROM items
         WHERE orderid < 1000
```

```
  GROUP BY orderid
      ORDER BY orderid;
   ordernumber INTEGER;
   ordertotal REAL;
BEGIN
  OPEN ordercursor;
  LOOP
    FETCH ordercursor INTO ordernumber, ordertotal;
    ... other application-processing logic ...
    EXIT WHEN ordercursor%NOTFOUND;
  END LOOP;
  CLOSE ordercursor;
END;
```

In this example, the PL/SQL block is interactive because it does something with each row returned by the cursor's query, one row at a time. Because there is the potential for Oracle7 to total all of the line items for up to 1000 sales orders, it might take Oracle7 a long time to completely identify the return data for the cursor's query before even returning control for the first row. Consequently, the application or user waits and wastes valuable time.

In interactive mode applications, it's best if Oracle7 optimizes the query for fastest response time rather than for maximum throughput. This way Oracle7 quickly finds the first set of rows that satisfy the query and returns those rows to the application, which can then immediately begin other processing using the rows. Meanwhile, Oracle7 can find the remainder of the rows for the cursor. When Oracle7 optimizes statements like this for better response time, applications or users can be more productive.

An Oracle7 client application can dynamically tune when Oracle7 optimizes application statements for a goal of maximum throughput or faster response time. An application session can set the optimization goal after application startup (or at any time) by issuing an ALTER SESSION command with the SET OPTIMIZATION clause and one of the following options:

```
ALTER SESSION
  SET OPTIMIZER_GOAL = FIRST_ROWS

ALTER SESSION
  SET OPTIMIZER_GOAL = ALL_ROWS
```

The FIRST_ROWS option tunes the optimizer's goal for faster response times. The ALL_ROWS option tunes the optimizer's goal for maximum throughput. After issuing an ALTER SESSION statement, Oracle7 optimizes application statements according to the setting unless a statement specifically overrides the setting. (The next section explains how individual statements can override the current optimizer setting for an application session.)

Note that as a database administrator, you determine the Oracle7 optimizer's default tuning goal for all applications, using the OPTIMIZER_MODE initialization parameter:

```
OPTIMIZER_MODE = FIRST_ROWS
```

Influencing Statement Execution with Hints

In most situations, Oracle7 executes an application's statements in the way that delivers the best performance possible for the application. However, if after diagnosing a statement's execution plan you find that the server executes an application statement in a way you feel is less than optimal, you can influence or force Oracle7 to execute an application statement the way you want by including hints in SQL statements. A *hint* is a directive enclosed within a comment of a SQL statement that instructs Oracle7 to execute the statement using a particular approach.

The following sections explain how to specify hints in SQL statements and describe the hints that are available in Oracle7.

Expressing Hints within SQL Statements

To specify an Oracle7 hint, you include the hint within a comment of a SQL statement. Unlike SQL comments that do not contain hints, Oracle7 requires that you code a comment with a hint in a specific location within a statement. Also, the comment must include a plus sign (+) to tell Oracle7 that the comment contains a hint. The following examples illustrate the correct locations and syntax for SQL comments that contain hints within SELECT, UPDATE, and DELETE statements:

```
SELECT /*+ INDEX(customers stateindex) */
    lastname, firstname
    FROM customers
    WHERE state = 'WA'
```

```
UPDATE --+ INDEX(customers stateindex)
  customers
  SET ...

DELETE --+ INDEX(customers stateindex)
  FROM customers
  WHERE state = 'WA'
```

All of the preceding statements include a hint to force Oracle7 to use the STATEINDEX index of the CUSTOMERS table.

Notice that SQL comments can either begin with two hyphens (--) or begin with a slash and asterisk (/*) and end with an asterisk and slash (*/). In either case, the beginning comment delimiter must be immediately followed by the plus sign (+). Also, a comment with a hint must immediately follow the SELECT, UPDATE, or DELETE command keyword.

TIP You can indicate multiple hints in the same SQL comment by separating the different hints with one or more blank spaces.

Now that you know how to specify a hint in an application's statement, let's learn the different hints that you can use with Oracle7.

Controlling the Optimizer's Goal with Hints

The section "Dynamically Controlling Oracle7's Optimizer for Different Applications" earlier in this chapter discusses how an application can determine when Oracle7 optimizes SQL statements for maximum throughput or faster response times. To override an application session's optimizer goal setting for individual SQL statements, you can use the FIRST_ROWS and ALL_ROWS hints. Like the options for the ALTER SESSION command, the FIRST_ROWS hint forces the optimizer to execute a statement for a faster response time, and the ALL_ROWS hint forces the optimizer to execute a statement for maximum throughput.

```
SELECT /*+ ALL_ROWS */ SUM(total)
  FROM items
  WHERE orderid < 1000
```

```
DECLARE
  CURSOR ordercursor IS
    SELECT --+ FIRST_ROWS
      orderid, SUM(total)
      FROM items
      WHERE orderid < 1000
      GROUP BY orderid
      ORDER BY orderid;
... remainder of the PL/SQL block ...
```

NOTE
The second example shows that hints can be included within PL/SQL blocks, including anonymous blocks, stored procedures, database triggers, and so on. However, hints are identified and used only with those Oracle products that support PL/SQL version 2.0 or greater (for example, Oracle7) and not those that support PL/SQL 1.x (for example, SQL*Forms 3.0).

When a SQL statement does not contain either the FIRST_ROWS or ALL_ROWS hint, Oracle7 executes the statement according to the current session setting optimizer behavior.

Controlling Table Access Methods Using Hints

Depending on the situation, Oracle7 can execute a SQL statement by accessing a table using a full table scan or using an index, indexed cluster, or hash cluster. Oracle7 has several hints that allow you to suggest a table-access method for a statement. If the suggested table-access method is available, Oracle7 will use it.

Here are some of the hints you can use to suggest table-access methods:

Hint	When You Use It
FULL(*table*)	When you want Oracle7 to perform a full table scan on a table rather than use an index or a cluster.

Hint	When You Use It
CLUSTER (*table*)	When you want Oracle7 to use the cluster index associated with a table in an indexed cluster rather than a full table scan or a separate table index.
HASH(*table*)	When you want Oracle7 to use a hash scan rather than an index or a full table scan for a table in a hash cluster.
INDEX (*table index(es)*)	When you want Oracle7 to use an index scan for a table rather than a full table scan, an index scan using a different index, or a hash scan. If you include a list of indexes, Oracle7 considers the listed indexes and picks the one that delivers the lowest execution cost. If you do not specify indexes, Oracle7 considers all indexes and picks the one that delivers the lowest execution cost.
INDEX_ASC (*table index(es)*)	When you want Oracle7 to use an index scan for a table, scanning the index in ascending order of index values, rather than other types of table-access methods (similar to the INDEX hint).
INDEX_DESC (*table index(es)*)	When you want to scan an index in descending order (similar to INDEX_DESC).
AND_EQUAL (*table index(es)*)	When you want Oracle7 to merge index scans from several single-column indexes.

Now that you know the different hints that can control table-access methods for a SQL statement, let's take a look at how and when you might use them.

Considering the CUSTOMERS table and the STATEINDEX index described earlier in this book, what do you think would be the best way for Oracle7 to execute the following statement?

```
SELECT lastname, firstname
  FROM customers
  WHERE state = 'NY'
```

If customers are uniformly distributed across many states and there are many customers in the table, the best method might be for Oracle7 to perform an index scan using the STATEINDEX to find the ROWIDs of all customers in the state of New York and then access those rows using their ROWIDs. However, if the table contains clients located mostly in New York, a full table scan would deliver a lower cost than using the STATEINDEX.

Let's consider the former case. You would expect Oracle7 to use the STATEINDEX index for the query. However, when you use the EXPLAIN PLAN command, you find that Oracle7 is using a full table scan to get the New York customers:

```
EXPLAIN PLAN
  INTO plan_table
  FOR
    SELECT lastname
    FROM customers
    WHERE state = 'NY';

SELECT cost, operation, options
  FROM plan_table;

COST OPERATION              OPTIONS
---- ------------------     --------
   1 SELECT STATEMENT
   3 TABLE ACCESS           FULL
```

To reveal the cost of executing the same query when using the STATEINDEX index, include a hint in the EXPLAIN PLAN statement:

```
EXPLAIN PLAN
  INTO plan_table
  FOR
    SELECT --+ INDEX(customers stateindex)
    lastname
    FROM customers
    WHERE state = 'NY';

SELECT cost, operation, options
  FROM plan_table;
```

```
COST OPERATION             OPTIONS
____ _____  _____
   1 SELECT STATEMENT
   3 TABLE ACCESS          FULL
   3 SELECT STATEMENT
  10 TABLE ACCESS          BY ROWID
   5 INDEX                 RANGE SCAN
```

Aha! Maybe your customers are not as equally distributed as you thought they were. The cost of using the STATEINDEX index to find the New York customers is more than four times greater than the cost of performing a full table scan. In this case, using the hint to force the SQL statement to execute using an index is not the correct choice.

Controlling Joins with Hints

Joins are among the more complicated statements that SQL supports. Oracle7 includes four hints that allow you to affect the execution of queries that join information:

Hint	When You Use It
USE_NL (*table*[*s*])	To make Oracle7 join tables using a nested-loops join strategy. A *nested-loops join* means that Oracle7 picks the first row from the *inner* or *driving* table. Then it finds the rows in the outer table to join, returns the results, finds the second row in the driving table, finds the rows in the outer table to join, returns the results, and so on. A nested-loops join has the advantage of returning the first results early and the disadvantage of requiring more overall work to complete the join.
USE_MERGE (*table*[*s*])	To make Oracle7 join tables using a sort-merge join strategy for an *equality-join query* (that is table1.column1= table2.column2). A *sort-merge join* means that Oracle7 first sorts data from both tables (in the order of the joining attributes) and then merges the sorted results to perform the join. A sort-merge join has the advantage of reduced overhead to complete the join but the disadvantage that the first set of results cannot be returned until much of the sorting work is complete.

Hint	When You Use It
ORDERED	To make Oracle7 join tables according to the order in which a query lists them. In other words, the ORDERED hint lets you pick the driving table in a join.
USE_HASH (*table*[s])	Available only with release 7.3 of Oracle7, a *hash join* reads the two tables of a join operation and splits them into smaller partitions that can fit in server memory, builds a hash table to point to specific partitions in memory, and then performs joins using the hash table and corresponding partitions. A hash join can outperform a sort-merge join in many cases and a nested-loops join in cases where an index is several levels deep in a join operation. The administrator must set several initialization parameters that begin with the prefix HASH_ to determine the characteristics of hash joins.

When should you use the different hints to influence the nature of joins? As always, it's best to let the Oracle7 optimizer pick the right join strategy for you. However, if you feel that for some reason Oracle7 is not executing a join query as it should, check its execution with the EXPLAIN PLAN feature. Then suggest a new approach with any of the preceding hints.

In particular, the USE_NL or USE_MERGE hint can come in handy when applications want to optimize statement execution for faster response time or optimal throughput, respectively (similar to the FIRST_ROWS and ALL_ROWS hints). Note that nested-loops joins return the first set of results more quickly that do sort-merge joins, but sort-merge joins deliver better overall throughput than do nested-loops joins. With release 7.3 of Oracle7, hash joins are optimal in many cases.

Tuning Transaction Behavior

A key to good application performance is not only good SQL statement design but good transaction design. Especially in an OLTP environment where many users are modifying a single database at the same time, poorly implemented OLTP transactions can dramatically slow down overall application performance. This section addresses some issues to think about when designing transactions for your applications.

Designing Transactions Correctly

Remember that a database transaction is a logical unit of work that completes or fails as a unit. When you sit down to design a client application, not only must you consider how you program the application's SQL statements, you must also consider the transactions that encompass them, for two key reasons:

- The locks a transaction's SQL statements acquire are held for the duration of the transaction.

- The rollback segment space that a transaction's SQL statements consume is held for the duration of the transaction.

With these two points in mind, let's consider how a client/server database system would perform when an application uses either short or long transactions. If an application uses short transactions, data locks and rollback segment space are released shortly after they are acquired by each transaction. Therefore, application users are less likely to contend for the same data and rollback segment space. However, if a client application uses long transactions, data locks and rollback segment space are held for longer periods of time, increasing the likelihood that users will bump into each other when trying to accomplish work. In other words, the longer an application's transactions, the better the chances that users will have to wait for one another to complete work.

A key goal of transaction design is to make sure each transaction is in fact a "unit" of work, not "units" of work. This in turn will keep database transactions as short as possible, reduce resource contention in the system, and deliver maximum performance.

Overriding Oracle7 Default Locking Mechanisms to Improve Application Performance

Chapter 2 described how Oracle7's automatic row-level locking and multi-versioning mechanism works to create data concurrency in a multi-user database system. Although most applications will perform well with Oracle7's default locking mechanisms, there are situations in which manual locking strategies can improve application performance. This section describes when and how transactions can manually lock data in an Oracle7 database to improve application performance.

Explicitly Locking Tables to Improve Application Performance

If a single statement or transaction is going to update many or all of the rows in a table, Oracle7's row-level locking mechanism can result in extra server overhead and force application users to sit idle.

Here's the scenario: Assume that an application is about to issue an UPDATE statement to update all of the rows in a table. When the application starts the update of the table, Oracle7 acquires exclusive row locks on each of the rows in the table, one at a time. Since the statement is eventually going to exclusively lock all of the rows in the table, Oracle7 ends up taking many exclusive row locks when a single exclusive table lock would do the trick much more efficiently and with much less overhead. Furthermore, if Oracle7 encounters a row that is currently locked, it waits indefinitely until the transaction that has the row locked completes and releases the lock; an application user might sit around unproductively while waiting for one lock out of a thousand.

To avoid these problems, when an application transaction is going to issue one or more statements that modify a large majority or all of the rows in a table, the transaction should attempt to acquire a lock on the table instead of on individual rows, one at a time. Acquiring a table lock accomplishes two goals:

- Applications can specify that they do not want to wait if an attempt to acquire a table lock does not immediately complete. In this case, when an application attempts to acquire a table lock but other locks prohibit the table lock, the application can attempt to acquire the lock again or move on to another operation instead of sitting idle.

- The application acquires a single table lock instead of many row locks to accomplish the same thing. One table lock is much more efficient than many row locks, and this leads to reduced server overhead and better overall system performance.

To explicitly acquire table locks, an application can use the SQL command LOCK TABLE:

```
LOCK TABLE orders IN EXCLUSIVE MODE

LOCK TABLE orders IN EXCLUSIVE MODE NOWAIT

LOCK TABLE orders, items IN EXCLUSIVE MODE NOWAIT
```

The first two examples show how an application can exclusively lock the ORDERS table. The first statement will wait when Oracle7 cannot immediately acquire the table lock because of other table or row locks on the ORDERS table. The second example returns control to the application if Oracle7 cannot immediately acquire the table lock on the ORDERS table. The third example shows how you can lock more than one table at a time if a transaction needs to acquire table locks on related tables.

These examples show one of the most common types of table locks Oracle7 can acquire using the LOCK TABLE command: an exclusive table lock. However, Oracle7 allows you to acquire several types of table locks using the LOCK TABLE command, including exclusive, share row exclusive, share, row exclusive, and row share table locks. Let's focus on the two types of table locks that most applications explicitly acquire to improve application performance: exclusive and row exclusive table locks.

Exclusive Table Locks   An *exclusive table lock* prohibits other transactions from performing DML operations on the locked object, including other types of table- and row-level locks. To improve performance, an application might acquire an exclusive table lock before updating or deleting all (or many) of the rows in a table, as explained earlier in this section. Oracle7 takes an exclusive table lock only when an application specifically requests one.

Row Exclusive Table Locks   A *row exclusive table lock* is a sort of counter-balance to the exclusive table lock because it ensures that no other transaction can exclusively lock the table for its own purpose. Oracle7 automatically acquires a row exclusive table lock when a transaction updates or deletes one of the rows in the table, explicitly acquires a row exclusive lock on a row in the table (see the next section), or when a user explicitly requests a row exclusive table lock using the LOCK TABLE command:

```
LOCK TABLE orders ROW EXCLUSIVE MODE
```

The only time an application can improve its performance by acquiring a row exclusive table lock is when the same or other applications are acquiring exclusive table locks. Performance gains can be achieved for transactions that want to modify tables but don't want to wait behind transactions that acquire exclusive table locks.

Explicitly Locking Rows to Improve Application Performance

The preceding section explained how the acquisition of table locks can help application performance. Likewise, there are application situations in which explicitly acquiring row-level locks can improve application performance.

Here's a common scenario in which this type of locking can help performance: Assume that an application opens a cursor and then selectively updates some or all of the rows in the return set of the cursor. Unless the application locks all of the rows in the cursor's return set when opening the cursor, there is a chance that another transaction will lock one of the rows in the cursor's return set while the application processes other rows in the cursor. Then, when the application tries to update the row in the cursor's return set that is locked by the other transaction, the application must wait until the other transaction completes and releases the lock on the desired row. As a result, application users can sit idle, waiting for other users to finish their work.

To avoid this type of situation in your applications, an application transaction can explicitly lock the rows in the return set of a cursor (or a query) using the FOR UPDATE OF clause of the SELECT command, thereby guaranteeing that the transaction has exclusive rights to update the row before all other transactions:

```
DECLARE
CURSOR ordercursor (orderid INTEGER) IS
SELECT orderdate, shipdate, paiddate
  FROM orders
  WHERE id = orderid
  FOR UPDATE OF orderdate, shipdate, paiddate;
... remainder of the PL/SQL block ...
```

In this example, the PL/SQL block acquires an exclusive row-level lock for the specified sales order to make sure no other transaction can intervene to update the order while the program finishes processing the row. As with other row locks, the transaction holds the lock on the sales order until the transaction commits.

Explicitly Locking Other System Resources to Improve Application Performance

Rows and tables are database resources that applications rely on to accomplish work done on behalf of system users. However, applications sometimes rely on other types of resources to get work done. For example, reporting applications make extensive use of a shared system printer. If several users want to print several reports at the same time, then they can contend for a resource—in this case, a printer.

You can use the procedures in a utility package called DBMS_LOCK to help you manage other types of resources that applications might use. For example, users of one or more applications can use the following package to coordinate the use of up to five shared peripherals (printers, modems, and so on):

```
CREATE PACKAGE sharedperipherals AS
  FUNCTION lockperipheral (peripheral IN VARCHAR2, handlenum IN OUT VARCHAR2)
    RETURN VARCHAR2;
  FUNCTION releaseperipheral (handlenum IN VARCHAR2)
    RETURN VARCHAR2;
  peripheralhandle1 VARCHAR2(50);
  peripheralhandle2 VARCHAR2(50);
  peripheralhandle3 VARCHAR2(50);
```

```
   peripheralhandle4 VARCHAR2(50);
   peripheralhandle5 VARCHAR2(50);
END sharedperipherals;

CREATE PACKAGE BODY sharedperipherals AS

-- This function attempts to acquire an exclusive lock on the specified
-- peripheral. Success or failure is indicated by the function's return value.
FUNCTION lockperipheral (peripheral IN VARCHAR2, handlenum IN OUT VARCHAR2)
   RETURN VARCHAR2 IS
   resourceflag INTEGER := 9;
   returnvalue VARCHAR2(50) := 'Peripheral '||peripheral||' could not be locked';
BEGIN
   dbms_lock.allocate_unique(peripheral, handlenum);
   resourceflag := dbms_lock.request(handlenum);
   IF resourceflag = 0 THEN
     returnvalue := 'Peripheral '||peripheral||' successfully locked';
   END IF;
   RETURN returnvalue;
END lockperipheral;

-- This function attempts to release a lock on the specified
-- peripheral. Success or failure is indicated by the function's return value.
FUNCTION releaseperipheral (handlenum IN VARCHAR2)
   RETURN VARCHAR2 IS
   resourceflag INTEGER := 9;
   returnvalue VARCHAR2(50) := 'Lock on peripheral could not be released';
BEGIN
   resourceflag := dbms_lock.release (handlenum);
   IF resourceflag = 0 THEN
     returnvalue := 'Lock on peripheral successfully released';
   END IF;
   RETURN returnvalue;
END releaseperipheral;

END sharedperipherals;
```

For example, a reporting application can call the LOCKPERIPHERAL function before it prints a report to make sure it has exclusive access to a printer:

```
x := sharedperipherals.lockperipheral
   ('PRINTER1', sharedperipherals.peripheralhandle1);
```

The return value of the function tells the application if the requested printer is available so the application can provide feedback to the user. Once the application is finished with the printer, it can use the RELEASEPERIPHERAL function to release the lock on the printer so other applications can use it:

```
x := sharedperipherals.releaseperipheral
  (sharedperipherals.peripheralhandle1);
```

These examples illustrate just a few of the procedures and functions in the DBMS_LOCK utility package that you can use to manage resources in a client/server application environment.

However, the programs in the DBMS_LOCK utility package do not actually lock any real resources. For instance, in the preceding example, if one application acquires a lock on a printer, another application can still send a report to the printer without checking for locks on the printer. If the printer is not busy, the application without the lock might very well be able to use the printer ahead of the application that has the lock. That's because the locks acquired by the DBMS_LOCK utility package are just a way of managing locks for external system resources within the database server. Therefore, locking of arbitrary system resources external to the database can work only when all applications acquire a named set of resource locks using the DBMS_LOCK utility package.

Using the SET TRANSACTION Command to Control Transaction Behavior

Oracle7 offers another feature that application developers should consider to help the performance and behavior of application transactions: the SQL command SET TRANSACTION. This command allows you to set several transaction characteristics when you begin a new database transaction. The following sections explain some of these options of the SET TRANSACTION command. Keep in mind that you must always make sure the SET TRANSACTION statement is the first one in a new transaction; otherwise, Oracle7 will return an error.

```
... statements of transaction ...
COMMIT                   -- end of transaction
SET TRANSACTION ...      -- beginning of new transaction
... statements of new transaction ...
.
.
.
```

Now let's learn about some of the most important transaction characteristics that the SET TRANSACTION command allows you to control: read consistency and rollback segment usage.

Using SET TRANSACTION to Control Read Consistency

In Chapter 2, you learned how Oracle7 uses multi-versioning instead of read locks to guarantee read consistency—a consistent, accurate set of results for every query. To deliver read consistency, Oracle7 uses rollback segments and multi-versioning to hide the work that other transactions might concurrently be performing on the data you query. By default, Oracle7's multi-versioning mechanism guarantees statement-level read consistency because every row in a single query's result set is consistent with respect to a specific timepoint—in Oracle7, the time that the query begins.

In most application situations, Oracle7's default of statement-level read consistency is acceptable. However, some applications might require a higher degree of read consistency: transaction-level read consistency. Transaction-level read consistency means that for the duration of a transaction, no matter how many queries you issue and no matter how many tables are involved, all query results are consistent with respect to the same point in time (the beginning of the transaction). Transaction-level read consistency is often important for decision support/reporting applications that issue many long-running complicated queries that must return consistent, accurate results.

One way to establish transaction-level read consistency is to exclusively lock tables of interest using the LOCK TABLE command. After a transaction exclusively locks tables, other transactions cannot modify the tables until the locking transaction ends and releases the locks.

```
-- exclusively lock tables to prevent other transactions
-- from using the same tables and ensure
-- transaction-level read consistency
LOCK TABLE orders, items EXCLUSIVE

-- return initial query results for locked tables
SELECT ... FROM orders, items ...

... other transaction statements ...
```

```
-- subsequent query results see same data as the first query
-- because other transactions cannot modify the tables
SELECT ... FROM orders, items ...
.
.
.
COMMIT
```

While exclusive table locks allow you to create transaction-level read consistency, this method has one primary disadvantage: it eliminates data concurrency with respect to the locked tables because no other users can modify the locked tables. If you want transaction-level read consistency without the penalty of lost data concurrency, consider a read-only transaction. Using the READ ONLY option of the SET TRANSACTION command, a transaction can issue any number of queries against any number of tables and see read-consistent results without locking any data, thus preserving complete data concurrency in a multi-user/multi-transaction environment.

```
COMMIT                        -- end of transaction
SET TRANSACTION READ ONLY     -- begin new read-only transaction
SELECT ... FROM orders, items -- return initial query results
.
.
.
SELECT ... FROM orders, items -- return same query results
.
.
.
```

To guarantee transaction-level read consistency, Oracle7 extends its multi-versioning model for all queries in the transaction. The only limitation of read-only transactions is that they are just what their name indicates—read-only transactions. If you attempt to issue anything other than a SELECT statement, Oracle7 returns an error.

Using SET TRANSACTION to Target Specific Rollback Segments

In Chapter 10, you learned a lot about rollback segments: how the administrator must plan, create, and manage them to support client applications, and how different-size rollback segments can have different performance and behavioral results when applications use them. Normally, Oracle7 assigns a transaction to a rollback segment according to availability and on a round-robin basis to make sure that all rollback segments carry a similar transaction load. However, Oracle7 allows you, as the application developer, to target specific rollback segments for transaction use with the USE ROLLBACK SEGMENT clause of the SET TRANSACTION command:

```
COMMIT                          -- end transaction
SET TRANSACTION                 -- begin new transaction
  USE ROLLBACK SEGMENT rs2
... other transaction statements ...
    .
    .
    .
COMMIT
```

When you design your application, you can use the SET TRANSACTION...USE ROLLBACK SEGMENT command to improve the performance of the application in several ways. For example, OLTP applications might decide to target transactions for small rollback segments cached in memory so that Oracle7 never needs to write rollback segment information to disk. Alternatively, batch operations like bulk data loads that contain long transactions might target extremely large rollback segments to reduce the likelihood of dynamic extent allocation/deallocation for rollback segments.

Pinning Application Code in Database Server Memory

In Chapter 12, you learned about the memory caches of the Oracle7 database server and how the administrator can tune them to minimize processing and the amount of disk I/O that is necessary for client/server applications to function. One such memory area is the shared pool, a buffer cache that holds shared, parsed, optimized application code (SQL statements and stored procedures) in memory so that repeated executions work much more quickly. But no matter how well the administrator tunes the size of the shared pool, if application code is somewhat large and not regularly used, Oracle7 will likely flush it out of the shared pool when it is necessary to make room for other code not in memory. Therefore, if an application executes a SQL statement or procedure that is no longer in the shared pool, extra processing (optimization and so on) and possibly disk I/O are necessary to complete the request, which can slow application performance.

When developing applications, consider using the DBMS_ SHARED_POOL utility package that has several procedures to allow you to control which pieces of application code can and cannot be flushed from the shared pool. Therefore, you can pin important pieces of application code in server memory to maximize application performance. The following list describes the different procedures available in the DBMS_SHARED_POOL package:

Procedure	Description
sizes (*minsize* NUMBER)	Prints a report of all objects in the shared pool larger than *minsize*. The report lists the name and size of each object, as well as whether or not the object is to be pinned in the shared pool. Execute this procedure in a Server Manager SQL worksheet or SQL*Plus after enabling server output.
keep (*name* VARCHAR2)	Pins the named object in the shared pool.
unkeep (*name* VARCHAR2)	Releases the pin on the named object in the shared pool.

To illustrate the use of the DBMS_SHARED_POOL package, let's look at one way that applications commonly use the utility. Most client/server applications typically use individual stored procedures, or packages of stored procedures, to reduce network I/O and improve application performance. Therefore, it's reasonable to pin an application's package in the shared pool. For example, upon application startup, a developer might include the following procedure calls to pin an application's packages in the shared pool:

```
dbms_shared_pool.keep('sales.customermanager')
dbms_shared_pool.keep('sales.partmanager')
 .
 .
 .
```

Likewise, when terminating an application, it's best to unpin an application's packages to free unused space in the shared pool:

```
dbms_shared_pool.unkeep('sales.customermanager')
dbms_shared_pool.unkeep('sales.partmanager')
  .
  .
  .
```

Array Processing: Another Way of Reducing Network Traffic

Reducing network I/O between clients and a database server has been a primary focus throughout this book. That's because network traffic in a heavily loaded client/server system can quickly saturate the network to slow application performance. We have already seen that SQL functions, integrity constraints, triggers, stored procedures, and database alerts are key Oracle7 features that all client applications should take advantage of to minimize network traffic in a client/server system. However, one Oracle7 client/server feature not yet discussed in detail is the ORACLE array-processing interface.

Figure 16.2 illustrates how array processing can improve client/server application performance. Instead of sending network packets with single rows when a client application inserts a row or requests a row from the server with a query, *array processing* allows applications to reduce network traffic by buffering rows for insert or retrieval into arrays and then send the arrays in very few network packets across the network. The end result is less network traffic and improved database system performance for all applications.

Array processing is built into many Oracle tools, including Oracle Forms and SQL*Plus. The Oracle precompilers and OCI 3GL development environments also contain commands you can include in an application to take advantage of array processing.

FIGURE 16.2:

Oracle7's array-processing interface can dramatically reduce network traffic for INSERT and SELECT statements in a client/server system.

This chapter has discussed several issues to focus on when tuning the logic of an Oracle7 client application for better performance, including the following:

- SQL statement design tips

- Hints to influence statement execution

- Transaction design to reduce contention among transactions for data and roll-back segment space

- Manual locking options to optimize application locking strategies

- How to pin pieces of application code in the shared pool

- The Oracle7 array-processing interface to reduce network traffic for INSERT and SELECT statements in a client/server system

The next chapter discusses how to use the programmatic constructs of Oracle7 in a client/server database system, including stored procedures and packages, database triggers, and database alerts.

CHAPTER

SEVENTEEN

Centralizing Application Logic
in the Database Server

- Using stored PL/SQL programs in Oracle7 client/ server systems

- Creating and managing stored procedures, functions, packages, and triggers

- Using Oracle7 programmer utility packages to enhance client/server applications

Chapter 14 showed you how to plan, create, and manage the foundation of an application's schema—the tables, integrity constraints, and views the application uses to work with a database system. This chapter explains other types of application schema objects you can use to enhance the performance and functionality of a client/server system by centralizing selected bits of application logic in the database. This chapter discusses the following:

- Creating and using database procedures

- Creating and using database functions

- Creating and using packages

- Creating and managing triggers

- Using programmer utilities, including database alerts and database pipes

If you are not familiar with the concepts of procedures, functions, packages, and triggers, see Chapter 2.

Using Database Procedures and Triggers Effectively

As you already know, planning is an important part of any complicated project, especially client/server application development and database design. When designing a client database application and its underlying schema, you must consider the opportunities where you can store application logic inside the database using procedures, functions, packages, and triggers. The following sections explain some of the most common situations in which you can use procedures, functions, packages, and triggers to encapsulate application logic inside an Oracle7 database.

Using Procedures and Triggers to Reduce Client/Server Network Traffic

Throughout this book, one of the recurring themes for client/server application development has been the focus on reducing network I/O between clients and the database server to eliminate the network as a bottleneck to application performance. Procedures and triggers can be significant players in accomplishing this goal because applications that use them rather than SQL statements generate much less network traffic. (Chapter 13 showed a good example of how procedures and triggers generate much less network traffic than equivalent SQL statements.)

Using Procedures and Triggers to Enforce Data Integrity

Procedures and triggers are also useful for enforcing complex data integrity rules. A procedure is a compiled method of data access that users cannot dynamically change. Therefore, if a procedure includes both an operation and an integrity rule, you force all applications that use the procedure to also abide by the integrity rule. For example, the DELETECUSTOMER procedure makes sure to log a customer's ID and name into a customer history table before deleting the customer record from the CUSTOMERS table:

```
CREATE PROCEDURE deletecustomer (custid IN INTEGER) AS
-- This procedure deletes the specified customer from the CUSTOMERS table.
-- Before deleting the customer, the procedure inserts the customer's ID and
-- name into a history table.
  last VARCHAR2(50);
  first VARCHAR2(50);
BEGIN
  SELECT lastname, firstname INTO last, first
    FROM customers WHERE id = custid;
  INSERT INTO customerhistory VALUES (custid, last, first);
  DELETE FROM customers WHERE id = custid;
EXCEPTION
  WHEN NO_DATA_FOUND THEN
    raise_application_error (-20100, 'Invalid Customer ID');
END deletecustomer;
```

You can also use triggers to enforce complex integrity rules. The next example shows how to enforce the integrity rule in the DELETECUSTOMER procedure using a database trigger:

```
CREATE TRIGGER deletecustomer
BEFORE DELETE ON customers
FOR EACH ROW
BEGIN
  INSERT INTO customerhistory
```

```
        VALUES (:old.id, :old.lastname, :old.firstname);
    END deletecustomer;
```

Using Procedures to Increase Object Security

Procedures are a great way to add an additional level of security to a database system. That's because users never require the object privileges to access database objects directly (for example, SELECT, INSERT, UPDATE, and DELETE object privileges); they require only the privilege to execute procedures that access the database objects (EXECUTE). And because a procedure is a compiled method of data access, you can be sure that users access an object only by using a method included in the procedure.

Using Procedures and Triggers for Complex Security Checks

Procedures and triggers are also useful for enforcing complex security checks. For example, consider the following trigger, which does not permit users to update or delete customer records before 7 A.M. or after 7 P.M.:

```
CREATE TRIGGER timecheck
BEFORE UPDATE OR DELETE ON customers
BEGIN
   IF TO_CHAR(SYSDATE, 'HH24') NOT BETWEEN 7 AND 18 THEN
     raise_application_error(-20108, 'Customer changes not allowed at this
time');
   END IF;
END timecheck;
```

Using Procedures and Triggers for Enhanced Functionality

You can use procedures and triggers to enhance the functionality of an application. Part II of this book includes several listings with stored procedures that the administrator can use to generate and print reports about a database and its configuration.

Procedures versus Triggers

If you can use both procedures and triggers to enforce complex integrity rules and security checks, how do you decide which approach to use? In general, if you need to apply a rule or check across all applications that might access the database, including ad hoc query environments, use a database trigger to centralize and automate the process in the database. This way, you are sure that Oracle7 always enforces the check no matter how someone gets to the data, whether through the use of a procedure or by issuing a SQL statement. On the other hand, if you only need to enforce an integrity rule or security check for one or just some applications, create a procedure and make the interested applications call the procedure. This way, other applications can access the database without being subject to the integrity rule or check.

NOTE   Also consider that you can call database stored procedures from within triggers.

Individual Procedures and Functions versus Packages

When creating procedures and functions, you can create them as stand-alone, individual stored procedures and functions or as procedures and functions that are encapsulated inside a package. How do you decide which approach to use? If you are creating an application that will use several different database procedures and functions to consistently perform work, it's best to code the PL/SQL programs as part of a package that corresponds to the application. The many benefits include the following:

- Organization: Encapsulation of related application procedures and functions inside a package makes the PL/SQL development process easy to manage.

- Additional functionality: Using packages permits database server-managed global variables that have a persistent state for the life of an application user's database session.

- Enhanced performance: Calling an object in a package loads the entire package into the shared pool of the server, thereby eliminating individual disk I/Os for each first call to a procedure or function.

Creating, Managing, and Using Procedures, Functions, and Packages

Now that you have a good idea of when to use PL/SQL programs for storing application logic within an Oracle7 database, the following sections explain the details of creating, managing, and using database stored procedures, functions, and packages. These sections provide a number of examples to show you how to enhance an application by using database-stored PL/SQL programs.

Using a Text Editor for Programming Productivity

When programming in 3GL development environments such as C, you typically use some type of an integrated development environment that includes a source code editor and a compiler. You use a source code editor to create the source file for an application. After you save the source file, you can try compiling it with the compiler. Unless you code a program absolutely correctly on the first try, the compiler returns messages to indicate all of the compile errors it finds in the source file. Next, you fix the problems the compiler identified by editing the source file in your editor, and then try to compile the application's source file again. You repeat this process until you eliminate all syntax and logic errors and get everything working just the way you want.

PL/SQL is a 3GL that adds procedural functionality to Oracle SQL. Therefore, when developing an application's PL/SQL programs like procedures and triggers, you can use the same development approach as for a 3GL compiler.

If you have Oracle's Developer/2000 suite of development tools, you can use Procedure Builder as your development environment, which includes an integrated source code editor, compiler, and so on. Without Procedure Builder, you can use a simple text editor to write and save the source code for procedures, functions, packages, and triggers, and then run the source files as command scripts from an Oracle tool such as SQL*Plus. If you ever need to change the functionality of an application's PL/SQL programs, you can retrieve the source files in an editor, modify them, and then recompile the new source code in the Oracle7 database server.

> **NOTE** Several independent companies offer development tools for database 3GL environments such as Oracle PL/SQL. Such tools offer debugging environments, code versioning and control systems, and so on. If you do a lot of PL/SQL coding, the use of such programming utilities can greatly improve the productivity of application development.

Creating Procedures, Functions, and Packages

To create procedures, functions, and packages, you use the SQL commands CREATE PROCEDURE, CREATE FUNCTION, and CREATE PACKAGE, respectively. The following statements show how to create a procedure and a function:

```
CREATE PROCEDURE sales.newcustomer (company IN VARCHAR2 DEFAULT null,
  last IN VARCHAR2, first IN VARCHAR2, street IN VARCHAR2 DEFAULT null,
  city IN VARCHAR2 DEFAULT null, state IN CHAR DEFAULT null,
  zipcode IN VARCHAR2 DEFAULT null, phone IN VARCHAR2 DEFAULT null,
  fax IN VARCHAR2 DEFAULT null) IS
-- This procedure adds a new customer to the CUSTOMERS table. At a
-- minimum, the caller must provide the new customer's last and first
-- name. The procedure uses a sequence to generate a new customer ID.
BEGIN
  INSERT INTO sales.customers
    VALUES (customersequence.NEXTVAL, UPPER(company), UPPER(last), UPPER(first),
      INITCAP(street), INITCAP(city), INITCAP(state), zipcode, phone, fax);
END newcustomer;

CREATE FUNCTION findcustomerid (last IN VARCHAR2, first IN VARCHAR2)
  RETURN INTEGER AS
-- This function returns a customer's ID given the customer's last
-- and first names.
custid INTEGER;
```

```
BEGIN
  SELECT id INTO custid FROM customers
    WHERE lastname = UPPER(last) AND firstname = UPPER(first);
  RETURN custid;
EXCEPTION
  WHEN NO_DATA_FOUND THEN
    raise_application_error (-20101,'Invalid Customer Name');
END findcustomerid;
```

> **NOTE**
>
> To create a procedure, function, or package in an application schema, you must have the CREATE PROCEDURE system privilege. To create a procedure, function, or package in another schema, you must have the CREATE ANY PROCEDURE system privilege.

If you create a PL/SQL program in one schema that references objects in another schema, privilege requirements can become a bit complicated. In this case, the owner of the PL/SQL program must have the necessary privileges to access the objects in the other schema. This way, Oracle7 prevents a simple procedure definition from bypassing the internal security controls for object access.

For example, assume that you create the SALES.NEWCUSTOMER procedure shown earlier in this chapter to access the CUSTOMERS table, which is in another user's schema. Oracle7 will not compile the SALES.NEWCUSTOMER procedure unless SALES has the INSERT object privilege for the CUSTOMERS table.

These caveats should not concern you when you are creating an application schema that contains all the objects necessary for an application. Because the owner of all application objects, including procedures and underlying base tables and views, is one and the same, you will never need to consider these tricky privilege requirements.

Specifying Procedure and Function Parameters

After you specify a new procedure's or function's name, you must specify the procedure's or function's parameters—the values you want to pass into the body of the program. A parameter specification includes a name and a datatype. For each parameter, you should indicate whether the parameter is an IN, OUT, or IN OUT parameter. See the section "Defining Procedure and Function Parameters" in Chapter 5 if you need a review of parameter types.

Notice that the package specification for the CUSTOMERMANAGER package shows that you can also assign default parameter values for the parameters of procedures or functions. If an application calls a procedure or function and does not supply a value for a parameter that has a default value, Oracle7 automatically substitutes the parameter's default value to complete the program call.

Specifying a Function's Return Value

Unlike a procedure definition, a function definition must indicate the datatype of the function's single return value and use the PL/SQL command RETURN to relay the function's return value. For example, the preceding statement defines the return value for the FINDCUSTOMERID function as an integer. The body of the function returns the value of the CUSTID variable, using a RETURN statement.

Separating a Package's Specification and Body

Creating packages of procedures and functions is similar to creating and managing stand-alone procedures and functions. However, there are some differences because each package has two parts: a specification and a body. A package's specification is a simple declaration of all the package components that the outside world can access. Procedures, functions, variables, cursors, and constants that you declare in a package's specification are public because applications can reference them to accomplish work.

To create a package specification, you use the SQL command CREATE PACKAGE. For example, this statement creates the specification for the CUSTOMERMANAGER package:

```
CREATE PACKAGE sales.customermanager IS
  PROCEDURE newcustomer (company IN VARCHAR2 DEFAULT null,
    last IN VARCHAR2, first IN VARCHAR2, street IN VARCHAR2 DEFAULT null,
    city IN VARCHAR2 DEFAULT null, state IN CHAR DEFAULT null,
    zipcode IN VARCHAR2 DEFAULT null, phone IN VARCHAR2 DEFAULT null,
    fax IN VARCHAR2 DEFAULT null);
  FUNCTION findcustomerid (last IN VARCHAR2, first IN VARCHAR2) RETURN integer;
  PROCEDURE updatecustomer (custid IN INTEGER, fieldtype IN CHAR,
    newvalue IN VARCHAR2);
```

```
   PROCEDURE deletecustomer (custid IN INTEGER);
   PROCEDURE deletecustomer (last IN VARCHAR2, first IN VARCHAR2);
   PRAGMA RESTRICT_REFERENCES(findcustomerid, WNDS, WNPS, RNPS);
END customermanager;
```

The specification of the CUSTOMERMANAGER package declares four public procedures and one public function. Notice that the package specification includes only the arguments for each public procedure and function, not the logic of each. When you code public procedures and functions in the body of a package, the arguments must match those in the package specification.

> **NOTE**　Notice that you can *overload* the procedure or function names in a package. For example, the CUSTOMERMANAGER package contains two public procedures named DELETECUSTOMER. One version of the procedure deletes a customer when you supply the customer's ID; the other version deletes a customer when you supply the customer's name. When an application calls the DELETECUSTOMER procedure, Oracle7 automatically determines which version of the procedure to execute, based on the types and number of arguments the call supplies.

The body of a package specifies the logic of all the procedures and functions within the package. A package body must define all public procedures and functions—those included in the package specification. A package body can also define other procedures, functions, variables, constants, and cursors that the package specification does not declare. Objects that the package body defines but that the package specification does not declare are private, not available to the outside world. However, procedures and functions in the package itself can make use of all private package objects.

To create a package body you use the SQL command CREATE PACKAGE BODY. For example, this statement creates the body for the CUSTOMERMANAGER package:

```
CREATE PACKAGE BODY sales.customermanager AS
   errnum INTEGER := -20000;
   errmess VARCHAR2(2000) := 'Standard Error';
---------------------RETURNERROR procedure ----------------------------
PROCEDURE returnerror (errorstring IN VARCHAR2) IS
```

```
-- This private procedure sets the error number and message for the error
-- asked for by a package procedure or function.
BEGIN
  SELECT errornumber, errormessage
    INTO customermanager.errnum, customermanager.errmess
    FROM usererrors
    WHERE errormessage LIKE errorstring||'%';
  raise_application_error(customermanager.errnum, customermanager.errmess);
EXCEPTION
  WHEN NO_DATA_FOUND THEN -- if no matching error message, use standard error
    raise_application_error(-20000, 'Standard error');
END returnerror;
---------------------NEWCUSTOMER procedure ---------------------
PROCEDURE newcustomer (company IN VARCHAR2 DEFAULT null, last IN VARCHAR2,
-- This procedure adds a new customer to the CUSTOMERS table.  At a
-- minimum, the caller must provide the new customer's last and first
-- name.  The procedure uses a sequence to generate a new customer ID.
    first IN VARCHAR2, street IN VARCHAR2 DEFAULT null,
    city IN VARCHAR2 DEFAULT null, state IN CHAR DEFAULT null,
zipcode IN VARCHAR2 DEFAULT null, phone IN VARCHAR2 DEFAULT null,
    fax IN VARCHAR2 DEFAULT null) IS
BEGIN
  INSERT INTO customers
    VALUES (customersequence.NEXTVAL, company, last, first,
    street, city, state, zipcode, phone, fax);
END newcustomer;
---------------------FINDCUSTOMER function ---------------------
FUNCTION findcustomerid (last IN VARCHAR2, first IN VARCHAR2)
  RETURN INTEGER IS
-- This function returns a customer's ID given the customer's last
-- and first names.
  custid INTEGER;
BEGIN
  SELECT id INTO custid FROM customers
    WHERE lastname = last AND firstname = first;
  RETURN custid;
EXCEPTION
  WHEN NO_DATA_FOUND THEN
    customermanager.returnerror ('Invalid Customer Name');
END findcustomerid;
---------------------UPDATECUSTOMER procedure ---------------------
PROCEDURE updatecustomer (custid IN INTEGER, fieldtype IN CHAR,
  newvalue VARCHAR2) IS
-- This procedure updates a customer record given the customer's ID,
-- field to update, and a new field value.
```

```
BEGIN
  IF UPPER(fieldtype) = 'C' THEN -- update the customer's company name
    UPDATE customers
      SET companyname = newvalue
      WHERE id = custid;
  ELSIF UPPER(fieldtype) = 'L' THEN -- update the customer's last name
    UPDATE customers
      SET lastname = newvalue
      WHERE id = custid;
  ELSIF UPPER(fieldtype) = 'F' THEN -- update the customer's first name
    UPDATE customers
      SET firstname = newvalue
      WHERE id = custid;
  ELSIF UPPER(fieldtype) = 'A' THEN -- update the customer's address
    UPDATE customers
      SET address = newvalue
      WHERE id = custid;
  ELSIF UPPER(fieldtype) = 'T' THEN -- update the customer's city
    UPDATE customers
      SET city = newvalue
      WHERE id = custid;
  ELSIF UPPER(fieldtype) = 'S' THEN -- update the customer's state
    UPDATE customers
      SET state = newvalue
      WHERE id = custid;
  ELSIF UPPER(fieldtype) = 'Z' THEN -- update the customer's zip code
    UPDATE customers
      SET zipcode = newvalue
      WHERE id = custid;
  ELSIF UPPER(fieldtype) = 'P' THEN -- update the customer's phone number
    UPDATE customers
      SET phone = newvalue
      WHERE id = custid;
  ELSIF UPPER(fieldtype) = 'X' THEN -- update the customer's fax number
    UPDATE customers
      SET fax = newvalue
      WHERE id = custid;
  ELSE
      customermanager.returnerror ('Invalid Field Type');
  END IF;
  IF SQL%NOTFOUND THEN
    customermanager.returnerror ('Invalid Customer ID');
```

```
  END IF;
END updatecustomer;
---------------------DELETECUSTOMER procedure ----------------------
PROCEDURE deletecustomer (custid IN INTEGER) IS
BEGIN
  DELETE FROM customers
    WHERE id = custid;
  IF SQL%NOTFOUND THEN
      customermanager.returnerror ('Invalid Customer ID');
  END IF;
END deletecustomer;
---------------------DELETECUSTOMER procedure ----------------------
PROCEDURE deletecustomer (last IN VARCHAR2, first IN VARCHAR2) IS
BEGIN
  DELETE FROM customers
    WHERE lastname = last AND firstname = first;
  IF SQL%NOTFOUND THEN
    customermanager.returnerror ('Invalid Customer Name');
  END IF;
END deletecustomer;

END customermanager;
```

The CUSTOMERMANAGER package body defines all of the public procedures and functions in the package specification, as well as the private procedure RETURNERROR. The CUSTOMERMANAGER package body also declares two private global variables, ERRNUM and ERRMESS, that work with the private RETURNERROR procedure.

Logic Restrictions within PL/SQL Programs

Oracle7 places relatively few significant restrictions on the types of logic you can include in PL/SQL programs. For example, a database PL/SQL program can include any PL/SQL statement and any DML SQL statement, including SELECT, INSERT, UPDATE, and DELETE. A PL/SQL program can also include SQL transaction control statements, such as COMMIT, ROLLBACK, and SAVEPOINT. However, a PL/SQL program cannot include any DDL statements (for example, CREATE, ALTER, and DROP) or DCL statements (for example, GRANT and REVOKE).

Calling Procedures and Functions

Once you have created a procedure, function, or package, you need to know how to call it from an application to make use of its logic. The following sections explain several methods applications can use to call database procedures and functions.

Calling Database Procedures and Functions Directly inside an Application

You can have an application call a database procedure or function directly. For example, to call the SALES.NEWCUSTOMER procedure an Oracle Forms application might issue this call from inside a procedure or trigger in a forms application:

```
sales.newcustomer('NBC','Gumble','Bryant')
```

Since the call to the NEWCUSTOMER procedure does not include all of the procedure's parameters, Oracle7 substitutes the default parameter values for those that are absent and executes the procedure.

Calling a public procedure or function that is part of a package is no different than calling a stand-alone procedure or function, except that you must include the program's package name as a prefix to the program name. For example, an application can call the CUSTOMERMANAGER.NEWCUSTOMER package procedure using this call:

```
sales.customermanager.newcustomer('NBC','Gumble','Bryant')
```

Applications can also access a package's public package variables to get a value or assign a variable a new value.

NOTE To execute a procedure or function, you must own the procedure, function, or package that encapsulates the program or have the EXECUTE object privilege for the PL/SQL program. By requiring a user to have only the EXECUTE privilege for a PL/SQL program, Oracle7 lets you create an additional level of security in your system. Application users do not need the object privileges to any objects; they need only the privilege to execute application procedures.

Referencing PL/SQL Functions in SQL Expressions

Releases 7.1, 7.2, and 7.3 of Oracle7 support SQL statements that call database functions. Consider this query, which uses a subquery to determine the ID of Thomas Brokaw and then return the ID of all the sales orders placed by him:

```
SELECT id
  FROM orders
  WHERE customerid =
    (SELECT id FROM customers
      WHERE lastname = 'Brokaw'
      AND firstname = 'Thomas')
```

Instead of using the subquery, the SQL statement can call the CUSTOMERMAN-AGER.FINDCUSTOMERID function to return the value needed in the SQL statement's WHERE clause:

```
SELECT id
  FROM orders
  WHERE customerid =
      sales.customermanager.findcustomerid('Brokaw','Thomas')
```

Package State

Package variables are different from their stand-alone procedure and function counterparts because the *state* of package variables (current values) persists for the life of a database session that uses the encompassing package. For example, in the CUSTOMERMANAGER package, Oracle7 initializes the ERRNUM and ERRMESS private package variables the first time a user's session makes a call to the package. Oracle7 retains the error number and error message values on behalf of the session until the session closes. Each database session that uses a package has its own state values for all package variables.

Replacing Procedures, Functions, and Packages

During the life of an application, the application's procedures, functions, or packages might become out of date as a result of changes in the underlying application schema or the application logic. It is common to need to replace the current version of a procedure, function, or package with a new version to account for such changes.

If you need to replace a procedure, function, or package with a new version, you can do so without dropping the current program version, using the OR REPLACE option of the CREATE PROCEDURE, CREATE FUNCTION, or CREATE PACKAGE command:

```
CREATE OR REPLACE PROCEDURE newcustomer ...

CREATE OR REPLACE FUNCTION findcustomerid ...

CREATE OR REPLACE PACKAGE customermanager ...

CREATE OR REPLACE PACKAGE BODY customermanager ...
```

Dropping Procedures, Functions, and Packages

In certain situations, a procedure, function, or package will become obsolete. For example, if you remove an application from an Oracle7 database system, the application's package is no longer needed. In such cases, you should drop procedures, functions, and packages to clean up the corresponding database's data dictionary and release some space in its SYSTEM tablespace.

To drop a procedure, function, or package, you use the SQL command DROP PROCEDURE, DROP FUNCTION, or DROP PACKAGE:

```
DROP PROCEDURE newcustomer

DROP FUNCTION findcustomerid

DROP PACKAGE customermanager
```

NOTE To drop both the specification and body of a procedure, function, or package, you must own the program or have the DROP ANY PROCEDURE system privilege.

If you want to drop only a package's body, not its specification, use the DROP PACKAGE BODY command:

```
DROP PACKAGE BODY customermanager
```

Before dropping a database procedure, function, or package, consider the problems that might result if other procedures, packages, or applications depend on the program to be dropped. For example, if an Oracle Forms application relies on a database procedure to do some work and you drop the procedure, the application cannot function correctly; you must modify the application to account for the drop of the procedure.

Within the database itself, Oracle7 has a sophisticated mechanism that tracks the dependencies of all objects within the database. For example, if procedure A calls procedure B and you drop procedure B, Oracle7 immediately marks procedure A as "invalid." The next time an application calls procedure A, Oracle7 automatically tries to recompile the invalid procedure and finds that procedure B is no longer available. In this case, Oracle7 returns the error message to the application, which alerts the administrator that the application logic is no longer valid and requires modification.

> **TIP**
>
> The administrator can identify invalid objects by querying the DBA_OBJECTS data dictionary view for objects that have STATUS = 'INVALID'.

Creating and Managing Triggers

The following sections explain the details of how to create, manage, and use database triggers.

Creating Triggers

To create a database trigger, you use the SQL command CREATE TRIGGER:

```
CREATE TRIGGER updatepartquantity
-- This trigger makes sure that when users insert, update,
-- or delete line items for sales orders, an appropriate
-- change is made to the on-hand quantity of the line item's part.
--------------------- TRIGGERING STATEMENTS ---------------------
AFTER INSERT OR UPDATE OF quantity OR DELETE ON items
--------------------- ROW TRIGGER --------------------------------
FOR EACH ROW
--------------------- TRIGGER RESTRICTION -----------------------
--------------------- TRIGGER BODY ------------------------------
BEGIN
  IF INSERTING THEN
    UPDATE parts
      SET onhand = onhand - :new.quantity
      WHERE id = :new.partid;
ELSIF UPDATING THEN
    IF :new.quantity > :old.quantity THEN
      UPDATE parts
        SET onhand = onhand - (:new.quantity - :old.quantity)
        WHERE id = :new.partid;
    ELSE
      UPDATE parts
        SET onhand = onhand + (:old.quantity - :new.quantity)
        WHERE id = :new.partid;
    END IF;
  ELSE
    UPDATE parts
      SET onhand = onhand + :old.quantity
      WHERE id = :new.id;
  END IF;
END updatepartquantity;
```

The comments in the trigger example show the different parts of a trigger definition. The following sections explain the different parts of a trigger.

TIP

Releases 7.0, 7.1, and 7.2 of Oracle7 do not store a trigger's body as a compiled PL/SQL code block as with procedures, functions, and packages. Instead, the first time an operation fires a trigger, Oracle7 reads the trigger's source code from the data dictionary, compiles the trigger, and stores the compiled version in the shared pool. Therefore, it might take a bit longer to complete an operation when it is the first time a specific trigger is fired. To avoid such performance hits when triggers are particularly large (for example, more than 60 lines of code), developers can put all trigger logic inside a stored procedure and have the trigger body simply call the stored procedure. When using release 7.3 of Oracle7, the size of database triggers are less of a concern because the server stores database triggers in compiled form.

Specifying a Trigger's Triggering Statement

A trigger's *triggering statement* indicates which statement automatically fires (executes) a trigger. A trigger's triggering statement can be an INSERT, UPDATE, or DELETE statement for a specific table. One trigger can have multiple triggering statements, as the example of the UPDATEPARTQUANTITY trigger earlier in this chapter shows. To minimize the complexity of how multiple triggers fire, it's best to include the logic for a number of triggering statements all together in one trigger, if possible. The next section discusses how to execute different blocks of logic in a trigger body based on the type of triggering statement that fires a trigger.

If you indicate that a trigger's triggering statement includes UPDATE statements, you can optionally indicate specific columns to fire on. That way, the trigger does not unnecessarily fire when a statement updates the target table but not a column of interest. If you omit the "OF column-list" clause after UPDATE, the trigger fires when a user updates any column in the target table.

Specifying a Trigger's Execution Time

A trigger can fire its body either before or after the triggering statement executes. Decide which type of trigger to use based on when you want to perform the trigger's logic in relation to the triggering statement. For example, if you use a trigger to perform a security check before allowing an UPDATE to occur, it makes sense to use a BEFORE trigger. If you use a trigger to check the integrity of a table after inserting a new row, it might make more sense to use an AFTER trigger.

If you specify the BEFORE keyword at the start of the triggering statement specification, Oracle7 fires the trigger body before executing a triggering statement. If you specify the AFTER keyword at the start of the triggering statement specification, Oracle7 fires the trigger body after the triggering statement completes.

Specifying Row and Statement Triggers

Oracle7 supports two types of triggers: row triggers and statement triggers. A *row trigger* fires its body once for every row that the triggering statement touches. A *statement trigger* fires its body only once, no matter how many rows the triggering statement affects. Which type of trigger should you use? That depends on the logic you include in a trigger's body. For example, if you use a trigger to perform a security check before allowing a user to insert, update, or delete rows in a table, the security check needs to occur only once, not for every row the triggering statement touches.

To specify a row trigger, include the FOR EACH ROW clause after specifying the triggering statement in the CREATE TRIGGER statement. To specify a statement trigger, simply omit the FOR EACH ROW clause. (See the TIMECHECK trigger in the section "Using Procedures and Triggers for Complex Security Checks" earlier in this chapter for an example of a statement trigger.)

Specifying a Trigger Restriction for a Row Trigger

If you have a row trigger that should fire only in select situations based on the values in a row, you can improve application performance by eliminating otherwise unnecessary trigger firings with a trigger restriction. A *trigger restriction* is a simple Boolean condition that Oracle7 checks before actually firing the body of a trigger.

You specify a trigger's restriction right after the FOR EACH ROW clause. For example, the REORDER trigger presented in the section "The DBMS_ALERT Package" later in this chapter shows a restriction that compares two field values in the target table. In the next example, if the value of a row's ONHAND column is less than that of the REORDER column, the condition evaluates to TRUE and Oracle7 fires the trigger:

```
WHEN (new.onhand < new.reorder)
```

Special PL/SQL Extensions for Trigger Bodies

To enhance the capabilities of triggers, there are some special PL/SQL extensions you can use in a trigger body: conditional predicates and correlation values.

The *conditional predicates* INSERTING, UPDATING, and DELETING allow you to conditionally execute different blocks of statements, depending on the type of triggering statement that fires a trigger. You need to use conditional predicates only when a trigger's condition includes two or all three types of triggering statements. The previous example of the UPDATEPARTQUANTITY trigger demonstrates the use of all the conditional predicates.

Correlation values allow statements in the body of a row trigger to use the old and new column values of the row on which the trigger is currently positioned when the trigger is firing. For example, the UPDATEPARTQUANTITY trigger uses the new and old QUANTITY values of the ITEMS table to adjust corresponding stock onhand quantity values in the PARTS table when someone inserts, updates, or deletes line items in the ITEMS table.

NOTE When the triggering statement is an INSERT statement, the old correlation values are NULL (there is no old row from which to obtain values); when the triggering statement is a DELETE statement, the new correlation values are NULL (there is no new version of the row from which to obtain values); and when the triggering statement is an UPDATE statement, both old and new correlation values are available.

Logic Restrictions within Trigger Bodies

Oracle7 restricts the logic within the body of a trigger more than that of a procedure or function. A trigger body can contain any DML SQL statement, including SELECT, INSERT, UPDATE, and DELETE statements, but cannot include any transaction control SQL statements (for example, COMMIT and ROLLBACK), DDL SQL statements (for example, CREATE, ALTER, and DROP) or DCL SQL statements (for example, GRANT and REVOKE). Also, Oracle7 returns an error when a trigger calls a procedure that includes a transaction control statement such as COMMIT or ROLLBACK.

Mutating and Constraining Tables   Triggers have specific logic restrictions to correctly handle complicated situations in which one session tries to perform many operations at the same time as a result of triggers being fired and/or integrity constraints being enforced. To avoid run-time application errors, you must consider these restrictions when designing triggers. This section explains some new terms and these special restrictions.

Oracle7 considers a table as *mutating* when a session is currently modifying the table in some way—for example, with an UPDATE, DELETE, or INSERT statement, or as the result of delete cascade referential integrity constraint action. For example, when your session updates one or more rows in a table with an UPDATE statement and the same statement also fires a row trigger, the table is mutating with respect to the trigger. To prevent row triggers from seeing an inconsistent set of data, Oracle7 prohibits the statements in a trigger body to read or modify a mutating table. See the section "Debugging Oracle7 PL/SQL Programs" a little later in this chapter for an example of a mutating table error condition.

Oracle7 considers a table as *constraining* when a session issues a SQL statement that fires a trigger and the trigger needs to read the table on behalf of a statement in the trigger's body or on behalf of an integrity constraint. For example, when your session issues a SQL statement that fires a trigger and the trigger includes a query of the PARTS table, the PARTS table is a constraining table. To prevent order- and index-dependent success and failure of SQL statements, Oracle7 prevents the statements of a row trigger from changing the values in any key (primary, unique, or foreign) of a constraining table.

Replacing Triggers

In much the same way that you can replace procedures and packages, you can use the OR REPLACE option of the CREATE TRIGGER command to replace the current version of a trigger with a new one:

```
CREATE OR REPLACE TRIGGER updatepartquantity ...
```

Dropping Triggers

If you want to remove the operation performed by a database trigger, you can drop the trigger by using the DROP TRIGGER command:

```
DROP TRIGGER updatepartquantity ...
```

If you drop a table that has triggers, Oracle7 automatically drops all of the triggers associated with the table.

Debugging Oracle7 PL/SQL Programs

If you've programmed in a third-generation programming language before, you know that bug-free code is an oxymoron, even with the smallest of programs. One of the most time-consuming and important jobs that face the application developer is the process of debugging a program so it works as intended. Programming with Oracle's PL/SQL is no different.

If you have Developer/2000 and use Oracle Procedure Builder to create your PL/SQL programs, the tool's integrated debugger will automatically check the syntax of your code, dependencies on database objects, and so on, and then report any problems that it finds. On the other hand, if you don't have access to Procedure Builder, debugging your code is a much more laborious process. In this case, you need to learn some debugging tricks to be productive at PL/SQL development. This section explains some basic ways to get started in debugging PL/SQL programs.

Types of Errors and Oracle7 PL/SQL Error Messages

Unless you are a programming wizard, the first time you try to compile a PL/SQL program (a procedure, function, package, or trigger) using an interactive database-access tool such as SQL*Plus or a Server Manager SQL worksheet, it's likely that Oracle7 will spit out error messages galore to tell you all that is wrong with your program. The error messages serve as the starting point from which you must debug your program.

Parse Errors

Oracle7 can return two rounds of PL/SQL error messages when you try to compile a PL/SQL program. The first wave of error messages will be the parse errors that Oracle7 finds in the program. *Parse errors* are those that result from incorrect use of command syntax—both PL/SQL commands and SQL commands. For example, see if you can find the parse error in the following code example for the CUSTOMERID function:

```
CREATE FUNCTION customerid (last IN VARCHAR2, first IN VARCHAR2)
RETURN INTEGER AS
  customerid  INTEGER;
BEGIN
  SELECT id INTOO customerid FROM customer
    WHERE lastname = last AND firstname = first;
  RETURN customerid;
END customerid;
```

If you can't find the parse error, take a close look at the SELECT command in the function. Notice that the INTO keyword has an extra "O" at the end. Such a syntax error results in a parse error. If you tried to compile the previous version of the CUSTOMERID function from within Server Manager, you would receive the following error message:

```
DBA-00072: Warning: FUNCTION CUSTOMERID created with compilation errors.
```

To reveal PL/SQL errors when using SQL*Plus or Server Manager, you can use the special SHOW ERRORS command. Use this command to see the errors that result from any CREATE PROCEDURE, CREATE FUNCTION, CREATE PACKAGE, CREATE PACKAGE BODY, CREATE TRIGGER, or CREATE VIEW statement. For example, the following command reveals the parse error identified in the previous example:

```
SHOW ERRORS FUNCTION customerid

Errors for FUNCTION CUSTOMERID:
LINE/COL ERROR
---------------------------------------------------------------------------
5/19     PLS-00103: Encountered the symbol "CUSTOMERID" when expecting one
of the following: , into
```

> **TIP**
>
> If you use the SHOW ERRORS command of SQL*Plus or Server Manager without specifying an object, the command returns the errors present for the most recently created procedure, function, package, package body, trigger, or view.

Notice from the preceding example that Oracle7 typically is not outstanding at telling you exactly what you did wrong, even with simple parse errors. Often, you'll need to interpret what the error message reveals to identify a problem. In this case, Oracle7 didn't expect the CUSTOMERID variable reference because it didn't interpret the INTO keyword correctly. After you work with Oracle7 PL/SQL for a while, your experience will help interpret Oracle7 PL/SQL error messages so you can identify problems more readily.

Using SHOW ERRORS, find and fix all of the parse errors in the source file for your PL/SQL program. Then resubmit the code and see if it works. Remember to first drop the older version of the code that has the errors, or simply use the OR REPLACE option of the respective CREATE command to replace the older, bug-ridden version of the program, as the following example shows:

```
CREATE OR REPLACE FUNCTION customerid (last IN VARCHAR2, first IN VARCHAR2)
RETURN INTEGER AS
  customerid  INTEGER;
BEGIN
  SELECT id INTO customerid FROM customer
    WHERE lastname = last AND firstname = first;
  RETURN customerid;
END customerid;
```

Compile-Time Errors

The next round of errors that Oracle7 identifies is compile-time errors. *Compile-time errors* happen when Oracle7 tries to compile the object but encounters some type of error. Common compile-time errors include things like incorrect object references or trying to reference an object for which you have no privileges. If you read the earlier chapters in this book and have a good memory and an outstanding eye for detail, you'll be able to identify the compile-time error in the example shown in the "Parse Errors" section. When trying to create this CUSTOMERID function with Server Manager, you'll find the following error is returned:

```
DBA-00072: Warning: FUNCTION CUSTOMERID created with compilation errors.

SHOW ERRORS

Errors for FUNCTION CUSTOMERID:
LINE/COL ERROR
-------------------------------------------------------------------------------
5/34      PLS-00201: identifier 'CUSTOMER' must be declared
5/3       PL/SQL: SQL Statement ignored
```

Now do you remember? The table name is CUSTOMERS, not CUSTOMER. Another quick fix, and the procedure will finally compile correctly:

```
CREATE OR REPLACE FUNCTION customerid (last IN VARCHAR2, first
IN VARCHAR2)
RETURN INTEGER AS
  customerid   INTEGER;
BEGIN
  SELECT id INTO customerid FROM customers
    WHERE lastname = last AND firstname = first;
  RETURN customerid;
END customerid;
```

Run-Time Errors

Run-time errors occur when your program compiles successfully but then returns errors when someone uses it. Oracle7 cannot identify and tell you about run-time errors until you actually run the program. To learn more about run-time errors, let's take a close look at a perfect example of a run-time error condition: a mutating table situation. Consider the following procedure and trigger definitions:

```
CREATE PROCEDURE restockpart (partid IN INTEGER) AS
  reorderstatus    INTEGER := 0;
```

```
  quantity          INTEGER := 0;
  reorderpt         INTEGER := 0;
BEGIN
-- First, check to see if part hasn't already been reordered.
  SELECT count(*) INTO reorderstatus FROM reorder WHERE id = partid;
-- If the part hasn't already been reordered, then reorder it now.
  IF reorderstatus = 0 THEN
    SELECT onhand, reorder INTO quantity, reorderpt
      FROM parts WHERE id = partid;
    INSERT INTO reorder VALUES (partid, quantity, reorderpt);
  END IF;
END restockpart;

CREATE TRIGGER reorder
AFTER UPDATE OF onhand ON parts
FOR EACH ROW
  WHEN (new.onhand <= new.reorder)
BEGIN
  restockpart(:new.id);
END;
```

Now consider what happens when someone updates the PARTS table to update a part's onhand quantity to be less than the part's reorder point:

1. The REORDER trigger fires. At this point, the PARTS table is mutating with respect to the user session that fired the trigger.

2. The REORDER trigger calls the RESTOCKPART procedure. The RESTOCK-PART procedure attempts to query the PARTS table, which, as previously stated, is mutating.

When Oracle7 identifies that the PARTS table is mutating, it returns the following run-time error messages:

```
ORA-04091: table SALES.PARTS is mutating, trigger may not read
or modify it
ORA-06512: at "SALES.REORDERPART", line 10
ORA-06512: at line 2
ORA-04088: error during execution of trigger 'SALES.REORDER'
```

Logic Errors

Logic errors occur when the program compiles successfully but doesn't work as you intended it to. These errors might be caused by anything from an unhandled exception to certain conditions that you didn't foresee. For example, consider the previous version of the CUSTOMERID function and how it works with the CUSTOMERS table. If all customers' last and first names are stored in initial capital letters in the CUSTOMERS table, what do you think would happen when an application (in the following case, an anonymous PL/SQL block) calls the CUSTOMERID function as follows:

```
DECLARE
  x INTEGER;
BEGIN
  x := customerid('BROKAW', 'THOMAS');
  dbms_output.put_line(x);
END;
```

The answer: The CUSTOMERID function will not find any customer records with the requested name, THOMAS BROKAW, even though there is a customer named Thomas Brokaw. The previous situation describes a simple logic error—the CUSTOMERID function doesn't account for variances in the case of function parameters. The addition of a SQL function or two can quickly fix this error condition:

```
CREATE OR REPLACE FUNCTION customerid (last IN VARCHAR2, first
IN VARCHAR2)
RETURN INTEGER AS
  customerid  INTEGER;
BEGIN
  SELECT id INTO customerid FROM customers
    WHERE lastname = INITCAP(last) AND firstname = INIT-
CAP(first);
  RETURN customerid;
END customerid;
```

The previous examples of a mutating table error condition and a logic error are just two of many possible types of errors you might encounter after successfully compiling a PL/SQL program. As with any programming project, one of the most important steps is to thoroughly test and validate the system to make sure the program works as intended.

Using the DBMS_OUTPUT Utility Package to Debug PL/SQL Programs

If you debug a 3GL program without the use of a nice debugger, it's hard to tell what is going on when the program is running. Therefore, it's hard to debug the program and get it working correctly. To get around the limitations of your compiler, you can include statements that produce output and tell you what is going on. For example, when using C, you might include some printf statements to reveal the values of several program variables as they change during program execution. You can then look at the output and figure out what is happening.

As described earlier, Oracle7 doesn't include a debugger to help you program with PL/SQL. Therefore, you might consider using the previous method of program output to reveal what is happening as a PL/SQL program executes. To produce output from a PL/SQL program, use the functions of the DBMS_OUTPUT utility package. If you are not familiar with the DBMS_OUTPUT package, see the section "Providing Terminal Output from PL/SQL" later in this chapter.

Using the Oracle7 Programmer Utilities

Oracle7 ships with several scripts that create useful programmer utilities in the form of PL/SQL packages. These packages contain a number of procedures and functions you can call to increase the functionality of an application's stored procedures, functions, and database triggers. The following sections describe each of these programmer utilities.

Supplementing SQL Functionality Inside PL/SQL

Oracle7 includes several utility packages for increasing the functionality of SQL inside PL/SQL programs. The following sections explain the packages you can use to add specific SQL functionality to your PL/SQL programs.

The DBMS_SESSION Package

The DBMS_SESSION package contains several procedures and functions that applications can use to control an application user's session. Two useful utilities are the SET_ROLE procedure, which allows a PL/SQL program to change an application user's current database role, and the IS_ROLE_ENABLED function, which allows an application to determine whether or not a specified role is enabled. Chapter 18 includes a discussion of how to use the SET_ROLE and IS_ROLE_ENABLED programs in the DBMS_SESSION package.

The DBMS_SESSION package also includes the RESET_PACKAGE procedure, which allows an application to reinitialize the state of all a session's current packages. For example, an application can use the RESET_PACKAGE procedure to reinitialize the current values for all global package variables in an application session:

```
dbms_session.reset_package
```

Another useful function in the DBMS_SESSION package is UNIQUE_SESSION_ID, which assigns a unique session ID to an application session. The UNIQUE_SESSION_ID function is useful for applications that open multiple connections to the server and must coordinate processing among the open sessions. Applications can keep track of each connection with variables that receive the unique session ID assigned by Oracle7:

```
session1 := dbms_session.unique_session_id;
```

NOTE The UNIQUE_SESSION_ID function merely assigns unique ID values among currently connected sessions; the function doesn't guarantee to create different session IDs each time someone calls it. For example, you might connect, get a session ID, disconnect, reconnect, and then get the same session ID as the first time or a different one.

The DBMS_TRANSACTION Package

The DBMS_TRANSACTION package permits a PL/SQL program to perform restricted transaction control. Here are some of the more useful procedures:

Procedure	Description
COMMIT	Commits a transaction
ROLLBACK	Rolls back a transaction
SAVEPOINT	Declares a transaction savepoint

Procedure	Description
ROLLBACK_SAVEPOINT	Rolls back a transaction to a declared savepoint
USE_ROLLBACK_SEGMENT	Specifies a specific rollback segment for a new transaction

However, many of these procedures have limited usefulness because of usage restrictions. For example, you cannot use any of these procedures inside database triggers, and you can use only one, the USE_ROLLBACK_SEGMENT procedure, in procedures called by Oracle Forms.

The DBMS_DDL and DBMS_UTILITY Packages

The DBMS_DDL and DBMS_UTILITY packages also contain procedures and functions that extend the functionality of PL/SQL with a limited number of DDL operations and other internal server operations. Several of the procedures in these packages will be of more interest to database administrators than to application developers. For example, the administrator can use the DBMS_UTILITY.ANALYZE _SCHEMA procedure to update the statistics for all objects in a specified application schema (see Chapter 10 for more information about this procedure).

Providing Terminal Output from PL/SQL

Oracle7 includes several utility packages to provide output from within PL/SQL programs. The following sections explain the utility packages you can use to generate application output from within PL/SQL programs.

The DBMS_STANDARD Package

For the most part, the procedures and functions in the DBMS_STANDARD utility package are used by other utility packages. However, applications can directly call one procedure, RAISE_APPLICATION_ERROR, to raise user-defined errors and error messages. (Chapter 5 discusses how to use the RAISE_APPLICATION_ERROR procedure, and several code listings throughout this book demonstrate the use of the procedure.)

The DBMS_OUTPUT Package

The DBMS_OUTPUT utility package contains several procedures and functions that applications can use to produce terminal output from database procedures and triggers. For example, the ENABLE procedure creates a buffer to enable output from other DBMS_OUTPUT procedures, the PUT_LINE procedure puts a specified text string as a new line in the output buffer, the GET_LINE procedure retrieves a single line from the output buffer, and the GET_LINES procedure retrieves an array of lines from the output buffer.

A Server Manager SQL worksheet and SQL*Plus make the management of the output buffer transparent with the SERVEROUTPUT option of the SET command. Several examples of stored procedures throughout this book demonstrate how to use cursors and the PUT_LINE procedure to return multiple rows of output from a stored procedure.

Providing File Input/Output from PL/SQL

Similar to the DBMS_OUTPUT utility package, you can use the procedures and functions of the UTL_FILE utility package to read and write text files located on the server computer. Available only with release 7.3 of Oracle7, the UTL_FILE package includes many routines to handle different file I/O related operations, including FOPEN, FCLOSE, GET_LINE, PUT, NEW_LINE, PUT_LINE, and PUTF.

Passing Information among Database Sessions

Oracle7 includes several utility packages to allow communication among different database sessions. The following sections explain the different utility packages you can use to allow database sessions to communicate.

The DBMS_LOCK Package

The DBMS_LOCK utility package allows applications to coordinate access to shared resources that are external to the database server. Chapter 16 includes examples that show how to use several of the procedures and functions in the DBMS_LOCK utility package to coordinate application access to a number of shared system peripherals, such as printers and modems.

The DBMS_ALERT Package

Most types of client applications require user interaction to get work done with a database system. For example, a forms-based application might provide entry fields, where users can enter new records of information, as well as a button that, when pressed, notifies the application to send the new data records to the database server. In this case, the application user drives the communication between the client and the server to get work done. But intelligent applications include two-way communication logic so the database server can alert an application user when certain conditions exist in the database. For example, a powerful inventory management application might alert an inventory manager that the stock on a particular product has dropped below its reorder point, or even worse, to nothing. If the inventory management application did not include such alerting logic, the inventory manager would not discover an inventory crisis unless the inventory manager frequently and consistently remembered to query the database for problem situations.

One way an Oracle7 client application can identify an alert condition is to regularly poll the database server for an alert situation using a SQL query. For example, an inventory management application might issue this query every five minutes to check for parts below their reorder point:

```
SELECT id, description
  FROM parts
  WHERE onhand < = reorder;
```

The primary drawback of such polling is that it can significantly degrade system performance, especially when many client applications all poll for many alert conditions. If this happens, the database server is subject to an extraordinary burden just in checking for alert conditions that might never exist, not to mention a significant amount of extra network traffic.

A much more efficient way to identify and signal alert conditions in an Oracle7 database is by using database alerts. As Chapter 13 discusses, database alerts allow applications to create, register for, and signal when alert conditions arise in an Oracle7 database without polling. Because database alerts do not perform any polling to identify alert conditions, database alerts can keep application users abreast of any alert situations while placing no extra burden on the Oracle7 database server and keep network traffic to a minimum. Figure 17.1 contrasts the different methods of identifying and signaling database alert conditions.

FIGURE 17.1:

Database alerts place much less burden on the database server and the network than does polling to alert applications of specific conditions.

Applications can create, register for, and signal database alerts using the procedures and functions in the DBMS_ALERT utility package. Here is a list of the primary procedures:

Procedure	Description
REGISTER	Used by an application to register interest in a named database alert
WAITONE and WAITANY	Used by an application to wait for a signal that a specific database alert or any database alert has occurred for which the application has registered
SIGNAL	Included by the developer in an application procedure or database trigger to identify when an alert condition happens

One of the best ways to learn how to use database alerts is to look at a sample application that uses the procedures and functions of the DBMS_ALERT package. The following examples show how to include database alert logic in an inventory management application to notify an inventory manager when the stock is low on a part in inventory.

To be signaled when an alert condition happens, the first thing an application needs to do is register for the alert using the DBMS_ALERT.REGISTER procedure. For example, the inventory management application can register for the alert named STOCKLOW by making this procedure call after application startup or when a menu item is selected:

```
dbms_alert.register('STOCKLOW');
```

Oracle7 keeps track of sessions that register for an alert and makes a note to signal these sessions when something triggers the alert condition. However, registering for named alerts is not enough for an application to be signaled when the alerts happen. Because the Oracle7 server does not support *synchronous communication* (communication independent of user directives), Oracle7 can notify an application of an alert condition only when the application is waiting for an alert signal. To wait for one or more alert conditions, an application should create a dedicated connection to the database apart from the primary focus of the application.

For example, the inventory application might create a second database session when opening a separate window that has some indicators to show the current status of several alert situations. The session tied to the alert window simply waits for alert conditions to happen. When there are no alert conditions, the window might show an array of green lights to indicate that all systems are in good shape. When an alert condition arises, the application can beep and change a light to a flashing red to indicate that the corresponding alert condition has occurred.

To wait for an alert signal for a registered alert, an application can use the DBMS_ALERT.WAITONE procedure or the DBMS_ALERT.WAITANY procedure. The WAITONE procedure waits for a signal from a specific registered alert, while the WAITANY procedure waits for a signal from any registered alert. For example, this PL/SQL block shows how a database session in an inventory management application might use an endless loop to wait for a signal that the STOCKLOW alert condition has occurred:

```
DECLARE
  message VARCHAR2(256);
  status INTEGER;
BEGIN
  LOOP
    dbms_alert.waitone('STOCKLOW', message, status, 5);
```

```
      IF status = 0 THEN
         dbms_output.put_line(message);
      END IF;
   END LOOP;
END;
```

Notice that the return status of the WAITONE (and WAITANY) procedure indicates whether or not an alert condition is positive; 0 indicates that an alert occurred, and 1 indicates that a time-out occurred. When calling the WAITONE (and WAITANY) procedure, you can indicate the time to wait, in seconds. In the previous example, the WAITONE procedure waits for five seconds.

> **NOTE**
>
> If a session waiting for alert signals uses a lengthy time-out period, the session should connect to the database server using a dedicated server connection rather than a multithreaded, shared server connection. That's because while a session is waiting for an alert to occur, Oracle7 binds a shared server to the waiting session and prevents all other sessions from using the shared server.

The previous examples show what is necessary from the perspective of client-side application logic. However, one last thing is necessary to make a database alert work: a procedure or trigger that actually signals an alert condition. This is the trick that makes polling unnecessary and saves all of the overhead on the server.

For example, consider the following rewrite of the REORDER trigger shown in Chapter 5. Recall that the REORDER trigger inserts a new row into a table called REORDER that keeps track of all the parts in inventory where the part's stock has fallen below its reorder point. The only modification we will make in this version of the REORDER trigger is to add a line to signal that a STOCKLOW alert condition exists:

```
CREATE or replace TRIGGER reorder
AFTER UPDATE OF onhand ON parts
FOR EACH ROW
WHEN (new.onhand <= new.reorder)
```

```
BEGIN
  INSERT INTO reorder VALUES (:new.id, :new.onhand, :new.reorder);
  dbms_alert.signal('STOCKLOW','Part '||:new.id||' reordered;
    low on stock');
END;
```

When an application transaction updates the PARTS table to lower a part's inventory supply, the preceding version of the REORDER trigger checks to see if the part's new inventory supply is lower than its reorder point. If so, the trigger automatically reorders the part and signals an alert condition, which might appear as a flashing red beacon on the inventory manager's terminal:

```
UPDATE parts
  SET onhand = onhand - 100
  WHERE id = 7
```

NOTE Alert signals wisely depend on the outcome of transactions. Therefore, Oracle7 does not immediately signal registered sessions when a procedure or trigger signals the alert. Instead, Oracle7 signals registered sessions only if the transaction that signals the alert commits. This logic can be very important. For instance, consider what happens if an application user's transaction updates the PARTS table to lower a part's inventory quantity below its reorder point, but then the user rolls back the transaction. Since the transaction never really happened, Oracle7 does not signal the alert condition, so the inventory manager does not see an alert that didn't really happen.

The inventory management alert example is just one way you can use database alerts to enhance the functionality and power of your Oracle7 database applications. As you plan an application, discuss with users the different types of alerts that would make the application better for their job. If you use database alerts wisely in an application, you can positively affect the productivity of application users.

The DBMS_PIPE Package

The DBMS_PIPE utility package allows different database sessions connected to the same database instance to communicate with one another using *database pipes*—channels for intersession communication. For example, an application might open multiple sessions to a database server as in the database alert example shown in the preceding section. To allow communication among the different application sessions, you can use database pipes.

The more important procedures and functions in the DBMS_PIPE package include the following:

Procedure	Description
PACK_MESSAGE	Places a specified message text string, number, or date into the message buffer
UNPACK_MESSAGE	Extracts a message from the message buffer into a specified local variable
SEND_MESSAGE	Sends a message in the message buffer to a named pipe
RECEIVE_MESSAGE	Receives a message sent to a named pipe

To send and receive intersession messages, client applications must execute the different procedures and functions in the DBMS_PIPE package in specific orders. For example, to send a message to a pipe, client applications should first place the message in the message buffer using the PACK_MESSAGE procedure and then assign the message to a named pipe using the SEND_MESSAGE function. This PL/SQL block illustrates the importance of the order of DBMS_PIPE calls:

```
DECLARE
  x integer;
BEGIN
  dbms_pipe.pack_message('Here is an example of a message');
  x := dbms_pipe.send_message('PIPE1'); -- send message to PIPE1
  IF x = 0 then
    dbms_output.put_line('Success');
```

```
   ELSE
     dbms_output.put_line('Failure');
   END IF;
END;
```

Similarly, to receive messages on a pipe, client applications need to check for a message on a named pipe using the RECEIVE_MESSAGE function and, if present, extract the message into a local application variable using the UNPACK_MESSAGE procedure. This PL/SQL block demonstrates these operations:

```
DECLARE
  x INTEGER;
  message VARCHAR2(256);
BEGIN
  LOOP
    x:= dbms_pipe.receive_message('PIPE1',60); -- wait 60 secs for
      PIPE1 messages
    IF x = 0 then
      dbms_pipe.unpack_message(message); -- extract message into
          variable MESSAGE
      dbms_output.put_line(message);
      EXIT;
    END IF;
  END LOOP;
END;
```

The explanations and examples in this chapter have given you an understanding of the powerful features available for application development in Oracle7, including the following:

- How and when to use database stored procedures, functions, packages, and triggers effectively in an application design

- How to create, manage, and use database stored procedures, functions, packages, and triggers

- How to use special utility packages included with Oracle7 (for example, DBMS_OUTPUT, DBMS_STANDARD, DBMS_ALERT, and DBMS_PIPE packages) to enhance the functionality of Oracle7 client/server applications

CHAPTER

EIGHTEEN

Securing Applications

- Granting and revoking access to database objects

- Using roles to manage privileges for applications

- Enabling and disabling roles for applications

After reading all of the chapters in Part II of this book, you must feel like there is an endless array of things to consider when developing a client application for an Oracle7 database system. After designing the application interface, defining the application's schema and application logic, and then tuning the application's performance, what else could there possibly be? Add to the list handling application security issues. This chapter explains how to control access to the data in an application schema using roles and database object privileges.

The ABCs of Application Security

Once you develop, test, and install an application in an Oracle7 client/server database system, it's ready to be put into action—into the hands of the real workers, the application users. However, not just any database user can run an application to accomplish work. There are many security controls that prevent unauthorized users from executing an application.

In many environments, the operating system presents the first security hurdle to an application user: a user must have the appropriate file system privileges to run the application's executable file. For example, if a user intends to use a UNIX workstation to run a client application, the user must have the necessary file permissions on the application executable. Most multi-user operating systems have similar security checks.

NOTE   If a client application executes on a single-user operating system like DOS, Microsoft Windows, or Apple Macintosh, there is probably no way to control who can execute the specific application on a PC.

After getting past the operating system, an application user must be able to connect to the Oracle7 database server. This requires the application user to have a valid database username and password and to be able to create a database session. (See Chapter 9 for a discussion of how the database administrator creates database usernames and passwords for application users, as well as an introduction of system privilege management for application users.)

Even after an application user has the necessary operating system file permissions and can connect to an Oracle7 database, there are other controls that prevent unauthorized use of an application's data: database object privileges. *Database object privileges,* such as SELECT, INSERT, UPDATE, DELETE, and EXECUTE, allow you to explicitly authorize which database users can manipulate an application's table data and execute an application's stored procedures. It is the Oracle7 database object privileges that the application developer needs to consider when putting together a security policy for an application. The following section explains the different object privileges that control access to the data in an Oracle7 database.

Understanding Database Object Privileges

An application schema can contain many different types of database objects, including tables, indexes, views, sequences, procedures, functions, and packages. To execute and use a client database application, an application user must have the necessary object privileges to many of the objects that the application uses. The following table lists the Oracle7 object privileges that are available for the different types of database objects:

Object	Privileges Available
Tables	SELECT, INSERT, UPDATE, DELETE, ALTER, INDEX, REFERENCES
Views	SELECT, INSERT, UPDATE, DELETE
Sequences	SELECT, ALTER
Procedures, functions, and packages	EXECUTE

In many cases, the access that each database object privilege protects will be obvious. For example, the SELECT privilege for a table authorizes a user to issue SELECT statements against the table. However, in some cases, it is not apparent what each object privilege corresponds to. The following list of the commonly misunderstood object privileges should help shed some light:

Privilege	Description
INDEX (table privilege)	Permits a user who does not own the table to create an index for the table
REFERENCES (table privilege)	Permits a user who does not own a table to reference the table in the declaration of a referential integrity constraint
SELECT (sequence privilege)	Permits a user who does not own the sequence to reference the sequence with the NEXTVAL and CURRVAL pseudo-columns

You should also check with a database's administrator to see if the server enforces privileges for searched updates. A *searched update* is an UPDATE or DELETE statement that includes a subquery to find the target rows. For example, the following UPDATE and DELETE statements qualify as searched updates because of the subqueries present as WHERE clauses:

```
UPDATE parts SET onhand = onhand - 100 WHERE id = 3

DELETE FROM parts WHERE id = 7
```

If an Oracle7 server enforces privileges for searched updates, a user needs the SELECT privilege to update a table with a searched update. For example, to execute the first of the two preceding statements, an application user needs both the UPDATE and SELECT object privileges for the PARTS table, not just the UPDATE privilege.

NOTE   The administrator can determine whether or not a server enforces privileges for searched updates using the SQL92_SECURITY initialization parameter. The possible values are TRUE and FALSE.

Database Object Privileges and Synonyms

Chapter 14 discussed how you can use synonyms to remove an application's direct dependence on tables, views, procedures, and other database objects. In terms of security for an application's objects, there are no special privileges to consider when referencing an object's synonym instead of the object itself; just as a user must have the privileges to reference an object by its name, the user must have the privileges to reference an object by a synonym. For example, to query data from the PARTS table, you must have the SELECT privilege for the PARTS table. To query data from the PARTS table using its INVENTORY synonym, you must still have the SELECT privilege for the PARTS table.

You can also grant (or revoke) an object's database object privileges to a user or role by referencing a synonym of the object. For example, the following two statements are equivalent, considering that the PARTS table has a synonym, INVENTORY:

```
GRANT SELECT ON parts TO tjefferson

GRANT SELECT ON inventory TO tjefferson
```

As you can see, there are many different object privileges to consider for an application, particularly for the most common types of objects that an application uses (tables and views). To make it easier to manage the privileges necessary to run an application for many different users, it is wise to take advantage of roles to manage an application's privileges. The following section explains how to use roles for application privilege management.

Using Roles for Application Privilege Management

A role is a collection of related privileges. Chapter 9 showed how the security administrator for a system can create and use roles to greatly simplify privilege management for the different types of database system users. In the same manner, an application developer can create roles to manage and group together the related object privileges necessary to run an application. Then, as part of application installation, the database security administrator grants the application's role to the users who need to run the application. If the privilege requirements for the application change at some time, it's no problem—all that is necessary is a quick change to the privileges in the application role, not to the privileges of many application users.

Use of roles in an Oracle7 client/server database system provides another important benefit: dynamic privilege management for application users. As a user moves from one application to another, each application's role ensures that the user has only the privileges necessary to run the current application and does not carry over privileges from another application.

When planning the security for an application, you might identify different types of application users. For example, it is common that some users will be responsible for creating reports only, not for changing data. Therefore, you should create an application role for these users so they can only read data using the application. Other users might need to use the application to insert new data. Likewise, you need another application role that has the privileges to insert new data using the application. A third application role is necessary if still other users need to have both read and write access to data using the application. And instead of granting an application's roles directly to users, the administrator might decide to grant application roles to other roles that define distinct sets of users in the database. Figure 18.1 shows how a hierarchy of roles can grow from the simple goal of managing application privileges.

Now that you have an idea of the issues to consider when managing an application's security, the following sections explain how to create roles for an application and manage its privilege domain.

Creating Roles to Manage Application Privileges and Application Users

Chapter 9 explained how you can use the Create Role dialog box in Server Manager to create a role and set its authentication method. However, as an application developer, you will probably want to include the definition of an application's roles in its DDL script. Therefore, you will most likely want to create application roles with the equivalent SQL command CREATE ROLE. For example, these statements demonstrate the different options available in the CREATE ROLE command:

```
CREATE ROLE ordersread

CREATE ROLE orderswrite
    IDENTIFIED BY gomitgomat

CREATE ROLE ordersreadwrite
    IDENTIFIED BY phloristigoo
```

Follow the guidelines for client/server systems presented in Chapter 9 concerning role authorization. For example, do not use operating system authentication; instead, use passwords that have no real meaning.

FIGURE 18.1:

Example of a hierarchy of roles used to manage application privileges

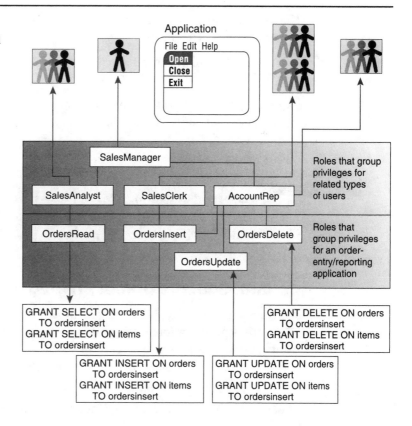

Granting Privileges to an Application's Roles

After you have created a role to manage an application's privileges, the next task is to establish the role's *privilege domain,* or set of privileges for the role. You manage a role's privilege domain using the SQL commands GRANT and REVOKE, along with the different object privileges for the application objects. For example, this set of statements creates a role for insert-only access using an order entry application:

```
CREATE ROLE ordersinsert
  IDENTIFIED BY wiffopnertu

GRANT INSERT ON orders TO ordersinsert

GRANT INSERT ON items TO ordersinsert
```

The next statements show how you can grant several object privileges for a single table all in one GRANT statement:

```
CREATE ROLE ordersreadwrite
  IDENTIFIED BY phloristigoo

GRANT SELECT, INSERT, UPDATE, DELETE ON orders
  TO ordersreadwrite
```

NOTE
As Chapter 9 shows, you can also grant system privileges to any database role. However, most application users should not have the access that powerful system privileges supply. Use extreme caution when considering the grant of a system privilege to an application role.

Column-Specific Object Privileges

The examples of the GRANT command in the preceding section show how to grant object privilege access for all columns in a table or view. As an alternative, you may want to grant object privilege access for specific columns in a table or view. Oracle7 supports object privilege access for specific columns with the INSERT, UPDATE, and REFERENCES privileges only.

```
GRANT UPDATE (shipdate, paiddate) ON orders TO ordersupdate
```

Although Oracle7 does not support granting the SELECT privilege for specific columns of a table, it's easy to work around this limitation by using views. For example, if you want some users to be able to see only the ID, LASTNAME, and FIRSTNAME columns of the CUSTOMERS table, create a view that selects these columns, and then grant the SELECT privilege on the view to the users:

```
CREATE VIEW customernames AS
  SELECT id, lastname, firstname
  FROM customers

GRANT SELECT ON customernames TO ...
```

Revoking Object Privileges from an Application's Roles

If an application's privilege requirements change, you might need to revoke a previously granted object privilege from the application's role. Revoking an object privilege is just as easy as granting it; you use the SQL command REVOKE:

```
REVOKE SELECT ON reorder FROM inventorymanager
```

If a grant exists for a table or view and you want to revoke access to only specific columns, you must first revoke access altogether and then regrant column-selective access:

```
REVOKE UPDATE ON orders FROM ordersupdate

GRANT UPDATE (shipdate) ON orders TO ordersupdate
```

Enabling Application Roles on Application Startup

After you have created an application's roles and defined the privilege domains for each role, you need to create a mechanism in the application to enable the application's role. This ensures that an application user has the correct privileges to successfully run the application. Enabling a specific role for an application also disables a user's other roles, including the user's default roles. (See Chapter 9 for a discussion of default roles.) Most commonly, an application enables its roles at application startup. The following sections explain how an application can enable specific roles for application privilege management.

TIP A user can enable an application role only after the database administrator has granted the role to the user. When you hand over an application to an administrator for installation, make sure the administrator knows to grant the application roles to the application users directly, or indirectly through other database roles that group related users. See Chapter 9 for more information about granting roles to users.

Using the SET ROLE Command

To enable a role, an application can use the SQL command SET ROLE:

```
SET ROLE ordersread

SET ROLE orderswrite
  IDENTIFIED BY gomitgomat
```

Notice that if the role is protected by a password, a SET ROLE statement must also include an IDENTIFIED BY clause to specify the role's password.

The SET ROLE command also allows an application to enable multiple roles:

```
SET ROLE
  ordersread
  orderswrite IDENTIFIED BY gomitgomat

SET ROLE
  orderswrite IDENTIFIED BY gomitgomat,
  ordersreadwrite IDENTIFIED BY phloristigoo
```

In the first example, one role requires a password while the other does not. The second example shows how to enable multiple roles that all have passwords.

NOTE When an application uses the SET ROLE command to explicitly enable one or more roles, Oracle7 implicitly disables all other roles that the user currently has enabled.

Using the DBMS_SESSION Package to Work around Development Environment Limitations

Many application development environments do not support the use of the SQL command SET ROLE. This can make life difficult when trying to use roles for application security. However, if an application development environment permits calls to database stored procedures, an application can work around this problem by calling the SET_ROLE procedure in the DBMS_SESSION utility package.

The DBMS_SESSION.SET_ROLE procedure allows access to the SET ROLE command through a procedural interface. For example, an Oracle Forms application can use the SET_ROLE procedure in a pre-form trigger to enable a specific role for the form application:

```
dbms_session.set_role('orderswrite IDENTIFIED BY gomitgomat');
```

Notice in this example that you need to specify a role's password in the SET_ROLE procedure. If you code a role's password into an application, as the previous example shows, you can open up a potential security hole—a malicious user could look at the application's source code or reverse-engineer the application's code to discover a role's password. To work around this potential security hole, create a dialog box that appears at application startup and prompts the user for the application's role and password, and then feed the entered values as variables in a call to the SET_ROLE procedure:

```
dbms_session.set_role(:rolename||' IDENTIFIED BY '||:rolepassword);
```

If a role does not have a password, call the SET_ROLE procedure without the IDENTIFIED BY part of the parameter:

```
dbms_session.set_role('ordersread')
```

This chapter has described how to approach security for individual Oracle7 applications, including the following topics:

- What database object privileges are, as well as how to grant them to and revoke them from users and roles

- How to use roles to manage the group of related object privileges necessary for users to run a database application

- How an application can enable and disable application roles using the SET ROLE command and the procedures in the DMMS_SESSION utility package

CHAPTER

NINETEEN

Rapid Application Development with Oracle's Designer/2000: A Tutorial

- **Designing, documenting, and validating the Oracle7 application development process**

- **Generating an application schema and all application models**

- **Enhancing a generated Oracle7 application for client/server systems**

This chapter shows you how to rapidly develop custom Oracle7 client/server applications from start to finish, using a subset of the tools in the Oracle Designer/2000 tool set:

- Process Modeller

- Entity Relationship and Function Hierarchy Diagrammers

- Repository Object Navigator

- Server Generator

- Oracle Forms Generator

Rather than teaching you how to press buttons and choose menu items, this chapter presents a brief tutorial that steps you through a simple application development process to illustrate some important benefits of using the Oracle application development tools. You will see how you can use the Oracle Designer/2000 tools to:

- Design, document, and validate an Oracle7 application development process for better-designed applications the first time

- Automatically generate an application schema and all application modules

This tutorial shows how you might design and create simple form applications for the sample sales order application schema used throughout this book. To begin, let's learn about the fundamentals of the client/server application development process.

Computer-Aided Software Engineering (CASE) and Systems Development

The overall goal of computerizing a business's operations with a client/server database system like Oracle7 is to make the business run more efficiently than it otherwise would. For the computer system to successfully meet this high-level objective, the system designers must study and understand the exact needs of the business and its workers and then design and implement a system that adequately addresses these needs. Only then will the business benefit from the computer system that controls the lifeblood of the business, the business's information.

Computer-aided software engineering (CASE) is a formal, methodical approach to systems development. Just as computer-aided design (CAD) tools allow architects and mechanical engineers to design good physical structures, CASE techniques and tools allow application developers to quickly and easily analyze, design, validate, implement, and document superior client/server systems.

System Development Stages

CASE methodology addresses the life-cycle stages in the system development process, which include the strategy, analysis, design, implementation, test, and production stages. The following sections briefly explain each stage in more detail.

Strategy

The strategy stage is the initial stage of a business system's life cycle. At this stage, you focus on developing an initial, high-level description of the business and its operations. To gain the insight into a business's operations, a good strategy phase always includes initial and follow-up interviews of company personnel to identify and validate key requirements of the system. During the strategy stage, it is appropriate to study the operations that the business is currently performing to determine which ones are efficient and which ones could benefit from improvement; this particular strategy is commonly known as *business process reengineering* (BPR).

Analysis

After strategizing, you can gather specific information, analyze the specific requirements of the business and its workers, and then produce a set of clear-cut functional requirements that the software application system must address. During the analysis stage, you'll identify the particular business functions that the company's software system must address and the corresponding data elements necessary to support the applications. Like the strategy stage, the analysis stage requires interviews of company personnel to help fill in the details and point out missing information.

Design

Once the analysis stage is successful, you can map identified system requirements to specific application schema and module components to form an initial system design. It is during the design phase that the front-end client applications and the back-end application schema/database start to take shape.

Implementation

Once a system design is available, you can build the actual database and client applications to support the system design. Implementation of new applications typically takes place in a test system to protect current production application systems.

Testing

After implementation, you should thoroughly test the system, validating its operations and seeking feedback on user interfaces. If necessary, modify the components of the system to adjust for any problems uncovered during the test stage.

Production

Once you validate a new system, you can move the system from the test environment to the production environment so the business can realize the many benefits of computerizing the associated operations.

What Are CASE Tools?

CASE tools like Oracle's Designer/2000 are software development tools that specifically address the different stages of the application system life cycle. CASE tools incorporate modeling techniques so system developers can easily represent the processes and data required to make a system work. As a result, CASE tools make system development a logical, documented, and thorough yet reasonably quick process. Better still, CASE tools really pay off because you can develop sound systems from the start. This way, users can be productive with the first version of the application, and developers and administrators don't need to spend lots of time correcting for unforeseen problems or bad application design not considered during development.

CASE tools typically have other features that can help you save time maintaining a system once it is running. For example, Designer/2000 has impact analysis utilities that allow you to report answers to questions such as, "What application modules are affected when I change the definition of this table?"

Understanding Oracle's Designer/2000

Designer/2000 is Oracle's CASE development system that runs on a Microsoft Windows-based PC. Figure 19.1 shows the primary Designer/2000 window that provides access to many different tools within Designer/2000.

Before learning how to operate specific Designer/2000 tools, let's gain an overall understanding of the organization of the tools within the Designer/2000 development environment.

Repository Management and Documentation Tools

The foundation of the Designer/2000 application development system is the repository. A *repository* is schema of database tables and indexes in an Oracle database that stores *metadata*—the information about the application systems that you and other developers design throughout the many stages of the system development life cycle. Each Designer/2000 tool transparently communicates with the Designer/2000 repository to automatically record system development information as a business system takes shape.

Before developers can accomplish any work with Designer/2000, a *repository administrator* will need to create a repository in an Oracle7 database. The left column in the Designer/2000 window organizes the utilities that an administrator can use to work with a Designer/2000 repository. For example, using the Designer/2000 Admin utility, an administrator can create, manage, and control developer access to a Designer/2000 repository.

FIGURE 19.1:

The primary Designer/2000 window provides easy access to the various tools within the Designer/2000 development system.

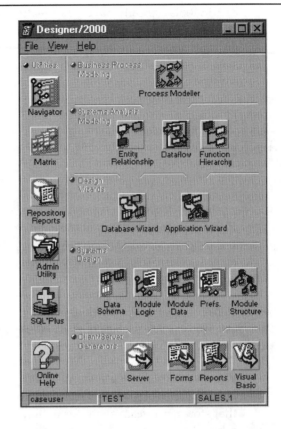

A Designer/2000 repository is a complicated schema of tables, views, and so on that hold the design information about Oracle databases and applications. An administrator can use the Designer/2000 Repository Object Navigator (RON) utility to view and modify information within a repository. For example, soon after repository creation, a repository administrator must use RON to create one or more application systems within the repository with which developers can work. An *application system* is the CASE development information that's associated with a specific client/server database application system. Developers can also use RON to view and manipulate the properties of different design objects and settings within application systems. Later in this chapter, you'll see some examples of how to use RON in the client/server application development process.

The tutorial in this chapter does not explain how to manage a repository with the Admin utility, create an application system in the repository, or provide developer access to an application system. The tutorial works with a fictitious application system named SALES within the Designer/2000 repository. If you want to follow along on your computer with this tutorial, ask an administrator to create a test application system in the Designer/2000 repository.

Business Process Modeling Tools

As you already have learned, the purpose of the strategy stage in systems development is to put together an initial, high-level description of the business and its operations. The Designer/2000 Process Modeller allows you to model the processes and flows of information and materials throughout a business system. By analyzing process models and making adjustments to a business's operations, you can be sure that you are headed in the right direction for the remainder of your systems development effort.

Analysis and Design Tools

After you get a good feel for the overall scope of your systems development project, you can move onto the analysis stage, then the design stage. Designer/2000 includes many tools that you can use to model the processes and data in an application system during the analysis and design stages of system development. Analysis tools include the Entity Relationship, Data Flow, and Function Hierarchy Diagrammers. Design tools include the Data Schema, Module Logic, Module Data, and Module Structure Diagrammers. Designer/2000 also includes Database and Application Wizards that help to make the transition between the analysis and design stages an easier task. This tutorial pays particular attention to the Entity Relationship and Function Hierarchy Diagrammers and several related design tools.

Server and Application Generation Tools

Once you complete the strategy, analysis, and design stages of system development, it's time to implement the system. The Designer/2000 Client/Server Generators make this an automatic process by using the information in the Designer/2000 repository to generate modules of application code, including menus, forms, and reporting applications—all without your having to type a single line of 3GL, 4GL, or SQL code. Meanwhile, the Designer/2000 Server Generator can generate DDL scripts that create the necessary database, tables, views, indexes, sequences, and other database objects that support an application schema.

Working with Designer/2000 Tools

Now that you have an overall understanding of the Designer/2000 development environment, it's time to get started and begin developing a simple application-system. To start Designer/2000 from within Microsoft Windows, click on the Designer/2000 icon in the Oracle Designer/2000 Program Manager group, or if you are using Windows 95, the Designer/2000 menu option on the Programs menu.

Once you start the program, Designer/2000 prompts you for your Oracle database username and password, as well as a connect string that points to the database containing the Designer/2000 repository. After you connect to an Oracle Server, Designer/2000 queries the repository and displays a dialog box that prompts you to indicate the application system with which you want to work. In this tutorial, we'll be using a fictitious system named SALES.

After choosing the application system, Designer/2000 presents you with the primary Designer/2000 window, as Figure 19.1 (earlier in the chapter) shows. From this window, you can choose a specific tool to work with by clicking on the corresponding button. When Designer/2000 starts a new tool for you, it uses your original Designer/2000 login information to conveniently make a separate connection to Oracle on behalf of your new tool session. The next section explains how to use the Designer/2000 Process Modeller to complete the strategy stage of systems development.

An Introduction to the Strategy Stage

The strategy stage is the initial, high-level definition of a business's application system. During the strategy stage, you study and document the processes and flow of information and materials that are necessary for a business to operate. After you understand what a business does and how the business currently accomplishes work, you can decide what is being done correctly and what could be done better as you design the new application system.

To complete the strategy stage for an application system, you'll use Designer/2000's Process Modeller. You start the Process Modeller by selecting the corresponding button in the primary Designer/2000 window. Figure 19.2 shows the Process Modeller with a diagram that describes the subset of the fictitious business system that is the focus of this tutorial.

FIGURE 19.2:

The Designer/2000 Process Modeller allows you to graphically represent the organization units, process steps, and flows of information and materials that make a business operate.

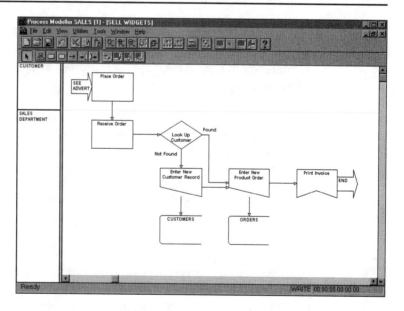

At the top of the Process Modeller window, there are toolbars that provide you with quick access to the tools that you will use to build process diagrams. When you hold the mouse pointer over a specific tool, a small help bubble appears to display the name of the tool. To display more detailed help about anything that you see in the Process Modeller window, choose the Help button at the far right of the top toolbar and then click on what you want more help on.

Process Model Diagram Elements

Before you learn to use the Process Modeller, you'll need to understand the elements that you can include on a process model diagram. The next few sections explain the different elements in a Process Modeller diagram like the one in Figure 19.2.

Organization Units   An *organization unit* is a part of an application system that has responsibilities. Good examples of organization units in an application system are divisions, departments, people within a company, or people external to the company that have a specific role or purpose in the system (for example, a customer). A Process Modeller diagram represents organization units as swim lanes to which you can add specific processes and other items. For example, the diagram in Figure 19.2 has the organization units Customer and Sales Department.

Process Steps   A *process step* is a specific task within a business process diagram. The Process Modeller allows you to indicate process steps in general or to be more specific by classifying each process step as one of three different types of process steps.

- A *data entry* step is a process that collects data. In Figure 19.2, Enter New Customer Record and Enter New Product Order are examples of data entry process steps.

- A *decision point* is a process that makes a choice. In Figure 19.2, Look Up Customer is an example of a decision point.

- A *report* is a process step that produces written or printed output. In Figure 19.2, Print Invoice is an example of a report.

Process diagrams typically represent the *process hierarchy* of a business system. In such a hierarchy, a *root process* is a business process that has no parent in the application system. For example, the most general, highest-level process in an application system, the overall objective of the business, might be the root process of a system.

From this root process or parent process, you can then refine the processes in a system with a hierarchy of child business processes. You can use the Process Modeller to create a process diagram for a process at any level in a process hierarchy.

Flows   A *flow* represents the work flow in a business operation. A *data flow* shows a movement of information; a *material flow* shows a movement of physical objects. For example, the diagram in Figure 19.2 shows how the information about customers and product orders flows among different process steps and stores in the sample sales order entry system.

Stores   A *store* is a collection of information or materials. A store can be a *data store*, such as a database or table of information, or a *material store*, such as a warehouse of goods. For example, the diagram in Figure 19.2 shows the data stores Customers and Orders.

Events   In a process diagram, you can represent important events that are related to individual process steps. A *trigger* is an event that initiates a business process. An *outcome* is an event that results from a business process. Events are optional elements of a business process model. When you include events, each business process can have only one trigger and one outcome. The diagram in Figure 19.2 shows the See Advertisement trigger that sets in motion the Place Order process, and the End outcome after the Print Invoice report.

Creating a Process Model Diagram

Now that you understand the components in a business process diagram, the next few sections explain how you can use the Process Modeller to put together a diagram such as the one in Figure 19.2. As you create a new process diagram, keep in mind that small, focused process diagrams are easier to understand than large, expansive diagrams that document an entire business system.

Opening a New Diagram

To create a new diagram, click on the New diagram button in the Process Modeller toolbar. A dialog box then asks you to indicate a root process as a reference point for the new diagram. When you begin putting together a new application system, there will not be any processes available in the dialog box list, so choose the Create

New Root Process dialog box button to create one. The Process Modeller presents the Create Process Step dialog box, as in Figure 19.3.

When you create a new process step, you must indicate two names for the new process: a short name and a label. Designer/2000 uses the label as an internal identifier for the process, and uses the name as a more descriptive identifier in diagrams. In this tutorial, we are creating an application system for a typical sales order entry system that sells a product called Widgets. Therefore, create a new root process of the system using the names Sell Widgets and SALES, as in Figure 19.3.

When you create a new process step, you can optionally indicate what type of process step it is, how long it takes to complete the process, and how much it costs to complete the step. For our root process, leave these settings as the defaults. We'll learn more about them later as we refine the business process diagram. Click on the OK button to create the new root process and open the new diagram, as Figure 19.4 shows.

Creating an Organization Unit

Every new Process Modeller diagram has a default "Unspecified" organization unit. Unless you want to include all of your diagram elements in this unclassified, catch-all organization unit, you can begin diagramming a system's processes by establishing the specific organization units in the business. To create a new organization unit, choose the Create Organization Unit button in the Process Modeller toolbar,

FIGURE 19.4:

A new process diagram has an unspecified organization unit.

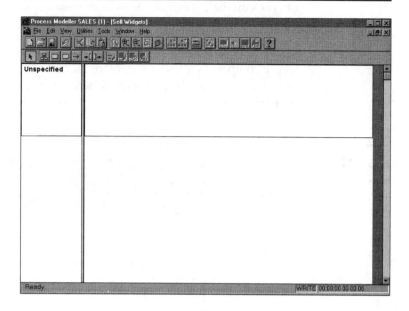

and then click on the unspecified organization unit. The Process Modeller presents the Create Organization Unit dialog box, as Figure 19.5 shows.

Again, you must indicate a complete name and a short name for the new organization unit. Figure 19.5 shows appropriate names for a Customer organization unit: Customer and CUST. After you fill out the names for the new organization unit, you

FIGURE 19.5:

Use the Create Organization Unit dialog box to create a new organization unit in a process diagram.

can click on the OK button to create the new organization unit and present it on the diagram.

In this tutorial, we are modeling the processes that happen when a customer contacts a company's sales staff to place an order for the company's products. Therefore, use the procedure described here to create two organization units in our tutorial diagram, Customer and Sales Department, as Figure 19.6 shows.

FIGURE 19.6:

A process diagram with two organization units: Customer and Sales Department

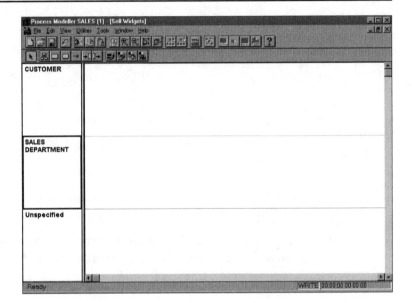

Creating Process Steps

Once the necessary organization units of a business appear on a process diagram, you can then start adding processes to describe the operations of the specific part of the business system that you are modeling. In this diagram, we need to document the process steps that occur when a customer places an order for a company's products. For example, the first step in the process might be when the customer contacts the sales staff to place an order. After receiving the order, a salesperson must determine whether the order is from a new or existing customer, and so on.

As this example illustrates, a process diagram is simply a document that describes what happens during a business operation.

When you are ready to create a new process step in a diagram, choose the Create Process Step button in the Process Modeller toolbar, move the mouse pointer to the swim lane of the organization unit that is responsible for the new process step, and click the mouse. The Process Modeller presents the Create Process Step dialog box again. Figure 19.7 shows the dialog box entries for a new Place Order process step.

As with other diagram elements, you must indicate a short name and a label for the new process step. Skip entering other, more specific information about the process step for now—you will attend to that later when revising the process diagram. Use this procedure to create the process steps in the sales order entry system as in Figure 19.8: Place Order, Receive Order, Enter New Customer Record, Look Up Customer, Print Invoice, and Enter New Product Order.

TIP

As you add process steps to a diagram, you might find that the swim lane for a particular organization unit is too narrow. To adjust the width of an organization unit's swim lane, click on the name area of the unit, press and hold down the Shift key, and use the up-arrow or down-arrow keys to decrease or increase the width of the organization unit, respectively.

FIGURE 19.7:

Use the Create Process Step dialog box to create each new process step in a process diagram.

FIGURE 19.8:

An early process diagram for a sales order entry system

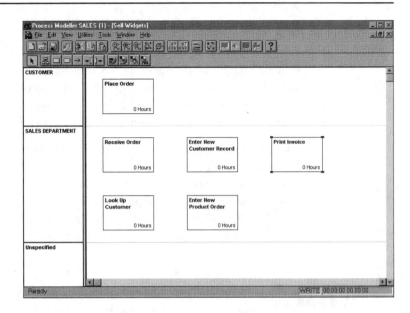

Creating Stores

Many types of process steps store data or materials as part of their function. To indicate data and material stores on a process diagram, choose the Create Store button on the Process Modeller toolbar, move the mouse pointer to the swim lane of the organization unit that is responsible for the new store, and click the mouse. The Process Modeller presents the Create Store dialog box, as in Figure 19.9.

For this part of the tutorial, indicate only a short name and a label for each new store that you add. Use this procedure to create two data stores, CUSTOMERS and ORDERS, in the sales order entry system, as Figure 19.10 shows.

TIP

If you accidentally add a process step, store, or other diagram element to the swim lane for the wrong organization unit, simply drag-and-drop the element to the correct swim lane to fix the diagram and update the Designer/2000 repository.

FIGURE 19.9:

Use the Create Store dialog box to create a new data or material store in a process diagram.

FIGURE 19.10:

A process diagram with two data stores

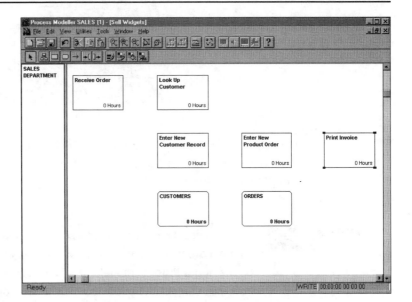

Adding Flows to a Diagram

The tutorial sales order entry system begins to take shape as you add process steps and stores to the diagram. However, it's hard to see how the different elements relate to one another without flows. To create flows for the system, first choose the Create Flow button in the Process Modeller toolbar. Next, draw a flow line from the origin process step to the destination process step or store. Draw a flow line using standard mouse drag-and-draw techniques as you would with a graphics program: start the line by clicking the primary mouse button inside the origin process step, drag the mouse pointer to extend the line over the destination process step or store, then press the primary mouse button again to complete the flow line. The Process Modeller then presents the Create Flow dialog box, as in Figure 19.11.

FIGURE 19.11:
Use the Create Flow dialog box to create a new data or material flow in a process diagram.

For this part of the tutorial, you need to indicate only a name for each new flow that you create. Use the steps above to create the flows that Figure 19.12 shows in the sample sales order entry system.

> **TIP**
>
> As a process diagram grows in size, it helps to focus on certain diagram areas by using the various zoom in and out buttons available on the upper Process Modeller toolbar. Play with these tools to see how they can change your view of a process diagram.

Creating Events

Optionally, you can enhance a process diagram by adding the events that trigger or result from the business process system that you are documenting. To add a trigger or outcome event to a process diagram, activate the respective tool from the Process

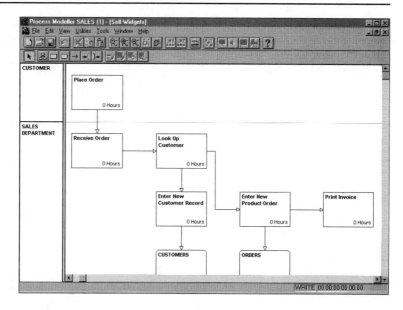

FIGURE 19.12:

A process diagram with flows shows how data or materials move among the process steps and stores within a business operation.

Modeller toolbar and click on the process step that relates to the new event. Figure 19.13 shows the previous process diagram after adding a trigger and an outcome event.

Saving a Process Diagram

As you add business system elements to a process diagram, the Process Modeller automatically updates the Designer/2000 repository. However, because a diagram layout is itself not a repository object, you must save the diagram independently. To save a process diagram, simply click on the Save button in the upper toolbar of the Process Modeller.

Refining a Process Diagram

At this point, we have a basic process diagram that shows the process steps, stores, flows, and events within a typical sales order entry system. The next few sections show how to make some simple adjustments that will make the existing Process Modeller diagram a much clearer representation of the system.

FIGURE 19.13:

Triggers and outcomes clearly represent the starting and end points of a business operation.

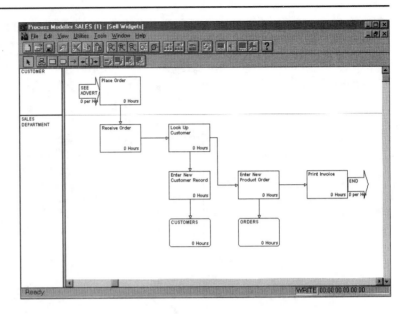

Rearranging Diagram Elements

As you add more and more elements to a process diagram, the arrangement of elements can make the diagram hard to read. Flows that criss-cross are particularly distracting. To move a diagram element such as a process step or store, simply drag-and-drop the element to any position that you like. Just make sure that the new position is not on top of another element and remains within the appropriate organization unit's swim lane. You'll find that as you move process steps and stores, the Process Modeller automatically moves associated flows and events.

TIP

The Process Modeller has an Autolayout tool that you can use to make the Modeller itself position diagram elements where it sees best. More often than not, however, the Autolayout tool does not do a good job of diagram layout, so you might want to avoid using this feature.

Removing Unwanted Diagram Elements

As you think about and model the processes of a business operation, you'll most likely make mistakes and add process steps, stores, and other elements that are not actually part of the particular system you are studying. If you do so, you should remove unrelated diagram elements to make the diagram focused and clear.

To remove an element from a diagram but keep its definition in the Designer/2000 repository, select the target element and cut it from the diagram by pressing Ctrl-X. To remove an element from a diagram and the Designer/2000 repository, select the target element and delete it from the diagram by pressing the Delete key.

Modifying the Characteristics of Diagram Elements

Up to this point, most elements in our process diagram have rather unspecific characteristics, primarily a name and a basic element type—process step, store, or flow. A process diagram can present a much clearer representation of a business system when you specify many characteristics about its process steps, stores, and other elements.

To modify the characteristics of a diagram element, double-click on the element. The Process Modeller presents a corresponding Edit dialog box for the element. Depending on how detailed your evaluation must be for the business system, you can set many different characteristics for each element. The specific characteristics that you can set for an element vary according to the type of element you are editing.

- You can change the name and label for an element.

- You can indicate how much time it takes to complete a process step, flow, and so on.

- You can indicate how much it costs per unit of time to complete a process step, flow, and so on.

- You can indicate several multimedia characteristics for a diagram element. For example, you can choose an icon to represent a process step or store.

This tutorial does not document each setting that is available for the different types of process diagram elements. At a minimum, you should edit the characteristics of each process step, flow, and store to indicate exactly what type of element it is. For example, a process step can be a data entry, decision, or report step, and a flow can be a data flow or a material flow. After you make such adjustments, the diagram will more clearly display exactly what types of processes, flows, and other elements are in the system. Adjust the diagram's view setting by choosing View ➤ Enhanced Symbol or Iconic. Once you edit the elements in the example, it might look something like the one in Figure 19.14.

FIGURE 19.14:

A process diagram that includes specific types of elements and appears in Iconic mode more clearly represents the system that it documents.

Business Process Reengineering

After you revise a business process diagram, it's time for you and other company personnel to analyze the business system as it currently functions. You can use the Process Modeller to print process diagrams and related reports for others to review. A process diagram that includes multimedia settings, such as icons, sounds, and animations, can be more effective when people review the diagram online.

In any case, reviewers should focus on issues similar to the following:

- Are all process steps, flows, and other elements included and accurately documented in the diagram?

- Which business operations are functioning efficiently, which ones could benefit from improvement, and which ones could be eliminated all together?

After reviewing your business's operations, you'll want to go back and modify your process diagrams accordingly. After additional reviews and modifications of the business's processes, you are ready to move on to the next stage of systems development: the analysis stage.

Introduction to the Analysis Stage

Using the information gained from the strategy stage, you can now put together more specific information and analyze the specific requirements of the business and its workers. The goal of the analysis stage is to produce the set of functional requirements that describe the functions and data that correspond to the application system.

To complete the analysis stage, you'll use two Designer/2000 tools: the Entity Relationship (ER) Diagrammer and the Function Hierarchy Diagrammer. You can start the each tool by choosing the corresponding button in the primary Designer/2000 window. Figures 19.15 and 19.16 show each diagrammer with diagrams that represent the analysis design elements of our fictitious business system.

ER and Function Hierarchy Diagram Elements

As with the Process Modeller, the ER Diagrammer and Function Hierarchy Diagrammer windows have toolbars that provide you with quick access to the tools for building corresponding diagrams. But before you can learn to use each tool, you'll need to understand the diagram elements that you can include on ER and function hierarchy diagrams. The next few sections explain these elements.

FIGURE 19.15:

The Designer/2000 Entity Relationship (ER) Diagrammer allows you to graphically represent the entities and relationships that provide the foundation of a business system.

FIGURE 19.16:

The Designer/2000 Function Hierarchy Diagrammer allows you to hierarchically organize the general and specific functions that make a business operate.

Entities and Attributes   An *entity* is a unit of information that has significance within the organization. *Attributes* are the details of an entity. For example, the ER diagram in Figure 19.15 includes the CUSTOMER entity, which you describe with the COMPANYNAME, FIRSTNAME, LASTNAME, and other customer-related attributes.

Relationships   A *relationship* indicates how two system elements relate to one another. ER diagrams describe the relationships among entities using different line symbols. For example, the relationship between the ORDER and ITEM entities in Figure 19.15 reads "A sales order may be made up of one or more line items," or conversely, "A line item must be on one and only one sales order."

Domains   A *domain* is a business constraint that determines acceptable values for an attribute or a set of attributes. For example, the COMPANYNAME, LASTNAME, and FIRSTNAME attributes in the CUSTOMER entity of Figure 19.15 are all bound by the same domain called NAME, which allows variable-length text strings up to 100 bytes long.

Functions   A *function* is a specific process that the business performs. The functions of a business can range from the general to the focused. For example, the overall purpose of a the business is its *root function*. By decomposing a business's root function, you will discover more elementary functions. The arrangement of general parent functions and more focused child functions establishes the function hierarchy of a business. For example, the root function of the function hierarchy diagram in Figure 19.16 is the Sell Widgets diagram, which you can decompose into more specific child functions, such as Place Order and Receive Order.

Creating an ER Diagram

Now that you understand the different types of elements that you will work with in the analysis stage of systems development, let's begin by putting together an ER diagram such as the one in Figure 19.15. As with the strategy stage, we'll focus on just those system components that correspond to this small subset of the overall business system presented in this simple tutorial.

When your application system is large and complex, you will probably have many different entities. For this reason, it is best to create a number of ER diagrams, each focusing on a specific area of the business. Since Designer/2000 allows you to place the same entity on any number of ER diagrams, you can easily show the relationships among many detailed ER diagrams.

Opening a New Diagram

After you start the Designer/2000 ER Diagrammer, choose the New diagram button in the toolbar to create a new diagram. The ER Diagrammer then presents a blank diagram, as Figure 19.17 shows.

Creating an Entity

After studying the processes of a business, you should have a pretty good idea of the data the system will generate. Business process diagrams that contain data stores even provide a start as to what entities the application system requires. With

FIGURE 19.17:

A new ER diagram is a blank canvas to which you can add entities and relationships.

this information, you can define the entities that represent how the system should store its data. For example, it's apparent from the earlier process diagrams that entities are needed to store information about the company's customers and the orders that they place for the company's products. Although not documented earlier in the process diagram, it will soon become apparent that you need a related entity to store line items for each order and another entity to store information about the company's products.

To create a new entity, choose the Entity button on the ER Diagrammer toolbar and then click anywhere in the diagram. The ER Diagrammer puts a new entity on the diagram and presents the Create Entity dialog box, as in Figure 19.18.

FIGURE 19.18:
Use the Create Entity dialog box to create a new entity in an ER diagram.

In the Create Entity dialog box, enter the complete name, short name, and plural name for the new entity. Figure 19.18 is an example of how you might fill out this dialog box for the CUSTOMER entity. Use the same procedure to create the CUSTOMER, ORDER, ITEM (for order line items), and PART entities. The resulting diagram should resemble the one in Figure 19.19.

TIP

The ER Diagrammer allows you to move, edit, and delete diagram objects just as you can with the other diagrammers in Designer/2000.

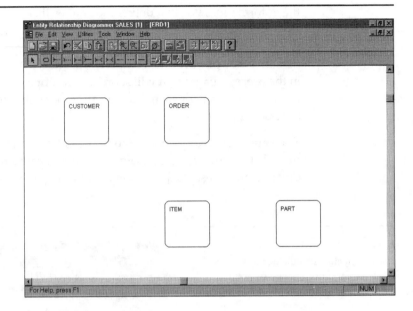

Creating a Relationship

Once you have the entities on your diagram, the next task is to indicate how these entities relate to one another. You can draw relationships using the different relationship tools of the ER Diagrammer toolbar. First, you must become familiar with the type of relationship that each tool declares. You can get a description of each tool using the diagrammer's help bubbles, or refer to Figure 19.20, which shows a key that defines the different relationship tools.

The next step is to determine what relationships exist among the entities of your system. The following relationships exist in our example business system:

- A customer may be the source of one or more sales orders.

- A sales order must be placed by one and only one customer.

- A sales order may be made up of one or more line items.

- A line item must be on one and only one sales order.

Key to the different relationship tools
of the ER Diagrammer

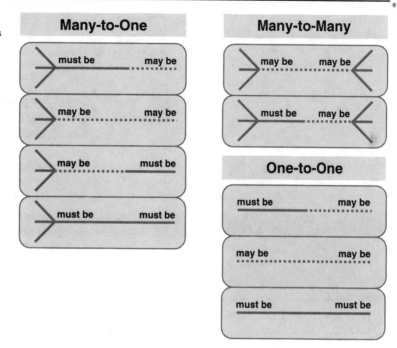

- A part may be on one or more line items.

- A line item must be for one and only one part.

Given these relationships, let's add them graphically to the ER diagram using the appropriate tools of the ER Diagrammer. For example, to add the relationship between the CUSTOMER and ORDER entities, select the leftmost relationship tool, the M:1 relationship tool. Next, place the mouse pointer inside the ORDER entity and press the mouse button to indicate the origin of the relationship. Then place the mouse pointer inside the CUSTOMER entity and end the relationship by pressing the mouse button again. When you complete the drawing of a new relationship, the ER Diagrammer presents you with the Create Relationship dialog box, as in Figure 19.21.

FIGURE 19.21:

Use the Create Relationship dialog box to indicate the name and labels for a new relationship.

Use the Create Relationship dialog box to indicate the labels for each side of the relationship (starting on the side of the first entity in which you clicked) so you can clearly represent the relationship on the diagram. Use the appropriate relationship tools to add relationships among the entities in our business system so that you end up with a diagram similar to the one in Figure 19.22.

FIGURE 19.22:

An ER diagram with relationships

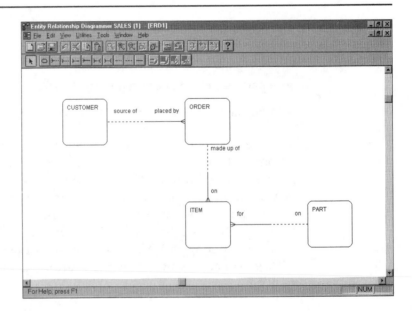

Saving an ER Diagram

Once you complete an ER diagram, be sure to save it so you don't lose any of your work. To save an ER diagram, select File ➤ Save.

Refining an ER Diagram

After you draft an ER diagram, you can then go back and revise the diagram to specify more detail about the entities and relationships in the system. Most of time you spend revising an ER diagram will focus on adding the attributes for the entities in the system. Therefore, before you can revise an ER diagram, it's necessary to scope out what attributes are necessary to describe each entity in the system. From your preliminary analysis, you can also identify entity attributes that have similar domains and justify the definition of user-defined domains. The next few sections explain how to add more information to the sample ER diagram.

Creating Domains for a Business System

As you analyze each entity to assemble a list of corresponding attributes, you should also determine the characteristics for each attribute. In doing so, you'll most likely find that many attributes share common characteristics. When several entity attributes in a business system have similar domains of acceptable values, you can develop more consistent applications by first creating user-defined domains. For example, many attributes in the CUSTOMER entity describe a name of some type— a customer's company name, last name, and first name. When you first declare a user-defined domain NAME, you can then more easily and consistently create the name-type attributes in the CUSTOMER table, specifically the COMPANYNAME, LASTNAME, and FIRSTNAME attributes. All attributes defined with a domain can also be easily modified with one change to the domain rather than many identical changes to individual attributes.

To create a user-defined domain in a business system using the ER Diagrammer, select Edit ➤ Domains to display the Edit Domains dialog box, as in Figure 19.23.

FIGURE 19.23:

Use the Edit Domains dialog box to create user-defined domains for a business system.

From the Edit Domains dialog box, you can edit any existing domain and create new domains. Among other settings, you can describe each domain's name, format, attribute length, datatype, column length, and description. You can even create a new domain as a subtype of an existing domain using the Supertype setting.

For this simple tutorial, create just one domain called NAME, with the following characteristics.

Supertype	Format	Attribute Length	Datatype	Column Length
None	VARCHAR2	100	VARCHAR2	100

After you create the NAME domain, you can turn your attention to better describing the entities in the business system.

Adding Details about Entities

You can add many details for the entities in an ER diagram. Simply double-click on an entity in an ER diagram to display the Edit Entity dialog box, as in Figure 19.24.

By clicking on the tabs of the Edit Entity dialog box, you'll quickly notice that you can establish many details about an entity. You'll work most efficiently if you work with the tabs of the Edit Entity dialog box in the following order:

1. Use the dialog box controls of the Attributes and Att Detail tabs to declare and describe all attributes for an entity. Additionally, use the dialog box controls in the Att Values tab to declare more complex domains for an attribute— for example, you might want to indicate that the STATUS attribute of the ORDER entity can only contain the values "F" to indicate a filled order or "B" to indicate a backlogged order.

2. Next, use the Synonyms tab to declare synonyms, if any, for the entity.

The UIDs tab allows you to declare any alternate keys for an entity. You can use the Definition tab to change the entity's name and add other miscellaneous details

FIGURE 19.24:

Use the Edit Entity dialog box to, among other things, add attributes to an entity, change an entity's name, and establish synonyms for an entity.

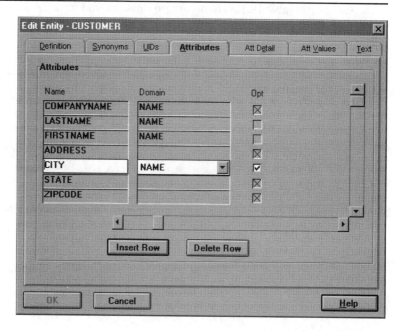

about the entity. The Text tab allows you to enter comments about the entity and its purpose in the system. For the purposes of this tutorial, we'll skip using the other tabs of the Edit Entity dialog box.

> **WARNING**
>
> As you create attributes, be sure *not* to include columns that specifically serve as a primary key or to relate different entities in the system. For example, do not create attributes in the ORDER entity such as ID (to serve as a primary key) and CUSTOMERID (to specifically relate each order to a customer). When you generate an application schema, Designer/2000 automatically creates a surrogate primary key for an entity that does not specifically declare one, as well as a corresponding sequence that applications can use to generate values for the primary key. Additionally, Designer/2000 automatically creates foreign key attributes using the relationships that you define in an ER diagram.

Edit the CUSTOMER, ORDER, ITEM, and PART entities using the information in Table 19.1. When you are finished, the new ER diagram should look like the one in Figure 19.25.

TABLE 19.1: Attribute Descriptions for the CUSTOMER, ORDER, ITEM, and PART Entities

Entity	Attribute Name	Sequence	Optional	Format	Length	Dec Pl
CUSTOMER	COMPANYNAME	2	y	VARCHAR2	50	-
	LASTNAME	3	N	VARCHAR2	50	-
	FIRSTNAME	4	N	VARCHAR2	50	-
	ADDRESS	5	y	VARCHAR2	100	-
	CITY	6	y	VARCHAR2	50	-
	STATE	7	y	CHAR	2	-
	ZIPCODE	8	y	VARCHAR2	10	-
	PHONE	9	y	VARCHAR2	20	-
	FAX	10	y	VARCHAR2	20	-

TABLE 19.1: Attribute Descriptions for the CUSTOMER, ORDER, ITEM, and PART Entities (continued)

Entity	Attribute Name	Sequence	Optional	Format	Length	Dec Pl
ITEM	QUANTITY	2	N	INTEGER	5	-
	UNITPRICE	3	N	MONEY	10	2
	TOTAL	4	N	MONEY	10	2
ORDER	ORDERDATE	2	N	DATE	-	-
	SHIPDATE	3	y	DATE	-	-
	PAIDDATE	4	y	DATE	-	-
	STATUS	5	y	CHAR	1	-
PART	UNITPRICE	2	N	MONEY	10	2
	ONHAND	3	y	INTEGER	5	-
	REORDER	4	y	INTEGER	5	-
	DESCRIPTION	5	y	VARCHAR2	2000	-

Notice in Figure 19.25 that each attribute in the diagram has a symbol prefix.

FIGURE 19.25:

An enhanced ER diagram reveals the attributes for each entity in the business system.

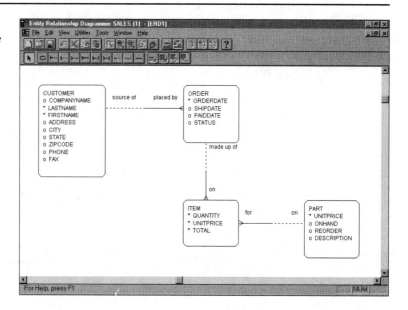

- A pound sign (#) indicates that the attribute is part of the entity's primary key (none are present in this diagram).

- An asterisk (*) indicates that the attribute is not optional.

- A lowercase letter *O* (*o*) indicates that the attribute is optional.

ER diagrams can reveal only so much information about each entity and its attribute. For example, the revised ER diagram in 19.25 does not reveal specific details about attributes. For this tutorial, you should also configure the following attribute details:

- For the STATE attribute in the CUSTOMER entity, configure attribute values that correspond to all state codes for the states in the United States.

- For the STATUS attribute of the ORDER entity, configure the attribute values "F" and "B" (short for "Filled" and "Backlogged"), and make "F" the default value.

- For the TOTAL attribute of the ORDER entity, configure the derivation of the attribute as "QUANTITY * UNITPRICE."

After you complete the steps above, you are finished with the ER Diagrammer. Save the diagram, exit the tool, and continue to the next stage of system analysis: business function analysis.

Creating a Function Hierarchy Diagram

The next step in the analysis stage of system development is to decompose and arrange a hierarchy of the functions that are at work in the business environment. The root of a function hierarchy is typically the business's high-level function. By refining and analyzing the specific functions of a business, a developer can determine which ones to automate with the application system under development.

When a function hierarchy is complete, it is a tree of related business functions. Using your understanding of each business function, you can define a function in the hierarchy by describing the events that trigger the function, as well as the associated entities that are necessary to support each function. The next section explains how to get started by creating a new function hierarchy diagram.

Opening a New Diagram

To create a new diagram, start the Designer/2000 Function Hierarchy Diagrammer and click on the New diagram button in the Function Hierarchy Diagrammer toolbar. The Function Hierarchy Diagrammer then presents the New Diagram dialog box, as in Figure 19.26.

FIGURE 19.26:

Use the New Diagram dialog box to indicate the root function for a new function hierarchy diagram.

The purpose of the New Diagram dialog box is to allow you to indicate a root function as a starting point for the new diagram. If you've completed the strategy stage of systems development as presented in earlier sections of this tutorial, you'll see a lone function, Sell Widgets, in the list of available functions for the diagram. Choose this function as the basis for the new function hierarchy diagram, and then choose the OK button to create the new diagram. Figure 19.27 shows what the initial function hierarchy diagram should resemble.

You'll quickly notice that Designer/2000 automatically builds the initial function hierarchy for the new diagram from the process steps that you created during the

Designer/2000 automatically builds the initial functions in a function hierarchy diagram from the process steps that you created during the strategy stage of systems development.

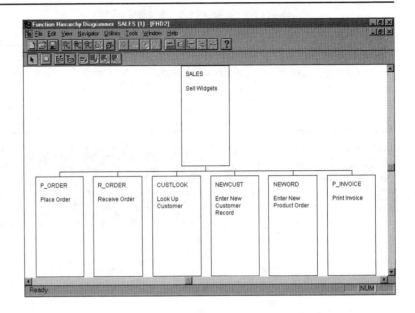

strategy stage of systems development. Where do you go from here? Well, if the existing function hierarchy is complete and accurate, all that's necessary to do for the new diagram is to add details about each function in the tree. Alternatively, if you want to decompose functions more completely or rearrange the relationship of one function to another, you need to make some modifications to the diagram. The next few sections explain how to work with the Function Hierarchy Diagrammer tools.

Decomposing Functions

The process steps from the strategy stage of systems development provide a good basis for a function hierarchy diagram. However, unless your process diagrams contain extreme detail, you most likely will need to further decompose the general functions on the initial version of a function hierarchy diagram. This section explains how to add new, more elementary, business functions to a function hierarchy diagram.

Before you can add child functions to a function hierarchy diagram, you must decide which of the existing functions require further decomposition. For example, the function Enter New Product Order really contains two, more elementary, child functions: Generate New Order Record and Generate New Order Line Item Record.

To add these new functions to the parent function, select the New Function tool from the Function Hierarchy Diagrammer toolbar, then click the mouse pointer inside the parent function Enter New Product Order. The Function Hierarchy Diagrammer then presents the Create Function dialog box, as in Figure 19.28.

FIGURE 19.28:
Use the Create Function dialog box to specify the name of a new function.

Use the Create Function dialog box to name and describe the new function. When you finish, click on the OK button to create the new function. Use these steps to add the two new child functions of the Enter New Product Order parent function. When you finish, the function hierarchy diagram should resemble the diagram in Figure 19.29.

Continue to develop a function hierarchy diagram until it reveals all elementary-level business functions.

TIP

As a function hierarchy diagram becomes more detailed, you can change your view of the function tree to make it easier to focus on specific parts of the diagram. The + (plus sign) or - (minus sign) icon adjacent to each parent function allows you to expand or collapse, respectively, the function hierarchy underneath a parent function.

FIGURE 19.29:

A more complete revision of the previous function hierarchy diagram

Adding Details to Business Functions

One of the most important steps to complete when building a function hierarchy diagram is to identify which functions will correspond directly with application modules in the new application system. For example, a business function such as Receive Order does not translate well into an application module, because the process of receiving an order is the simple act of receiving a communication such as a telephone call, fax, or e-mail message. In contrast, the functions Enter New Customer Record and Enter New Product Order are most definitely functions that will translate into screen modules of the new application system, primarily because they are data entry steps.

After you know the functions that are candidates for modules in the new database application system, describe each of these functions in terms of the entities and attributes necessary to support them. You can edit a function's properties by double-clicking on the function in a function hierarchy diagram. The Function Hierarchy Diagrammer then presents the Edit Function dialog box, as in Figure 19.30.

FIGURE 19.30:

Use the Edit Function dialog box to indicate the entities and attributes that are necessary to support the function in the application system.

There are many tabs for the Edit Function dialog box. For the purposes of this tutorial, focus just on the Entity Usages and Attribute Usages tabs. Tables 19.2 and 19.3 list the settings that you should modify for the functions in this tutorial.

TABLE 19.2: Entity Usages for the Enter New Customer Record, Generate New Order Record, and Generate New Order Line Item Record Functions

Function	Entity	Create	Retrieve	Update	Delete	Archive	Other
Enter New Customer Record	CUSTOMER	Yes	Yes	Yes	Yes	-	-
Enter New Product Order	ORDER	Yes	Yes	Yes	Yes	-	-
	ITEM	Yes	Yes	Yes	Yes	-	-

TABLE 19.3: Attribute Usages for the Enter New Customer Record and Enter New Product Order Functions

Function	Entity	Attribute	Insert	Retrieve	Update	Nullify	Archive	Other
Enter New Customer Record	CUSTOMER	COMPANY-NAME	Yes	Yes	Yes	Yes	-	-
		LASTNAME	Yes	Yes	Yes	Yes	-	-
		FIRSTNAME	Yes	Yes	Yes	Yes	-	-
		ADDRESS	Yes	Yes	Yes	Yes	-	-
		CITY	Yes	Yes	Yes	Yes	-	-
		STATE	Yes	Yes	Yes	Yes	-	-
		ZIPCODE	Yes	Yes	Yes	Yes	-	-
		PHONE	Yes	Yes	Yes	Yes	-	-
		FAX	Yes	Yes	Yes	Yes	-	-
Enter New Product Order	ORDER	ORDERDATE	Yes	Yes	Yes	Yes	-	-
		SHIPDATE	Yes	Yes	Yes	Yes	-	-
		PAIDDATE	Yes	Yes	Yes	Yes	-	-
		STATUS	Yes	Yes	Yes	Yes	-	-
	ITEM	QUANTITY	Yes	Yes	Yes	Yes	-	-
		UNITPRICE	Yes	Yes	Yes	Yes	-	-
		TOTAL	Yes	Yes	Yes	Yes	-	-

After you edit a function's properties, its appearance on the function hierarchy does not change. You are now finished analyzing the functions in the system for the purposes of this tutorial. Save the function hierarchy diagram and exit the Function Hierarchy Diagrammer.

What about Dataflow Diagramming?

Another task that you can complete during the analysis stage of systems development is to create dataflow diagrams using the Designer/2000 Dataflow Diagrammer. Dataflow diagrams show how data flows throughout a company. Dataflow diagrams are often used to represent data dependencies for system components.

Many development projects do not complete the task of creating dataflow diagramming. While dataflow diagramming can be helpful, it is not required to create repository objects that are necessary to later implement the system. Therefore, this tutorial does not describe how to use the Designer/2000 Dataflow Diagrammer.

Circulating Analysis Stage Information for Review

Just as with the strategy stage, it is very important to now distribute the detailed analysis stage information for review. This way, you can identify problems and make any necessary modifications before putting a lot of work into the design stage of system development.

Use the printing and reporting functions of the ER Diagrammer and Function Hierarchy Diagrammer to generate printouts of your system analysis. Distribute the reports to different types of workers throughout the organization, asking for feedback to help you make sure you have correctly identified all the entities and functions that the business performs. Based on this feedback, you probably will need to modify diagrams to produce final, working drafts of ER and function hierarchy diagrams.

An Introduction to the Design Stage

Once you have defined and refined the business model for a system with the strategy and analysis stages, you are ready to begin the design stage of system development. The design stage is when you put together the designs for the system data model (the application schema) and the system process model (the application's modules).

To move quickly from the analysis to the design stage, you can use the Designer/2000 design wizards.

- The Database Wizard allows you to quickly generate first-draft table definitions from entities in the repository.

- The Application Wizard allows you to quickly generate first-draft module definitions from the business functions in the repository.

After using the Designer/2000 wizards to put together quick definitions for tables and application modules, you will then want to use other Designer/2000 design tools to fine tune the design of the application and corresponding database schema. Although all Designer/2000 design tools have an important function, this introductory tutorial focuses on how to complete a quick design stage of application development using the design wizards, the Data Schema Diagrammer, and the Module Data Diagrammer. The next section explains how to get started by designing the tables for the application system.

Using the Database Wizard

To move quickly from the analysis stage to the design stage for a system's tables, you can use the Database Wizard. Start the Database Wizard from the main Designer/2000 window. Figure 19.31 shows the Database Wizard.

Notice in Figure 19.31 that the Database Wizard automatically shows all the candidate entities that you can map to table definitions. The In Set? column in the Table Mappings tab indicates the entities that you would like to map to table definitions in this run (execution) of the Database Wizard. To quickly select all entities for mapping, choose the Include All button. Then to build the table definitions from the corresponding entities, choose the Run button. After a bit of work, the Database Wizard builds table definitions in the Designer/2000 repository. These table definitions correspond to the entities in the system; the table designs that the Database Wizard builds are not actually tables in any Oracle database. When the wizard is finished, briefly browse the other dialog box controls in the other tabs of the Database Wizard. Notice that the Designer/2000 Database Wizard automatically defines objects that relate closely to the new tables, including primary keys, foreign keys, and indexes.

FIGURE 19.31:

You can quickly map an application's systems entities into tables using Designer/2000's Database Wizard.

Later on, this tutorial will show you how to use the Designer/2000 Data Schema Diagrammer to view the first-draft table designs created by the Database Wizard. However, before doing so, first turn your attention to building the modules for an application system.

Using the Application Wizard

As with the Database Wizard, you can quickly move from the analysis stage to the design stage for a system's application modules using the Application Wizard. Start the Application Wizard from the main Designer/2000 window. Figure 19.32 shows the Application Wizard.

To translate a candidate business function into an application module using the Application Wizard, select the function from the Start Function drop-down list and choose the Generate button. The Application Wizard then builds a corresponding module definition in the Designer/2000 repository. For this tutorial, use the Application Wizard to build a module from the Enter New Customer Record (NEWCUST)

FIGURE 19.32:

Use Designer/2000's Application Wizard to quickly translate an application's business functions into application modules.

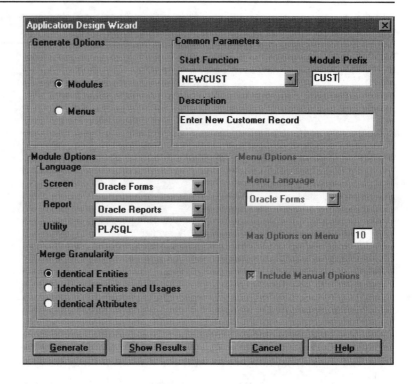

and Enter New Product Order (NEWORD) functions. A section later in this chapter explains how to view and modify the first-draft module designs using the Module Data Diagrammer.

WARNING   Make sure to indicate a unique Module Prefix (six characters or less) before generating each function with the Application Wizard. If you do not do so, the utility will not be able to generate unique module names.

Viewing Generated Table and Module Designs Using the Repository Object Navigator

To view and modify information in the Designer/2000 repository, you can always use the Designer/2000 Repository Object Navigator (RON). To start RON, click on the Navigator button in the primary Designer/2000 window. Figure 19.33 shows RON for our test application system SALES.

RON presents information about an application system using an interface of three windows:

- The Application window contains a menu, toolbar, an Object Hierarchy window, and a Properties window for a specific application system. You can change the application for RON using the Open Application tool in the Application window toolbar.

- The Object Hierarchy window reveals the objects in the application system using a hierarchical structure. You can quickly expand or collapse nodes to see more or less information about objects in the application system.

FIGURE 19.33:

Use Designer/2000's Application Wizard to quickly translate an application's business functions into application modules.

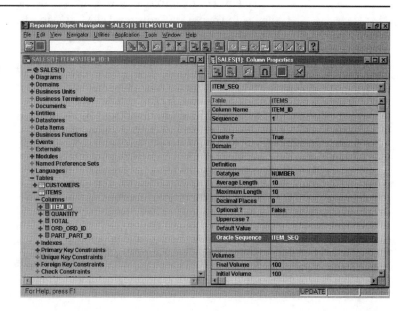

- The Properties window displays the property values for the object that is currently selected in the Object Hierarchy window. You can select and modify an object's individual properties using the corresponding text or drop-down list that appears at the top of the Properties window, and then commit your changes to the repository using the Commit button in the Properties window toolbar.

For example, Figure 19.33 shows part of the object hierarchy for the SALES application system. The Properties window reveals the properties for the ITEM_ID column of the ITEMS table, which is selected in the Object Hierarchy window.

Now that you understand the interface of RON, you can explore the properties of the objects in the SALES application system to observe the accomplishments of the Database and Application Wizards.

- The Database Wizard created the CUSTOMERS, ITEMS, ORDERS, and PARTS tables to correspond with the CUSTOMER, ITEM, ORDER, and PART entities, respectively. Each table's columns correspond to the attributes of the related entity.

- The Database Wizard created a surrogate primary key for every table in the application system, as well as a sequence to correspond with each table's primary key. For example, Figure 19.33 shows how the ITEMS table's primary key is the generated column ITEM_ID, and that this column is associated with the Oracle sequence ITEM_SEQ.

- The Database Wizard created columns to support the foreign keys of each table. For example, Figure 19.33 reveals that the ITEMS table contains the column ORD_ORD_ID to serve as a foreign key that references the primary key of the ORDERS table (the ORD_ID column), as well as the column PART_PART_ID to serve as a foreign key that references the primary key of the PARTS table (the PART_ID column).

- The Application Wizard created modules that correspond to the NEWCUST and NEWORD functions.

You can use RON at anytime to modify and add repository objects in the SALES application system. For example, one design stage change that you need to make using RON is to "accept" the first-cut module designs in the system so that we can edit them using the Module Data Diagrammer later in the development process. To accomplish this, expand the Module node to view each generated module and then change the Candidate property for each module to null, as Figure 19.34 demonstrates for the CUST0010 module.

FIGURE 19.34:

You can use RON to add or modify repository objects and their corresponding properties.

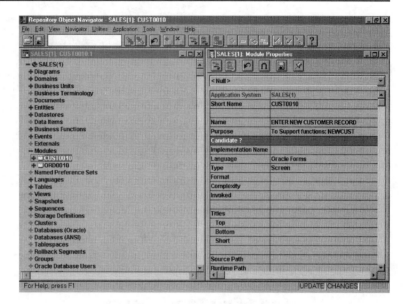

Another change that's necessary to make with RON is to create a new database in the repository. During the next stage of application development, you will implement the table designs of the application system. However, before you can implement the tables for the application system, you must indicate what database will contain the tables. To create a new database in the Designer/2000 repository, double-click on the Databases (Oracle) node in the Object Hierarchy window of RON. RON reacts by creating a new database node in the object hierarchy. Fill out the Properties window according to the information shown in Figure 19.35.

After making changes with RON, don't forget to commit your modifications to the repository by choosing the Commit button.

You could continue to use RON to make some other changes to the design elements in the repository. However, Designer/2000 has graphical design tools, including

FIGURE 19.35:

Use RON to quickly create a new database called TEST.

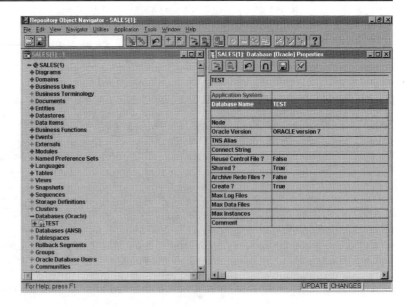

the Data Schema Diagrammer and the Module Data Diagrammer, which you can use to refine the design elements of the system. The next two sections of this chapter quickly introduce how to use these tools.

Modifying Table Designs

To modify the initial table designs created by the Database Wizard, we'll use Designer/2000's Data Schema Diagrammer. To start the Data Schema Diagrammer, click on the Data Schema button in the primary Designer/2000 window. At this point in the tutorial, you should recognize many elements of the Data Schema Diagrammer, which has an interface very similar to the other diagrammers of Designer/2000.

To start a new data schema diagram, choose the New button. Rather than diagram all of our table designs manually, we can just include the first-cut table designs present in the Designer/2000 repository by selecting Edit ➤ Include ➤ Table/ View/Snapshot. The Data Schema Diagrammer then presents the Include Tables/ Views/Snapshots dialog box, as in Figure 19.36.

FIGURE 19.36:

The Data Schema Diagrammer's Include Tables/Views/Snapshots dialog box allows you to quickly paste first-cut table designs from the Designer/2000 repository into a new schema diagram.

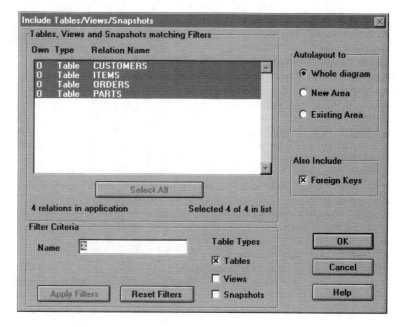

The table designs generated earlier by the Database Wizard should be present in the list box of the dialog box. To paste these designs into our new schema diagram, choose the Select All button and click on the OK button. The diagram in the Data Schema Diagrammer should appear, similar to the diagram in Figure 19.37.

Notice that a schema diagram is extremely similar to an ER diagram. The primary difference to remember is that an ER diagram models entities and relationships, while a schema diagram represents corresponding tables, foreign keys, and other design elements of an application's schema.

At this point, we can edit the properties of a diagram element by simply double-clicking on it and then using the subsequent dialog box that appears. For example, when you click on the CUSTOMERS table, the Data Schema Diagrammer presents the Edit Table dialog box, as Figure 19.38 shows.

FIGURE 19.37:

A data schema diagram represents the tables, foreign keys, and other design elements of an application's schema.

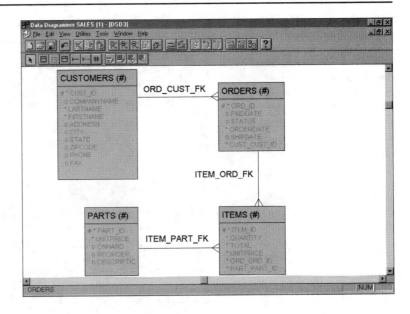

FIGURE 19.38:

The Edit Table dialog box allows you to edit the properties of a table in a schema diagram.

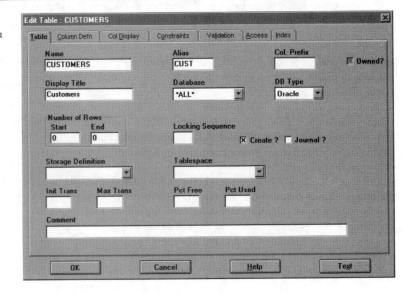

Edit the following properties using the Edit Table dialog box of the Data Schema Diagrammer:

- For each table, set the target database to TEST in the Table tab.

- For each table column, review and adjust all display settings in the Col Display tab as you see appropriate.

- For the ITEMS table, set the Oracle Sequence property of the ITEM_ID column to null in the Column Defn tab. It does not make sense to use a sequence for this column.

- For the ITEMS table, set the AutoGen type property of the ORD_ORD_ID column to Seq in Parent in the Col Display tab. This property setting allows the foreign key of child records to reuse the generated sequence number of the parent record.

- For the ITEMS table, set the Delete Rule property for the ITEM_ORD_FK foreign key to Cascades in the Constraints tab. This way, when a user deletes an order, Oracle will automatically delete all corresponding line items.

- For the CUSTOMERS table, add a unique key constraint called CUST_NAME using the Constraints tab. The new constraint should include the LASTNAME and then the FIRSTNAME columns as key components. Since these key components are both mandatory columns for each customer record, make sure to also indicate that the unique key is mandatory by checking the Mandatory checkbox.

As you work with the tabs and corresponding dialog box controls, notice that you can set an incredible number of properties for each table, column, and integrity constraint that is present in an application schema. The information in the previous chapters of this book should have prepared you to quickly recognize the meaning for most of the settings in the Edit Table and other related dialog boxes that you can access using the Data Schema Diagrammer. The settings in this example merely set a few essential parameters that are necessary to complete this tutorial, but don't be afraid to experiment.

At this point, we are finished making modifications to the table designs in our simple application schema. Save the diagram, print a copy of the diagram for review, and then exit from the Data Schema Diagrammer.

Modifying Module Designs

Before generating application modules during the implementation stage, you must make some refinements in the data usages of the modules. To modify the initial module designs created by the Application Wizard, we'll use Designer/2000's Module Data Diagrammer. To start the Module Data Diagrammer, click on the corresponding button in the primary Designer/2000 window. Again, you should recognize many elements of the Module Data Diagrammer, since it closely resembles the interface of the other Designer/2000 diagrammers.

To start a new diagram, click on the New button. The Module Data Diagrammer then presents the New Diagram dialog box asking you to indicate the module on which you want to base the diagram. If you followed the steps outlined earlier with RON, you should see the names of the two first-draft module designs built earlier by the Application Wizard. Pick a module and click on the OK button. The Module Data Diagrammer then presents a new diagram for the chosen module, as Figure 19.39 shows for the Enter New Customer (CUST0010) module.

FIGURE 19.39:

The Module Data Diagrammer allows you to refine the table and column usages for a module.

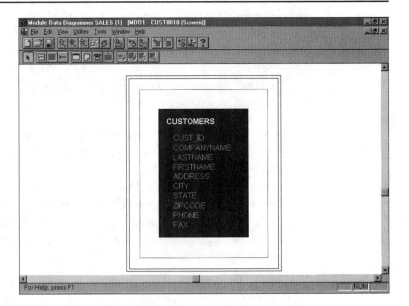

A module in a module data diagram is represented by the outer double-lines. Inside the module's borders are the detailed table and column usages. When using the Module Data Diagrammer, the goal is simply to refine the table and column usages for each module that you want to later implement.

To edit the properties of a table that's already in use by a module, double-click on the table. For example, double-click on the CUSTOMERS table of the Enter New Customer module to display the Detailed Screen Usages for Screen Module dialog box, as Figure 19.40 shows.

The dialog box contains many tabs that you can explore. For the purposes of this tutorial, make the following essential changes for the CUSTOMERS table in the CUST module.

- In the Table Layout tab, set the Rows Displayed property to 1 to display a single customer record in the screen module.

- In the Usage tab, turn the display property on for the CUST_ID column.

FIGURE 19.40:

Use the Detailed Screen Usages for Screen Module dialog box to edit the properties of the table usages in a module.

- In the Column Detail tab, reorder the columns of the CUSTOMERS so that they appear as in Figure 19.40. Also, set the ordering direction for the CUST_ID column to Ascending as in Figure 19.40.

- In the Column Display tab, adjust the prompts and display widths for each column as you see appropriate.

After you finish refining the CUSTOMERS table usage for the Enter New Customer module, save the diagram, print it, and close the diagram. Then turn your attention to creating a similar diagram for the Enter New Product Order module. When you open a new diagram for the Enter New Product Order module, it should appear similar to the diagram in Figure 19.41.

The Enter New Product Order module is fundamentally different than the Enter New Customer module because it is based on more than one table. As Figure 19.41 shows, the primary tables that the Enter New Product Order module uses are the master-detail ORDERS and ITEMS tables. At first, you can concentrate on refining these existing table usages, but later on, you'll see how to add table usages to the module data diagram.

FIGURE 19.41:

The data usages for the Enter New Product Order module as they appear after opening a new diagram

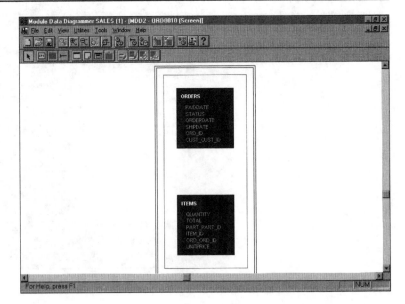

The first modification to make for the Enter New Product Order module data diagram is to include the relationship that exists between the master and detail tables. The Designer/2000 repository must include this fact to properly generate the module later on in the implementation stage. Accomplish this step quickly by selecting Utilities ➤ Generate Default Links, and then accepting the defaults in the subsequent Generate Default Links dialog box. The Module Data Diagrammer adds the foreign key to the diagram.

Next, you need to make a number of detailed modifications to the ORDERS table usage:

- In the Table Layout tab, set the Rows Displayed property to 1 to display a single order record in the screen module.

- In the Usage tab, turn the display property on for the ORD_ID and CUST_CUST_ID columns.

- In the Column Detail tab, sequence the columns so that they appear as in Figure 19.42. Also, set the ordering direction for the ORD_ID column to Ascending.

- In the Column Display tab, adjust the prompts and display widths for each column as you see appropriate.

Continue by making the following modifications to the ITEMS table usage:

- In the Table Layout tab, set the Rows Displayed property to 5 to display multiple line items per order.

- In the Usage tab, turn the display property on for the ITEM_ID and PART_PART_ID columns.

- In the Column Detail tab, sequence the columns so that they appear as in Figure 19.42. Also, set the ordering direction for the ITEM_ID column to Ascending.

- In the Column Display tab, adjust the prompts and display widths for each column as you see appropriate.

After you complete the above steps, the diagram should appear as in Figure 19.42.

We could stop here with modifying this module's design, but let's make a couple more adjustments to make it a bit more user-friendly. Specifically, the CUST_CUST_ID column of the ORDERS table references customer IDs that most users will not be able to remember. Similarly, the PART_PART_ID column of the ITEMS table references part IDs. Let's add a couple of detailed table usages to the module that will serve as lookup lists for these reference-type columns.

To add a new table usage to a module data diagram, start by choosing the Detailed Table Usage button. The cursor changes to a box outline that you can position on the diagram. The position at which you add the new table usage will determine the default type of table usage. In this case, we want to add the CUSTOMERS table as a lookup table related to the ORDERS table. To achieve this type of table usage by default, position the new table just to the right and slightly below the top of the

FIGURE 19.42:

The Enter New Product Order module data diagram after making a number of modifications to the ORDERS and ITEMS table usages

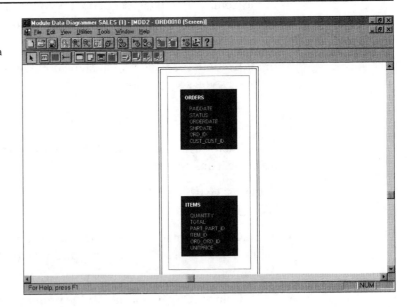

ORDERS table before pressing the primary mouse button. The Module Data Diagrammer presents the Use Table/View/Snapshot dialog box, asking you to indicate the table in the system that you want to add to the diagram at the chosen position. Select the CUSTOMERS table and choose OK. The Module Data Diagrammer adds the CUSTOMERS table to the module, as well as the foreign key that relates the table to the ORDERS table. Repeat these steps to add the PARTS table adjacent to the ITEMS table, and then you should have a diagram similar to the one in Figure 19.43.

Notice that when you add a new table usage to a diagram, it does not have any corresponding column usages. Edit the properties of each table usage to add the columns that you want for the corresponding lookup lists.

FIGURE 19.43:

Use the Detailed Table Usage button to quickly add new table usages to a module data diagram.

- Using the Column Detail tab of the Detailed Usages for Screen Module dialog box, add the COMPANYNAME, LASTNAME, and FIRSTNAME columns for the lookup list that corresponds to the CUSTOMERS table, and the DESCRIPTION column for the lookup list that corresponds to the PARTS table.

- Adjust the display characteristics of all columns that you add in the above step. Keep in mind that you are adjusting the column displays for lookup lists.

When you complete the above steps, the Enter New Product Order module data diagram should appear similar to the one in Figure 19.44. You can now save and print the diagram, and then exit the Module Data Diagrammer.

FIGURE 19.44:

The Enter New Product Order module data diagram after adding column usages to lookup tables

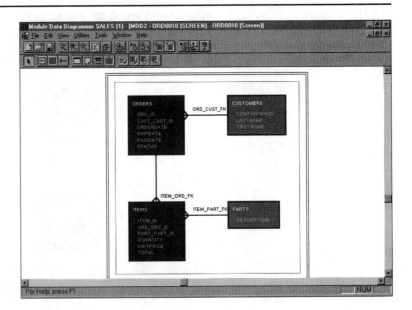

Reviewing Design Stage Information

Just as when you completed the strategy and analysis stages, it is critical that you obtain feedback on the design of your new system before actually implementing the system. Along with the printouts of the data schema and module data diagrams, you might also want to distribute related reports that are available from each of the Designer/2000 design stage tools. Based on the feedback that you receive, go back to make the necessary adjustments to your table and module designs before implementing the system.

An Introduction to the Implementation Stage

The implementation stage takes the system design and turns it into a real system—an application schema and corresponding application modules that users can use to get work done. The following sections show you how to use Designer/2000 to automatically generate the DDL script for the application system schema and the corresponding Oracle Forms applications for customer maintenance and sales order entry. First, the next section explains how to use the Designer/2000 Server Generator to create command scripts and use them to build the schema for our sample application system. After this, you'll see how to implement the front-end application modules.

Using the Server Generator

The first step in the implementation stage is to create the underlying data structures necessary for the application modules. The Server Generator is the tool that you use to accomplish this step quickly and easily. To start the Designer/2000 Server Generator, click on the corresponding button in the primary Designer/2000 window. The Server Generator Generate DDL dialog box appears, as shown in Figure 19.45.

FIGURE 19.45:

Use the Designer/2000 Server Generator to implement an application system's schema.

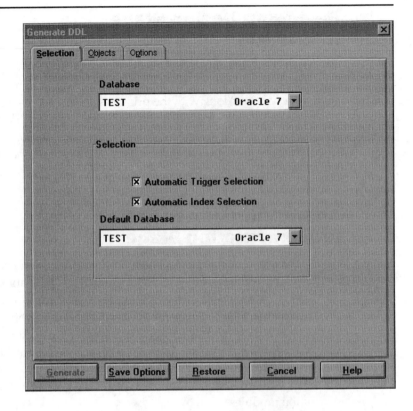

In the Selection tab of the Generate DDL dialog box, select the database TEST as the target database. Next, move to the Objects tab, as Figure 19.46 shows.

The Name list reveals every object in the application system of the type selected in the Type list. Using the up and down buttons, you can move specific or all objects in the Name list to and from the list of objects to build in the Objects list.

Work with the controls of the Objects tab to create an object list like the one in Figure 19.46. Then choose the Generate button to create SQL command scripts that will build the selected objects.

FIGURE 19.46:

Use the Objects tab of the Generate DDL dialog box to indicate what objects to build with the Server Generator.

Implementing the Application Schema

After the Server Generator completes its work, it will display the DDL Generated Files window, with a list of the SQL command scripts that it has built at your request. Figure 19.47 shows the DDL Generated Files window.

Every filename begins with the name of the corresponding database, but the names have different file extensions to indicate what type of objects they build.

- Files with the *tab* extension are SQL command scripts that build tables.

- Files with the *seq* extension are SQL command scripts that build sequences.

FIGURE 19.47:

Use the DDL Generated Files window to view and execute the SQL command scripts that the Designer/2000 Server Generator builds for you.

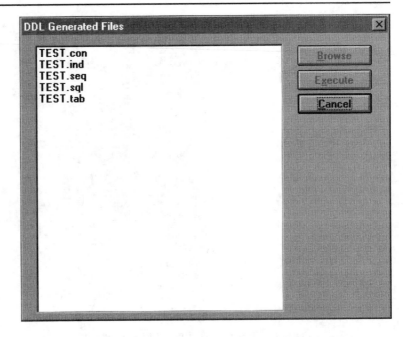

- Files with the *ind* extension are SQL command scripts that build indexes.

- Files with the *con* extension are SQL command scripts that build constraints.

The file with the *sql extension is a special SQL command script that executes all of the listed SQL command scripts.*

NOTE　　The Server Generator will create SQL command scripts with other file extensions when other types of database objects (for example, views) are included in a run. The list of file types here indicates the type of files created in this tutorial.

The DDL Generated Files window is also a convenient tool that you can use to view and execute the SQL command scripts in the list. After selecting a file in the list, click on the Browse button to see a report that shows the script, or click on the Execute button to start a SQL*Plus session and run the script. Use the DDL Generated Fileswindow to execute the TEST.sql file, which builds all objects for our test application schema. Once you build the application system's schema, you are halfway home—you have implemented the data for the new application system!

Using the Oracle Forms Generator to Implement Application Modules

The next step in the implementation phase is to generate the form and report application modules for our business system. In this simple tutorial, you'll see how to implement the Enter New Customer and Enter New Product Order form modules using Designer/2000's Oracle Forms Generator.

To start the Forms Generator, choose the corresponding button in the primary Designer/2000 window. The Oracle Forms Generator window (labeled Generate Form) appears, as in Figure 19.48.

FIGURE 19.48:

Use Designer/2000's Oracle Forms Generator to generate Oracle Forms applications from modules in the Designer/2000 repository.

The defaults of the Oracle Forms Generator are fine for most application-generation activities. However, be sure to investigate the many tabs and controls in the dialog box, so that you know what options are available to you in the future. To generate one or more modules in the repository, select the modules to implement from the Module(s) list box in the Generate tab of the Generate Form dialog box and choose Start. The Forms Generator then carries out many activities to create and compile the selected application modules. In certain circumstances, the Generator will prompt you with basic questions regarding application module design characteristics; reply as you see fit.

After generation is complete, the Oracle Forms Generator will ask if you want to run the application right away using the Oracle Forms runtime version. Select Yes to get a look at the new application. The screens in Figures 19.49 and 19.50 show the first version of the form applications with some data.

At this point, the front-end applications are a bit rough and need improvement. Obvious problems include general design characteristics, such as item layout and block and label fonts. However, don't let this first-cut of the applications take away from your accomplishments up to this point. Realize that without having to type a single line of 3GL code or playing around with a 4GL screen development tool, you

FIGURE 19.49:

The first generation of the Customers form application

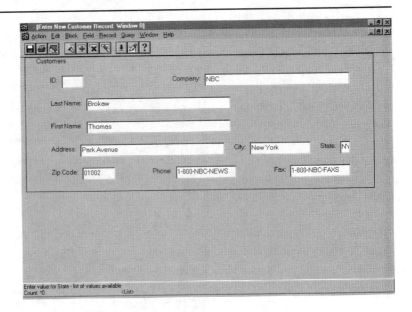

FIGURE 19.50:

The first generation of the Orders
form application

have generated functional form applications that provide an interface to a database
schema.

Improving the Look and Feel of Applications

In most cases, you should attempt to make all modifications to your application
system using the Oracle Designer/2000 environment. Oracle Server, Designer/2000,
and Developer/2000 are tightly integrated, and you should be able to capture all
application development activities within the Designer/2000 repository. By doing
so, you can automatically repeat all system-generation steps as the application system evolves with later versions.

To make most appearance-type modifications to application modules, you need to
become intimately familiar with the Designer/2000 Preferences Navigator. The
Preferences Navigator is a design stage tool that allows you to set hundreds of
global or module specific "preferences." For example, if you change two simple
preferences (BLKMLF and BLKVFL) and then regenerate the Enter New Customer
module, it will appear as in Figure 19.51.

FIGURE 19.51:

After altering the BLKMLF and BLKVFL preferences in the Designer/2000 repository, the layout of items in a regenerated version of the Customers form will appear very different.

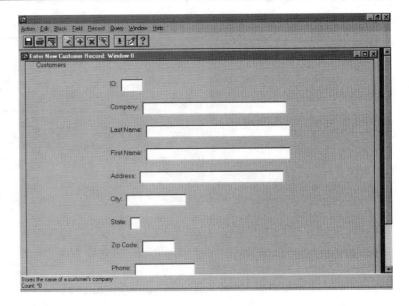

Although this tutorial does not provide detailed instructions on how to use the Preferences Navigator, don't be afraid to see how it works on your own. The interface of the Preferences Navigator is similar to RON. Keep experimenting with the settings for the various preferences and regenerate your application modules until they appear just the way that you want.

NOTE　　In rare circumstances, you might need to use the actual design module of the application development tool itself (for example, Oracle Forms or Oracle Reports) to make finer adjustments to application modules. This book does not discuss how to work with the Developer/2000 designer products, such as Oracle Forms Designer and Oracle Reports Designer.

You can continue system development by automatically developing other form applications (for example, one for maintaining inventory), reporting applications, and menu applications to tie together all related applications—and all without complicated programming.

The Remaining Stages of System Development: Testing and Production

After you develop your application in a test environment, you are responsible for validating the behavior and performance of each application module. You should also solicit user feedback on the user interface and possible enhancements you can incorporate before creating the first production version of the application.

This chapter has given you a head start in developing good applications quickly with Oracle's Designer/2000 suite of CASE tools. More important, you have gained an understanding of how to assemble the front-end and back-end components of a client/server system that uses an Oracle7 database server. Now you can use this knowledge to create your own Oracle7 client/server system.

APPENDIX

A

Quick Reference Tables for Oracle7

This appendix includes a number of lists to use as references when working with Oracle7, including:

- SQL commands (Table A.1)

- PL/SQL commands (Table A.2)

- SQL functions (Tables A.3 through A.8)

- Data dictionary views (Tables A.9 through A.11)

- Datatypes (Table A.12)

- System privileges (Table A.13)

- Object privileges (Table A.14)

Oracle7 SQL Commands

Table A.1 includes quick descriptions for all of the Oracle7 SQL commands (not including embedded SQL commands). In the table, † next to a command name means the command is available only with the Oracle7 Distributed Database option.

TABLE A.1: Oracle7 SQL Commands

SQL Command	Description
ALTER CLUSTER	Modifies the structure of an indexed or a hash cluster.
ALTER DATABASE	Modifies the structure and/or operational mode of an Oracle7 database; allows database recovery.
ALTER FUNCTION	Manually forces a function to recompile.
ALTER INDEX	Modifies the storage parameters for an index.
ALTER PACKAGE	Manually forces a package to recompile.
ALTER PROCEDURE	Manually forces a procedure to recompile.
ALTER PROFILE	Modifies the resource limits of a profile.
ALTER RESOURCE COST	Modifies the weighting costs for the composite resource limits.
ALTER ROLE	Modifies a role's password or authentication method.

TABLE A.1: Oracle7 SQL Commands (continued)

SQL Command	Description
ALTER ROLLBACK SEGMENT	Modifies the availability or storage parameters of a rollback segment.
ALTER SEQUENCE	Modifies the characteristics of a sequence.
ALTER SESSION	Modifies database session settings.
ALTER SNAPSHOT†	Modifies a snapshot's refresh mode and/or time, or storage characteristics.
ALTER SNAPSHOT LOG†	Modifies a snapshot log's storage characteristics.
ALTER SYSTEM	Dynamically modifies several current database server system settings.
ALTER TABLE	Modifies a table's physical structure, storage parameters, and/or integrity constraints.
ALTER TABLESPACE	Modifies a tablespace's availability, backup mode, or storage parameters, or adds data files to increase tablespace capacity.
ALTER TRIGGER	Enables or disables a trigger.
ALTER USER	Modifies a user's account settings, password, or authentication method.
ALTER VIEW	Manually recompiles a view.
ANALYZE	Generates optimizer statistics or lists chained rows for a table, an index, or a cluster and can also validate the structure of an index.
AUDIT	Sets audit options for the system and database objects.
COMMENT	Creates in the data dictionary a comment for a table, view, snapshot, or column.
COMMIT	Commits a transaction to make transaction changes permanent in the database.
CREATE CLUSTER	Creates an indexed or a hash cluster.
CREATE CONTROLFILE	Creates a new database control file to replace a damaged or badly sized control file.
CREATE DATABASE	Creates a database.
CREATE DATABASE LINK†	Defines a named path to a remote database. Database links are available without the Distributed Database option, but for read operations only.
CREATE FUNCTION	Creates a stored function.

TABLE A.1: Oracle7 SQL Commands (continued)

SQL Command	Description
CREATE INDEX	Creates an index for a table.
CREATE PACKAGE	Creates a stored package specification.
CREATE PACKAGE BODY	Creates a stored package body.
CREATE PROCEDURE	Creates a stored procedure.
CREATE PROFILE	Creates a named profile of resource limits.
CREATE ROLE	Creates a role to group related privileges.
CREATE ROLLBACK SEGMENT	Creates a rollback segment.
CREATE SCHEMA	Creates a number of tables and views, all in one statement, in a current database account.
CREATE SEQUENCE	Creates a named sequence of numbers.
CREATE SNAPSHOT[†]	Creates a snapshot of a remote table.
CREATE SNAPSHOT LOG[†]	Creates a refresh log for a snapshot.
CREATE SYNONYM	Creates a synonym for a database object.
CREATE TABLE	Creates a new database table.
CREATE TABLESPACE	Creates a new tablespace.
CREATE TRIGGER	Creates a database trigger for a table.
CREATE USER	Creates a new database username and password.
CREATE VIEW	Creates a view of a table or other views.
DELETE	Deletes one or more rows from a database table.
DROP CLUSTER	Drops an indexed or a hash cluster.
DROP DATABASE LINK[†]	Drops a named path to a remote database.
DROP FUNCTION	Drops a stored function.
DROP INDEX	Drops an index on a table.
DROP PACKAGE	Drops a stored package specification and body.
DROP PACKAGE BODY	Drops a stored package body.
DROP PROCEDURE	Drops a stored procedure.
DROP PROFILE	Drops a named profile of resource limits.
DROP ROLE	Drops a role of related privileges.
DROP ROLLBACK SEGMENT	Drops a rollback segment.

TABLE A.1: Oracle7 SQL Commands (continued)

SQL Command	Description
DROP SEQUENCE	Drops a named sequence of numbers.
DROP SNAPSHOT[†]	Drops a snapshot of a remote table.
DROP SNAPSHOT LOG[†]	Drops a log for a snapshot.
DROP SYNONYM	Drops a synonym for a table or view.
DROP TABLE	Drops a database table.
DROP TABLESPACE	Drops a tablespace.
DROP TRIGGER	Drops a trigger on a table.
DROP USER	Drops a database username, as well as the user's objects.
DROP VIEW	Drops a view.
EXPLAIN PLAN	Puts into a database table the optimization strategy for a SQL statement.
GRANT	Grants roles, system privileges, and/or object privileges to users and/or roles.
INSERT	Inserts one or more new rows into a database table.
LOCK TABLE	Manually locks a table.
NOAUDIT	Disables audit options for the system and database objects.
RENAME	Renames a table, view, sequence, or synonym.
REVOKE	Revokes roles, system privileges, and/or object privileges from users or roles.
ROLLBACK	Rolls back the changes made by the current transaction.
SAVEPOINT	Identifies an intermediate transaction savepoint.
SELECT	Retrieves all or specific column and row information from one or more tables or views.
SET ROLE	Enables one or more specific roles of related privileges and disables all others.
SET TRANSACTION	Specifies transaction characteristics.
TRUNCATE	Deletes all rows from a table and optionally releases all space allocated to the table.
UPDATE	Updates all or specific rows in a table.

[†]Available only with the Oracle7 Distributed Database option.

PL/SQL Commands

Table A.2 provides a quick reference to the Oracle7 PL/SQL commands.

NOTE PL/SQL also supports the DML SQL commands, such as INSERT, UPDATE, DELETE, and LOCK TABLE, as well as transaction control SQL commands, such as COMMIT, ROLLBACK, and SAVEPOINT. Also, Table A.2 does not include other PL/SQL functionality, such as variable declarations and assignment statements (assigning values to variables), because they are not commands.

TABLE A.2: Oracle7 PL/SQL Commands

PL/SQL Command	Description
CLOSE	Closes a cursor.
EXCEPTION_INIT	Associates a declared exception name with an Oracle error number to trap and handle an Oracle error with a PL/SQL exception handler.
EXIT	Exits a loop.
FETCH	Fetches the next row from a cursor.
GOTO	Goes to a named block of PL/SQL code.
IF	Conditional statement to execute a PL/SQL block.
LOOP	Creates a loop to execute one or more statements a number of times.
NULL	Performs no action.
OPEN	Opens a declared cursor.
RAISE	Raises a declared exception.
RETURN	Completes the execution of a PL/SQL program and, if in a function, returns a value to the calling environment.
SELECT INTO	Retrieves one or more column values from a single row in a table into specified PL/SQL variables.

Oracle7 SQL Functions

Tables A.3 through A.8 are quick references to the various Oracle7 SQL functions. The tables organize the SQL functions by type:

- Numeric SQL functions

- Character SQL functions

- Date SQL functions

- Conversion SQL functions

- Miscellaneous SQL functions

- Group SQL functions

TABLE A.3: Oracle7 Numeric SQL Functions

SQL Function	Description
ABS(x)	Returns the absolute value of x.
CEIL(x)	Returns the smallest integer greater than or equal to x.
COS(x)	Returns the cosine of x.
COSH(x)	Returns the hyperbolic cosine of x.
EXP(x)	Returns e raised to the xth power.
FLOOR(x)	Returns the largest integer less than or equal to x.
LN(x)	Returns the natural logarithm of x.
LOG(x,y)	Returns the base x logarithm of y.
MOD(x,y)	Returns the remainder of x divided by y.
POWER(x,y)	Returns x raised to the y power.
ROUND(x[,y])	Returns x rounded y places to the right of the decimal place. Default y is 0. If y is negative, x is rounded to the left of the decimal place.
SIGN(x)	Returns the sign of x as -1 if negative, 0 if 0, and 1 if positive.
SIN(x)	Returns the sine of x.

TABLE A.3: Oracle7 Numeric SQL Functions (continued)

SQL Function	Description
SINH(x)	Returns the hyperbolic sine of x.
SQRT(x)	Returns the square root of x.
TAN(x)	Returns the tangent of x.
TANH(x)	Returns the hyperbolic tangent of x.
TRUNC(x[,y])	Returns x truncated to y decimal places. Default y is 0. If y is negative, x is truncated to the left of the decimal place.

TABLE A.4: Oracle7 Character SQL Functions

SQL Function	Description
ASCII(x)	Returns the decimal representation of the character x.
CHR(x)	Returns the character in the database character set that corresponds to integer x.
CONCAT(x,y)	Returns x concatenated with y.
INITCAP(x)	Returns the string x, with the first letter in each word in uppercase and the remaining letters in each word in lowercase.
INSTR(w,x[,y[,z]]).	Returns the starting character position of string x in string w, if present. Returns 0 if string x is not present in string w. If you specify y, search starts at character position y in string w. If you specify z, search looks for the zth occurrence of string x in string w, starting at character position y.
INSTRB(w,x[,y[,z]])	Same as INSTR, except that y and the return value are expressed in bytes instead of character position. Useful only when using multibyte character strings for w and x.
LENGTH(x)	Returns the string length of x.
LENGTHB(x)	Returns the byte length of x.
LOWER(x)	Returns x with all letters in lowercase.

TABLE A.4: Oracle7 Character SQL Functions (continued)

SQL Function	Description
LPAD(x,y[,z])	Returns x left-padded with spaces with length y. Use the optional argument z to specify a padding string.
LTRIM(x[,y])	Trims characters from the left of string x and returns the resulting string. Use z to specify a set of characters to be trimmed. Default y is a blank space to remove left blank padding from strings.
NLS_INITCAP (x[,y])	Same as INITCAP, except optional argument y allows you to specify a language for consideration in the function.
NLS_LOWER(x[,y])	Same as LOWER, except optional argument y allows you to specify a language for consideration in the function.
NLSSORT(x[,y])	Returns the string of bytes used to sort x based on the language specified by y. Useful for comparing strings in different languages.
NLS_UPPER (x,[y])	Same as UPPER, except optional argument y allows you to specify a language for consideration in the function.
REPLACE(x,y[,z])	Returns x with all occurrences of y replaced by z. If z is omitted, all occurrences at y are simply removed.
RPAD(x,y,z)	Returns x right-padded with spaces to length y. Use the optional argument z to specify a padding string.
RTRIM(x[,y])	Trims characters from the right of string x and returns the resulting string. Use y to specify a set of characters to be trimmed. Default y is a blank space to remove right blank padding from strings.
SOUNDEX(x)	Returns the phonetic representation of x (a four-character representation of how the first part of x sounds).
SUBSTR(x,y[,z])	Returns the portion of x beginning with the character y. If you specify z, returns the portion that is z characters long. If y is negative, Oracle7 counts backward from the end of x.
SUBSTRB(x,y[,z])	Same as SUBSTR, except that arguments y and z are expressed in bytes rather than characters. Useful only when using multibyte character strings.
TRANSLATE(x,y,z)	Translates the values of x as seen in set y to the corresponding values in set z and returns the result.
UPPER(x)	Returns x with all letters in uppercase.

TABLE A.5: Oracle7 Date SQL Functions

SQL Function	Description
ADD_MONTHS(x,y)	Returns the date of x plus y months.
LAST_DAY(x)	Returns the last day in the month specified by the date x.
MONTHS_BETWEEN(x,y)	Returns the number of months between the dates x and y.
NEW_TIME(x,y,z)	Returns the corresponding time in time zone z of the time of x in time zone y.
NEXT_DAY(x,y)	Returns the date of the first day of the week named y after the date x.
ROUND($x[,y]$)	Returns x rounded to the nearest day to the format model specified by y (for example, month or year).
SYSDATE	Returns the current date and time.
TRUNC($x[,y]$)	Returns x with the time portion of the day truncated to the specification of the format model y.

TABLE A.6: Oracle7 Conversion SQL Functions

SQL Function	Description
CHARTOROWID(x)	Converts a character string x to an Oracle7 ROWID.
CONVERT($x,y[,z]$)	Converts the character string x using the character set y. Use the optional argument z to specify the source character set.
HEXTORAW(x)	Converts the character string of hex digits x to raw (binary) data.
RAWTOHEX(x)	Converts raw data x to a hexadecimal character string.
ROWIDTOCHAR(x)	Converts the Oracle7 ROWID value x to a hexadecimal character string.
TO_CHAR($x,[y]$)	Converts a date or number to a character string. When x is a date, y is a format model; when x is a number, y is a format model for varying character strings.
TO_DATE($x[,y]$)	Converts the character string x to a date using the format model y.
TO_LABEL($x[,y]$)	Converts a character string to a value for the MLSLABEL datatype using the format model y. Useful only with Trusted Oracle7.
TO_MULTI_BYTE(x)	Converts the character string x with single-byte characters to multibyte characters.
TO_NUMBER($x[,y]$)	Converts the character string x to a number using the format model y.
TO_SINGLE_BYTE(x)	Converts the character string x with multibyte characters to single-byte characters.

TABLE A.7: Oracle7 Miscellaneous SQL Functions

SQL Function	Description
DUMP(w[,x[,y[,z]]])	Returns a character string containing the datatype code, length in bytes, and internal representation of w. Specify the optional argument x to indicate the return value notation (8=octal, 10=decimal, 16=hexadecimal, and 17=single characters). The optional argument y indicates the start position in w. The optional argument z indicates the length of w starting at y to dump.
GREATEST(x[,y][, ...])	Returns the greatest of x, y,... values. Type comparisons are based on the datatype of the first value or expression x.
GREATEST_LB(x[,y][, ...])	Returns the greatest lower bound of the list of labels x, y,.... Useful only with Trusted Oracle7.
LEAST(x[,y][, ...])	Returns the least of x, y,... values. Comparisons are based on the first value or expression x.
LEAST_UB(x[y],[, ...])	Returns the least upper bound of the list of labels x, y,.... Useful only with Trusted Oracle7.
NVL(x,y)	Returns y if x is NULL; otherwise, returns x. Useful for representing NULLs in queries.
UID	Returns the integer that uniquely identifies the current user.
USER	Returns the database username of the current user.
USERENV(x)	Returns environment information about the current database session. For example, when x is LANGUAGE, Oracle returns the language in use by the session. Possible values for x include ENTRYID, LABEL, LANGUAGE, SESSIONID, and TERMINAL.
VSIZE(x)	Returns the number of bytes in the internal representation of x.

TABLE A.8: Oracle7 Group SQL Functions

SQL Function	Description
AVG([DISTINCT|ALL] x)	Returns the average expression value for x. When you specify DISTINCT, Oracle considers only distinct column values in x; when you specify ALL, Oracle considers all column values in x. ALL is the default.
COUNT(* | [DISTINCT|ALL] x)	Returns the number of rows returned by the query. If you specify *, the count includes all duplicate and NULL values found. If you specify the column argument x rather than *, the count is the number of rows where column x is NOT NULL. The optional DISTINCT and ALL work as with AVG.
GLB([DISTINCT|ALL] x)	Returns the greatest lower bound of label x. DISTINCT and ALL work as with AVG.
LUB([DISTINCT|ALL] x)	Returns the least upper bound of x. DISTINCT and ALL work as with AVG.
MAX([DISTINCT|ALL] x)	Returns the maximum column value for column x. DISTINCT and ALL work as with AVG.
MIN([DISTINCT|ALL] x)	Returns the minimum column value for column x. DISTINCT and ALL work as with AVG.
STDDEV([DISTINCT|ALL] x)	Returns the standard deviation of the number column x. DISTINCT and ALL work as with AVG.
SUM([DISTINCT|ALL] x)	Returns the sum of the number column x. DISTINCT and ALL work as with AVG.
VARIANCE([DISTINCT|ALL] x)	Returns the variance of the number column x. DISTINCT and ALL work as with AVG.

Oracle7 Data Dictionary Views

Table A.9 lists the prefixed Oracle7 data dictionary views. Views prefixed with ALL_ are available to all users and show things specific to the privilege domain of the user issuing the query. Views prefixed with DBA_ are available only to users with the SELECT ANY TABLE system privilege and show everything in the database. Views with the USER_ prefix are available to all users and show things specific to the user issuing the query. Words in parentheses are synonyms for the preceding view. For example, the following view name table entry means that there are ALL_CATALOG, DBA_CATALOG, and USER_CATALOG dictionary views, along with the CAT synonym for the USER_CATALOG view:

```
CATALOG (ALL_, DBA_, USER_ (CAT))
```

TABLE A.9: Oracle7 Data Dictonary Views

View Name	Description
2PC_NEIGHBORS (DBA_)	Information about incoming and outgoing connections for pending distributed transactions.
2PC_PENDING (DBA_)	Information about pending distributed transactions.
AUDIT_EXISTS (DBA_)	Audit trail entries made on behalf of the AUDIT EXISTS command.
AUDIT_OBJECT (DBA_, USER_)	Audit trail entries for audited database objects.
AUDIT_SESSION (DBA_, USER_)	Audit trail entries concerning database sessions.
AUDIT_STATEMENT (DBA_, USER_)	Audit trail entries for audited statements.
AUDIT_TRAIL (DBA_, USER_)	Collection of all audit trail entries.
BLOCKERS (DBA_)	Sessions whose locks are blocking other transactions from performing work. See related view DBA_WAITERS.
CATALOG (ALL_, DBA_, USER_ (CAT))	Information about database tables, views, synonyms, and sequences.
CLU_COLUMNS (DBA_, USER_)	Relation of table columns to cluster keys.
CLUSTERS (DBA_, USER_ (CLU))	Information about indexed and hash clusters in the database.
COL_COMMENTS (ALL_, DBA_, USER_)	Comments for table and view columns.

TABLE A.9: Oracle7 Data Dictionary Views (continued)

View Name	Description
COL_PRIVS, (ALL_, DBA_, USER_)	Information about grants on specific columns.
COL_PRIVS_MADE (ALL_, USER_)	Information about grants made on specific columns.
COL_PRIVS_RECD (ALL_, USER_)	Information about grants received on specific columns.
CONS_COLUMNS (ALL_, DBA_, USER_)	Information about columns involved in integrity constraints.
CONSTRAINTS (ALL_, DBA_, USER_)	Information about integrity constraints in the database.
DATA_FILES (DBA_)	Information about the database's data files.
DB_LINKS (ALL_, DBA_, USER_)	Information about database links in the database.
DDL_LOCKS (DBA_)	Information about locks taken on behalf of DDL operations.
DEF_AUDIT_OPTS (ALL_)	Information about default object auditing options.
DEPENDENCIES (ALL_, DBA_, USER_)	Information about object dependencies in the database.
DML_LOCKS (DBA_)	Information about DML locks in the server.
ERRORS (ALL_, DBA_, USER_)	Information about compile errors detected for procedures, functions, package specifications, and package bodies in the database.
EXP_FILES (DBA_)	Description of export files.
EXP_OBJECTS (DBA_)	Information about objects that have been incrementally exported with the Export utility.
EXP_VERSION (DBA_)	Version number of the last Export utility session.
EXTENTS (DBA_, USER_)	Information about the extents for objects in the database.
FREE_SPACE (DBA_, USER_)	Information about the free extents in the tablespaces of a database.
IND_COLUMNS (ALL_, DBA_, USER_)	Information about the columns that correspond to table indexes.
INDEXES (ALL_, DBA_, USER_ (IND))	Information about indexes in the database.
LABELS (ALL_)	Information about system labels. Useful only with Trusted Oracle7.
LOCKS (DBA_)	Information about all DDL and DML locks in the database server.

TABLE A.9: Oracle7 Data Dictionary Views (continued)

View Name	Description
MOUNTED_DBS (ALL_)	Information about all mounted databases. Useful only with Trusted Oracle7.
OBJ_AUDIT_OPTS (DBA_, USER_)	Information about auditing options set for database objects.
OBJECT_SIZE (DBA_, USER_)	Size information for all procedures, functions, package specifications, and package bodies in the database.
OBJECTS (ALL_, DBA_, USER_ (OBJ))	Information about database objects in the database.
PRIV_AUDIT_OPTS (DBA_)	Information about auditing options set for privileges.
PROFILES (DBA_)	Information about resource limit profiles in a database.
RESOURCE_LIMITS (USER_)	Information about resource limits for the current user session.
ROLE_PRIVS (DBA_, USER_)	Information about roles granted to a user.
ROLES (DBA_)	Information about roles in the database.
ROLLBACK_SEGS (DBA_)	Information about rollback segments in the database.
SEGMENTS (DBA_, USER_)	Information about segments in the database.
SEQUENCES (ALL_, DBA_, USER_ (SEQ))	Information about sequences in the database.
SNAPSHOT_LOGS (DBA_, USER_)	Information about snapshot logs in the database.
SNAPSHOTS (ALL_, DBA_, USER_)	Information about snapshots in the database.
SOURCE (ALL_, DBA_, USER_)	Source code of procedures, functions, package specifications, and package bodies in the database.
STMT_AUDIT_OPTS (DBA_)	Information about auditing options set for statements.
SYNONYMS (ALL_, DBA_, USER_ (SYN))	Information about synonyms in the database.
SYS_PRIVS (DBA_, USER_)	System privileges granted to a user.
TAB_COLUMNS (ALL_, DBA_, USER_ (COLS))	Information about the columns of tables and views in the database.
TAB_COMMENTS (ALL_, DBA_, USER_)	Comments for tables and views in the database.
TAB_PRIVS (ALL_, DBA_, USER_)	Information about object privilege grants.
TAB_PRIVS_MADE (ALL_, USER_)	Information about object privileges that were granted.

TABLE A.9: Oracle7 Data Dictionary Views (continued)

View Name	Description
TAB_PRIVS_RECD (ALL_, USER_)	Information about object privileges that were received.
TABLES (ALL_, DBA_, USER_ (TABS))	Information about tables in the database.
TABLESPACES (DBA_, USER_)	Information about tablespaces in the database.
TRIGGER_COLS (ALL_, DBA_, USER_)	Information about the columns that database triggers use.
TRIGGERS (ALL_, DBA_, USER_)	Information about triggers in the database.
TS_QUOTAS (DBA_, USER_)	Information about user tablespace quotas.
USERS (ALL_, DBA_, USER_)	Information about users in the database.
VIEWS (ALL_, DBA_, USER_)	Information about views in the database.
WAITERS (DBA_)	Information about sessions waiting on a lock held by another session.

Table A.10 provides a list of miscellaneous Oracle7 data dictionary views, and Table A.11 gives you the virtual Oracle7 data dictionary views.

TABLE A.10: Oracle7 Miscellaneous Data Dictionary Views

View Name	Description
AUDIT_ACTIONS	Mapping of audit trail action numbers to descriptions.
CHAINED_ROWS	Output information about chained rows from the ANALYZE command. Created by the UTLCHAIN.SQL administrative script.
COLUMN_PRIVILEGES	Information about column grants.
DBMS_ALERT_INFO	Information about registered alerts created by the DBMS_ALERT utility package.
DBMS_LOCK_ALLOCATED	Information about user-defined locks created by the DBMS_LOCK utility package.
DEPTREE	Information about object dependencies. Created by the UTLDTREE.SQL administrative script.
DICT_COLUMNS	Information about data dictionary columns.

TABLE A.10: Oracle7 Miscellaneous Data Dictionary Views (continued)

View Name	Description
DICTIONARY (DICT)	Information about data dictionary tables and views.
EXCEPTIONS	Output information for integrity constraint exceptions. Created by the UTLEXCPT.SQL administrative script.
GLOBAL_NAME	Information about the global name of the database.
IDEPTREE	Information about object dependencies. Created by the UTLDTREE.SQL administrative script.
INDEX_HISTOGRAM	Statistical information about indexes generated from the ANALYZE INDEX...VALIDATE INDEX command.
INDEX_STATS	Statistical information about indexes generated from the ANALYZE INDEX...VALIDATE INDEX command.
LOADER_COL_INFO	Information for SQL*Loader regarding columns.
LOADER_CONSTRAINT_INFO	Information for SQL*Loader regarding integrity constraints.
LOADER_INDCOL_INFO	Information for SQL*Loader regarding indexed columns.
LOADER_IND_INFO	Information for SQL*Loader regarding indexes.
LOADER_PARAM_INFO	Information for SQL*Loader regarding parameters.
LOADER_TAB_INFO	Information for SQL*Loader regarding tables.
LOADER_TRIGGER_INFO	Information for SQL*Loader regarding triggers.
NLS_DATABASE_PARAMETERS	Information about database NLS (National Language Support) settings. Useful only if the server uses NLS.
NLS_INSTANCE_PARAMETERS	Information about database server NLS settings. Useful only if the server uses NLS.
NLS_SESSION_PARAMETERS	Information about session NLS settings. Useful only if the server uses NLS.
PLAN_TABLE	Output information about optimizer execution plans from the EXPLAIN PLAN command. Created by the UTLXPLAN.SQL administrative script.
PUBLIC_DEPENDENCY	Information about object dependencies.
RESOURCE_COST	Information about the costs of system resources.
ROLE_ROLE_PRIVS	Information about roles granted to other roles.

TABLE A.10: Oracle7 Miscellaneous Data Dictionary Views (continued)

View Name	Description
ROLE_SYS_PRIVS	Information about system privileges granted to roles.
ROLE_TAB_PRIVS	Information about object privileges granted to roles.
SESSION_PRIVS	Information about privileges available to a session.
SESSION_ROLES	Information about roles available to a session.
STMT_AUDIT_OPTION_MAP	Mapping of audit trail action numbers to descriptions.
SYSTEM_PRIVILEGE_MAP	Mapping of system privilege numbers to descriptions.
TABLE_PRIVILEGES	Information about object privilege grants.
TABLE_PRIVILEGE_MAP	Mapping of object privilege numbers to descriptions.

TABLE A.11: Oracle7 Virtual Data Dictionary Views

View Name	Description
V$ACCESS	Information about objects currently in use.
V$ARCHIVE	Information about the archived transaction log of the database.
V$BACKUP	Information about the backup status of all online tablespaces in the database.
V$BGPROCESS	Information about all background server processes of the database server.
V$CIRCUIT	Information about all circuits (user connections) in a multithreaded server configuration.
V$DATABASE	Information about a database from the database's control file.
V$DATAFILE	Information about the database's data files.
V$DBFILE	Information about the database's data files.
V$DB_OBJECT_CACHE	Information about objects in the database server's object cache, including tables, views, indexes, and procedures.
V$DISPATCHER	Information about dispatcher background server processes currently up in a multithreaded database server.

TABLE A.11: Oracle7 Virtual Data Dictionary Views (continued)

View Name	Description
V$ENABLEDPRIVS	Information about enabled privileges.
V$FILESTAT	Statistical I/O information about database files.
V$FIXED_TABLE	Information about all fixed tables in the database.
V$INSTANCE	Information about the current state of the database server (instance) .
V$LATCH	Information about the internal locks (latches) in the database server.
V$LATCHHOLDER	Information about sessions that currently hold internal locks (latches).
V$LATCHNAME	Information about internal locks (latches) in the database server.
V$LIBRARYCACHE	Statistical information about library cache management.
V$LICENSE	Information about Oracle software license limits.
V$LOADCSTAT	Information about SQL*Loader statistics compiled during a direct path load.
V$LOADTSTAT	Information about SQL*Loader statistics compiled during a direct path load.
V$LOCK	Information about DML locks in the database server.
V$LOG	Information about a database's transaction log.
V$LOGFILE	Information about a database's transaction log files.
V$LOGHIST	Information about a database's transaction log sequence history.
V$LOG_HISTORY	Information about a database's transaction log.
V$MTS	Tuning information for the multithreaded server configuration.
V$NLS_PARAMETERS	Information about current NLS (National Language Support) parameter values.
V$OPEN_CURSOR	Information about each database session's open cursors.
V$PARAMETER	Information about each database server initialization parameter.
V$PROCESS	Information about currently active processes.
V$QUEUE	Information about the multithreaded server queues.
V$RECOVERY_LOG	Information about the archived transaction log groups needed to perform database recovery.
V$RECOVER_FILE	Status information about data files needing recovery.
V$REQDIST	Statistical information about request times.

TABLE A.11: Oracle7 Virtual Data Dictionary Views (continued)

View Name	Description
V$RESOURCE	Information about system resources.
V$ROLLNAME	Information about all online rollback segments.
V$ROLLSTAT	Statistical information about all online rollback segments.
V$ROWCACHE	Statistical information about data dictionary activity.
V$SECONDARY	Information about secondary mounted databases. Useful only with Trusted Oracle7.
V$SESSION	Information about database sessions.
V$SESSION_EVENTS	Wait statistic information for each session and each event.
V$SESSION_WAIT	Information about resources that sessions are waiting for.
V$SESSTAT	Statistics information about database sessions.
V$SESS_IO	Information about each session's I/O usage.
V$SGA	Information about the database server's SGA memory area.
V$SGASTAT	Statistical information about the database server's SGA memory area.
V$SHARED_SERVER	Information about shared foreground servers of a multithreaded database server.
V$SQLAREA	Information about shared cursors.
V$SQLTEXT	Information about statements corresponding to shared cursors.
V$STATNAME	Descriptions for session statistic codes shown in V$SESSTAT.
V$SYSLABEL	Information about system labels. Useful only with Trusted Oracle7.
V$SYSSTAT	Information about system-wide statistics for each statistic in V$SESSTAT.
V$SYSTEM_EVENTS	System information of all per-session event statistics.
V$THREAD	Information about threads of the database's transaction log.
V$TIMER	The current system time in hundredths of a second.
V$TRANSACTION	Information about current database transactions.
V$TYPE_SIZE	Information about low-level data components to aid in the prediction of space usage estimates.
V$VERSION	Information about versions of core software libraries of the Oracle7 server.
V$WAITSTAT	Statistical information about data block contention among transactions.

Oracle7 Datatypes

Table A.12 lists the Oracle7 datatypes. In parentheses are equivalent ANSI and/or IBM DB2 or SQL/DS datatypes that you can use.

TABLE A.12: Oracle7 Datatypes

Datatype	Description
CHAR(*size*) (CHARACTER, CHAR)	Stores fixed-length character strings.
DATE (DATE)	Stores time-related information, including dates and times.
LONG (LONG VARCHAR)	Stores large, variable-length character strings, up to 2 gigabytes.
NUMBER(*precision, scale*) (FLOAT, NUMERIC, DECIMAL, DEC, INTEGER, INT, SMALLINT, REAL, DOUBLE PRECISION)	Stores numbers of all types, including integer, floating point, and so on.
LONG RAW	Stores long binary strings, up to 2 gigabytes.
MLSLABEL	Stores the binary format of an operating system label. Useful only with Trusted Oracle7.
RAW(*size*)	Stores small binary strings, less than 2000 bytes.
ROWID	Stores hexadecimal ROWID values that correspond to Oracle table ROWIDs. Note that columns declared with the ROWID datatype should not be confused with the pseudo-column of a table, ROWID, which stores the ROWIDs for all rows in a table.
VARCHAR2(*size*) (VARCHAR, CHARACTER VARYING)	Stores variable-length character strings.

Oracle7 System Privileges

Table A.13 lists the Oracle7 system privileges. Prefixed system privileges have the available prefixes in parentheses. For example, the following system privilege table entry:

```
CLUSTER (CREATE, CREATE ANY, ALTER ANY, DROP ANY)
```

translates to these system privileges:

```
CREATE CLUSTER
CREATE ANY CLUSTER
ALTER ANY CLUSTER
DROP ANY CLUSTER
```

TABLE A.13: Oracle7 System Privileges

System Privilege	Description
ANALYZE ANY	Analyzes any table, index, or cluster in the database using the ANALYZE command.
AUDIT ANY	Sets audit options for any database object.
AUDIT SYSTEM	Permits auditing of system operations.
CLUSTER (CREATE, CREATE ANY, ALTER ANY, DROP ANY)	Creates, alters, and drops clusters.
DATABASE (ALTER)	Modifies the database using the ALTER DATABASE command.
DATABASE LINK (CREATE, CREATE PUBLIC, DROP PUBLIC)	Creates and drops database links.
INDEX (CREATE ANY, ALTER ANY, DROP ANY)	Creates, alters, and drops indexes.
PRIVILEGE (GRANT ANY)	Grants any system privilege.
PROCEDURE (CREATE, CREATE ANY, ALTER ANY, DROP ANY, EXECUTE ANY)	Creates, recompiles, drops, and executes procedures.
PROFILE (CREATE, ALTER, DROP)	Creates, alters, and drops resource limit profiles.

TABLE A.13: Oracle7 System Privileges (continued)

System Privilege	Description
RESOURCE COST (ALTER)	Sets costs for session resources.
ROLE (CREATE, ALTER ANY, DROP ANY, GRANT ANY)	Creates, alters, drops, and grants roles.
ROLLBACK SEGMENT (CREATE, ALTER, DROP)	Creates, alters, and drops rollback segments.
SESSION (CREATE, ALTER, RESTRICTED)	Creates and alters database sessions. RESTRICTED corresponds to creating restricted database sessions.
SEQUENCE (CREATE, CREATE ANY, ALTER ANY, DROP ANY, SELECT ANY)	Creates, alters, drops, and uses sequences.
SNAPSHOT (CREATE, CREATE ANY, ALTER ANY, DROP ANY)	Creates, alters, and drops snapshots.
SYNONYM (CREATE, CREATE ANY, CREATE PUBLIC, DROP ANY, DROP PUBLIC)	Creates and drops synonyms.
SYSTEM (ALTER)	Alters the database server settings using the ALTER SYSTEM command.
TABLE (CREATE, CREATE ANY, ALTER ANY, BACKUP ANY, DROP ANY, LOCK ANY, COMMENT ANY, SELECT ANY, INSERT ANY, UPDATE ANY, DELETE ANY)	Creates, alters, backs up, drops, locks, comments, or manipulates tables.
TABLESPACE (CREATE, ALTER, MANAGE, DROP, UNLIMITED)	Creates, alters (extends), manages (backup, availability), drops, or uses space in tablespaces.
TRANSACTION (FORCE, FORCE ANY)	Manages the outcome of pending distributed transactions.
TRIGGER (CREATE, CREATE ANY, ALTER ANY, DROP ANY)	Creates, alters, or drops triggers.
USER (CREATE, BECOME, ALTER, DROP)	Creates, alters, or drops users. BECOME is required for performing full database exports using the Export utility.
VIEW (CREATE, CREATE ANY, DROP ANY)	Creates or drops views.

Object Privileges

Table A.14 provides a quick reference to the Oracle7 object privileges.

TABLE A.14: Oracle7 Database Object Privileges

Object	Privileges Available
Tables	SELECT, INSERT, UPDATE, DELETE, ALTER, INDEX, REFERENCES
Views and Snapshots	SELECT, INSERT, UPDATE, DELETE
Sequences	SELECT, ALTER
Procedures, functions, and packages	EXECUTE

APPENDIX

B

Configuring and Using the Oracle7 Parallel Query Option

Releases 7.1, 7.2, and 7.3 of the Oracle7 database server includes the Parallel Query option, which can dramatically enhance the performance of Oracle7 database systems that use multiprocessor computers. The Parallel Query option permits Oracle7 to take full advantage of the combined power in a multiprocessor computer to speed up complicated, time-consuming database operations. In this appendix, you will learn about parallel query processing and the Oracle7 Parallel Query option.

What Is Parallel Processing?

Whether or not you realize it, parallel processing is all around us. For example, you've probably never considered how a publisher might produce a book like this one. Let's examine the steps in this type of job to learn what parallel processing is. One way to produce a book would be as follows:

1. The author writes the entire manuscript and then sends it to the publisher. Meanwhile, the editors sit idle waiting for the author to finish the book manuscript.

2. The editors review the entire manuscript, make comments, and then send it back to the author for final review. Meanwhile, the author sits idle waiting for the editors to finish editing the manuscript.

3. The author incorporates the changes suggested by the editors and then sends the entire edited manuscript back to them. Meanwhile, the editors sit idle waiting for the author to finish reviewing the edits.

4. The editors finalize the manuscript from the edits and produce the book.

In this situation, only one activity (writing, editing, and so on) is occurring at any one time. Additionally, valuable resources often sit idle instead of doing productive work. Consequently, the time to complete the overall process is the sum of the times necessary to complete each subtask. This situation is an example of *serial processing* —only one task in the book production process is carried out at a time.

Now let's study parallel processing. *Parallel processing* is just what it sounds like: multiple processes work in parallel (at the same time) to finish a job more quickly than it would otherwise take. For example, consider how parallel processing can speed up the job of producing a book. After writing a chapter, the author immediately sends it to the publisher. Then the author can continue writing subsequent chapters. Meanwhile, the publisher's editors will be busy editing finished chapters. Consequently, the parallel processing situation utilizes all resources at the same time to produce the book much more quickly.

The objective of parallel computer processing is literally the same as that of the book production process: to split up one large, complex job into many smaller jobs and then have multiple workers complete each smaller job in parallel to complete the entire operation quickly. In the case of parallel database query processing, the "workers" are multiple computer processors, and the "complicated operations" are relational database server operations, such as relational queries and index builds.

First, let's take a look at a fundamental issue for parallel processing—multiprocessor computers and how they work.

The Foundation of Parallel Processing—Multiprocessor Computers

An implicit requirement for parallel processing is a *multiprocessor computer*. Computers that have multiple processors come in several varieties. Figure B.1 shows some different types.

Perhaps the most common type of multiprocessor computer is the *symmetric multiprocessor (SMP)* computer. An SMP computer usually has between 2 and 16 processors, all of which share the computer's single memory source and storage devices. Because of their design regarding memory usage, SMPs are commonly referred to as *tightly coupled multiprocessor systems.*

Another type of multiprocessor computer shown in Figure B.1 is a *clustered multiprocessor system.* In clustered systems, each processor has its own, private memory area, but all processors can share the same storage devices. Because of their design regarding memory usage, clustered systems are commonly referred to as *loosely coupled multiprocessor systems.*

An extension of the loosely coupled architecture is the *massively parallel processing system,* or *MPP.* An MPP is characterized by many loosely coupled processors— perhaps 50 or even hundreds of processors—all of which can share the same storage devices or work with their own private storage devices.

FIGURE B.1:

Multiprocessor computer architectures

Symmetric Multiprocessors (SMPs)
(Tightly Coupled Systems)

Clustered Multiprocessors
(Loosely Coupled System)

Massively Parallel
Processing Systems (MPPs)

> **NOTE** Hybrid multiprocessor architectures are also common; that is, systems that have loosely coupled clusters of tightly coupled systems.

Choosing a Multiprocessor Computer for an Oracle7 Database System

Now that you know a little about the different types of multiprocessor systems, you are probably asking yourself about the advantages and disadvantages among the different varieties when considering the design of a database management system like Oracle7. First, let's take a look at SMPs.

SMPs of up to 16 processors are a popular choice for database management systems for several reasons. First of all, SMPs are very cost effective, considering the price-to-performance gains they can deliver. This, coupled with the fact that SMPs are the most mature multiprocessor architecture and have lots of available software, makes SMP machines a good choice for many application environments. However, because of their tightly coupled processor/memory design, SMPs tend to top out on performance, as a result of disk I/O or memory contention problems, after reaching a certain number of processors.

If a database system tops out on performance of an SMP, the next move up is usually to an MPP system. Because MPPs have a loosely coupled processor architecture and, perhaps, a non-shared disk design, they do not suffer from the performance limitations inherent in SMPs. If the database software can take advantage of the many processors in an MPP computer, you can use literally thousands of processors to complete complicated database operations at lightning-fast speeds. Naturally, because MPPs have more processing power than smaller SMPs, their cost is greater—but you get what you pay for.

The only real disadvantage of MPPs is that they are a relatively new and complicated hardware model for which to develop software, which means that there is limited software available that takes advantage of their tremendous processing power. For example, MPPs have traditionally been used for scientific applications that are extremely computing intensive. However, as more and more software companies learn how to take advantage of the power of MPPs, they will no doubt become more popular in all types of computing environments, including database processing systems.

Understanding Linear Performance Speedup

One of your most important goals when using any type of multiprocessor computer should be to notice *linear speedup* as you add more and more processors to attack a single computing task. Linear speedup occurs when a doubling of resources (in this case, processors) halves response time. Linear speedup is important; if response time does not decrease by a factor of 1 each time you add a new processor to the operation, you are not getting your money's worth from each processor on the system. Figure B.2 shows some graphs that represent linear and nonlinear speedup for multiprocessor systems.

FIGURE B.2:

Linear speedup occurs when the multiprocessor computer reduces an operation's response time by a factor of 1 for every processor you use to handle the operation.

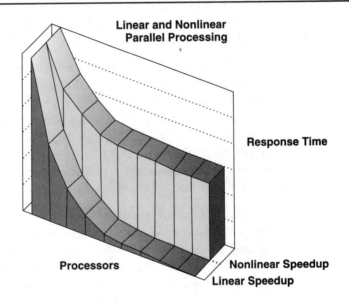

To make multiprocessor computing systems deliver near linear speedup, special versions of computer operating systems are available. For example, many UNIX vendors offer multiprocessor versions of the UNIX operating system to explicitly take advantage of SMP, clustered, and MPP systems. Microsoft Windows NT is another popular operating system that supports multiprocessor systems.

Much like an operating system, relational database management software must have special features to take advantage of multiprocessor computers and deliver linear speedup. In fact, that's what the remainder of this appendix focuses on: the features of the Oracle7 Parallel Query option that allow you to tap into the power of all types of multiprocessor computers.

Parallelizing Database Operations for Maximum Performance

To review, the objective of parallel processing is to take a single and perhaps complicated database operation, intelligently break it down into logical subtasks, and then feed the subtasks to multiple computer processors that can work in parallel to reduce the overall time necessary to complete the database operation. Without parallel processing features, a database server executing on a multiprocessor computer is really not much better than a database server using a single-processor computer. The illustration in Figure B.3 contrasts parallel and nonparallel database query processing models using a multiprocessor computer.

FIGURE B.3:

Without parallel query processing, a single processor of a multiprocessor computer completes all parts of a query while other processors sit idle. Parallel query processing takes advantage of all available processors to speed up response time.

Figure B.3 compares how a full table scan and sort are performed by serial and parallel processing models. Notice that with serial processing, the time it takes to complete one large operation is the sum of the time necessary to complete each subtask (scan and sort) in the larger operation. A parallel processing database server identifies each relational operator (scan and sort), breaks down each operator into subtasks, and then assigns the subtasks to individual processes for processing. In Figure B.3, scans and sorts can happen simultaneously to decrease the overall time necessary to complete the SQL query.

Relational database management systems such as Oracle7 are perfect candidates for parallel processing. That's because they already hide the complexities of data access from the developer. Developers can design client database applications without ever considering what type of computer will be used to run the application or the database server. Also, existing applications automatically benefit from parallel processing enhancements added to the server. For example, a SELECT statement issued to a database server has the same syntax whether the server uses a single-processor or multiprocessor computer. If the database server happens to use a multiprocessor computer, the internal mechanisms of the server automatically take advantage of parallel processing capabilities to deliver maximum performance for all applications.

As you might guess, parallel database processing makes its biggest impact on demanding database operations rather than simple ones. For example, decision-support applications that regularly issue complicated join queries or queries that access a lot of data will see greater performance improvements from parallel processing than will online transaction-processing applications that issue simple INSERT statements.

Capabilities of the Oracle7 Parallel Query Option

Oracle7 with the Parallel Query option automatically parallelizes almost every type of relational database operation, including all types of SQL operations, such as joins, scans, sorts, aggregates, groupings, and any mix of these. Users and developers never need to consider the complexities of parallel processing because Oracle7 transparently parallelizes these operations for all SELECT statements, as well as for subqueries in INSERT, UPDATE, DELETE, and CREATE TABLE statements. Oracle7 also uses parallel processing to build indexes much more quickly. This is particularly useful when a database has particularly large tables and the corresponding indexes take a very long time to create.

The Oracle7 Parallel Query Process Architecture

To parallelize database operations, Oracle7 with the Parallel Query option uses a special operating system process architecture, as shown in Figure B.4.

FIGURE B.4:

Process architecture of Oracle7 with the Parallel Query option

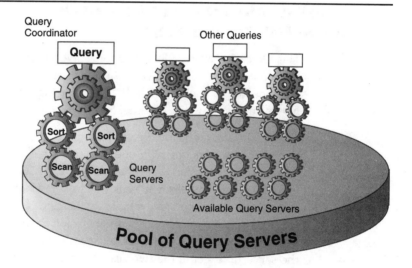

Notice that the Oracle7 parallel query process architecture contains some special processes: a query coordinator and query servers. A *query coordinator* is similar to a typical shared foreground server process of a nonparallel Oracle7 system. It is the process that receives a database request from the dispatcher. However, a query coordinator is a foreground server process that has special capabilities, making it the focal point of a parallelized operation. A query coordinator's job is to read a query (or any other type of statement), intelligently break it down into smaller requests that will execute efficiently, coordinate sending out the requests to available query servers, and merge request results.

A *query server* simply performs the request that a query coordinator asks of it. As Figure B.4 shows, Oracle7 keeps a pool of shared query servers available for use by any query coordinator that needs work done. As parallel processing loads fluctuate in the database system, Oracle7 automatically tunes its parallel processing architecture by starting and stopping more query servers as necessary to vary the size of the query server pool according to current demands. Therefore, the database administrator does not need to constantly monitor the parallel processing architecture to make sure things are running smoothly.

Partitioning Data to Eliminate Disk I/O Bottlenecks

The Oracle7 Parallel Query option solves the problem of processing database operations in parallel. However, another critical bottleneck that can limit performance speedup is disk I/O bandwidths. For example, consider the parallel processing examples shown in Figure B.5.

Figure B.5 shows what happens when an Oracle7 server with the Parallel Query option executes the same SQL query (a full table scan with a sort) using nonpartitioned and partitioned table data. In both cases, Oracle7 parallelizes the query into two degrees of parallelism (it breaks the scan and sort operators into two scans and two sorts). However, when all the table's data resides on a single disk, the disk head can serve the request of only one scan operation at any given time. Consequently, even though the server did a great job of parallelizing the query, the single disk forces the server to execute the two scan operations serially, thus limiting the response time for the query. Alternatively, when the table data is partitioned on two disks, two scan operations can happen in parallel, and the response time for the query is much better.

Figure B.5 also shows a system with database partitioning. *Database partitioning* means that the data in a single database is physically spread across multiple disk drives to reduce the limiting effects of disk I/O bandwidths. In the example, the table to scan is spread across different disk drives therefore the database server can complete two table scans in parallel to reduce the overall time needed to scan the table, taking perhaps half the time it would to perform them with a nonpartitioned database.

FIGURE B.5:

No matter how well a database server can parallelize database operations, data that is not partitioned can be a significant bottleneck in performance speedup.

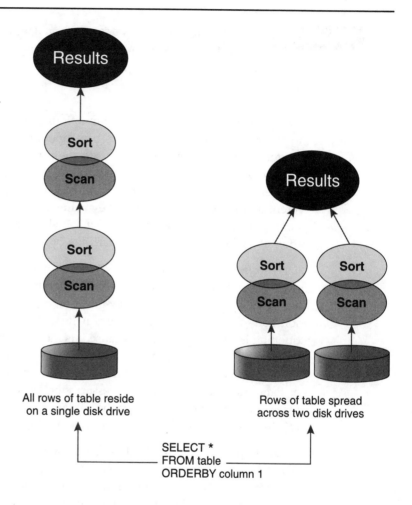

All rows of table reside on a single disk drive

Rows of table spread across two disk drives

SELECT *
FROM table
ORDERBY column 1

Several database partitioning strategies are possible. Chapter 12 discusses one strategy you should be using to some degree—schema partitioning, or the separation of different objects within a single application schema across different disks—and mentions one form of schema partitioning—storing a table's indexes on a different disk drive from the drive that stores the table, thus permitting Oracle7 to read index data and table data in parallel.

TIP

Schema partitioning provides no advantage for Oracle7 with the Parallel Query option. Instead, focus on the other types of partitioning mentioned in this section.

Adequately eliminating disk I/O limitations in parallel processing database systems for almost every type of database operation requires granular partitioning strategies, such as *horizontal table partitioning,* or separating the rows of a single data table across multiple disks. You can partition the rows of a single table using several different strategies. For example, *key partitioning* separates a table's rows into different partitions according to the key value in each row. Another horizontal partitioning strategy is *round-robin partitioning,* where the system randomly scatters the rows of a table in available table partitions.

Each horizontal partitioning strategy has its own calling, depending on application characteristics. For example, if an application frequently processes rows in groups according to key values, then key partitioning is not the appropriate partitioning solution—all the rows in a group are on the same disk. In this case, round-robin partitioning is a better approach because it is more likely to spread rows with similar key values across multiple disk drives. Round-robin partitioning is essential for temporary work areas (used for sorts, joins, and so on) where the characteristics of temporary data might not necessarily be known beforehand. In fact, in most cases round-robin partitioning is the best approach because it can adequately separate the rows that any type of application might request or work with.

An alternative to internal database partitioning that can yield the same results for parallel processing is external operating-system disk striping. Many multiprocessor operating systems support utilities that can perform *disk striping,* which is randomly distributing the pages of files across many different disks. Since striping is done at the operating-system level, all types of files, including those related to the database, can be spread out on different disks for better performance in a parallel processing environment. Many system administrators prefer to use external disk striping because it allows a multiprocessor to reduce disk I/O bottlenecks associated with database files as well as other types of application files, and because it centralizes administration at the operating-system level.

Now that you have a solid understanding of parallel database processing and data partitioning, the following sections explain how to configure and use the Oracle7 Parallel Query option and set up your data-partitioning strategy.

Configuring and Tuning the Parallel Query Option

Configuring the Oracle7 Parallel Query option is not too complicated. The database administrator needs to set only a few initialization parameters and consider some unique options when creating tables and indexes. Once you accomplish this, you are ready to begin exploiting the full power of a multiprocessor Oracle7 database server. First, let's learn how to configure the size of the query server pool.

Setting Thresholds to Limit the Size of the Query Server Pool

Oracle7 automatically tunes its parallel processing architecture by starting and stopping query servers to vary the size of the query server pool according to current processing demands. Therefore, you never need to spend lots of time monitoring and tuning Oracle7's Parallel Query option. However, you must pay attention to the minimum and maximum number of query servers allowed by Oracle7's dynamic architecture. If you allow too many query servers, the process overhead on the server can become excessive and actually degrade system performance. If you permit too few query servers, there won't be enough processes to adequately parallelize concurrent user requests.

To set the thresholds for the minimum and maximum number of query servers in the query server pool, you use the two initialization parameters PARALLEL _MIN_SERVERS and PARALLEL_MAX_SERVERS. The following excerpt from an initialization parameter file shows how easy it is to set these parameters:

```
PARALLEL_MIN_SERVERS=10
PARALLEL_MAX_SERVERS=100
```

As with other parameters, configuring the thresholds for the query server pool takes a bit of trial and error at first. When setting the initial thresholds for the query server pool, consider the characteristics of both the hardware and the database system. For example, the maximum number of processes your multiprocessor computer can adequately support might serve as an upper limit for the query server pool. Likewise, the average number of users who concurrently access the database system at any given time might serve as the lower bound for the query server pool.

Once Oracle7 with the Parallel Query option is up and running, it is useful to monitor how Oracle7 varies the pool of query servers according to normal system demands. Throughout a normal day, you might query the Oracle7 data dictionary to get a quick idea of how many query servers are up at any given time. However, just as when tuning the thresholds for shared servers in a multithreaded Oracle7 server, it is useful to record the fluctuation of query servers in a parallel processing environment over a time period. You can do this by creating a table and a stored procedure similar to the ones shown in Chapter 8 (Listing 8.2). You can even create a single stored procedure to gather dispatcher, shared server, and query server information at the same interval for the same amount of time. This way, you will need to dedicate only one session to monitoring the multithreaded server and query server pool at the same time.

Once you have gathered fluctuation information for the query server pool, use the information along with the current settings for the initialization parameters PARALLEL_MIN_SERVERS and PARALLEL_MAX_SERVERS to tune the threshold settings. For example, if any of the query counts touch the current thresholds, consider lowering the lower threshold or raising the upper threshold to allow more fluctuation in query server counts. Continue to monitor the fluctuation of the query server pool until you feel you have correctly tuned the system.

Another initialization parameter to consider for query servers is the PARALLEL _SERVER_IDLE_TIME parameter. This parameter determines how long Oracle7 will let a query server sit idle before removing the process from the query server pool. Setting this time interval correctly avoids the processing overhead associated with constantly starting and stopping query servers. The PARALLEL_SERVER _IDLE_TIME parameter is set as a number of minutes. For example, this setting instructs Oracle7 to terminate a query server process only after it has been idle for at least 10 minutes:

```
PARALLEL_SERVER_IDLE_TIME=10
```

Controlling Runaway Parallelism

As the old saying goes, it's possible to have too much of a good thing. The parallelism of database operations is no different. For example, if one statement unnecessarily hoards too many available query servers to parallelize its work, other queries will suffer in performance because they end up needing to execute using serial processing.

Parallelism can get out of control, particularly for table scan operations. Theoretically, you could have one scan process for every row requested by a statement. To prevent such situations, Oracle7 includes several mechanisms to control the *degree of parallelism,* or the number of query servers used to process a single statement. The following sections discuss the controls for the degree of parallelism in an Oracle7 database server.

System-Wide Control of Parallelism

As an administrator, you can set a default degree of parallelism for all database tables using the PARALLEL_DEFAULT_SCANSIZE initialization parameter. Oracle7 uses this setting only when table- or statement-level controls for parallelism are not in use (see the next two sections).

To set the system-wide default for parallelism correctly, it's important to understand how Oracle7 calculates the degree of parallelism using the PARALLEL_DEFAULT _SCANSIZE initialization parameter. When a user requests data from a table, Oracle7 calculates the degree of parallelism using this formula:

```
degree of parallelism = # blocks in the table ÷
PARALLEL_DEFAULT_SCANSIZE
```

Consequently, Oracle7 gives greater degrees of parallelism for larger tables. But how do you correctly set PARALLEL_DEFAULT_SCANSIZE? One way might be to determine the average table size in the database and how many disks hold rows for the average table. Set the PARALLEL_DEFAULT_SCANSIZE parameter such that the degree of parallelism equals the average number of disks that contain blocks for the average table.

The PARALLEL_DEFAULT_MAX_SCANS parameter determines the maximum degree of parallelism for any operation in the system. No matter what control you use to determine the degree of parallelism, nothing can exceed the setting for PARALLEL_DEFAULT_MAX_SCANS.

Controlling the Degree of Parallelism on a Per-Table Basis

To set the default degree of parallelism for all parallel database operations concerning a specific table, you can create the table with the PARALLEL option. For example, this statement creates the ITEMS table, setting the default degree of parallelism for the table to 10:

```
CREATE TABLE items
(... column specifications ...)
PARALLEL DEGREE 10
```

If you partition a table across multiple disks, an appropriate setting for the PARALLEL option of a CREATE TABLE statement is the number of disks you use to store the table. Be sure not to set PARALLEL higher than the current system-wide maximum degree of parallelism—the setting of the PARALLEL_DEFAULT _MAX_SCANS initialization parameter—since nothing can override this system setting.

Alternatively, if by default you do not want Oracle7 to parallelize operations on a table, you can specify the NOPARALLEL option. This option is appropriate for small lookup tables where parallelism is not likely to improve performance of scan operations.

```
CREATE TABLE parts
( ... column specifications ...)
NOPARALLEL
```

NOTE If you create a table without specifying a default degree of parallelism, Oracle7 automatically uses the system-wide default degree of parallelism when parallelizing an operation.

Controlling the Degree of Parallelism on a Per-Statement Basis Using Hints

If you are an application developer, you have the power to explicitly control the degree of parallelism for each table referenced in an individual statement using the PARALLEL and NOPARALLEL hints. These hints are the tuning knobs you can use to maximize application performance by making wise use of available database server resources. You can increase parallelism for demanding statements and reduce or eliminate parallelism for less-demanding statements.

```
SELECT --+ PARALLEL(sales.items, 10)
  MAX(SUM(linetotal)), MIN(SUM(linetotal)), AVG(SUM(linetotal))
  FROM sales.items
  GROUP BY orderid

SELECT --+ NOPARALLEL(sales.parts)
  description
  FROM sales.parts
  WHERE id = 5
```

In the first example above, a reasonable degree of parallelism is warranted because the query must perform a complete table scan of a large table to get the necessary values for the aggregate functions (SUM). The statement also needs to perform grouping. Alternatively, it is unlikely that parallelism will increase the response time of the second statement, because the query accesses a small table using an index to find a single row.

NOTE
If you issue a statement and do not use hints to control the degree of parallelism, Oracle7 first uses the degree of parallelism specified for the tables in the statement. If a referenced table does not have a specific degree of parallelism, Oracle7 then uses the system-wide default degree of parallelism.

Controlling the Degree of Parallelism when Building Indexes

Building and rebuilding indexes is a common undertaking for database administrators because an index can get out of balance as a result of frequent DML operations on the corresponding table. To reduce the time it takes to build an index for a large table, Oracle7 with the Parallel Query option automatically builds indexes using parallel processing.

By default, Oracle7 builds each index using the degree of parallelism specified for the corresponding table. If you wish, you can override this setting and indicate a specific degree of parallelism to use when building an index. For example, you can use the PARALLEL option of the CONSTRAINT clause of the CREATE TABLE command or the PARALLEL option of the CREATE INDEX command. The following set of statements rebuilds the index behind the PRIMARY KEY for the ITEMS table:

```
-- drop the primary key index by disabling the primary
-- key constraint
ALTER TABLE items
  DISABLE PRIMARY KEY
-- rebuild the primary key index by enabling the primary key,
-- using a degree of parallelism equal to 10
ALTER TABLE items
  ENABLE PRIMARY KEY
    USING INDEX PARALLEL DEGREE 10
```

The PARALLEL option for an index allows you to explicitly specify the degree of parallelism to use when building the index. In the preceding example, the degree of parallelism for the index build is 10.

Alternatively, the NOPARALLEL option of the CONSTRAINT clause of the CREATE TABLE command or the NOPARALLEL option of the CREATE INDEX command permits you to create an index without any parallel processing at all. Use the NOPARALLEL option to avoid unnecessary parallelism on small tables that might otherwise hurt overall system performance.

Relieving Disk I/O Limitations to Maximize the Performance of Parallel Processing

As mentioned earlier, disk I/O can significantly limit the performance speedup of parallel database processing. The following sections explain ways you can remove disk I/O as a bottleneck and realize the maximum performance speedup possible from parallelizing database operations with the Oracle7 Parallel Query option.

Caching Tables in Memory to Avoid Disk I/O

One way to remove disk access as a performance bottleneck is to avoid disk I/O altogether with data caching. That's just what the data buffer in an Oracle7 database server does for the most frequently requested blocks of database data (see Chapter 12). Building on this capability, the Oracle7 Parallel Query option offers special options of the CREATE TABLE and ALTER TABLE commands that allow you to specifically control the caching of a table's data in memory: the CACHE and NOCACHE options.

```
CREATE TABLE parts
  (... column specifications ...)
  CACHE
  NOPARALLEL

CREATE TABLE items
  (... column specifications ...)
  NOCACHE
  PARALLEL DEGREE 10
```

When you specify the CACHE option of the CREATE TABLE or ALTER TABLE command, Oracle7 caches the entire table in the SGA of the Oracle7 database server. Unless you have an incredibly large amount of memory available to the database server, the CACHE option is appropriate only for small lookup tables in an application schema. That's because caching large tables in memory can quickly consume the available shared memory of the database server and hurt overall system performance. With large tables, it is more appropriate to use the NOCACHE option of the CREATE TABLE or ALTER TABLE command.

Notice the relationship of the PARALLEL and NOPARALLEL options of the CREATE TABLE and ALTER TABLE commands with the CACHE and NOCACHE options. If you decide to cache an entire table in memory with the CACHE option, the PARALLEL option is not appropriate because all table data is in memory, thereby making it unnecessary to consider the number of physical parallel table scans. Likewise, if you specify NOCACHE, you should take time to appropriately set the PARALLEL option, as described in the preceding section.

TIP

If you use the Oracle7 Parallel Query option as well as the Oracle7 Parallel Server option for loosely coupled multiprocessor systems, you can also use the CACHE PARTITIONS option of the CREATE TABLE or ALTER TABLE command. This option allows you to cache the table in all instances of a parallel server configuration.

Schema Partitioning

Partitioning database data is another way to minimize disk I/O bottlenecks in a parallel database processing system. The easiest way to physically partition data in an Oracle7 database is by schema partitioning. Unfortunately, schema partitioning does not offer any significant benefits for the Oracle7 Parallel Query option. Therefore, we will instead focus on other ways of partitioning data in an Oracle database.

Horizontal Table Partitioning

The Oracle7 Parallel Query option offers no built-in mechanism to make sure Oracle7 horizontally partitions the rows of a single table across multiple disks as users insert new rows into tables. However, if your database is primarily a decision-support database (that is, a static, read-only database), you can be clever and use SQL*Loader to load a single table's rows in different data files throughout the same tablespace. Therefore, if you place the data files of a single tablespace on multiple disks, you can, in effect, use SQL*Loader to partition the rows of a table across multiple disks. Following are the steps necessary to accomplish horizontal table partitioning in a decision-support database:

1. Use Server Manager's Create Tablespace dialog box to create a tablespace with multiple data files. Each data file should be on a different disk drive. The number of data files you choose for the tablespace can be no more than the number of disks that are available and should correspond to the degree of data partitioning you want to create for any table that resides in the tablespace. For example, the SALES tablespace might have ten different data files, all of which reside on different disks.

2. Create the table you want to partition in the previously created tablespace.

3. Use a text editor or a custom-written program to partition the table's rows among several different SQL*Loader input files. For example, the rows for the ORDERS table might end up in the SQL*Loader input files named ORDERS1.DAT, ORDERS2.DAT,...ORDERS10.DAT. The number of SQL*Loader input files you create determines the degree of data partitioning for the table and should be no greater than the number of data files in the table's corresponding tablespace. You can partition the table's rows using any of the previously described horizontal partitioning strategies, such as key partitioning or round-robin partitioning.

4. Use SQL*Loader to load each input file into the table. Be sure to use the SQL*Loader control file option FILE to specifically target the data file that should store the new table rows being loaded. For example, here are excerpts from two different SQL*Loader control files that correspond to the ORDERS table:

```
LOAD DATA
INFILE 'orders1.dat'
FILE = '/disk1/dbs/sales1.dbf'
INSERT INTO TABLE orders

LOAD DATA
INFILE 'orders2.dat'
FILE = '/disk2/dbs/sales2.dbf'
INSERT INTO TABLE orders
    .
    .
    .
```

When you have completed all the data loads for the same table, repeat the operation for the other tables in the database that you want to horizontally partition.

Database Partitioning Using the Operating System Disk Striping

Disk striping is the easiest way to horizontally partition an Oracle7 table's data across multiple disks. Furthermore, it is the only way to horizontally partition an Oracle7 table if users continue to update its data. Many multiprocessor operating systems have utilities that allow you to physically scatter the pages of one or more files across a number of available disks. For example, the Pyramid DC/OSx operating system has the vdisk utility, and the Sequent DYNIX/ptx operating system has the Sequent Volume Manager (ptx/SVM). If your multiprocessor operating system has such a utility, you should consider using it to partition the data in your database.

Using the Parallel Query Option

Once you have configured a system for the Oracle7 Parallel Query option and have partitioned the database's data, applications automatically start benefiting from parallel database processing. That's because Oracle7 automatically parallelizes most database operations, including SELECT statements; the subqueries of INSERT, UPDATE, and DELETE; and CREATE TABLE statements. Therefore, the performance enhancement from the Oracle7 Parallel Query option is in effect but transparent to users. On the other hand, developers should consider explicit use of the PARALLEL and NOPARALLEL hints to control and maximize parallel processing performance, as described earlier in this appendix.

APPENDIX

C

What's On the Disk

The files on this disk are SQL command scripts that will build the listings in this book:

File	Description
LIST7-1.SQL	Listing 7-1
LIST7-2.SQL	Listing 7-2
LIST8-1.SQL	Listing 8-1
LIST8-2.SQL	Listing 8-2
LIST9-1.SQL	Listing 9-1
LIST9-2.SQL	Listing 9-2
LIST9-3.SQL	Listing 9-3
LIST10-1.SQL	Listing 10-1
LIST10-2.SQL	Listing 10-2
LIST11-1.SQL	Listing 11-1
LIST12-1.SQL	Listing 12-1

The disk also contains the file TABLES.SQL, which will build the example tables used throughout the book.

INDEX

Note to the Reader: First level entries are in **bold**. Page numbers in **bold** indicate the principal discussion of a topic or the definition of a term. Page numbers in *italic* indicate illustrations.

Numbers and Symbols

3GL and 4GL development tools, 79–80, 516–517
* (asterisk), in SQL statements, 491
-- (hyphens), in SQL statements, 491
/ (slash), in SQL statements, 491

A

access privileges. *See* privileges; security
accessing
    Server Manager Dispatcher monitor, 260–263, *260*
    Server Manager Shared Server monitor, 264, *265*
activating standby databases, 377–378
adapter cards for networks, 97
ADD clause, ALTER TABLE command, 441–442
Add Datafile dialog box, in Server Manager, 213–214, *213*
Add Redo Logfile Group dialog box, in Server Manager, 339–341, *340*
Add Redo Logfile Member dialog box, in Server Manager, 343–344, *343*
adding
    data files to tablespaces, 213–214, *213*
    details to business functions in function hierarchy diagrams, 602–604, *603*
    entity details to ER diagrams, 595–598, *595*, *597*
    integrity constraints, 442
    log groups, 339–341
    log members, 343–344, *343*
addresses, port addresses for listener process, 256

Administration Manager, in Server Manager, 167–168, *167*
administrative utilities, **82–84**. *See also* Network Manager utility; Server Manager utility; SQL*Loader utility; utilities
Advanced Replication option, for Oracle7, 64
AFTER triggers, 150
alert conditions, 421, 543–547, *544*
aliases. *See also* synonyms
    naming view columns with, 451
ALTER ANY SEQUENCE system privilege, 476
ALTER DATABASE command, 214–215, 347, 348, 355, 374, 375, 377
ALTER DATABASE system privilege, 50, 215, 340, 344, 345, 348, 355
ALTER INDEX command, 463–464
Alter Profile dialog box, in Server Manager, 292–293, *293*
ALTER PROFILE system privilege, 293
Alter Rollback Segment dialog box, in Server Manager, 332, *333*
ALTER ROLLBACK SEGMENT system privilege, 331
ALTER SEQUENCE command, 475–476
ALTER TABLE command, **440–442**, 443
ALTER TABLESPACE command, 399
ALTER TABLESPACE system privilege, 213, 355
Alter User dialog box, in Server Manager, 276–277, *277*, 289, *289*
ALTER USER system privilege, 277
altering. *See* changing; modifying
alternate keys, 33, 429–430
analysis stage of application development, **565**, 569, **585**, *586*, **605**. *See also* Designer/2000
ANALYZE command, 463, 486–488
anonymous PL/SQL blocks, **140–141**

B

C

D

E

F

L

M

N

P

Q

R

S

T

u

Oracle7 Multimedia Courseware Training

Training can determine the success or failure of a client/server project. Make sure your developers and administrators get the training they need to succeed.

➢ **Comprehensive Training**
50+ hours, including the very latest release.

➢ **Visual Training Techniques**
Animated graphics and sound make learning fun and retention excellent.

➢ **Cost Effective and Convenient** Only $149 per module, unlimited users.

Download a demo from our web site *www.animatedlearning.com*
or call us toll free for more information
1-800-235-3030
(1-408-688-7735 outside the USA)

Oracle7 SQL Commands

SQL Command	Description
DROP ROLE	Drops a role of related privileges.
DROP ROLLBACK SEGMENT	Drops a rollback segment.
DROP SEQUENCE	Drops a named sequence of numbers.
DROP SNAPSHOT[†]	Drops a snapshot of a remote table.
DROP SNAPSHOT LOG[†]	Drops a log for a snapshot.
DROP SYNONYM	Drops a synonym for a table or view.
DROP TABLE	Drops a database table.
DROP TABLESPACE	Drops a tablespace.
DROP TRIGGER	Drops a trigger on a table.
DROP USER	Drops a database username, as well as the user's objects.
DROP VIEW	Drops a view.
EXPLAIN PLAN	Puts into a database table the optimization strategy for a SQL statement.
GRANT	Grants roles, system privileges, and/or object privileges to users and/or roles.
INSERT	Inserts one or more new rows into a database table.
LOCK TABLE	Manually locks a table.
NOAUDIT	Disables audit options for the system and database objects.
RECOVER	Initiates recovery of a damaged database, tablespace, or data file.
RENAME	Renames a table, view, sequence, or synonym.
REVOKE	Revokes roles, system privileges, and/or object privileges from users or roles.
ROLLBACK	Rolls back the changes made by the current transaction.
SAVEPOINT	Identifies an intermediate transaction savepoint.
SELECT	Retrieves all or specific column and row information from one or more tables or views.
SET ROLE	Enables one or more specific roles of related privileges and disables all others.
SET TRANSACTION	Specifies transaction characteristics.
TRUNCATE	Deletes all rows from a table and optionally releases all space allocated to the table.
UPDATE	Updates all or specific rows in a table.

[†]Available only with the Oracle7 Distributed Database option